Personality, Political Leadership, and Decision Making

A GLOBAL PERSPECTIVE

Jean Krasno and Sean LaPides, Editors

An Imprint of ABC-CLIO, LLC
Santa Barbara, California • Denver, Colorado

Library of Congress Cataloging-in-Publication Data

Personality, political leadership, and decision making : a global perspective / Jean Krasno and Sean LaPides, editors.
pages cm
Includes bibliographical references and index.
ISBN 978–1–4408–3910–8 (hard copy : acid-free paper) — ISBN 978–1–4408–3911–5 (ebook) 1. Personality and politics—Case studies. 2. Political leadership—Psychological aspects—Case studies. 3. Decision making—Psychological aspects—Case studies. I. Krasno, Jean E., 1943– II. LaPides, Sean.
BF698.9.P6P53 2015
303.3′4—dc23 2015009800

ISBN: 978–1–4408–3910–8
EISBN: 978–1–4408–3911–5

19 18 17 16 15 1 2 3 4 5

This book is also available on the World Wide Web as an eBook.
Visit www.abc-clio.com for details.

Praeger
An Imprint of ABC-CLIO, LLC

ABC-CLIO, LLC
130 Cremona Drive, P.O. Box 1911
Santa Barbara, California 93116-1911

This book is printed on acid-free paper ∞

Manufactured in the United States of America

Contents

1

Introduction: Laying Out the Conceptual Framework

Jean Krasno

INTRODUCTION

This book undertakes an examination of the personalities of a selected group of political leaders, analyzes the forces that formed their personalities, and then demonstrates how their personality has shaped important political decisions that these leaders have made. The study of personality, decision making, and leadership falls under the relatively new field of political psychology, which recognizes that state actors comprise individual leaders, and the personalities of political elites can influence decision making and foreign policy to a degree far greater than what realist theories propose. Embedded within personality lie the characteristic behaviors that inform management style, worldview, motive, and decision making skills. This research draws upon the literature on leadership personality theory, crisis decision making, and cognitive biases in belief systems. Prevailing personality typologies have historically originated exclusively in the field of psychology. Consequently, the focus has been on psychopathology—personality traits predicated on diagnosable symptoms of illness. In the last several years, the field of political psychology has produced some very useful theoretical frameworks and case studies that go beyond pathology and address the study of healthy, or at least functional, leadership personality types. This study is based on this more recent tradition and builds on it to propose some new ideas by introducing more studies of international leaders and expanding the theoretical framework of analysis.

The approach of this study draws on behaviorist learning theory, which explains that the learning of sustained habits over time guides future decision making and that these patterns can be observed. The theoretical framework used here also assumes that cognition, how the mind works, is integrally related to emotion, especially those emotions that drive motives such as the need for power, achievement, or affiliation.

The leadership studies included in this volume are, as David Winter would describe, "studies of personality at a distance."[1] Winter also states that "psychobiography at a distance" involves the "systematic application of psychological theory . . . to the explanation of certain biographical facts."[2] The biographical information on specific leaders included in this volume uses both early childhood experiences and adult experiential learning. Some psychobiographers who look at leaders from a distance may prefer not to use early childhood experiences because they can be very speculative. Nevertheless, we have adopted the approach used by Alexander and Juliette George in their analysis of Woodrow Wilson, which relates Wilson's power-seeking behavior to his struggle to overcome low self-esteem brought about by a severe and domineering father.[3]

All leaders exhibit certain traits in common. They must be relatively charismatic and enjoy attention or they could hardly survive the political process. These common traits manifest themselves regardless of their respective political cultures or where elites fall within the political spectrum. More specifically, we identify four broad personality types: authoritarian, chaotic/impulsive, delegative, and flexible/pragmatic. The authoritarian personality requires almost total control and obedience. It manifests tremendous ego defensiveness and narcissism to the point of aggression. The management style of this type exhibits deference to superiors but abuse to subordinates, coupled with dogmatic defense for his/her belief system and an obsession with details. Power becomes an end in itself and the authoritarian type will resort to manipulation and secrecy to maintain it. The chaotic/impulsive type is self-confident and independent but vacillates between compulsive behavior and disorganization. Decision making tends toward nonideological choices but the inability to focus leads to frequent changes in position. These individuals also display an inflated sense of personal efficacy in their role and may like to think of themselves as "mavericks." The delegative leader enjoys the public image and opportunities of office but often delegates policy and management decisions to others. This personality manifests less enthusiasm for governance, power, or handling details. He/she remains loyal to an inner circle of advisers but consequently may be prone to manipulation. Flexible/pragmatic personalities present an innovative, open-minded approach to issues. Their ability to manage disagreement and synthesize perspectives into a larger picture makes this type more willing to listen to subordinates or peers. High self-esteem and a natural curiosity of differing belief systems create an interest in examining multiple alternatives.

We test these personality types by means of qualitative examinations of world leaders—past and present, men and women—from childhood through adult experiences. Against this genesis, we assess personal characteristics, or traits, such as a sense of efficacy, interest in power, open- or closed-mindedness, compulsiveness, self-esteem, ego-defense, and so forth. We then derive a personality type based on these traits gathered from personal writings, interviews, speeches, and impromptu comments and biographies. Understanding the personality type and psychology of a political leader allows analysts to predict plausible responses to crisis situations or international negotiations. It can also give elites the tools to counter their own misperceptions and cognitive biases in making foreign policy.

RATIONALE

Realist theories, based on power struggles in an anarchic world, have been the dominant paradigm of political thought since the end of World War II. While realism and its state-centric approach have offered explanatory meaning to world events, the position of this study is that states do not make decisions; individual leaders set policy and direct the actions of states. Leaders arrive on the scene with differing cognitive skills, personal motives, unique life experiences, worldviews, belief systems, and different personality types. While world events and their environments may call for leaders to act on state interests, how those interests and events are perceived and processed will depend on the personality and skills of leaders. Therefore, realist theories, which depend on the abstraction of a rational actor and a symbolic state, are insufficient in explaining why leaders make decisions in the way they do. This study attempts to explore the relationship of leadership personality and decision making, building upon previous, and very useful, research.

As Valerie Hudson explains, the point of intersection in the formation of foreign policy is not the state; it is the human decision maker and the state is an abstraction.[4] The rational actor model assumes that a leader has all the complete information and preset goals, and is not acting in an environment of uncertainty. On the contrary, choices come from culture, personality, shared organizational understandings, domestic politics, and how the situations and problems are framed.[5] Studying political leadership and personality presents a complex intellectual puzzle, crossing a number of disciplines: politics, psychology, behavioralism, cultural theory, history, and international relations, among them. Therein lies the dilemma. The field of political psychology attempts to bridge that gap but again the expertise is found generally in either political science, with a somewhat lacking grasp of personality theory, or psychology, which has generally focused, as stated earlier, on pathology rather than on the personality of leadership. Where very useful studies have been done, they have generally focused on U.S. presidential leaders and American leadership styles. This study builds on those cases, integrates and expands their theoretical frameworks, and enriches this area of study by adding a cross-cultural examination of international leaders from several continents and political traditions.

BUILDING ON PREVIOUS THEORETICAL STRUCTURES

Fred Greenstein, agreeing with Graham Allison, explains that we can approach the examination of decision making at three levels: the state, the bureaucracy, and the individual decision maker.[6] The personality of the individual decision maker interacts with situations, cultures, organizational structures, class, gender, and any number of other factors. Greenstein calls for more research in studying the interaction of personality and politics, and this study attempts to add to this body of research. Greenstein offers a useful definition of personality for our purposes: "Personality is a pattern of behavior that includes inner conflicts, ego-defense, and their behavioral manifestations."[7] Personality addresses how a person interacts with reality, expresses feelings, relates to other individuals, and maintains a sense of self-esteem and a sense of efficacy on the job. Greenstein also proposes that there can be three types of studies: (1) the single case study, (2) a typological or multicase study (e.g., a study of authoritarianism); and (3) an aggregate study such as looking at national character or bureaucratic culture.[8] The three forms of examination can interact as in the study of President Woodrow Wilson by Alexander and Juliette George in which the authors described Wilson as a compulsive type. President Wilson's compulsive behavior enabled him to reach high levels of achievement but also interfered with accomplishing important goals such as the Senate ratification of the League of Nations Covenant, largely written by Wilson. His dream of creating a world organization for peace was thwarted by the lack of U.S. membership, as George and George describe, due to his stubbornness and unwillingness to compromise with Senate leaders.[9] In examining the sources of Wilson's compulsive behavior, George and George drew on his early childhood relationship with his father.

Early childhood experiences can play an important role in shaping personality, but Greenstein, James Barber, Stanley Renshon, and others argue that personality development is a lifelong process and dramatic events or even self-examination over time can reshape behavior. Renshon also describes the influence of cultural identity on group personality, explaining that there may be a common or collective self-image based on group myths of past glories or traumas.[10] The leadership studies included in this research draw on the theories of these scholars in the field. In addition, Milton Rokeach's *The Open and Closed Mind*, though written in the 1960s, also provides a very useful framework for the study of the formation of personality. Rokeach examines the extent to which a leader is open-minded by examining his or her willingness to learn more about, or differentiate, information about the nonbelief system as well as one's preferred beliefs. Open- or closed-mindedness becomes a personality trait and has an impact on decision making. For example, stereotyping the enemy, by not being open-minded enough to understand the capabilities or motivations of the other group, can lead to poor decision making with disastrous results.[11]

Along with their study of Wilson, George and George lay out three presidential management models that this study uses as a framework for analyzing management styles of various leaders. Their model framework includes: (1) the formalistic, hierarchical model, which gives the leader the most direct control over advisers and cabinet heads who have to report separately to him/her (used by President Harry Truman) or through a gatekeeper/chief of staff (used by Dwight Eisenhower); (2) the competitive model, which allows a free flow of ideas to the extent that advisers, cabinet heads, and even other staff members are encouraged to compete for the president's attention (used by Franklin Roosevelt); and finally (3) the collegial model in which advisers meet regularly with the president as a group and discuss openly the issues at hand, either forming a consensus or providing the president with various sources of information for the leader's ultimate decision (used by John Kennedy). Our analysis of leadership personality types and their management styles that emerge from those types builds on George and George and modifies their ideas.

Work by David Winter has added depth and rigor to the study of leadership personality. Winter differentiates between personality traits: (1) those that he refers to as stylistic behavior and (2) those that represent the underlying dynamic characteristics or motives for behavior. Therefore, in our study, when we refer to ego-defense or the need for power for the sake of power, we are describing motives or dynamic traits. Winter emphasizes that motives—underlying factors we cannot visibly observe—are more variable than traits that are patterns of observable behavior. "How a motive is expressed in behavior will depend on many factors, such as obstacles and opportunities, the time since last satisfaction, the functional substitutability of different incentives for satisfying that motive, and conflicts and fusion with other motives."[12] While Winter does not refer to Rokeach's concept of the *Open and Closed Mind*, he does seem to support the idea of "open-mindedness." Winter uses the term "cognitive complexity" to mean the ability to differentiate complex situations, or the capacity to be open minded toward the behavior of other nations. He claims that the greater a leader's capacity for cognitive complexity, the more that leader can differentiate the motivations of others, and the greater this leader can integrate this information into a vigilant decision making style, for example, not stereotyping the enemy. Studies demonstrate that leaders who display a capacity for cognitive complexity show a greater tendency to seek peaceful solutions to conflict rather than resorting to an escalation of the conflict or the use of force.

Winter goes on to suggest that in studying personality one ought to look at four domains: traits, motives, cognition, and social contexts. He explains that social contexts are not only the environment the decision maker occupies, but also the community dynamics that have shaped personality during the leader's lifetime.[13] Winter also gives a warning, which we here humbly acknowledge, that predicting a leader's policy choices is very difficult "because we cannot know future situations, especially the surprising and improbable ones, that they may encounter. . . . My final lesson from studying leaders at a distance, then, is that in such an enterprise (as in the rest of life), a certain sense of humility is both necessary and becoming."[14]

Margaret Hermann tells us that predictions of political decision making are more reliable when using a combination of factors. She supports a more integrative model when making an analysis of personality as a determinant of foreign policy formation that should include: motives, beliefs, cognitive style (complexity), and temperament, including competitiveness, dominance, and the tendency to trust or not to trust. She also broadened the study of foreign policy creation to include not only orientations toward war and peace, but also the varied ways in which a leader may search for information, select advisers, and cope with disagreement and opposition.[15]

The previous studies do not adequately apply to a secretary-general, who is essentially a world leader without a state. The work of Kent Kille in examining decision making by UN secretaries-general, therefore, is very useful to our work here. Kille examines a secretary-general's ethical framework, which he defines as a: "combination of personal values that establish the beliefs, forms of reasoning, and interpretation of the world that guide an individual when making judgments about proper behavior in specific contexts."[16] Values and ethics can play a formative role in how a leader frames a decision or situation. Kille explains that values come from a wide range of sources, for example, family, education, culture, personal history and experience, and religion. But leaders can give more weight or less weight to these influences. He acknowledges that the job position and the expectations of the role of a secretary-general, of course, shape behavior once in office. But each secretary-general has approached the office in a different way.

Some secretaries-general, such as Kofi Annan, have seen the role as an opportunity to take advantage of this very public position to act as a bully pulpit and launch such value-rich ideas as promoting human rights, combating poverty, promoting ethical values in the corporate community, and so forth. Others have seen their role as taking a low profile and acting behind the scenes privately to secure the confidentiality of the office in resolving international disputes. One might argue that the constraints of the Cold War would have prohibited previous secretaries-general from promoting values in such a public manner, but we have now had three secretaries-general since the end of the Cold War, and each has taken a different approach. Kille's book explores, through different contributing authors, the relationship between ethics, religion, and decision making among the various secretaries-general and provides a rich case history to build upon.

Kille's other book, *From Manager to Visionary: The Secretary-General of the United Nations*, provides a comparative analysis of leadership style, in general, among three of the United Nations' top officeholders. In this study, Kille undertakes an extensive and very useful review of the literature on personality and leadership, which does not need to be repeated here, but the reader is welcome to refer to his scholarly review. Kille points out that historically, most scholars have held the view that the political context and not the individual is the ultimate determinant of a secretary-general's influence—not his ethical framework, belief system, or personality. On the other hand, Kille refers to Brian Urquhart, who served several secretaries-general over the years, who claims that because the secretary-general has few resources and little real authority, the strength of the office depends on the personal character of the individual.[17]

Kille agrees with Urquhart's observation and creates three leadership styles: managerial, strategic, and visionary. Categorizing each secretary-general into one of the three types, according to Kille, depends on an assessment of his character based on six characteristics: (1) responsivity, (2) belief that he has influence, (3) need for recognition, (4) need for relationships, (5) supranationalism, and (6) problem-solving emphasis.[18] Although these concepts are interesting, the language used is less helpful. Building on other scholarly work by such people as Greenstein, George and George, and Irving Janis, we might find a clearer understanding of what Kille is most likely driving at. An effective leader needs to be perceptive and have good cognitive skills as well as a strong sense of efficacy, or what might be referred to as self-confidence in his/her leadership abilities. A leader who is sociable is perhaps more able to build networks and constituencies for new ideas. On the other hand, low self-esteem and a compulsive need for ego-defensive behavior would be counterproductive, as we saw in the case of Woodrow Wilson and the U.S. failure to join the League of Nations. All leaders are involved in problem-solving, so this does not appear to be a distinctive characteristic. Rather we might look at a leader's approach to problem-solving using Janis's analysis of the "vigilant" decision maker[19] or Kille's research on the influence of ethics or religion on shaping a leader's values and policy goals. Kille's inclusion of the characteristic "supranationalism," which refers to a secretary-general's emphasis on promulgating the values and legitimacy of the United Nations and the common good, is a useful contribution for evaluating UN leaders and perhaps other leaders who are presented with making decisions on global issues.

All this analysis, while interesting in describing past behavior, becomes more useful if it has predictive power. Dean Keith Simonton writes on U.S.

presidents and their leadership successes in an attempt to use empirical evidence to support the relationship between personality and eventual presidential success. Simonton offers a useful description of the field of political psychology in his introduction to presidential leadership.

> Unlike the pure political scientist, the political psychologist considers such factors as motivation, cognitive style, intelligence, childhood experience, age, attitude, and environmental stimuli; unlike the pure psychologist, the political psychologist is also concerned with significant acts of political leadership.[20]

Simonton uses personality as a means of predicting presidential success in two important areas: foreign policy and domestic affairs. He claims that an important attribute that can lead to success is flexibility. A flexible leader can interact with prevailing political situations, for example, in foreign affairs by maintaining the peace through diplomatic relations, and avoiding war, unless absolutely necessary. In domestic affairs, flexibility can facilitate relationships with Congress in negotiating productive outcomes. Simonton bases some of his analysis on other scholars. He uses James Barber's two-dimensional personality scheme: active/passive and positive/negative, developed in Barber's classic book *Presidential Character* to propose that the most successful leader would be both active and positive. The least successful would be negative and passive, while others would fall somewhere in between. Simonton also uses Lloyd S. Etheredge's theories of dominance-oriented personalities versus those that are more conciliatory. As an example, Teddy Roosevelt (a dominant personality) took Panama from Colombia while Jimmy Carter (a conciliatory personality) gave Panama its independence.[21]

Behavioral Traits and Personality Types

All leaders, regardless of position on the political spectrum or their domestic political culture, enjoy attention and are charismatic. Otherwise, they would not have risen to the positions they achieved. This study, therefore, takes that as a basic assumption. We use the concept of traits to describe observable, patterned behavior. For example, one end of the spectrum finds behavior that is controlling, dogmatic, or narcissistic, and on the other end, behavior that is more flexible, open-minded, and even humble. We then group these traits into leadership personality types: (1) authoritarian, (2) chaotic/impulsive, (3) delegative, and (4) flexible/pragmatic. Of course, no leader falls directly or perfectly into one type nor are traits always at one end of the continuum. Therefore, there will be overlap, but the accumulation of traits will place a leader generally into one of the four types. We then compare these four types to George and George's management models. We assume that (1) our authoritarian type would utilize George and George's formalistic model; (2) our chaotic/impulsive type might have a confusing management style that would vacillate from one style to another, which by default may emerge as the competitive model but with less control at the output end than Roosevelt maintained; (3) the delegative type would most likely use the Eisenhower version of the formalistic model where a chief of staff manages the task of delegation and filters all input before it reaches the leader; and (4) our flexible/pragmatic type would use the collegial management model.

We hope that this examination of traits, types, and management models can form a useful framework for analyzing international leaders, and move beyond the heretofore U.S.-centric case studies. The previous studies and models have been based on democratic systems where there is greater transparency, where totalitarianism is not tolerated, and where leaders have to periodically stand for election. Therefore, previous models may not be applicable in societies where, at least historically, leaders have not been elected, there is little or no transparency, and despotic, authoritarian rule, even through brutal means, is accepted or even expected.

This framework of analysis focuses on various international leaders who come from different governmental systems and geographical locations, and also includes women.

An Outline of Traits and Types

The following lists clarify the ideal images of how traits fit into the larger classification of personality type.

The Authoritarian Type and Its Traits

The "ideal" traits of an authoritarian leader:

- Controlling; requires the agreement and obedience of inner circle at all costs, despite reality
- Dogmatic; closed-minded, highly ideological
- Ego-defensive
- Megalomania; leader cannot be wrong
- Power is an end in itself; a preoccupation with maintaining power
- Narcissistic; self-aggrandizement, must be the center of attention; cult of personality
- Obsessive-compulsive
- Intractable; exhibits extreme stubbornness
- Secretive; waits to announce decisions until the opposition has no time to disagree
- Aggressive

- Manipulative
- Deferential to superiors, but abusive to subordinates
- Obsessed with details

The Chaotic/Impulsive Type

The "ideal" traits of the chaotic/impulsive type:

- Inability to focus; often changes mind
- Vacillates between compulsive and impulsive behavior
- Self-confident
- Independent; considers himself/herself a "maverick"
- Accepts the first policy alternative that satisfies the need for a choice
- Nonideological
- Strong sense of personal efficacy
- No tolerance for details

The Delegative Type

The "ideal" traits of the delegative type:

- Likes the prestige of the office, and may use it to promote new norms
- Is not especially interested in governance or administration
- Delegates policy and decisions to others, may show confidence in trusted persons to act without his/her control
- Interest in control is limited, and is only sought to promote a goal
- In weaker leaders, may be easily manipulated, often taking the advice of the last person he/she talks to
- Loyal to inner circle of friends and advisers, whom are relied upon to make decisions
- May or may not be ideologically oriented, depending on political supporters

The Flexible/Pragmatic Type

The "ideal" traits of the flexible/pragmatic type:

- Open-minded
- Strong sense of efficacy; high level of self-esteem
- Curiosity and the capability to find differentiation in disbelief systems
- Innovative
- Listens to others
- Ability to handle disagreement and synthesize perspectives into a larger picture

- Tolerant of different points of view
- Nonideological
- Capacity to see the big picture and still retain a structural focus
- Power is sought to be able to implement policy, not simply for the sake of power

These are what we consider the ideal types and any one individual will not fit neatly into one type. Nevertheless, there will be a tendency to fall into one or another with some overlap. In a democracy, you will not find the extremes of authoritarian leadership, but this enables us to use this type to describe leaders internationally. While we claim that authoritarian leaders will choose the formalistic model of management, this does not mean that every leader who chooses this model is an extreme example of the authoritarian type. But it does mean that, within democratic leadership, there is a role for leaders who want more control, and who perhaps do not have the kind of personality that can tolerate the lack of order or even chaos in the competitive model or the self-confidence of a more collegial interaction.

What Factors Shape Personality?

We attempt here to describe personality as patterns of behavior, offer a list of personality traits, group traits into types, and then link these types to management models. But the challenge remains: what factors shape personality to begin with? George and George bravely address this issue by delving into the early childhood relationship Woodrow Wilson had with his domineering father. Fred Greenstein provides a useful methodology for examining personality and the single political actor, which includes three approaches: (1) phenomenology, a survey and description of observable behavior; (2) dynamics, an analysis of what is responsible in general for patterns of behavior; and (3) genesis, the specific causes within a leader's life experiences, from early childhood through adult experience that determine behavioral outcomes. For our study, we use Greenstein's three levels as: a description of a leader's behavior, the underlying dynamics of the leader's personality type, and finally the origin or causes of these underlying dynamics.

Of course, leaders have characteristics that rest on innate cognitive skills and perhaps even other genetically determined personality factors that are beyond the scope of this study. We acknowledge the whole debate on the nature/nurture phenomenon and some explanatory power will be locked up in that biological interaction. Nevertheless, we believe that we should not be held hostage by what we cannot know in order to develop a better understanding of leadership personality. The examination of each leader in this study is done with the humble awareness that this will probably just scratch the surface and may in some cases be wrong. However, through examining cross-cultural leaders, we can add to the body of case studies that might provide data for future work.

Jerrold Post views the history of the study of personality as taking two paths: the academic interdisciplinary path undertaken by political psychology used here and the applied use of personality study by governments.[22] Not only have scholars found this type of study provocative, but also the importance of this work has been recognized by practitioners within the U.S. government. For example, the U.S. Office of Strategic Services (OSS) followed by the U.S. Central Intelligence Agency (CIA), which replaced the OSS after World War II, has utilized at-a-distance personality assessments over the years to provide a greater understanding of leaders such as Adolf Hitler, Saddam Hussein, Anwar Sadat, Menachem Begin, and others in order to predict behavior. In addition, U.S. government personality studies were used to guide mediation and peace-making processes. Post describes his 21 years in this service and emphasizes the importance given by the U.S. government to this field of study.[23] The creation of a special interdisciplinary office to take up the endeavor, the Center for the Analysis of Personality and Political Behavior, illustrates the value that the U.S. government places on the study of personality.[24] President Jimmy Carter utilized this unit's preparation of personality studies on Anwar Sadat and Menachem Begin in his 1978 Camp David mediation process that ended successfully with the Camp David Accords and peace between Egypt and Israel. Post explains:

> After his diplomatic triumph, President Carter conveyed his appreciation to the CIA for the intelligence support provided him and singled out the personality profiles for special praise.[25]

Nevertheless, from his years of experience of analyzing political personalities, Post expresses an important observation that we will take up again within the conclusion of this volume:

> Yet political leaders from different political cultures differ profoundly, and understanding those differences would be of inestimable value to our senior leaders both in negotiating with them and in dealing with them in politico-military crises.[26]

In conclusion, this book builds on previous work and adds to the field by creating new ways of examining political personalities and bringing together a cross-section of leaders of both genders. We draw from countries around the world and from the past and present, adding to qualitative case studies and exploring how cultural differences, as Post suggests, impact personality and political decisions. In addition, the chapter contributors who have undertaken the examination of the leaders included in this volume are in many cases native speakers or fluent in the language of the subject, enabling the use of primary sources not previously available in English.

NOTES

1. David G. Winter, "Assessing Leaders' Personalities: A Historical Survey of Academic Research Studies," in *The Psychological Assessment of Political Leaders*, ed. Jerrold M. Post (Lansing, MI: University of Michigan Press, 2003), 12.

2. Ibid., 12–13.

3. Ibid., 14–18.

4. Valerie Hudson, "Chapter One: Foreign Policy Decision Making," in *Foreign Policy Decision Making (Revisited)*, ed. Richard Snyder, H. W. Bruck, and Burton Sapian (New York: Palgrave/MacMillan, 2002), 3–4.

5. Ibid., 5–10.

6. Fred Greenstein, *Personality and Politics: Problems of Evidence, Inference, and Conceptualization* (Princeton, NJ: Princeton University Press, 1987), Introduction.

7. Ibid., 3.

8. Ibid., 16.

9. Alexander George and Juliette George, *Presidential Personality and Performance* (Boulder, CO: Westview Press, 1998).

10. Stanley Renshon, ed., *The Political Psychology of the Gulf War: Leaders, Publics, and the Process of Conflict* (Pittsburgh, PA: University of Pittsburgh Press, 1993), Chapter One.

11. Milton Rokeach, *The Open and Closed Mind: Investigations into the Nature of Belief Systems and Personality Systems* (New York: Basic Books, 1960).

12. David G. Winter, "Things I've Learned about Personality from Studying Political Leaders at a Distance," *Journal of Personality*, 73, no. 3 (June 2005): 567.

13. Ibid., 572.

14. Ibid., 579.

15. Margaret Hermann, "Assessing the Foreign Policy Role Orientations of Sub-Saharan African Leaders," in *Role Theory and Foreign Policy Analysis*, ed. S. G. Walker (Durham, NC: Duke University Press, 1992), 161–198; also see Winter, "Assessing Leaders' Personalities," 33–35.

16. Kent Kille, ed., *The UN Secretary-General and Moral Authority: Ethics and Religion in International Leadership* (Washington, D.C.: Georgetown University Press, 2007), 20.

17. Kent Kille, *From Manager to Visionary: The Secretary-General of the United Nations* (New York: Palgrave Macmillan, 2006), 11.

18. Ibid., 20.

19. Irving Janis, *Crucial Decisions: Leadership in Policymaking and Crisis Management* (New York: Free Press/Macmillan, 1989).

20. Dean Keith Simonton, *Why Presidents Succeed: A Political Psychology of Leadership* (New Haven: Yale University Press, 1987), 3.

21. Ibid., 98–110.

22. Jerrold M. Post, Stephen G. Walker, and David G. Winter, "Profiling Political Leaders: An Introduction," in *The Psychological Assessment of Political Leaders*, ed. Jarrold M. Post (Ann Arbor, MI: University of Michigan Press, 2003), 3.

23. Ibid., xi.

24. Ibid., 51–52.

25. Ibid., 59.

26. Ibid., xi–xii.

Part I

AUTHORITARIAN LEADERS IN NONDEMOCRATIC SOCIETIES

2

Colonel Gaddafi: The Political Psychology of a Mad Dog?

Peter Marcus Kristensen and Salem B. S. Dandan

THE PUZZLE OF COLONEL GADDAFI[1]

Dressed in a golden robe and dark sunglasses, and surrounded in his Bedouin tent by female *Amazon* bodyguards—an elite unit in high heels and makeup, allegedly all virgins—Colonel Gaddafi was indisputably a unique personality in international relations. He was the young revolutionary leader who removed a dictator from power to become one of the world's longest ruling heads of state until he was ironically removed from power by young revolutionaries. He was a leading figure of anti-Western resistance during the Cold War, yet defiantly raised his Bedouin tent in Western capitals.[2] He financed an eclectic array of terrorist groups, at least until he joined the U.S. War on Terror. He overtly pursued weapons of mass destruction (WMD), but then in 2003 voluntarily disarmed these programs, under some pressure from the West. To complicate things further, the leaders with whom Gaddafi, as president of the African Union, had shaken hands at the G8 summit in 2009 ended up demanding him to step down just two years later. To say that Gaddafi's foreign policy behavior was enigmatic is perhaps an understatement. Early on, he earned titles such as "rogue criminal" (Henry Kissinger),[3] "the lunatic of Libya" (Anwar Sadat),[4] "a split personality—both evil" (Gaafar Nimeiry),[5] "a reckless adventurer" (Fidel Castro),[6] and, most famously, "the mad dog of the Middle East" (Ronald Reagan).[7] These pejorative portraits, mostly from the 1980s, depict an irrational megalomaniac whose political ambitions were infinite and whose sense of reality was entirely absent. This perception seemed to change when Colonel Gaddafi made a surprising return to the international stage in 2003, after the United States invaded Iraq, until the Arab Spring—a period where he made more headlines with his eccentric behavior abroad than his authoritarian politics at home.

In this chapter, we apply the type of analysis offered by political psychology, which we find more nuanced than the traditional "rational actor" model. Through this lens, an examination of Gaddafi's foreign policy reveals a prudent political calculator who was certainly brutal and dangerous, but not mad. Gaddafi's decisions to support the U.S. War on Terror in 2001 and to dismantle Libya's WMD program in 2003 represented a break with the "terror" and "rogue" foreign policy of his three previous decades in power. But this approach dramatically changed again with the Arab Spring, the Libyan civil war, UN Resolution 1973, and the intervention led by the very Western capitals he had been courting for almost a decade. The question, then, is whether Gaddafi changed or whether the *international perception* of Gaddafi changed. Is it possible to map a consistent political psychological analysis of Gaddafi throughout his rise and fall on the international stage or was he an entirely unpredictable madman with an equally unpredictable foreign policy? How did this seemingly contradictory behavior relate to Gaddafi's personality, ideology, and previous foreign policy behavior? Although it is definitely challenging to paint a coherent picture of Gaddafi, we argue that although he appeared dogmatic in his ideological stance, Gaddafi continuously revised his ideology in order to maintain power. His leitmotif was neither dogmatism nor madness, but to "survive in power" and he managed to do so until both domestic and international pressure in the wake of the Libyan civil war proved too great an obstacle. Before we move on to the analysis of Gaddafi, the following section outlines the theoretical framework.

PERSONALITY, BELIEF SYSTEMS, AND FOREIGN POLICY

In the standard economic definition of "rationality," the decision maker with full information on preferences, possible options, and outcomes chooses the option with the highest benefit. However, these assumptions not only are highly unrealistic, but also inhibit analysis. Instead of posing the question of whether Gaddafi was rational or not, a political psychological approach moves beyond rationality to the analysis of reasoning processes. This move rests on the assumption that "choice is the product of reason."[8] In other words, "a rational choice is one that is based on reasons, irrespective of what these may be."[9] "Reasoning" is defined as a human process of seeking, processing, and concluding from information. This poses the question of how Gaddafi formulated his thoughts and reasoning. Utilizing theories of personality, psychology, and decision making, this chapter aspires to provide "an account of the subject's personality that gives coherence and depth to the explanation of his behavior in a variety of situations and that illuminates the more subtle patterns that underlie whatever seeming 'inconsistencies' of character and behavior he displayed."[10] More specifically, it aims to map out Gaddafi's personality type to provide an explanation for his inconsistent or (in less negative terms) changing foreign policy behavior.[11]

How do we explain Gaddafi's apparently contradictory and changing foreign policy behavior? The theory of belief systems developed by Milton Rokeach, and later introduced into the field of international relations (IR) by Ole Holsti, seems useful here.[12] Rokeach argued that despite any contradiction between them, statements and actions can reveal a belief system—not necessarily a logical one, but a psychological one.[13] He generally distinguishes between open-mindedness and closed-mindedness. At the closed extreme, new information is interpreted to fit existing beliefs, out-groups are rejected and vilified, and cognition tends to be more rigid, narrow, and has a tendency for premature closure.[14] At the open-minded extreme, change is more likely and new information can change the belief system.[15] A belief system representing beliefs, hypotheses, and expectancies about the world is always accompanied by a disbelief system. The disbelief system is a series of subsystems containing disbeliefs and information regarded as false and thus has a low degree of differentiation.[16] A closed-minded personality is expected to isolate and reject contradictory information in the disbelief system.[17]

Another useful theoretical distinction is that of central, intermediate, and peripheral regions. The central region consists of primitive beliefs closely related to *self-image* and perception of the social world as either hostile or friendly.[18] The intermediate region describes nonprimitive beliefs dependent on external authorities for information.[19] A closed-minded person is expected to rely heavily on absolute authority and thus make hard distinctions between the self and the other, in-group and out-group, friend and enemy, and faithful and unfaithful.[20] When faced with new information, the individual may screen its compatibility with primitive beliefs and if incompatible may prefer to distort the new information rather than have to change a core, primitive belief. One can also rationalize this distortion by relying on either an authority figure or the person's own assessment.[21] The central region is fundamental and therefore not prone to change and revisions in the light of new information, while the intermediate and peripheral regions are more open because they do not threaten core beliefs. In sum, at the closed-minded extreme, "it is the new information that must be tampered with—by narrowing it out, altering it, or containing it within isolated bounds. In this way, the belief-disbelief system is left intact."[22] While at the open-minded extreme, new information is assessed as is, potentially producing genuine change in the belief system.[23] Lastly, belief systems rely on a certain temporality—beliefs about the past, present, and future, and their interrelation. Here, a closed-minded person fixates on one temporality rather than "appreciating the continuity and the connections that exist among them."[24]

From available data sources (biographies, interviews, and official statements), the following analysis attempts to establish the degree of closed-mindedness in Gaddafi's personality by initially mapping out the organization of his belief system, and subsequently analyzing changes.[25] It should be noted that the focus on personality and political psychology rests on an assumption that personality has political consequences and thus inscribes itself into a long-standing level-of-analysis discussion in IR.[26] While a more in-depth theoretical discussion is beyond the scope of this chapter, it can be argued that the "personality matters" assumption may be more plausible in authoritarian cases where power is highly concentrated. The Libyan case has been particularly accentuated in this regard: "Libya's foreign policy has to a large extent been determined by the personality in power."[27] With this in mind, we move onto the psychological biography of Muammar Gaddafi.

FORMATION OF THE PRIMITIVE BELIEF SYSTEM: THE BEDOUIN HERITAGE

Born in a Bedouin tent south of the desert town of Sirte, Muammar Gaddafi grew up under poor conditions in the North African desert. One must analyze Gaddafi's character and primitive belief system within the context of these conditions.[28] His family belonged to the Gaddafa tribe, and was respected, but underprivileged and illiterate.[29] Despite the Gaddafa humble living conditions as stock herders, they placed high value on education and sent their only son to a Koranic elementary school in Sirte, where he received a strongly Islamic education, much of it under Egyptian teachers.[30] Since his family could afford neither accommodation nor transportation, he slept in a mosque during school days and trekked the 18 miles home on the weekends.[31] The humble upbringing in an environment most people would consider uninhabitable affected Gaddafi decisively. In his own words "The desert teaches you to rely on yourself ... the values I learned there have remained with me all my life."[32] His emphasis on desert values is worth quoting at length:

> Bedouin society made me discover the natural laws, natural relationships, life in its true nature and what suffering was like before life knew oppression and exploitation ... I have known and lived life in its very primitive stages. Because of that early life, a very simple life, I have lived life in its various stages right up to this modern age of imperialism when life became very complicated, very abnormal and unnatural ... I had a general idea how to make the masses free, how to make man happy. After that, things started to get clearer.[33]

Though Gaddafi's description certainly also served his propaganda purposes of creating an image of a simple and humble desert man, most biographers have stressed the importance of the self-reliance and endurance he learned from the desert.[34] This trait is possibly the most essential component of Gaddafi's primitive belief system and thus crucial to the understanding of his later foreign policy maneuvers. After finishing elementary school, he attended high school in Sebha where he was the oldest boy in class. According to biographers, Gaddafi was seen as a country boy and ostracized by his classmates.[35] In Anderson's account these early encounters with townspeople strongly influenced the young nomad:

> His schoolmates, mostly children of trading townspeople, apparently ostracized and persecuted the young nomad, probably causing much of Qadhafi's antagonism for the urban commercial class and his determination to achieve and hold a position consistent with the positive self-image he would have developed as the son of tribal leader in the desert. The effect of such a negative social experience for a child whose family had given him an extremely positive self-image can be to generate a strong desire for personal power.[36]

According to Middle East scholar Milton Viorst, Gaddafi's tribal Bedouin upbringing also made him "suspicious of outsiders, committed to customary ways, and Arab rather than global in orientation."[37] And while North Africa was a battleground between the Allies and the Axis powers in World War II, Gaddafi's father would tell proud stories about their tribe and its heroes. In biographical accounts, this resulted in a "profound identification and communion with the Libyan people"[38] and simultaneously planted the "seeds of anti-imperialism, the suspicion and dislike of foreigners."[39] Repeatedly faced with conflicting messages about his personality, background, and very nature, however, the young Gaddafi's positive image of himself and his tribe suffered a vital defeat in his formative years. Such experiences contributed to the formation of a victimized personality. The strong tribal affinity among the Gaddafa tribe arguably made him prone to glorification of the in-group while creating a strong us-versus-them attitude. Though the dynamics of a closed *primitive* belief system seemed to consolidate, the young Gaddafi's disbelief system was yet to be differentiated in his encounters with other cultures in his teenage years.

The Formation of an Intermediate Belief System: Nasser, Authority, and Out-groups

The tribal affiliation appears to be the main source of authority when considering Gaddafi's intermediate belief system. However, he was also a pious Muslim, and from his Islamic education derived devout and austere morals, which would later guide his leadership style and be incorporated in his revolutionary ideology.[40] But the young Bedouin's intermediate belief system was arguably most affected by a charismatic leader in a neighboring country. Exposed to the powerful rhetoric of the Egyptian leader Gamal Abdel Nasser—soon to become Gaddafi's greatest idol—the young Muammar developed a strong revolutionary zeal founded in his Bedouin identity and pride of being an Arab.[41] Nasser's vision of Arab nationalism and unity became crucial to Gaddafi's *intermediate belief system.* Nasserism became the primary source of authority against which all new information was assessed. Inspired by Nasser, Gaddafi in his high school years agitated to drive the British out of Libya and put an end to the monarchy. He was expelled (by ministerial order) from school in Sebha for conspiring with classmates to carry out a Nasserite, anti-imperial revolution.[42] The expulsion certainly fueled Gaddafi's alienation from the sociopolitical system and his revolutionary zeal. Upon his father's appeal, however, he was allowed to attend another secondary school despite being 19 and thus too old. In addition to Nasser's influence, other events in the Middle East, such as the 1948 Arab defeat in Palestine, the 1956 Suez crisis, and the 1958 Egypt–Syria union, also had a determining impact on the formation of Gaddafi's pan-Arab and anti-Western ideology.[43] The admiration of Nasser's pan-Arabic foreign policy was hardly unique, but what separated Gaddafi from the rest was his determination to bring a similar revolution to Libya.[44]

Emulating Nasser, Gaddafi entered the army and even received training in England. However, as biographers suggest, he enjoyed neither being a soldier nor visiting England, but was offended by racism and other features of English society while wearing his Bedouin robe in London.[45] In Anderson's analysis, this is credited as a crucial experience that "solidified and personalized his hatred for the West."[46] Gaddafi was reportedly not a good cadet: he was among the 2% failing the exam and he repeatedly disobeyed orders.[47] But as Simons notes, Gaddafi's goal was never to become a good soldier, but rather to use his charisma and rhetorical abilities to organize his military colleagues in a nonviolent coup to overthrow King Idris, which he did on September 1, 1969.[48] According to Anderson, Gaddafi's inspiration from Nasser was so evident that:

> In the first months after the September 1969 revolution, the new regime simply imported its government structure (centered on a "Revolutionary Command Council" of officers who had participated in the coup) and ideology from the model of Nasser's Egypt.[49]

A psychological profile of a charismatic young Gaddafi, strongly inspired by Nasser, began to emerge, dreaming of future achievements, and able to attract a circle of conspirators who were to follow him for the next 40 years.

Relying to a high degree on tribal, Islamic, Nasserite authority, and arguably above all on his personal defeats and the quest for survival in a hostile world, Gaddafi's peripheral belief system was prone to dogmatism and antagonism toward outsiders.

Consolidating the Peripheral Belief System: Toward a Dogmatic Rogue Foreign Policy

The peripheral belief system consists mostly of ideologies and beliefs and disbeliefs about the outside world. Before turning to Gaddafi's foreign policy, it is worth noting his ideological dogmatism in his domestic policy termed "Islamic Socialism." From 1975 to 1979, Gaddafi published his version of Mao's "Red Book"—*The Green Book*—outlining his ideology and leadership style. In 1977, Gaddafi proclaimed his self-invented ideology *Jamahiriya* (state of the masses), emphasizing egalitarianism, popular democracy, and his concept of "Islamic Socialism." Two years later, he announced that he was giving up all official prerogatives in keeping with the new egalitarian philosophy of the revolution.[50] However, in reality, he maintained control. Gaddafi's initial leadership reflected his Islamic moral framework by imposing a system of Islamic morals, outlawing alcohol and gambling. Even the Latin alphabet was banned after the revolution.[51] Despite egalitarian intentions, Gaddafi's Libyan revolution reflected his dogmatic personality.

Turning to Gaddafi's foreign policy, Arab nationalism seems to have been the leitmotif during his first years in power. When Nasser died in 1970, Gaddafi became the self-appointed guardian of Nasser's legacy, calling for a new era of Arab and Muslim unity.[52] Since the revolution, Gaddafi made numerous attempts to promote Arab unification. In line with the vision of pan-Arab unity, Gaddafi made attempts to unify Libya with Egypt, Sudan, Syria, Tunisia, Algeria, Morocco, and South Yemen—needless to say, none was successful.[53] But Gaddafi's Arab nationalist ideology (belief system) was also rooted in a strong anti-imperialist sentiment (disbelief system), and therefore, one of his first acts in power was to demand the departure of the British and Americans. Pan-Arabism thus soon turned into an anti-Western foreign policy.[54] Gaddafi was accused of providing financial backing for the group that carried out the Munich Olympic hostage crisis in 1972 and the bombing at La Belle nightclub in Berlin 1986. The latter prompted the United States to retaliate with bombings in Tripoli and Benghazi and a U.S. embargo on Libyan oil and petroleum products.[55] But it was Libya's connections to the 1988 Lockerbie bombing (leaving 270 dead) and the 1989 UTA bombing (leaving 171 dead) that resulted in the UN sanctions that isolated the country and its leader from international society.[56] Gaddafi responded by denying all responsibility and refusing to extradite the two Libyan intelligence agents, who were accused of planting the Lockerbie bomb.

Simultaneously, Gaddafi's Libya overtly pursued the acquisition of WMD. This became particularly evident in the aftermath of the 1986 U.S. bombings of Tripoli, where Gaddafi claimed that "regarding reciprocal treatment, the world has a nuclear bomb, so we should have a nuclear bomb."[57] Throughout the 1970s, Gaddafi tried to acquire nuclear weapons directly from China, Pakistan, and India, but without success.[58] Efforts then turned to developing indigenous WMD programs and chief among these was a nuclear weapon. Gaddafi succeeded in acquiring uranium yellowcake from Niger and a 10-megawatt nuclear reactor from the Soviet Union.[59] Although it fell short of developing a nuclear capability, the WMD programs combined with sponsoring terrorism made Libya the paradigm example of a rogue state in the eyes of the United States and its allies.[60]

All these foreign policy decisions to some extent reflected, and thus confirmed and consolidated, Gaddafi's dogmatic ideological character and closed-mindedness with regard to the out-group—the West. But while this hostile anti-Western policy might be a result Gaddafi's central belief system that perceived the "outside" world as hostile (with the exception of some other Arab countries included in the in-group), it does not provide the full picture of Gaddafi's motivations. Gaddafi achieved a reputation for impulsiveness and an image as an Arab madman (or hero) who would meet any challenge to his regional or ideological superiority with a call for retaliation, regardless of the costs.[61] However, his very madness and unpredictability could have been a way of keeping his enemies off guard. It might be argued that Gaddafi subscribed to a Nixonian madman theory—the Machiavellian maxim that it can be wise to simulate madness—or Thomas Schelling's idea on the rationality of irrationality. Gaddafi might therefore have reveled when Reagan denounced him as a "mad dog." But apart from the "dogmatic" and "madman theory" explanations, it is essential to question whether Gaddafi had nonideological reasons to affirm his intransigent opposition against the West and Israel, and his quest for Arab unity. A more pragmatic explanation would accentuate that Gaddafi's initial rogue policy added to his David-versus-Goliath image and was useful for international as well as domestic purposes.[62] Libyan scholar Lillian Craig Harris stresses how:

> the need for recognition—the drive to be on stage—infuses Qadhafi's behavior. His grandiose self-assessment allows him to define himself as an opposition figure on a worldwide scale. The fact that he is usually held at arm's length by other heads of state—including those whose admiration he desires . . . appears to have reinforced his dedication to his mission as well as his perception of himself as a chosen person.[63]

His image as a maverick facing the Western imperialists undoubtedly grew in his first decades in power. Close ties with the Red Army Faction (RAF), the Basque separatist organization Euskadi Ta Askatasuna (ETA), the Palestine Liberation Organization (PLO), the Irish Republican Army (IRA), Abu Nidal, the Japanese Red Army, and rebel movements in Sierra Leone and Liberia bolstered the international perception of Gaddafi as a terrorist/freedom fighter.[64] Domestically, Gaddafi faced the rising entrenchment and militancy of the revolutionary committees and could not easily ignore the legitimacy residing with this constituency. Internationally, the Cold War power balance provided him with an instrument to seek security from the U.S. threat and nuclear cooperation with the Soviet Union. Libya's vast oil wealth allowed him to pursue this policy.[65] In sum, during the 1970s and 1980s, Gaddafi embarked on a delicate navigation between domestic and international pressure, although his self-preservation and enduring instinct for survival were not put to the test until much later.

GADDAFI'S POLICY CHANGE: A SURVIVOR THREATENED FROM ALL SIDES

Despite his apparent dogmatism, and contrary to most observers' expectations, Gaddafi actually managed to manipulate the international threat perceptions of his leadership and accordingly his policy on terrorism and WMD.[66] Libya announced a commitment to fight al-Qaeda as early as 1999, and a U.S. State Department report on terrorism credited Gaddafi with having "repeatedly denounced terrorism" since the 9/11 attacks.[67] Having rejected taking the blame for the Lockerbie bombing since 1988, Libya accepted responsibility for the "actions of its officials" in 2003, renounced terrorism, and compensated the victims' families.[68] In December 2003, Gaddafi surprisingly announced the dismantlement of Libya's WMD programs and allowed International Atomic Energy Agency to inspect its facilities.[69] Three years later, the United States agreed to restore diplomatic relations for the first time in 25 years. With its expertise on combating local terrorists/freedom fighters, Libya joined the U.S.-led Global War on Terror.[70] Why did Gaddafi decide to engage in such a metamorphosis? Even more puzzling, how could he succeed in doing so? There were several rationales behind Gaddafi's decision. Domestically, he faced an ailing economy and a rising Islamic opposition. Strategically, he had become isolated in a potential conflict with a United States that just toppled Saddam Hussein in Iraq. Psychologically, Gaddafi observers have noted that he was "weary from a lengthy period of global isolation and longed to return to the international spotlight."[71] Initially, we shall analyze the external, environmental pressures on Gaddafi in order to then explain his internal, psychological motives.

External Pressure on a Dogmatic Personality: Righting the Rogue

Three environmental factors were crucial: the U.S. threat, UN sanctions, and rising Islamic opposition. First, the collapse of the Soviet Union deprived Libya of a power-balancing counterweight to the United States. In addition to this, the events in Iraq certainly provided Gaddafi with an impetus for reflection on his pursuit of WMD, support for terrorism, and the fate of his own, often fragile, regime.[72] Libyan scholar Luis Martinez stresses how "the rapidity of the Iraqi regime's collapse led the Libyan regime to doubt its own forces and its ability to resist."[73] American intelligence reports indicate that Gaddafi continuously perceived another U.S. air raid a constant possibility.[74] Gaddafi also expressed this fear with his characteristically bombastic rhetoric:

> We must comply with international legality even though it has been falsified and imposed by the United States, or we will be slaughtered.[75]
>
> When Bush has finished with Iraq, he'll turn on us. We shall see quickly enough whether Iran, Saudi Arabia and Libya will be targets. The American policy will drop the veil. It will be colonialism over again.[76]

Gaddafi's realignment of Libyan foreign policy was certainly affected by the threat of forced regime change. Gaddafi, who did not shy away from any means to survive in power, therefore presented a quid pro quo to the Americans: "if Libya abandoned its WMD program, the U.S. in turn would drop its goal of regime change."[77] Though negotiations had been going on for months, the announcement of the WMD disarmament on December 19, 2003, less than a week after the capture of Saddam Hussein, verifies the immense U.S. pressure on Gaddafi.

Second, many Libyan scholars have stressed the significance of U.S. and UN sanctions.[78] As a *rentier state*, the regime's primary legitimacy depends on its redistribution of oil revenues.[79] While high oil prices in the 1970s provided high legitimacy for Gaddafi, the sanctions in the 1990s restricted his access to international petroleum markets and caused an unemployment rise of 30 percent, inflation up to 50 percent in 1994, a GDP decrease of 30 percent in 1993, and an average GDP growth of 1 percent from 1992 to 1998.[80] Gaddafi was accused of mismanaging the economy and his legitimacy deteriorated accordingly.[81] This resulted in several coup attempts and a rising Islamic opposition.[82]

Third, he faced a growing Islamic opposition. According to Takeyh, Gaddafi's Libya was the Middle Eastern regime most threatened by Islamic fundamentalists.[83] The Libyan Islamic Fighting Group had declared Gaddafi's government un-Islamic and intended to overthrow it.[84] Groups such as Islamic Liberation Army, National Salvation Front, and Islamic Martyrdom Movement also posed a threat to Gaddafi's survival.[85] Most importantly, the radical Islamists were said to be establishing ties with the institution that has hitherto shielded Gaddafi's regime—the armed forces.[86] According to the U.S. head of negotiations, Martin Indyk, "Mr. Gaddafi had realized that Libya and the US faced a common threat from Islamic fundamentalism."[87] Whereas Gaddafi had considered the Islamists a by-product of imperialism before the conversion, he now associated the Islamists with al-Qaeda.[88] This redefinition indicates that Gaddafi had a very pragmatic attitude toward both his anti-imperialist and his Islamic ideology: whatever keeps his enemies off guard works. In line with this pragmatism, Solomon and Swart conclude that:

> The eccentric "Maverick of the Maghreb" has proved quite capable of adapting his political doctrines and rhetoric to suit the times and the political environment in which he finds himself, even the company he keeps. He has also proven quite cunning in adapting to prevent his demise as a relevant figure in international politics, albeit to stir up controversy and heated debate.[89]

Solomon and Swart also emphasize how Gaddafi's penchant for attention from the media and heads of state had produced an uncomfortable dual diplomacy, with "the colonel proving equally adept at entertaining Africa's elite, while dining with the West's strong men and still succeeding in making headlines."[90] Not only had Gaddafi managed to gain international support for his own war on Islamic terrorists, but he had also stepped back into the spotlight. The question is thus not whether his volte-face was driven by political self-preservation (rational statesman) or a pathological narcissism (madman); it was a combination both.

An Image Change from Within: Paranoid Narcissist and Political Survivor

Personally, Gaddafi had been isolated from the world stage most of the 1990s. He even acknowledged as early as 1999 that, "the world has changed radically and drastically. The methods and ideas should change, and being a revolutionary and a progressive man, I have to follow this movement."[91] According to Takeyh, a crucial psychological reason for the policy change was that Gaddafi realized that while his former compatriots Nelson Mandela and Yasser Arafat were feted in Washington and European capitals, his revolutionary anti-imperialism had become "hopelessly anachronistic."[92] Gaddafi has been described as the prototype of a narcissistic leader, willing to nurture his ego by taking excessive risks and indulging in macho adventures.[93] Such narcissism to some extent corresponds with Middle East scholar Cory Julie's psychological profile of a Gaddafi who had "orchestrated a cult of personality, designating himself al-qa'id al-mu'allim, the 'leader and teacher,' and exploited a combination of symbols and myths for the purposes of accentuating his charismatic nature, simultaneously hiding the realities of an increasingly exclusionary political system."[94] The displays of Gaddafi's portrait in heroic poses that once covered the roads in Libya seem to support this narcissism.[95]

Also, Gaddafi exhibited extreme attention to his personal security, which has been cited as evidence of his paranoia.[96] He reportedly took extraordinary security precautions against being attacked, such as moving constantly and sleeping in different locations; he also feared that the CIA was trying to assassinate him.[97] When leaving his compound, two convoys would take off: one as a decoy, one transporting Gaddafi. When he flew, two planes would take off hours in advance to check for altitude-triggered bombs. He often announced his arrival only shortly before landing.[98] Gaddafi was also notorious for being surrounded by female bodyguards (supposedly because Muslim assassins would have trouble shooting a woman).[99] This apparent security paranoia may very likely have been caused by pathological narcissism. Meanwhile, Gaddafi himself had tried to project an image of an austere leader who had given up all administrative obligations to provide philosophical guidance for the benefit of the people. He apparently saw himself "very much as an intellectual."[100] As he told a German interviewer, "I am a poet . . . From time to time, I weep, but only when I am alone."[101] Although little in his track record suggested that he felt a need for humility, prudence, or restraint, some biographers actually do portray Gaddafi as a modestly living man, rejecting all luxuries and vices. His tradition of receiving visitors in a tent in the desert was considered a conceit by critics and a sign of austerity by admirers.[102] Unlike other military revolutionaries, Gaddafi (again following Nasser) never promoted himself to the rank of general upon seizing power. Although Gaddafi was head of state or the "Leader," Viorst characterized power in Libya as decentralized.[103] But, as the charismatic leader he was, Gaddafi should not be misjudged. He was probably his own best PR agent, dropping details of his humble past in the desert to Western media while wearing designer sunglasses and extravagant robes. One must not forget that Gaddafi was one of the longest serving heads of state and enjoyed the benefits of the office until the very end.

However, although fading away from the world's TV screens due to Libya's isolation might have affected Gaddafi's decision, an explanation based solely on personality disorders such as pathological narcissism rests on uneasy ground. It risks giving his personality medical rather than political relevance and thus trivializing the analysis. Interpreting any selfish behavior as an outward expression of a narcissistic inferiority complex risks neglecting the possibility that Gaddafi's behavior (adventurism, security precautions, etc.) may have a foundation. Following Robert Jervis, it is crucial to avoid the fallacy of overpsychologizing, when behavior could be explained by political analysis. In his classic work, *Perception and Misperception in International Politics,* Jervis argues that in international relations there is an obvious incentive to be suspicious and mistrustful, and therefore, in this case, selfish behavior may be caused not only by Gaddafi's personality, but also by political pressure from the environment.[104] Gaddafi did face a real threat due to immense discontent among a middle class disillusioned by his failed economic distributions, Muslim clerics and fundamentalists deeming his version of Islam as un-Islamic, and military officers infuriated by plans that were to replace the army with a people's militia.[105] Prior to his volte-face, Gaddafi was targeted domestically by Islamist assassins and several military coup attempts, as well as internationally by U.S. air raids and reportedly CIA-trained rebel movements.[106] *Primary narcissism,* the Freudian term for the desire that drives one's instincts to survive, rather than pathological narcissism provides a more appropriate description of the principal features of Gaddafi's personality.[107] This corresponds with the analysis of his *primitive belief system* as being dominated by self-reliance, self-preservation, and survival, whereas his flamboyance and need for attention appear to have been products of later personality developments and a defensive reaction to his rejection at school.

FROM ROGUE TO RIGHTEOUS: A BREAK WITH THE BELIEF SYSTEM

The contradictions in Gaddafi's foreign policy behavior are obvious. In his metamorphosis, Gaddafi had modified, replaced, or discarded most of his ideological tenets: he had turned from an exceptionally anti-Western foreign policy to erecting his Bedouin tent on public squares in Belgium,[108] in France,[109] and at the G8 summit in Italy.[110] The support of Islamic terrorist groups had been replaced by the War on Terror. Pan-Arabism was discarded and was replaced with a vision of a "United States of Africa."[111] The socialist economic ideology was discarded alongside the admission that "the fashion now is the free market and investments."[112] As Takeyh succinctly observes, "the regular procession of visitors to the colonel's tent no longer includes guerrilla leaders and terrorists, but instead features investment consultants and Internet executives."[113] But the question here is whether Gaddafi's policy change represented a break with his belief system or whether one can identify a coherent narrative.

In order to understand Gaddafi's foreign policy change, it is necessary to understand his primitive belief system. Above all, Gaddafi was a survivor. Not surprisingly, the unique political system of "direct democracy" supervised by "the Leader" was the only ideological component impervious to change.[114] In theoretical terms, Gaddafi's policy change can be described as a *punctuated equilibrium* in his peripheral belief system. A punctuated equilibrium describes the compromise between the peak of prior beliefs and the model judged most likely by the data alone. It involves long periods of slow, gradual change, punctuated by relatively short periods of dramatic changes when a lack of logical consistency in previous ideology is suddenly exposed.[115] As Rokeach argues, a belief system (general) differs from ideologies (particular).[116] Thus, while Gaddafi's ideologies of Arab nationalism, socialism, and Islamism were subject to change and revision, the unifying component of his primary belief system remained intact—his endurance and pragmatic drive toward self-preservation. In light of new information on his environment and the perceived threats to his power position, Gaddafi proved more open-minded than the stereotypical image of his personality would expect. When his political survival was threatened by international pressure led by the United States as well as domestic opposition, he adapted his peripheral belief system to fit this information rather than adapting the information to a dogmatic, anti-Western belief system.

The personality explanation does not come without qualifications, though. It is important to note that Gaddafi's core belief system and drive for self-preservation were not only products of his Bedouin upbringing and early encounters with a hostile world, but also affected by the role he had occupied for the last 40 years of his rule. Kenneth Waltz has argued that statesmen under pressure internally and externally (whether authoritarian or not) are crafty: "You've got to carry them out in a box. They've got power and they want to hold it and they want to continue to hold it. They want to pass it on to their progeny, as a matter of fact."[117] As the analysis demonstrated, Colonel Gaddafi's foreign policy decisions corresponded closely with this statement. Several of his official statements support this finding: In one of his early speeches, he stated that "I have become the leader of this revolution by force, and you should know that I will not leave it except by force."[118]

The character trait of self-reliance is not the only source emerging from Gaddafi's Bedouin upbringing. Also, the high value placed on family ties has been characterized as particularly pronounced in Bedouin culture.[119] Not only had Gaddafi propelled members of his tribe and affiliated clans into key state positions, he had also appointed most of his children to official positions.[120] According to several Libyan experts, Gaddafi had long fostered dynastic ambitions.[121] His willingness to bring Libya back into the international community could indeed be interpreted as a preparatory step toward his own succession.[122] According to several sources, Gaddafi's son Seif El Islam, a Western- and reform-oriented philanthropist who held a PhD from the London School of Economics (on the role of civil society in global governance), had been positioned as the designated successor.[123] Or he would have shared power with Al-Mu'tassim, former leader of the advanced army division Force 70. This would have been in the interest of both the military and the Gaddafa tribe, and thus diminish the risk of a post-Muammar coup.[124] Theoretically, Gaddafi's move reveals that his *time perspective* was not only past oriented toward Nasserism and reuniting the Arab world, but was also future oriented toward his own succession and the establishment of a dynasty. The attempt to establish a Gaddafi dynasty was explained both by his tribal personality and by his authoritarian position. But before such dynastic ambitions would ever become relevant, the revolutionary tide that first struck Tunis in late 2010 and eventually made its way to Benghazi presented Gaddafi with an insurmountable challenge, again domestic as well as international, but this time the pressure was larger than before and would eventually end the reign of Gaddafi and his family.

THE ARAB SPRING AND THE FALL OF GADDAFI

Though Gaddafi had managed to reinvent himself as a friend and an ally of the West, he failed to deliver the genuine economic and political reforms that many ordinary Libyans were hoping would come as a result of rehabilitation and opening of the economy.[125] The enduring authoritarian domestic policy allowed discontent to manifest itself again, but unlike the previous rebellious movements, this more popular resistance movement rode on the winds of revolution that blew in from Tunisia and Egypt. The arrival of the Arab Spring in Libya not only would be more violent and bloodier, but would also put Gaddafi's tenacity and self-preservation to a test. The biggest blow came in the form of wide international condemnation and the adaptation of UN Security Council Resolution 1973, which would seal the fate of his regime. Eventually, what started as demonstrations, the likes of which had been seen many times before, would evolve into an all-out civil war and finally result in an international military intervention before it ended with the death of Colonel Gaddafi. The significance of the regional environment in the Arab Spring effect explains the difference between the Libyan Revolution of 2011 and earlier coup attempts that had failed to bring down Gaddafi. Not only did the idea of popular power, fueled by events in Tunisia and Egypt, manifest itself among many different social groups, it also changed the way the Arab world and the wider international community perceived Gaddafi and the legitimacy of his regime.

THE DOMESTIC CHALLENGE: FROM DEMONSTRATIONS TO REVOLUTION

For ordinary Libyans, the rehabilitation had not meant new opportunities or more rights, even though promises of reform and openness were being repeated on a regular basis. Instead they saw more wealth being accumulated and squandered within the high echelons of power and especially by Gaddafi and his family. Although Libya had been opened for foreign investments, the people had seen little to no change, and they felt cheated and angry.[126] Although dissatisfaction with Gaddafi's regime had led to protests and reprisals before, a demonstration planned for the 17th of February in Benghazi, the so-called Day of Rage, gained significant importance. Its purpose was to demand reforms and political rights and simultaneously mark the fifth year anniversary of the killing of demonstrators in Benghazi, an event that shook the regime and especially Gaddafi.[127] While a demonstration like the Day of Rage in its own right would usually have posed few problems for Gaddafi, its coincidence with the Arab Spring in Tunisia and Egypt caused concern. Measures were taken to prevent key activists from participating while Gaddafi planned his own preemptive rallies to be held on the 15th of February.[128] The protests that had managed to unify a broad spectrum of activists from Islamists to autocrats came under attack by Gaddafi's security forces that reportedly acted on orders to "put down the unrest by all means necessary."[129] As the number of martyrs started to mount on the side of the protesters, not only did the slogans change from pro reform to anti-regime, but also the protests turned into riots and then rebellion. Gaddafi's heavy-handed way of dealing with the demonstrators revealed a significantly different approach than that of his counterparts in Tunis and Cairo. Although both Ben Ali and Mubarak had used force against their rebellious populations, unlike Gaddafi they showed restraint and neither had seemed willing to hold onto power until the bitter end, whatever the costs. But Gaddafi—once again consistent with his primitive belief system, dominated by self-reliance, self-preservation, and survival—was determined to hold on to power.[130]

When the Arab Spring erupted in Tunisia and Egypt, Gaddafi was well aware of the risk that the protests might spread to Libya. In anticipation of the potential spillover, Gaddafi chose to condemn the uprising in Tunis as orchestrated by criminals who would destroy the country in their efforts to seize power. He insisted that only turmoil and destruction lay at the end of the journey Tunisians had embarked upon:

> Tunisia now lives in fear . . . families could be raided and slaughtered in their bedrooms and the citizens in the street killed as if it was the Bolshevik or American revolution . . . And for what? In order for someone to become president instead of Ben Ali?[131]

Furthermore, Gaddafi gradually seemed to return to elements of his previous ideological belief system. He argued, for example, that only one thing could justify the Jasmine Revolution, the establishment of a *Jamahiriya* state in Tunisia. Soon the rebellion in Benghazi began to spread in eastern Libya, while Gaddafi remained in control of most of the western part of Libya. The realization that the security forces in Benghazi and many of the eastern cities had disappeared or sided with the rebellion left him stunned. Again, he turned to previous elements of his belief system: suspicion of out-groups and others, notably Western imperialists and Islamic terrorists. Gaddafi blamed Western media and al-Qaeda, never once acknowledging any link to the Arab Spring. In his view, this was the work of Islamists and hostile easterners.[132] In an interview with the BBC, Gaddafi went as far as claiming that the rebels were young men drugged by al-Qaeda and that they would lay down arms as soon as the drugs wore off.[133] For Gaddafi, *the revolutionary*, the notion that his own people, ordinary Libyans, would rise up against him contradicted the central part of his belief system. It must have seemed unimaginable. In line with the theoretical framework, it is not surprising that he would interpret new information of that kind to fit existing beliefs or that he would reject and vilify out-groups. In his own view, Gaddafi had already relinquished power to the people in 1979; how could they even ask him to step down? Equally absurd was the notion of packing up the tent and leave his own country like the Tunisian leader had done. With his sight firmly set on reclaiming lost territory, Gaddafi (mistakenly) calculated that a Western intervention was unlikely due to war weariness from Afghanistan and Iraq.[134]

The fact that Gaddafi was able to launch a counteroffensive against Benghazi proved that he was still in control of much of the military. He had ordered his forces earlier to redeploy to the western cities, mainly to Tripoli. Gaddafi framed this move as security concerns but also as a way of showing restraint from attacking fellow Libyans, although the latter seems unlikely given his resolve and determination not just to survive, but to survive in power. The situations in Tunisia and Egypt had seen the armed forces siding with the protesters, but Gaddafi's model for guarding the regime, or coup-proofing, proved effective: relying on tribal relations that had helped him acquire power, rather than on the military. While we can only speculate whether the situation would have been different if the reliance on the army had been similar to that of neighboring countries, we would point to examples of desertion, especially in the east. Gaddafi himself had formulated his suspicion of the military as "always inclined to tyranny and even conspiracy."[135] By March 17, Gaddafi's forces had retaken several rebel-held towns and now found themselves on the outskirts of Benghazi itself.[136] It was here Gaddafi gave the radio speech that was to become one of the main arguments in favor of gathering international support for a UN-sanctioned intervention. No stranger to using fire-and-brimstone rhetoric, Gaddafi remained true to his image as a proud and uncompromising Bedouin warrior and lashed out at the rebel city of Benghazi and threatened that all opponents of his regime would be "hunted down street by street, house by house and wardrobe by wardrobe."[137]

MOUNTING EXTERNAL PRESSURES AND INTERNATIONAL INTERVENTION: WITH FRIENDS LIKE THESE

Another big blow to Gaddafi's self-image and primitive belief system came from the swiftness with which he fell from grace in the international community: the West, the Arab League, and finally the African Union turned against Gaddafi. On the same night that Gaddafi had broadcasted his warning, the UN Security Council adopted Resolution 1973, calling for a no-fly zone over Libya and authorizing the use of military force to protect Libyan civilians.[138] Baffled by the event, Gaddafi turned to condemnations and accusations reminiscent of his rhetoric from the 1980s and 1990s. European leaders who only a relatively short time ago had been cuing to meet with Gaddafi in order to secure lucrative oil deals had suddenly turned their backs on him. Among these were the Italian leader Silvio Berlusconi who had been his oldest and most trusted ally—and whom he had allegedly taught how to hold *Bunga Bunga* parties. Even more telling was the isolation from the leaders and heads of state of the other Arab states.[139] Unsurprisingly, Gaddafi returned to belligerent, anti-Western rhetoric founded in a central belief system that perceived the "outside" world as hostile. This time the outside was not only the West, however. Just as devastating was the fact that had it not been for the Arab League actively lobbying the Western states for a no-fly zone and going to the United Nations, Gaddafi's predictions of a West unwilling to intervene might have been accurate. The involvement of the Arab League in actively securing a resolution on Libya directly resulted in its adaptation, since the BRIC (Brazil, Russia, India, and China) countries that were all in the UN Security Council (as permanent or temporary members) chose only to abstain.[140] China quoted the regional backing as support for its decision to abstain, rather than veto, in the Security Council.

Gaddafi found himself isolated like never before, domestically, regionally, and internationally. He was certainly back in the international spotlight, but unwillingly in the image of a pariah, and unlike during the Cold War, this time there was no international power game to hide behind. The fact that the Arab League had sided with the West and eventually joined by the rest of the world meant not only that Gaddafi had lost his newly acquired place on the world stage but also that his dreams of Pan-Arab leadership lay shattered.[141] The final blow came in the form of an African Union peace delegation headed by Jacob Zuma of South Africa. During the delegation's visit, which had been welcomed by Gaddafi, the African heads of state made it clear that the time for him to step down had come.[142] Isolated in the international arena and under attack by rebels and NATO (North Atlantic Treaty Organization) strikes, Gaddafi, unsurprisingly given the psychological profile outlined earlier, stuck to his guns. When Tripoli fell in late August nearly six months after Benghazi, Gaddafi had already fled the capital for his hometown of Sirte.[143] When rebel forces finally attacked, they were met with heavy resistance and though the town had been home to many loyalists, suspicions of a high-profile regime target mounted. On October 20, Gaddafi's convoy tried to escape the town, but failed to get far when NATO planes attacked and struck his truck. A wounded Gaddafi, trying to preserve himself until the end, sought refuge in a concrete sewage pipe where rebel fighters found him. While being dragged away Gaddafi was beaten repeatedly; he kept asking his captors, "What did I do to you?" In the following euphoria and excitement over the capture of the leader, a young soldier shot the colonel in the head and chest.[144] Muammar Gaddafi died where he had been born—in the desert south of Sirte, never once contemplating to leave his Libya or relinquish power like Ben Ali and Mubarak.[145] In his final will he reemphasized his connection to his country and his self-image as the ever-vigilant leader of the revolution:

> I call on my supporters to continue the resistance, and fight any foreign aggressor against Libya, today, tomorrow and always . . . Let the free people of the world know that we could have bargained over and sold out our cause in return for a personal secure and stable life. We received many offers to this effect but we chose to be at the vanguard of the confrontation as a badge of duty and honour.[146]

CONCLUSION

Muammar Gaddafi was an enigmatic and colorful personality. His return to the world stage attracted an unmistakable amount of attention, as did his final days. The man who once called for pushing the "Zionists" into the sea turned proponent of a one-state solution to the Israel–Palestine issue called Isratine. Denied chairmanship of the Organization of African Unity in 1982, Gaddafi became chairman of its successor, the African Union.[147] He had proposed a "United States of Africa" and planned to act as screenwriter for a $40 billion epic on Italy's invasion of Libya. Despite his idiosyncrasies, Gaddafi was at the time of his demise the third longest serving head of state and the longest serving republican head of state, with a 42nd anniversary on September 1, 2011. And for almost as long, the West had tried to write his epitaph. Gaddafi survived more than four decades of embargoes, sanctions, U.S. bombings, rising domestic dissatisfaction, Islamic fundamentalism, and *Bunga Bunga* parties, but the Arab Spring and its domestic and international effects were too great a challenge. So if Gaddafi was an insane and irrational mad dog, how had he managed to stay in power for 42 years? Gaddafi's ability to obtain and retain power in Libya undoubtedly reflected his willingness to employ terror, but it also attested to his political skill.

On the other hand, Gaddafi was no stereotype of a rational statesman either. Most biographers concur that the young Gaddafi was a determined anti-imperialist and Arab nationalist inspired by the Egyptian president Nasser.[148] It is indeed obvious to identify the formation of a dogmatic ideological peripheral belief system from his very first years. However, this narrative ignores the complexities and flexibility of Gaddafi's personality and leadership. Politically, there is little doubt that Gaddafi was an authoritarian leader, but psychologically his personality was not unambiguously authoritarian. The analysis of Gaddafi's return to the world stage shows that he was not as closed-minded as the stereotypical image would suggest. Although maintaining power had been his leitmotif, Gaddafi proved susceptible to external pressures and had revised his seemingly dogmatic peripheral belief system. Gaddafi only pursued a rogue policy when he was in control of power resources. When his hold on power was seriously threatened, he changed strategy. His inability to circumnavigate the changes that came in the form of the Arab Spring was not a question of Gaddafi changing strategies, but rather one of the outside world reconstructing its perception of him. Although Gaddafi seemed to return to his previous belief system, particularly the antagonism toward out-groups, his latest actions were still consistent with his drive toward self-preservation. Nor does it change the fact that Libya actually dismantled its WMD program and supported the War on Terror. In the end it was the Arab Spring and how it was perceived in the West that would come to be the breaking point of relations with Libya. Nevertheless, Gaddafi's Libya provides a case of a rogue pursuing WMD, using bombastic anti-Israeli and anti-American rhetoric, and conducting a metamorphosis, in part because of serious domestic pressure and in part because the international community engaged him. A similar situation seems to be repeating in Iran with the nuclear deal and engagement with President Rouhani. The argument here is not that all dictators are susceptible to diplomatic pressure and other nonviolent measures, but simply that it is important to base policy assessments on thorough intelligence on the leader's reasoning and behavior and not to stereotype the enemy as an irrational "mad dog." It should also be noted that while the systematic variation of a specific leader's reasoning processes and behavior might seem perfectly clear in hindsight, prediction of future behavior is a very different matter.

NOTES

1. This chapter is based on original work done by Peter Marcus Kristensen in 2009. Salem B. S. Dandan has helped update the paper to events in the Middle East post-2009.

2. Paul Harris, "Muammar Gaddafi's Campsite Raises Hackles in Smalltown America," *Guardian*, September 23, 2009.

3. "Control of Libya Might Have Saved Sadat's Life, Kissinger Believes," *Free Lance–Star*, October 7, 1981, http://news.google.com/newspapers?id=LXQQAAAAIBAJ&sjid=m4sDAAAAIBAJ&pg=5367,1000335&dq=cannot-find-a-way-to-get-such-a-rogue-criminal.

4. Quoted in "Libya's Colonel Gaddafi Dreams of an Arab Empire—and Bankrolls Worldwide Terror," *People*, August 8, 1977, http://www.people.com/people/archive/article/0,,20068482,00.html.

5. Ogunbadejo, Oye, "Gaddafi and Africa's International Relations," *Journal of Modern African Studies*, 24, no. 1 (1986): 35.

6. "Scouring the Red Sea Floor," *Time Magazine*, August 27, 1984, http://www.time.com/time/magazine/article/0,9171,926817,00.html.

7. "Targeting Gaddafi," *Time Magazine*, April 21, 1986, http://www.time.com/time/magazine/article/0,9171,961140,00.html.

8. Arthur Lupia, Mathew D. McCubbins, and Samuel L. Popkin, eds., *Elements of Reason: Cognition, Choice, and the Bounds of Rationality* (Cambridge, UK: Cambridge University Press, 2000), 1.

9. Ibid., 7.

10. Alexander L. George and Juliette L. George, *Presidential Personality and Performance* (Boulder, CO: Westview Press, 1998), 27.

11. Ibid., 30.

12. Milton Rokeach, *The Open and Closed Mind: Investigations into the Nature of Belief Systems and Personality Systems* (New York: Basic Books Inc., 1960); O. R. Holsti, "The Belief System and National Images: A Case Study," *Journal of Conflict Resolution*, 6, no. 3 (1962), 244–252.

13. Rokeach, *Open and Closed Mind*, 4

14. Ibid., 16.

15. Ibid., 12.

16. Ibid., 33.

17. Ibid., 36–37.

18. Ibid., 40–41.

19. Ibid., 43.

20. Ibid., 45.

21. Ibid., 49.

22. Ibid., 50.

23. Ibid.

24. Ibid., 51.

25. Ibid., 19.

26. Fred Greenstein, *Personality & Politics: Problems of Evidence, Inference, and Conceptualization* (Chicago, IL: Markham Publishing Company, 1969), 1. However, the fact that the Decision Making level brings additional explanatory power does not preclude the level of the bureaucracy, the state, and the international system. See Robert Jervis, *Perception and Misperception in International Politics* (Princeton, NJ: Princeton University Press, 1976), 16–17.

27. Hussein Solomon and Gerrie Swart, "Libya's Foreign Policy in Flux," *African Affairs*, 104, no. 416 (2005): 470. See also Frank Anderson, "Qadhafi's Libya: The Limits of Optimism," *Middle East Policy*, VI, no. 4 (1999). Anderson stated 10 years ago that "The question of whether there will be a significant and lasting improvement in relations with the United States will, in fact, be resolved in the mind of Libyan leader Qadhafi . . . There are aspects of the nature of Libyan society, the Libyan state and Qadhafi's personality that make it virtually impossible for any person or political force in Libya to be able significantly to influence Qadhafi's decisions on major matters or to remove him from power, were they unable to accept his positions . . . The inescapable conclusion from this history is that Qadhafi and Qadhafi alone determines all significant policies of the Libyan government. So to understand what those policies are likely to be, we have to examine Qadhafi's personality, rather than the institutions of his country."

28. Janice Monti-Belkaoui and Ahmed Riahi-Belkaoui, *Gaddafi: The Man and His Policies* (Aldershot: Ashgate Publishing, 1996), 1.

29. Geoff Simons, *Libya: The Struggle for Survival* (London: MacMillan Press, 1993), 152; David Blundy and Andrew Lycett, *Gaddafi and the Libyan Revolution* (London: Weidenfeld & Nicolson, 1987), 33.

30. Craig R. Black, "Deterring Libya: The Strategic Culture of Muammar Gaddafi" (Report by the Counterproliferation Papers Future Warfare Series No. 8 USAF Counterproliferation Center, Air War College 2000), 7, http://www.au.af.mil/au/awc/awcgate/cpc-pubs/black.pdf.

31. Mohamed A. EL-Khawas, *Gaddafi: His Ideology in Theory and Practice* (Brattleboro, VT: Amana Books, 1986), 2; Monti-Belkaoui and Riahi-Belkaoui, *Gaddafi*, 6.

32. "Gaddafi: Obsessed by a Ruthless, Messianic Vision," *Time Magazine*, April 21, 1986, http://www.time.com/time/magazine/article/0,9171,961139,00.html.

33. Mohamed Berween, "The Political Belief System of Al-Gaddafi: Power Politics and Self-fulfilling Prophecy," *Journal of Libyan Studies*, 4, no. 1 (2003).

34. See El-Khawas, *Gaddafi*, 1–2; Blundy and Lycett, *Libyan Revolution*, 33–44; Monti-Belkaoui and Riahi-Belkaoui, *Gaddafi*, 18. In a BBC biography, political analyst Benjamin Barber describes him as "a Berber tribesman, somebody who came out of a culture informed by the desert, by the sand, and in some ways very atypical of modern leadership, and that's given him a certain endurance and persistence." "Profile: Muammar Gaddafi," *BBC News*, http://news.bbc.co.uk/2/hi/africa/7594790.stm.

35. El-Khawas, *Gaddafi*, 2; Simons, *Libya*, 152; Anderson, "Qadhafi's Libya."

36. Anderson, "Qadhafi's Libya."

37. Milton Viorst, "The Colonel in His Labyrinth," *Foreign Affairs*, 78, no. 2 (1999): 72.

38. Monti-Belkaoui and Riahi-Belkaoui, *Gaddafi*, 18.

39. Blundy and Lycett, *Libyan Revolution*, 35.

40. Monti-Belkaoui and Riahi-Belkaoui, *Gaddafi*, 19.

41. Simons, *Libya*, 153.

42. Ibid., 154; See also PBS "Libya's Gaddafi: From 'Mad Dog' to Global Player," *The Online Newshour*, August 4, 2008, http://www.pbs.org/newshour/updates/africa/july-dec08/Gaddafi_08-04.html.

43. Ronald Bruce St. John, "Redefining the Libyan Revolution: the Changing Ideology of Muammar al-Gaddafi," *Journal of North African Studies*, 13, no. 1 (2008): 92.

44. Ibid.

45. Monti-Belkaoui and Riahi-Belkaoui, *Gaddafi*, 8.

46. Anderson, "Qadhafi's Libya."

47. Monti-Belkaoui and Riahi-Belkaoui, *Gaddafi*, 7–8.

48. Simons, *Libya*, 155.

49. Anderson, "Qadhafi's Libya."

50. Luis Martinez, "Libya: The Conversion of a 'Terrorist State,'" *Mediterranean Politics*, 11, no. 2 (2006): 151.

51. Viorst, "The Colonel," 62.

52. Dirk Vandewalle, *A Modern History of Libya* (New York: Cambridge University Press, 2006), 80.

53. El-Khawas, *Gaddafi*, 11.

54. Viorst, "The Colonel," 64.

55. Bruce W. Jentleson and Christopher A. Whytock, "Who 'Won' Libya? The Force-Diplomacy Debate and Its Implications for Theory and Policy," *International Security*,

30, no. 3 (2005/06): 58. La Belle was a Berlin discotheque frequented by American soldiers during the Cold War. The bombings killed two Americans and a Turk. The United States avenged the bombing with an air raid on Libya 10 days later ("Flashback: The Berlin Disco Bombing," *BBC New online*, November 13, 2001, http://news.bbc.co.uk/2/hi/europe/1653848.stm).

56. The UN resolutions sanctioned flights to Libya (UNSCR 748), froze all Libyan assets abroad, and banned the sales of oil products and machinery to Libya (UNSCR 883). See also Tim Niblock, "The Foreign Policy of Libya" in *The Foreign Policies of Middle East States*, ed. Raymond A. Hinnebusch and Anoushiravan Ehteshami (Boulder, CO: Lynne Rienner Publishers, 2002), 229; Jentleson and Whytock, "Who 'Won' Libya?," 59.

57. Luis Martinez, *The Libyan Paradox* (London: Hurst & Company, 2007), 5.

58. Anthony Cordesman, *Weapons of Mass Destruction in the Middle East* (London: Brassey's, 1991), 152; Jentleson and Whytock, "Who 'Won' Libya?," 56.

59. Refers to the reactor in Tajoura that began operations in 1981/1982, See Cordesman, *Weapons of Mass Destruction*, 152.

60. Jentleson and Whytock, "Who 'Won' Libya?," 56. Tim Niblock also stresses that Libya has been considered a threat to Western interests and stability, and thus subject to more Western hostility than other Middle Eastern countries, except Iraq. See Niblock "The Foreign Policy of Libya," 214. It is estimated that more than 30 countries have been affected by terrorism sponsored by Libya. See Martinez, *Libyan Paradox*, 56.

61. Viorst, "The Colonel," 66.

62. Vandewalle, *A Modern History*, 133.

63. Lillian Craig Harris, *Libya: Qadhafi's Revolution and the Modern State* (Boulder, CO: Westview Press, 1986), 52.

64. See Monti-Belkaoui and Riahi-Belkaoui, *Gaddifi*, 20; "Libya's Gaddafi: From 'Mad Dog' to Global Player."

65. Ray Takeyh, "The Rogue Who Came in from the Cold," *Foreign Affairs*, 80, No. 3 (2001): 63

66. For a view of Gaddafi as extremely dogmatic, ideological, and not susceptible to pressure, see Anderson, "Qadhafi's Libya."

67. U.S. Department of State, *Patterns of Global Terrorism, 2001* (May 21, 2002), http://www.state.gov/s/ct/rls/pgtrpt/2001/.

68. Martinez, "Libya," 152; Jentleson and Whytock, "Who 'Won' Libya?," 68.

69. Anthony Cordesman, *The Military Balance in the Middle East* (Westport, CT: Greenwood Publishing Group, 2004), 451. The full agreement on dismantlement included: Libya committed to eliminate its chemical and nuclear weapons, declare its nuclear activities to the IAEA, eliminate ballistic missiles ranging more than 300 kilometers, accept international inspections to ensure the compliance with the Non-Proliferation Treaty, eliminate all chemical weapons, and accept the "Chemical Weapons Convention," allow immediate inspections, and surveillance of these actions See also Jentleson and Whytock, "Who 'Won' Libya?," 67.

70. Martinez, *Libyan Paradox*, 56.

71. Quoted in St. John, "Redefining the Libyan Revolution," 99. See also Viorst, "The Colonel"; and Takeyh, "The Rogue."

72. Solomon and Swart, "Libya's Foreign Policy," 484.

73. Martinez, *Libyan Paradox*, 6.

74. Gregory R. Copley, *Iraqi WMD Debate and Intelligence: The Links to Libya*, January 30, 2004, http://www.freerepublic.com/focus/f-news/1219953/posts.

75. Yahir H. Zoubir, "The United States and Libya: From Confrontation to Normalization," *Middle East Policy*, 13, no. 2 (Summer 2006): 57

76. Martinez, *Libyan Paradox*, 45.

77. Michael Hirsh, "Bolton's British Problem," *Newsweek*, May 2, 2005, www.newsweek.com/id/51894.

78. Viorst, "The Colonel," 60; Takeyh, "The Rogue," 64; see also Ronald Bruce St. John, "Libyan Foreign Policy: Newfound Flexibility," *Orbis*, 47, no. 3 (2003): 476.

79. Hazem Beblawi, "The Rentier State in the Arab World," in *The Arab State*, ed. Giacomo Luciani (London: Routledge, 1990): 85.

80. Jentleson and Whytock, "Who 'Won' Libya?," 65.

81. Cordesman, *The Military Balance*, 31.

82. Takeyh, "The Rogue," 65.

83. Ray Takeyh, "Qadhafi and the Challenge of Militant Islam," *Washington Quarterly*, 21, no. 3 (1998): 159.

84. Cordesman, *The Military Balance*, 411.

85. Takeyh, "Qadhafi and the Challenge," 168. And several other opposition movements could be mentioned: The Muslim Brotherhood, Islamic Jihad, Takfir wa-l Hijra, the non-Islamic National Front for the Salvation of Libya (NFSL), Libyan patriotic army (LPA), Libyan movement for change and reform (LMCR), Libyan National Alliance (LNA), and Libyan National Democratic Assembly.

86. Ibid., 159.

87. Martin Indyk, "The Iraq War Did Not Force Gaddafi's Hand" *Financial Times*, March 9, 2004, http://www.brookings.edu/opinions/2004/0309middleeast_indyk.aspx.

88. Martinez, "Libya," 157.

89. Solomon and Swart, "Libya's Foreign Policy," 491.

90. Ibid., 489.

91. Takeyh, "The Rogue," 66.

92. Ibid., 64.

93. See Aubrey Immelman, "The Assessment of Political Personality: A Psychodiagnostically Relevant Conceptualization and Methodology," *Political Psychology*, 14, no. 4 (1993): 736–737. Also, Gaddafi has been described as "a desert dandy, with a gold-embroidered and tasseled uniform for every conceivable occasion and all manner of robes, capes and turbans." "Gaddafi: Obsessed by a Ruthless, Messianic Vision."

94. Vandewalle, *A Modern History*, 124; Cory S. Julie, "What Makes Rogue States Rogue? Ideobalancing, Threat Perception, and Foreign Aggression" (working paper prepared for presentation at the Annual Mid-West Political Science Association Conference, 2009), 19, http://www.allacademic.com//meta/p_mla_apa_research_citation/3/6/3/5/0/pages363502/p363502-1.php.

95. Viorst, "The Colonel," 62.

96. Monti-Belkaoui and Riahi-Belkaoui, *Gaddafi*, 20.

97. Ibid. See also Bob Woodward, *Veil: The Secret Wars of the CIA 1981–1987* (New York: Simon & Schuster, 1987), 320.

98. Arnold M. Ludwig, *King of the Mountain* (Lexington: University Press of Kentucky, 2002), 250–251.

99. Woodward, *Veil*, 320.

100. BBC, "Profile: Muammar Gaddafi."

101. "Gaddafi: Obsessed by a Ruthless, Messianic Vision."

102. Viorst, "The Colonel," 65.

103. Ibid., 69.

104. Jervis, *Perception and Misperception*, 4.

105. Black, "Deterring Libya," 16; Jentleson and Whytock, "Who 'Won' Libya?," 66.

106. El-Khawas, *Gaddafi*, 107–113; Monti-Belkaoui and Riahi-Belkaoui, *Gaddafi*, 42–43; Viorst, "The Colonel," 62.

107. On primary narcissism, see Sigmund Freud, *On Narcissism: An Introduction* (1914; repr., London: Hogarth Press; 1957), 73–74.

108. "Consternation as Muammar Gaddafi Seeks to Pitch His Tent on Nicolas Sarkozy's Lawn," *Times Online*, November 24, 2007, http://www.timesonline.co.uk/tol/news/world/europe/article2933205.ece.

109. "Divided, France Welcomes and Condemns Gaddafi," *New York Times*, November 12, 2007, http://www.nytimes.com/2007/12/11/world/europe/11france.html.

110. "Obama Shakes Hands with Libya's Gaddafi," Sky News, July 10, 2009, http://news.sky.com/skynews/Home/World-News/President-Obama-Shakes-Hands-With-Colonel-Muammar-Gaddafi-At-LAquila-G8-Summit/Article/200907215334449?f=rss.

111. St. John, "Redefining the Libyan Revolution," 465.

112. Takeyh, "The Rogue," 65.

113. Ibid.

114. St. John, "Redefining the Libyan Revolution," 91.

115. Arthur T. Denzau and Douglass C. North, "Shared Mental Models: Ideologies and Institutions," in *Elements of Reason: Cognition, Choice, and the Bounds of Rationality* ed. Arthur Lupia, Matthew D. McCubbins, and Samuel L. Popkin (Cambridge, UK: Cambridge University Press, 2000), 41–42.

116. Rokeach, *Open and Closed Mind*, 29.

117. Kenneth Waltz, interview by Conversations with History; Institute of International Studies, UC Berkeley, http://globetrotter.berkeley.edu/people3/Waltz/waltz-con6.html.

118. Berween, "Political Belief System."

119. El-Khawas, *Gaddafi*, 32; Blundy and Lycett, *Libyan Revolution*, 98.

120. These positions range from head of the Libyan Olympic Committee (Muhammad); president of the Libyan National Association for Drugs and Narcotics Control, the Gaddafi International Foundation for Charity Associations, and negotiator on behalf of Muammar Gaddafi (Seif Al-Islam); head of the Libyan Football Federation (Saadi); national security adviser and leader of the advanced army division Force 70 (Mu'tassim); to defense lawyer of Saddam Hussein (Aisha). Little is known about his two youngest sons, Saif Al Arab and Khamis.

121. Martinez, *Libyan Paradox*, 152; Muhammed Ibrahim, "The Sons Also Rise," *Foreign Policy*, no. 139 (Nov–Dec, 2003), 38; Eben Kaplan, "How Libya Got Off the List," *Council of Foreign Relations*, http://www.cfr.org/publication/10855/.

122. Martinez, *Libyan Paradox*, 152.

123. Ibrahim, "The Sons Also Rise," 38; Martinez, *Libyan Paradox*, 152.

124. Ibrahim, "The Sons Also Rise," 38.

125. Daniel Kawczynski, *Seeking Gaddafi: Libya, the West and the Arab Spring* (London: Biteback Publishing, 2011), 229–231.

126. Alison Pargeter, *Libya: The Rise and Fall of Gaddafi* (New Haven: Yale University Press, 2012), 212.

127. Ibid., 214.

128. Ibid., 219.

129. Ibid., 220–221.

130. Ibid., 220.
131. Ibid., 221.
132. Ibid., 224.
133. Kawczynski, *Seeking Gaddafi*, 242; video interview available at: http://www.bbc.co.uk/news/world-middle-east-12607478.
134. Pargeter, *Libya*, 226.
135. Ibid., 224.
136. Ibid., 233.
137. Kawczynski, *Seeking Gaddafi*, 242.
138. Pargeter, *Libya*, 234.
139. Kawczynski, *Seeking Gaddafi*, 245.
140. UN Security Council statement, March 17, 2011, http://www.un.org/News/Press/docs/2011/sc10200.doc.htm.
141. Pargeter, *Libya*, 235.
142. Kawczynski, *Seeking Gaddafi*, 245.
143. Pargeter, *Seeking Gaddafi*, 242.
144. Ibid., 244–245.
145. Ibid., 246.
146. Pargeter, *Libya*, 246.
147. "Gaddafi Pushes for Power at Helm of African Union," *Independent*, February 18, 2009, http://www.independent.co.ug/index.php/reports/world-report/74-world-report-/596-gaddafi-pushes-for-power-at-helm-of-african-union.
148. See Simons, *Libya*, 152–154; Viorst, "The Colonel," 64.

3

Saddam Hussein: Violence and Terror

Charlotte Scaddan, Marcin Szudek, and Jean Krasno

Saddam Hussein's name appears high in the ranks of the most notorious twentieth-century dictators, frequently even referred to as the *Butcher of Baghdad* or the *Madman of the Middle East*. The epithets associated with his name are not baseless: from his accession to the top of the Iraqi government in 1979 until his fall in the U.S.-led invasion of 2003, Saddam ruled with an absolute disregard for human rights or justice. His rule was punctuated by acts of terror inflicted on friend and foe alike—from prison sentences imposed on political colleagues accused of propagating negative personal rumors, to the murder of those he feared were plotting against him, to the poisoning of thousands of Kurdish civilians, Saddam possessed the ability to perpetuate violence on every scale. This chapter examines Saddam's life experiences as an explanation for his decision making behavior and focuses particularly on his decisions that led to his demise in the 2003 Gulf War.

When political figures show a propensity for aggression, approaching the methods used by Saddam, Western political culture often labels them "irrational." Observers and analysts tend to view infamous leaders of the modern political era, from Hitler through Pol Pot to Kim Jong-un, as "insane," who lack the capacity to lead their regimes with logic or forethought. While this trend in political analysis tends to be effective for the media—sensationalism sells, after all—it is usually intellectually dishonest and counterproductive for policy makers. Viewing belligerent authoritarian leaders as irrational does not provide policy makers with the tools for effective prediction of future behavior. The widespread misperception that Saddam was an irrational actor to be

The views expressed herein are those of the authors and do not necessarily reflect the views of the United Nations.

feared by the West was a strong contributor to the creation of the political rationale to remove him from power through military force in the 2003 invasion of Iraq.

Saddam's personality and decision making, far from being irrational, were products of a difficult life in dangerous circumstances. Jerrold Post, offering what is perhaps the most accurate psychological profile of Saddam, characterized Saddam's early development as being most significantly affected by the failure to bond with his mother and the abuse he suffered from his stepfather. This produced what Post referred to as a "wounded self," leaving Saddam to identify himself as a victim at the hands of others from a very early age. Two possible responses usually follow in such situations: one is to give up and give in to abuse and depression, and the other is to develop a confrontational attitude, never allowing others to inflict pain on one's psyche. Saddam, or the "one who confronts," as his name is translated into English, followed the latter path.[1]

Certain facts concerning Saddam's childhood are vague; even such basic details as the date of his birth are unclear. Like many other authoritarian leaders, Saddam liked embellishing positives and disregarding negatives in his official biographies. While Saddam's exaggerations are not as egregious as other leaders—unlike Kim Jong-il, he does not claim to have shot a 38-under par on a golf course or learned to talk by the time he was 8 weeks old[2]—it is nonetheless difficult to accept the official word on Saddam's life as fact. There is little evidence to back some assertions made about Saddam's early life, but over time, historians have assayed some claims to be more plausible than others.

Saddam was most likely born on April 28, 1937. Some accounts place the year of his birth as 1935 or 1939, and the day and month of his birth are unclear as well. It is possible that Saddam is younger than the national holiday he created in his own name claims and that he changed his year of birth to make his marriage to his first wife, Sajida, less controversial (it is very unconventional in traditional Arab societies for a man to marry an older woman). It also seems that Saddam may have stolen his official birthdate from one of his peers, Abdul Karim al-Shaikhly, who, on account of being born into a family with considerable socioeconomic standing, possessed an official birthdate. Most rural authorities at this time did not bother recording the day and month of lower-class individuals.[3]

His birthplace was the village of al-Awja, some 8 miles south of the larger populated center of Tikrit. Life in Iraq, and especially in al-Awja, was extraordinarily miserable in the 1930s. There were no roads or schools, no running water or electricity. According to historical records, infant mortality rate in Iraqi cities in this era was 228 per 1,000 live births; and it is certain that rural areas experienced rates much higher.[4] Iraqis who did not perish in infancy experienced widespread malnutrition and epidemics of diseases such as malaria, tuberculosis, and nonvenereal syphilis. Most of the occupants of al-Awja worked as laborers on the estates of the more affluent residents of Tikrit; a large portion of the society engaged in illicit activities. The proximity of al-Awja to the Tigris River allowed it to become a hideout for bandits, whose main sources of loot were the *doba*, barges that traveled between Mosul and Baghdad with trade goods.[5] The village of al-Awja was a place that demanded of its inhabitants a social Darwinist perspective in order to prosper.

Saddam's familial circumstances did not foreshadow an easy life either. His father, a poor peasant named Hussein al-Majid, was not present at the time of Saddam's birth. His absence is the only certain fact about his person. While he most likely died of cancer or other natural causes, differing accounts allege that he was murdered due to his illegal activities or simply ran away from Saddam's mother. More extreme allegations also claim that he was never married to Saddam's mother, or that Hussein al-Majid did not exist as a person—there are accounts that claim that Saddam's mother engaged in prostitution and Saddam was a child of an unknown customer of hers.[6]

Regardless of the reasons, Hussein was not present for Saddam's birth, and his older brother had perished from a terminal disease shortly prior to Saddam's arrival. His mother, Subah Tulfah, unable to cope with her circumstances, fell into severe depression. Twice she attempted suicide to force a miscarriage. Both times a Jewish family that lived nearby prevented her from succeeding.[7] Once Saddam was born, Subah did not wish to care for him; regardless of her intentions, she was materially unable to provide for the newborn as well and she handed Saddam over to her brother, Khayrallah Tulfah. It was Khayrallah's presence, as well as his absence, that would have the biggest impact on the young Saddam.

Khayrallah Tulfah became Saddam's father figure as well as political mentor during his formative years. Khayrallah's only intellectual publication, "The Three Whom God Should Not Have Created: Persians, Jews, and Flies,"[8] provides the best summation of his political stance and psychology. Khayrallah was a military officer and a teacher. His extreme nationalism and hatred of British colonialism led him to become a Nazi sympathizer during late 1930s. By most accounts an ill-tempered man, he nonetheless cared for and made an impression on young Saddam from the very beginning. However, in 1941, Khayrallah began a jail sentence for his attempts to overthrow the British-supported Iraqi government.[9]

Saddam at this point was returned to his mother, who stabilized her life by marrying a distant relative, Hassan al-Ibrahim. It was rumored that Subah tempted Hassan to leave his first wife; the people that knew the family seemed to hold Hassan and her in contempt.[10] Whatever the circumstances of their marriage, the bond between the newlyweds was well-formed by the time Saddam returned, and his presence in the household was not welcome. Hassan was an abusive stepfather, berating Saddam, denying him an education, and coercing him to commit crimes. His mother did not step in to protect her child, favoring Saddam's newborn stepsiblings over him. Saddam, now about four to seven years old, suffered as a result of this treatment. In terms of child development theory and the impact on personality, response to this kind of harsh treatment can move in two directions: as a victim to surrender to circumstance on one end or aggressively reaffirm one's own personality at the other. Both results leave a child with a personality that is centered on protecting the ego. Post views Saddam as having developed "a psychological template of compensatory grandiosity, as if to vow, 'Never again, never again shall I submit to superior force.' "[11] This developmental path became evident very early on. Saddam, rejected by his family as well as by his village peers, began to carry around an iron stick, ready to use it against those who verbally or physically aggrieved him. While he still suffered at the hands of his stepfather, opportunities would soon open to Saddam that would drastically change his life.

By 1947, Khayrallah was out of jail and plotting to reenter the Iraqi political scene. Saddam's official biography states that desiring the education denied to him by his stepfather, he took off from his house in the middle of the night, seeking to rejoin his uncle Khayrallah and his older cousin. Whether Saddam actually escaped his own home and traveled by foot to Tikrit, or Saddam's mother and stepfather facilitated the decision, is uncertain. However, his uncle did greet Saddam with open arms and allowed him to begin his much-delayed academic and political education.[12]

THE MAKINGS OF AN ASSASSIN

Saddam had his first taste of violence at an early age, perhaps 20 or 21. Fittingly, the first homicide committed by Saddam was both a political and a personal assassination ordered by his uncle Khayrallah. Khayrallah managed by mid-1958 to receive an appointment as the director of education in Baghdad. As a Baathist, he faced opposition from the extant communists. Saadoun al-Tikriti, a communist party worker, informed Baghdad's authorities of Khayrallah's violent past, and Saddam's uncle quickly lost his appointment. Khayrallah decided to use Saddam to exact his revenge, and his nephew carried out the killing of Saadoun al-Tikriti in October 1958, shooting the communist in the head at point blank range as he was walking home from a social gathering. The subsequent investigation and arrest of Khayrallah and Saddam were fruitless; as the communists were not a well-liked political minority in Iraq, police held the pair in jail for several months and subsequently released them due to lack of evidence. While imprisoned, the two kept to themselves and did not disclose the details of

the murder even to fellow Baathists who passed through the same prison.[13] While Saddam has never officially acknowledged murdering al-Tikriti, much evidence points to him being the man behind it.[14]

The Baathists quickly recognized Saddam's violent abilities and Saddam joined Iraq's Baath Party in 1957. While the party was a miniscule political player in 1958, its ideologues already possessed ambitious plans for revolution at this time. Saddam thus received an official assignment from party officials: presidential assassination. However, after participating in a failed attempt to assassinate the Iraqi prime minister in 1959, Saddam fled to Egypt. He was able to return to Iraq when the Baathists gained power in 1963 but was jailed when they were overthrown. He escaped and helped reinstall the party in 1968. By 1979, Saddam Hussein had worked his way to becoming president of Iraq.

IRAN–IRAQ WAR, 1980–1988

Saddam's decision to invade Iran in 1980, one year after he became president, was motivated by his vision of Arab unity. Seeing himself as leader of the Arab world, Saddam, a Sunni, interpreted the Islamic Revolution of 1979 through his own belief system. His motives for initiating war with Iran were both offensive and defensive. First, there was the threat of Ayatollah Khomeini's revolution igniting a Shi'a rebellion within Iraq itself. Khomeini's defiance of Washington won him support in the Muslim world, and Saddam, always feeling besieged, feared a Shi'a popular uprising in his own nation.

He also had offensive motivations. He believed that his ultimate goal of becoming the symbol of Arab unity would be strengthened by a quick and decisive victory over Iran.[15] In addition, an Iraqi victory would leave Saddam controlling a disproportionally large percentage of global oil supplies, giving him incredible economic leverage.[16] Most likely, he calculated that the United States would decide not to interfere, as the American government was still reeling from its failures in Vietnam and the Iran hostage crisis. Additionally, he calculated that the Iranian government would be at its weakest vis-à-vis Iraq. Beyond the immediate strategic situation, his belief system switched once again to his siege mentality. Saddam stated in meetings that he believed the American government was behind the Islamic Revolution in Iran. Shortly prior to the breakout of the war he felt that "the change that took place in Iran was designed with the intentions to be against the interest of Iraq."[17]

His calculations of a quick victory over Iran proved wrong. As the war dragged on over eight years, Saddam's desperation caused him to employ tactics that showed complete disregard for even the most basic international human rights standards. Evidence is clear now that he used chemical weapons against Iran and against the Kurds in retaliation for a rebellion they had launched in northern Iraq.[18] His campaign against the Kurds in the north and Shi'as in the south during the war left almost 200,000 civilians dead.[19]

SADDAM'S USE OF MESOPOTAMIAN SYMBOLISM

Much like other Pan-Arabist leaders across the Middle East, Saddam made extensive use of ancient Mesopotamian symbolism in the development of his cult of personality. He used Iraq's extensive history, dating back to the beginnings of human civilization, as the backing for Iraqi nationalism, allowing him to place his country at the pinnacle of Arab states, its superiority due to its past greatness. The development of Saddam Hussein's cult of personality rested on two elements: the depth of Mesopotamian history and an extensive use of Iraqi Baathist insiders engaged with artistic and cultural circles to propel Saddam's image associated with legendary figures such as Nebuchadnezzar and Hammurabi.[20]

Saddam's motivation to reach absolute greatness and a permanent place in world history stemmed from the grandiose aspirations he developed as a result of a traumatic childhood. The actions he took to extend the power of his image across Iraq and the Arab world vividly express those desires. He appeared on art festival emblems, his profile next to that of Hammurabi, with cuneiform inscriptions around the two leaders. He replicated famous Mesopotamian art, adding himself (as well as modern military equipment) into battle scenes from antiquity. Archeological and historical conferences in Iraq had their contexts altered—Hammurabi's biography began to strangely resemble the official biography of Saddam Hussein.[21]

The affinity for association with ancient Mesopotamian heroes that Saddam developed was not only a public relations move (after all, even the most democratic of leaders love to hark back to past historical figures), but also a genuine aspect of his psychology, an element we can trace back to when Saddam first learned to talk. It was under the guidance of his uncle Khayrallah that Saddam first began to associate himself as a unique figure who was destined to restore the glorious past of Mesopotamian history.

THE 1990 INVASION OF KUWAIT

A full discussion of Saddam's motives for invading Kuwait in August 1990 is beyond the scope of this chapter; however, in short, after the war with Iran, Saddam found Iraq to be in tremendous debt, particularly to Kuwait. Saddam had appealed to regional organizations to cut the production of oil and raise prices, so he could earn back needed funds to pay off his debts. But these pleas fell on deaf ears, and Saddam decided aggressively to end the matter by invading Kuwait and taking over Kuwaiti oil fields. He believed that the United States was disinterested in these affairs, but, as we know, he was quite wrong and the 1991 Gulf War took place from January to April, ending his occupation. Saddam made similar miscalculations in 2003.

SADDAM'S EXTREME DECISION MAKING STYLE LEADING UP TO THE 2003 WAR

The policies of Saddam's government in the run-up to the U.S.-led invasion of Iraq in 2003 constitute a fascinating illustration of flawed decision making, contributing to the fall of his regime. It is counterfactual to speculate as to whether alternative decisions by Iraqi officials may have been able to avert the war altogether. But what is clear is that in Saddam's government, decisions were taken in an atmosphere of secrecy, deceit, and fear. The West would view Saddam as far from being a rational decision maker, yet, his assessment of the position of the United States before the 2003 war was fairly accurate. However, while displaying a few elements of rational thinking, Saddam's decisions were overwhelmingly dominated by psychological constraints. He transformed the Iraqi government into a defective decision making machine, the antithesis of vigilant problem solving.[22] How did this occur? And in what way did Saddam's personality traits impact governmental decisions? This section examines the constraints on Iraqi decision making that not only debilitated Saddam but caused him to inflict constraints on those around him, thereby creating a situation that rendered effective decision making unattainable at all official levels.

Saddam was a product of Iraq's violent culture and, as discussed, began his career as a hit man in the Baathist party, founded on a belief that the Arab world should be restored to its former glory. Saddam rose quickly through the ranks. In a climate of political instability in Iraq, he learned that maintaining power was more difficult than gaining it and he launched a regime of spying and purging political enemies, designed to defuse internal threats of a coup. For him, political devotion was by far the most important attribute in his officers and one that must be achieved at any cost. Upon gaining power, Saddam carried out the first of his purges of potential foes among his colleagues by having their 66 names announced at a party meeting before they were immediately executed.[23] A video of the event shows Saddam shedding tears as his purged colleagues were taken from the room.

Saddam's self-imposed image in the vein of Nebuchadnezzar and Saladin led him to believe that it was his destiny to liberate Jerusalem from the infidels and establish a new caliphate with himself as caliph. In this sense, Saddam displays his belief in what Marvin Zonis has called Arab "organizing myths," which serve to defend the state of Palestine and its people from Israel, and to pursue the notion of an Arab world unified under one powerful and charismatic leader. Saddam's invasion of Kuwait, however, shattered the idea of Arab unity. Furthermore, it was not a powerful Arab leader that came to Kuwait's rescue but a Western-led coalition of forces.[24] While Iraq's action trampled the Arab myth, Saddam nevertheless used myth to justify countless heinous acts. His belief in himself as the rightful leader of all Arab peoples fuelled his sense of invulnerability and his conviction that he would succeed against his enemies. He came to see himself as the foundation of the existence of the nation of Iraq; for Saddam, he and Iraq were indivisible.[25]

Saddam's closed belief system is evident, illustrated in part by his focus on the past glory of Iraq and in part by his willingness to justify any decision in order to retain power and therefore make Iraq great. Possessing an authoritarian leadership type, he showed no mercy to subordinates but could be charming and respectful to other leaders when politically expedient.[26] His focus on his own survival was obsessive; if Iraq was to survive as a great Arab nation, then he must remain in power.

Members of Saddam's inner circle have alluded to an emphasis on mysticism that was among the heuristics used in his decision making strategy. This involved Saddam finding inspiration in dreams and translating it into policy the next day—a method employed during the Iran–Iraq War, according to Abid Hamid Mahmud al-Khattarb, Saddam's personal secretary.[27] Such tactics are reflective of his overall tendency to take major decisions alone, consulting with only one or two of his most trusted aides, if anyone at all. He rarely sought advice from others, bolstered by an unfailing confidence in his own decision making abilities, which he believed superior to using facts gathered by intelligence agencies. Saddam boasted that situation analysis was his "specialty," which he used against Iran, "some of it out of deduction and some of it through invention and connecting the dots, all without having hard evidence."[28] For Saddam, numinous messages and instinct were of greater value than hard facts.

Despite his confidence, Iraq had faced severe military setbacks that warranted an explanation, at least in his own mind. This reality caused Saddam to turn to denial as a self-defense mechanism. He created the myth of Iraqi military might and reinterpreted recent history to create "chosen glories" that he had brought to Iraq.[29] Stating that the war with Iran had been a resounding success and that Iraq had defeated the United States and coalition forces in the 1991 Gulf War, he referred to the U.S. decision not to move upon Baghdad in the Gulf War as a sign of America's defeat and, more importantly, of Iraq's victory. Foreign Minister Tariq Aziz asserted that Saddam "lost touch with reality during the 1990s" and had adopted an "unrealistic outlook." For Aziz, it was his leader's denial over defeat in the Gulf War that led to the downfall of his regime.[30] Saddam attributed much of Iraq's supposed success to the spiritual superiority of his troops, which he believed would make up for the technological advantages of the United States. In February 2003, he told his officers that "Allah wanted to insult America by giving his strongest personal abilities to the materially weak Iraqis."[31] In the late 1990s, Saddam made a habit of recording all conversations with senior officials, providing clear evidence of the extent to which he had rewritten history in his own mind. Constantly reminding subordinates of the military victories to which he had led Iraq, he referred to Iraq's "heroic performance" in the "Mother of All Battles" (the Gulf War).[32]

The misperception that the United States and the United Kingdom did not have the stomach for war fed Saddam's conviction that their forces would never enter Baghdad. While inaccurate, however, the basis of Saddam's reasoning over the likelihood of war was not entirely irrational. Unimpressed by the U.S. failure to topple his regime in 1991, he saw numerous other instances of U.S. "weakness" in the years that followed, such as its withdrawal from Somalia after the death of 18 soldiers in Mogadishu (an inconsequentially low casualty rate in Saddam's view), as well as U.S. reliance on air combat in Kosovo. Furthermore, Saddam reportedly "saw no reason why the US would want to invade Iraq."[33] In this he was not alone as much Western opposition to the 2003 U.S.-led invasion was centered on the questionable motives of the United States and its allies. Saddam also firmly believed that Russia and France would prevent the United States from invading; the two countries would use their position on the Security Council to protect their trade and service contracts in Iraq, worth millions of dollars. Indeed, they had lobbied for sanctions against Iraq to be lifted. Saddam's presumption was therefore not unreasonable: Russia and France did oppose the war. What Saddam did not envision, however, was that the United States was prepared to act unilaterally and without UN backing.

The United States was, in fact, rather low down on Saddam's list of external threats to his regime. Even as the signals from Washington that an attack was imminent grew clearer, Saddam and his inner circle still believed that Iran posed the most prominent threat, closely followed by Israel and then Turkey, a view supported by reports of the National Security Committee.[34] The director general of Military Intelligence admitted after the war that "we were more interested in Turkey and Iran."[35]

It was this focus on the regional power balance that informed his policy of ambiguity over Iraq's weapons of mass destruction (WMD), which was designed to serve as a deterrent to Iran: "deterrence by doubt."[36] Saddam also believed that the threat of chemical weapons had prevented the United States from marching on Baghdad in 1991. While ordering cooperation with UN weapons inspectors, he thus desired a shred of doubt to remain; he would not, for example, allow Iraqi scientists to leave the country to be questioned, as stipulated by the Security Council. Perhaps the most extraordinary element of Saddam's WMD policy lay in the secrecy surrounding the fact that Iraq did not actually have WMD. Even top military officers believed that their country possessed this capability with only Saddam's sons and a few others knowing otherwise. In December of 2002, however, Saddam decided to announce the truth in a series of meetings with military leaders and top aides. Iraq's defense minister later stated that the generals had been stunned by the news and Tariq Aziz opined that the admission was a serious blow to morale.[37] On a fundamental level, then, Saddam's ruse subjected government and military officials to serious cognitive constraints, which thwarted the decision making process. Such secrecy, lack of trust, and ineffective communication extended into all areas of Iraqi policy making and its effect cannot be underestimated.

For Saddam, popular belief in the existence of WMD was also domestically expedient. By far the strongest influence on Saddam's decision making in terms of threats to his regime came in the form of the Shiite uprising in southern Iraq in 1991, which provoked a bloody suppression on the part of the government. The Shiite threat dominated Saddam's thoughts thereafter, remaining his top security concern. Policy planning revolved around preventing another uprising, such as the division of Iraq into four administrative sectors to facilitate the monitoring of domestic threats. While such policy served its internal purpose it proved disastrous in the face of external attack. Indeed, even as military officials prepared to defend Iraq, Saddam was more concerned with the deployment of the Fedayeen militias to contain the Shiite rebellion.[38] In late 2002, he met with his Revolutionary Command Council, senior officials, and heads of intelligent services to instruct them to "keep the internal situation under control."[39] The Shiite threat was a real one but it disproportionately influenced his decision making while he trivialized the more imminent danger gathering pace overseas. It is clear that preserving his status as Iraq's supreme leader was an all-consuming task for Saddam.

Indeed, Saddam displayed signs of paranoia over the threat of internal rebellion against his regime. Insurgents were not merely traitors to Saddam, but to Iraq itself. Any threat, more often perceived rather than real, was dealt with in the harshest possible way. Saddam did not shy away from having a subordinate tortured or murdered even on the basis that he merely predicted they were going to betray the regime. "If a military leader disappeared one did not ask to know what had happened, since it was known that the security services had dealt with the unfortunate individual," commented Tariq Aziz.[40]

An incident during a low point for Iraq during the war with Iran highlights the tightrope that those around him walked on a daily basis. In response to Saddam's request for advice, his health minister tentatively suggested that Saddam temporarily step down and resume power after the war was over. Saddam ordered him to be taken away immediately and the next day pieces of his body were delivered to the dead minister's wife.[41] This event is significant as it formed an early part of a fear campaign carried out by Saddam so as to ensure complete loyalty from his advisers, making clear to them that dissent, however mild, was not an alternative.

Saddam sought, and believed he needed for his personal security, complete control over all who worked for him; this extended to blocking foreign influences and outside information. Only a handful of carefully selected officials could access the Internet but, knowing that their every move was monitored by Saddam's security personnel and could be used against them, they rarely took advantage of the privilege.[42] Key information vital for quality decision making, therefore, did not filter through to even senior officials. Many military officers had no choice but to rely on official government channels for information after the U.S.-led invasion. One commander described his reaction at seeing a U.S. tank in central Baghdad: "I was absolutely astonished . . . I had no idea there were American tanks anywhere near the city."[43]

Saddam's paranoid fear of coup-plotting led him to restrict information flows in another sense: between his officers and military units. His Special Republican Guard, charged with the defense of Baghdad and the only force permitted to enter the capital, was not allowed to coordinate with other units. "I had no relation with any other units or fighting forces. No other units were ever allowed near our unit," explained one Republican Guard officer. As a further protective measure, the army was banned from possessing maps of Baghdad.[44] This continued during the war, with no communication allowed between commanders. In this way, Saddam was able to control the interaction of his military personnel to an extraordinary extent, using fear as a deterrent to form even friendships with fellow officers.

The climate of fear in Iraqi officialdom had disastrous consequences for decision making. First, officials would not dare to question or be seen to contravene Saddam's opinion, even when his judgment was clearly flawed. Toeing the party line under all circumstances became an accepted norm. Second, for fear of their leader's tendency to punish the bearer of bad news, military and government personnel lied to Saddam, to each other, and even to themselves. Lying was so endemic in the Iraqi government, in fact, that for most officials, keeping a hold on reality was near impossible. "Telling the truth was not to your own benefit," declared one military adviser. And a senior military commander interviewed after the war explained that during a conference attended by Saddam and his military leaders in 1995, the commander made a presentation in which he alluded to American military superiority. He went on to say that:

> Saddam was so mad at my presentation that the other presenters who were going to say something similar became too scared and changed their

> reports . . . It was around this time, 1996 and 1997, that everyone started lying. Everyone started lying a lot. They lied about things like "we won the 1991 war" and such as that. Since that time all military planning was directed by Saddam and a selected few.[45]

Even the highest echelons of Saddam's political inner circle were immersed in the culture of deceit. According to Kevin Wood's collection of interviews, one minister remembers that "[d]irectly disagreeing with Saddam Hussein's ideas was unforgivable. It would be suicide." Another official explained how Saddam did not have an accurate picture of Iraq's capabilities because "many reports were falsified. The ministers attempted to convey a positive perspective with reports, which were forwarded to Saddam's secretary, who in turn passed them up to Saddam." One group that seems to have excelled in its deceptive abilities were the members of the Military Industrialization Commission who carried out a range of military projects. The commission's leaders, under orders to develop weapons for which they knew they did not have the capability, promised success and then later faked plans and designs as proof of a program that did not exist.[46] As Tariq Aziz commented, "The people in the military commission were liars. They lied to you, and they lied to Saddam."[47]

Some of the trusted members of Saddam's inner circle worked hard to protect their leader from the little negative information that was forthcoming regarding the military's deficiencies and lack of preparedness for war. Saddam's personal secretary became a self-appointed mindguard to the president, seeking to protect Saddam from information that might undermine his confidence in the soundness of his policy decisions.[48] In December of 2002, some Republican commanders decided to present Saddam with a frank assessment of the country's military capability. Before their meeting with Saddam, however, his secretary warned them against doing so: "If you talk with Saddam, you must do so with high morale. You must make him happy," they were instructed.[49]

Saddam purposefully avoided placing anyone in powerful positions who had the personality type or intellectual capability to either question or overthrow him. Lieutenant General Raad Majid al-Hamandi, commander of the II Republican Guard Corps, said of Saddam that "by his decisions he threw out the clever men, or the clever men learned not to involve themselves in decision making. They were then replaced by sycophants who cared not for the people or army, but only cared about pleasing Saddam."[50]

In this vein, Qusay Hussein was made Honorable Supervisor of the Republican Guard and Special Republican Guard in 1995. Saddam viewed the Republican Guard as the military force most capable of overthrowing him, as opposed to the group best-equipped to defend Iraq. This distorted perception of the potential of the Republican Guard led him to appoint a trusted family member as its head. Qusay, however, had barely any military experience, and, according to the minister of defense, General Sultan Hashim Ahmad al-Tai, Qusay "knew nothing—he understood only simple military things like a civilian."[51] Yet, despite his obvious inadequacies, he continued to play a dominant role in the final planning for a U.S. invasion and had the final say in major military decisions. Qusay also lied to Saddam—perhaps so as not to incur Saddam's wrath or perhaps to protect his own prestige. He also played the part of mindguard to his father, refusing to inform Saddam of negative military reports.

It seems that the more important the military post, the more incapable the candidate Saddam found to fill it. After the war, many senior officials cited the appointment of Brigadier General Barzan 'abd al-Ghafur as Commander of the Special Republican Guard, responsible for defending Baghdad, as one of Saddam's most incredible appointments. Barzan was relatively inexperienced, had failed staff college, and was a notorious drunk who was not respected by other officers. However, based on Saddam's requirements he was perfect for the job: He was Saddam's cousin, he was not thought to be clever enough to organize a coup, and he was not considered brave enough to go along with the rebellious ideas of others. Nevertheless, Saddam could not be too careful and Barzan realized upon taking the job that Saddam would be watching closely: "I was ordered by Saddam to take the command; I had no choice. I was sick at the idea . . . it was the most dangerous job in the regime."[52]

Saddam went to extreme measures to monitor the activities of officials so as to foil the plans of those who might be plotting a coup. He developed a mechanism that involved at least five major security organizations. "The number of security personnel increased significantly after 1991" with sometimes more than one officer in every five reporting on his colleagues.[53] Furthermore, as one officer explained, senior military personnel were subjected to "constant technical monitoring and surveillance in and out of their homes" which "had a powerful negative effect on Republican Guard morale."[54] These security organizations conducted so much spying that officers spent much of their time ensuring that they did not come under suspicion. General Hamandi explained that he "spent considerable time finding clever ways to invite even the spies I was not supposed to know about" to meetings, adding that "the security situation in the last few years reached the point of the incredible. We could have no relationships with fellow commanders. This prevented even friendships."[55] Overall, in terms of the resulting cognitive constraints as well as psychological anguish, the regime's security apparatus was highly detrimental to Iraq's military effectiveness. Saddam's pathological need for self-preservation was at the heart of policy decisions that served only to make others fear for their own lives. Saddam's targets also acted primarily to preserve themselves rather than to defend the country.

This was certainly true in the case of General Sultan, who before being appointed as minister of defense was considered by most to be the best of Iraq's military leaders. While he did dare to contradict Qusay Hussein, Sultan remained silent during planning meetings before the U.S.-led invasion, even as more junior officers voiced their concerns.[56] This came as a disappointment to other officials who had believed Sultan would speak out—not an easy option for members of Saddam's inner circle. As we can see, toeing the party line was not simply a self-serving decision making tactic for these officials, but could literally be a matter of life or death. While some officials may have genuinely bought into regime propaganda, believing that U.S. forces could (or would) never reach Baghdad, General Sultan explained that: "Iraqi military professionals were not surprised at US actions at all. We knew what preparations were required, and what would happen if those preparations were not done properly."[57]

It is clear that the nature of the regime as well as Saddam's personality and his leadership style crippled effective decision making. The president himself was consumed by a pathological fixation on his "destiny" of becoming the leader of all Arabs, and the importance of his own survival for the existence of Iraq. Coupled with Saddam's growing paranoia over internal rebellion and the inclination to trust only those bound to him by family or blood ties, it resulted in the emergence of an environment in which Iraqi officials were crippled by fear, an inability to access even basic information, and a complete breakdown in communication within the government. This in turn led to a pattern of deceit and delusion that rendered successful decision making impossible. The reality of Saddam's Iraq was simply not conducive to developing efficient policy, and certainly not capable of defending the country against the enemy it faced in the United States. As General Hamandi articulated so well in the aftermath of the war:

> We understand the theory of proper decision making but are unable to do this in practice. Our academies teach the ideas of debate and discussion but for the last ten years or so our reality has been tribal. In a tribal situation you do not question things . . . Most commanders understood the nature and theory of warfare but in Iraq it was in conflict with tribal nature.[58]

CONCLUSION: SADDAM'S PERSONALITY TYPE

Most evident of Saddam's upbringing is his high level of comfort in regard to violence. His earliest childhood memories were replete with violent acts leveled against him by his stepfather, peers, and immediate community. His main father-figure, Khayrallah, was not a man who sheltered Saddam from the atrocities of the world around him; it was indeed Khayrallah who pushed Saddam toward becoming a murderer by his early 20s.

Saddam fits almost all of the ideal traits of an authoritarian leader: He required absolute obedience of his immediate government and his country; he held a closed-minded belief system; his megalomania was evident in most of his public actions; he acted in total secrecy and had no qualms disposing of subordinates who he felt had wronged him; and he showed no mercy to those who wronged him but was able to charm and respect others when it was politically expedient.[59] His focus on Iraqi preeminence justified all his actions; he was Iraq, and his actions were the actions of the nation, not of a leader.

Saddam's closed belief system was evident throughout his political career, illustrated by his focus on the past glory of Iraq and his willingness to justify his own actions in order to retain power and remake Iraq into a powerful Arab state. Since Saddam was Iraq, and Iraq was Saddam, any action that benefited Saddam in turn was the ideal strategy to pursue for the entire nation. Thus, subordinates who wronged him were disposed of not because of their personal slights against Saddam, but rather because Saddam perceived their actions against him as actions against the Iraqi nation. Conversely, Saddam was blind to the mistakes of subordinates and close associates whom he favored; their actions were excusable as he did not perceive them to be harmful to him or the nation.

Ultimately, the reality of Saddam's Iraq was simply not conducive to developing efficient policy, and certainly not capable of defending the country against any enemies, most certainly not the United States.

NOTES

1. Jerrold M. Post, "Saddam Hussein of Iraq: A Political Psychology Profile," in *The Psychological Assessment of Political Leaders*, ed. Jerrold M. Post (Lansing, MI: University of Michigan Press, 2003), 336.
2. Julian Ryall, "The Amazing Kim Jong-il and His Amazing Accomplishments," *The Telegraph*, January 30, 2011, http://www.telegraph.co.uk/news/worldnews/asia/north korea/8292848/The-Incredible-Kim-Jong-il-and-his-Amazing-Achievements.html.
3. Con Coughlin, *Saddam: The Secret Life* (London: Macmillan Press, 2002), 2–3.
4. Efrain Karsh and Inari Rautsi, *Saddam Hussein: A Political Biography* (New York: Free Press, 1991), 9.
5. Coughlin, *Saddam*, 2.
6. Ibid., 4.
7. Post, "Saddam Hussein of Iraq," 336.
8. 8 Joe Katz, "Saddam Hussein, Nephew of Khayrallah Tulfah, of the 1941 Pro-Nazi Coup in Iraq," www.eretzyisroel.org.
9. Post, "Saddam Hussein of Iraq," 336–346.
10. Coughlin, *Saddam*, 7.
11. Post, "Saddam Hussein of Iraq," 2.

12. Ibid., pages 336–345.
13. Coughlin, *Saddam*, 21.
14. Ibid., 22.
15. Kevin M. Woods, *The Saddam Tapes: The Inner Workings of a Tyrant's Regime, 1978–2001* (Cambridge: Cambridge University Press, 2011), 127.
16. Ibid.
17. Ibid., 131.
18. Julian Perry Robinson and Jozef Goldblat, "Chemical Warfare in the Iran–Iraq War 1980–1988," May 1984, in Stockholm International Peace Research Institute Fact Sheet.
19. Omar Sinan, "Iraq to Hang 'Chemical Ali,'" *Tampa Bay Times*, June 25, 2007, http://www.sptimes.com/2007/06/25/Worldandnation/Iraq_to_hang__Chemica.shtml.
20. Kamyar Abdi, "From Pan-Arabism to Saddam Hussein's Cult of Personality: Ancient Mesopotamia and Iraqi National Ideology," *Journal of Social Archaeology*, 8, no. 1 (2008): 3–36.
21. Ibid., 25–28.
22. Irving L. Janis, *Crucial Decisions: Leadership in Policy Making and Crisis Management* (New York: Free Press, 1989), chapter 1.
23. Kevin M. Woods, "Iraqi Perspectives Project: A View of Operation Iraqi Freedom from Saddam's Senior Leadership," US Joint Center for Operational Analysis, 2006, 4, http://www.foreignaffairs.org/special/iraq/ipp.pdf.
24. Marvin Zonis, "Leaders and Publics in the Middle East: Shattering the Organizing Myths of Arab Society," in *The Political Psychology of the Gulf War: Leaders, Publics and the Process of Conflict*, ed. Stanley A. Renshon (Pittsburgh, PA: University of Pittsburgh Press, 1993), 270–290.
25. Woods, "Iraqi Perspectives Project," 5.
26. Milton Rokeach, *The Open and Closed Mind: Investigation into the Nature of Belief Systems and Personality Systems* (New York: Basic Books, 1960), chapters 2 and 3.
27. Michael R. Gordon and General Bernard E. Trainor, *Cobra II: The Inside Story of the Invasion and Occupation of Iraq* (New York: Pantheon Books, 2006), 59.
28. Woods, "Iraqi Perspectives Project," 12.
29. Eileen F. Babbitt, "Ethnic Conflict and the Pivotal States," in *The Pivotal States: A New Framework for US Policy in the Developing World*, ed. Robert Chase, Emily Hill and Paul Kennedy (New York: W.W. Norton, 1999), 341.
30. Woods, "Iraqi Perspectives Project," 10.
31. Ibid., 29.
32. Ibid., 15, 47.
33. Gordon and Trainor, *Cobra II*, 65.
34. Ibid., 64.
35. Woods, "Iraqi Perspectives Project," 25.
36. Gordon and Trainor, *Cobra II*, 65.
37. Ibid., 118.
38. Ibid., 122.
39. Woods, "Iraqi Perspectives Project," 26.
40. Ibid., 7.
41. Ibid.
42. Ibid., 11.
43. Ibid., 10.

44. Ibid., 27.
45. Ibid., 8, 9.
46. Ibid., 42.
47. Ibid.
48. Irving L. Janis, *Groupthink* (Boston, MA: Houghton Mifflin Company, 1972), 40–42.
49. Woods, "Iraqi Perspectives Project," 42.
50. Ibid., 58.
51. Gordon and Trainor, *Cobra II*, 60.
52. Gordon and Trainor, *Cobra II*, 61 and Woods, "Iraqi Perspectives Project," 58.
53. Woods, "Iraqi Perspectives Project," 61–62.
54. Ibid., 62.
55. Ibid., 63.
56. Ibid., 58.
57. Ibid.
58. Ibid., 40.
59. Rokeach, *Open and Closed Mind*, chapters 2 and 3.

4

Fidel Castro: Philosopher-Despot

Sean LaPides

With even the most careful analysis, Fidel Castro embodies the quintessential authoritarian leadership style. For the preceding 50 years, he has given us scant evidence to the contrary. As a result I wondered at first, whether a chapter on Castro would make a good test case for this theoretical model. However, the research raises other interesting questions in addition to which archetype he fits. One question is *why* Fidel Castro became an authoritarian dictator when his origins were almost bourgeois and his earliest beliefs so democratic. The answer may provide insight into a half-century of foreign policy missteps by both the United States and Cuba, predicated on false cues, misplaced ideologies, and cognitive biases. With a more appropriate framework for analyzing the empirical data Castro has richly provided, future policy makers might avoid the pitfalls that have characterized America's relations with her third closest neighbor. This is the real value in analyzing the leadership archetype and political decision making of Fidel Castro.

THE COLONIAL CASTROS

Fidel Castro's father, Angel, first arrived in Cuba at the end of the nineteenth century as a cavalry quartermaster in the Spanish army. At the end of the war of independence, military authorities in Madrid required him to return to his native Galicia, a rugged, brutal corner of northwest Spain. He returned to Cuba of his own accord in 1905. Angel Castro was imbued with "the belief that physical work, strength of character, and the tolerance of hardship were important reflections of manliness and the route to success."[1] Reared in Spanish authoritarianism—from the same province as Franco—"Angel's word was law and . . . his style was tyrannical"[2] within his household. Orphaned at age 11, Angel always maintained his humble, Galician ways even as he built a modest holding of land in his adopted Cuba. The Castro farm constituted a considerable estate compared to the local peasantry, but foreigners, notably Americans, held the vast majority of agricultural land in Cuba at the time. Consequently, Fidel grew up as the son of a (comparatively) wealthy landowner—but an illiterate one, who eschewed luxury and comfort, and who identified with the peasantry rather than with the Spanish gentry. Nonetheless, he continued to feel a great loyalty to Spain and harbored a corresponding resentment toward the United States for the loss of Cuba.[3] Despite the success of the Castro sugar crop, Angel remained an often crude and belligerent man, who "tolerated little dissent from those around him and Fidel easily adopted that style."[4]

As is frequently the case in Latin American cultures, Fidel Castro held a reverence for his mother and a respect for his father tinged with conflict. Both men exhibited extraordinarily strong wills and Angel's authoritarian approach ruffled the younger Castro:

> I liked to be anywhere but at home. Home represented authority, and that got my dander up, and the rebel spirit in me began to emerge. I had several reasons for being [a rebel]. Faced with a certain Spanish authoritarianism, and even more so the particular Spaniard giving the orders . . . I didn't like authority, because at that time there was also a lot of corporal punishment . . . we gradually learned to defend ourselves.[5]

Castro sees this aversion to authority at such a young age as a reflection of his personality but it could be merely a facet of the masculine culture, still privileged in Latin American countries. Young males coming of age often resist a bridle of any sort. Fathers, no longer physically the strongest in the household, can feel a need to reassert their leadership roles by other means. The fact that Angel had contentious relationships with all of his sons would seem to bear out this notion. As if to bolster the idea personally, Castro claimed that he loved both his parents, "or at least respected them," but if he "felt more for [his] mother, it's only logical, she's the one you are closest to."[6]

Adding to the clash of wills, Angel conferred yet another burden on his eldest three children. Since they were born out of wedlock—in a deeply Catholic country—Fidel, Ramón, and Angela were denied a measure of social respectability, despite their father's influence and standing within their small fiefdom of Biràn. Fidel's mother, Lina, had entered the Castro household as a maid. Once she became pregnant by Angel, his first wife left with their two children. Lina and Angel married before the remaining four siblings arrived.[7] Lina had no formal education but matched Angel in strength of will. She was deeply religious and "combined warmth and affection with high expectations and determination that her children should succeed . . . [and] inculcated her tenacious belief that there was no level of success too lofty for her children to achieve."[8]

Fidel's education began in the inauspicious country school in Marcane, at the age of four. He was the son of the local gentry and his classmates—his childhood friends—were the children of the peasantry his father depended upon to harvest the sugar crop. Even at such a tender age, he noticed the deference with which he was treated, relative to the other children. He also noticed their bare feet, their shabby clothing, and their propensity to drop out of school. Conversely, Fidel "had learned to read faster . . . [and] was intellectually, socially, and physically superior to any other child. [H]e was exceptional, he saw himself in that light."[9] His high self-esteem and position led him into conflicts with his teacher, often for playing pranks. The punishments in the schoolhouse ranged from a smack with a ruler to kneeling with arms outstretched for a considerable period of time. Fidel referred to these tactics as torture, despite the complicity of the parents and the fact that the teacher frequently took meals at the Castro home.[10] She represented to Fidel yet another authority figure in his life at whom he rebelled. His tenure at the little school was rather short. By the time he had turned six, his parents decided to send him to Santiago de Cuba to school with his older sister. The teacher in the local school convinced Angel and Lina that the children of such esteemed landowners deserved a more rigorous education. She suggested they live with her sister, who was also a teacher, and receive private tutoring with room and board in exchange for a small monthly remuneration.[11] It appears the teacher's proposal may have been a scheme to garner funds from the wealthy Castro family by appealing to Lina's desire for the children to have a quality education. Fidel remembers that time period as a two-year waste of time:

> They didn't teach me a thing, I was never given a single lesson. They never sent me to any school. I was just there. The teacher's sister . . . was supposed to give me my first grade classes; elementary school. I never had *one*. . . . If you want, I'll tell you how I learned to add, multiply, subtract and divide, all by myself, from the back of a writing tablet . . . there were addition, subtraction, multiplication, and division tables. I'd sit down all by myself and study, and I memorized them, and that's how I learned arithmetic; but that was all I learned. Because they didn't even *teach* me that.[12]

The substance of Fidel's remarks clearly indicates that the experience was a scholastic waste. But in the language and repetition of the issues, we can hear the angry voice of a six-year-old, who had to sit *all by myself* because *they didn't teach me.* The words convey no sense of accomplishment for having mastered arithmetic without tutorials. Absent, too, is the characteristic Castro ego bragging about what a clever boy he had been. In fact, few school-age children would prefer mathematics to playing unsupervised so the sense of outrage in Castro's words is not over curriculum, but is rather the plaintive cry of abandonment by his parents to a group of adults who paid him no attention—he *was just there.* Perhaps this sense of abandonment was the reason young Fidel wet his bed the first night in Santiago.[13] Fidel's insistence that the "school" experience was tantamount to a scam appears to be accurate. He acknowledges that the family was poor and lived on the teacher's salary she sent home from Biràn. But despite billing the Castros for the children's full board, Fidel claims there was never enough to eat. The one daily meal was taken at lunch with whatever modest leftovers for supper. It provided a marked contrast with his home life, where his parents cajoled him to eat. In Santiago, however, he coveted every bite, down to the last grain of rice. When his shoes fell apart he had to attempt to sew them together himself. Occasional spankings were the means of keeping the children in line.[14]

When his mother discovered how thin the children had become she brought them home to Biràn but shortly thereafter, returned him to the teacher's family in Santiago to continue his schooling. This time, things were not as terrible, according to Fidel's version. The "teacher" (the sister of the real teacher in Biràn) had married the Haitian consul so the financial situation was much improved and with it came enough for everyone to eat and a roof that did not leak. Rather than continue the pretext of educating Fidel at the house, they sent him to the Colegio de La Salle, a French Marianist school in Santiago, as a day student.[15] Scholastically, the school represented a drastic improvement over his self-taught arithmetic; yet Fidel recognized the disadvantage his status as a day student conferred. Boarding students went on weekend excursions to the beach while Fidel remained at home with older adults who largely ignored him.[16] Thus, Fidel conspired to become a boarder. Despite the upgraded accommodations, he had tired of the rigid, "feudal" French-style discipline in the house:

> One day I rebelled—"I won't do it," whatever it was, "I refuse"; "I won't do this other thing, I refuse." My rebellion wasn't actually against the French manners and ways of doing things, it was against the abuses I'd been the victim of. What else could I do [but rebel]? It was instinctive. Really, it was the first conscious rebellion of my life . . . And it turned out the way I'd wanted it to. They sent me straight to the *Colegio de La Salle* as a boarding student . . . the second semester of first grade. . . . I was finally a happy boy.[17]

For all of Castro's insistence on scholastic rigor, he failed to pay attention in class once he got his way and became a "happy boy." He continued his practice of self-teaching from the text books, sometimes reading into the early morning hours, claiming that "mathematics and everything else I learned on my own."[18]

Fidel counts the manipulation of the teacher's family among his earliest rebellions, though he admits his intolerance for authority existed from an earlier age. His tenure at the La Salle school lasted until the end of fifth grade, when he engaged in his second rebellion. One of the Marianist brothers was in charge of boarding students. On two occasions, the monk hit Fidel hard enough for him to be dazed. The first time, Fidel had started a fight with another boy and the second time had talked in a queue. On the third occasion, Fidel erupted and attacked the monk "like a little tiger—biting and kicking him, hitting him with [his] fists."[19] Young Castro may have seen this as a rebellion against authority and injustice but it was more likely the humiliation that angered him to the point of violence. Apart from the feeling of helplessness against an aggressor (and especially a school official), his father pulled him out of school over the incident and punished him relentlessly at home "to settle accounts." Fidel felt that the most egregious punishment was the parents' refusal to allow him to return to school. He responded by threatening to burn down the family home.[20]

Through the intercession of his mother, Fidel once again prevailed in getting his way. His parents decided that a Jesuit school, the Colegio de Delores, with its strict military-style organization might benefit him. Fidel did not distinguish himself academically at Delores but continued to excel at sports. At age 15, however, Fidel succeeded in transferring to another Jesuit school, the prestigious Belén in Havana. There, Fidel lived among boys whose families represented the Spanish aristocrats in Cuba. He studied under the tutelage of priests, whose loyalties lay with those upper classes and the perpetuation of their privileged status. At last, Fidel's academic prowess matched his athletic abilities. He took a keen interest in sociology, geography, and agriculture, ultimately graduating third in his class. His favorite subject was history. He paid special attention to the great figures of history, which "under the Jesuits did not focus so much on ideology or personality, but rather on the exercise of power and their ability to shape events."[21] The school encouraged entrepreneurial thinking and individuality, even while maintaining strict adherence to scholastic fortitude. The Jesuits' tradition of rebelling against injustice appealed to Fidel. All the way back to Ignatius of Loyola, the patron saint of soldiers, Jesuits had fought for social justice as well as advocating excellence in education. Fidel described the priests at Belén as:

> Spaniards, [who] combined the traditions of the Jesuits—that military spirit, their military organization—with the Spanish character and personality. The Spanish Jesuits know how to inculcate a great sense of personal dignity in a boy, the sense of personal honour—they appreciate character, honest straightforwardness, uprightness, a person's courage, his ability to make sacrifices. Those are the values that they know how to instill, to bring out.[22]

Fidel credits his Jesuit educators with taking his *rebellious* temperament and forging it into his *revolutionary* personality. His youthful rebellions took the form of acting out against authority figures—teachers, caregivers, and priests—whom he perceived were treating him unjustly. This personal sense of justice ultimately extended to the social milieu as well. He noticed even as a child that his privileges did not extend to the peasantry. He noticed that bright people like his mother had no opportunity for education. And he noticed that the owners of Cuba's cash crops, including his own father, believed that the extraction of profits required a certain amount of exploitation of the peasants. The brutal poverty in which sugarcane workers lived provided a bitter juxtaposition to the abject wealth that expatriate managers of the United Fruit Company and their families enjoyed. His own family's prosperity could not match that of the American managers and the sight of "foreigners flaunting their affluence and protected by their own armed guards from the hungry eyes of the population . . . made a lasting impression on Fidel."[23] Nonetheless, his sense of social justice likely began with his mother's strict Catholicism and her "primitive rural Christianity emphasizing Christ's compassion for the poor and dispossessed."[24] Therein, the Jesuit tradition in Cuba created a paradox for him. Though Fidel admits the Society of Jesus "discriminated against blacks and [ran] a school for young men of the *haute bourgeoisie*,"[25] his own words credit them for being outspokenly defiant, insisting that they "rebelled against political authorities and hierarchies."[26] This rebellious sensibility may have suited Castro's sense of social justice as a high school student, but the Spanish Jesuits in Cuba were also fiercely pro-Franco and he came to view the church as an "institution of hypocrisy . . . and the maintenance of its own power and privilege."[27]

It seems clear that Castro's concern for ethics and fairness was not only genuine but also a personality trait early in his life: He recognized the special treatment he received at the parish school as a landowner's son, while his impoverished playmates went barefoot and hungry; and he noticed the misery of the men and women working for the American conglomerates.[28] However, that he always reacted with violence whenever he perceived himself to be the victim of injustice does not in itself augur a compassion for the exploited masses. Nonetheless, it is to Fidel's perception of his own victimhood that he credits his burgeoning social activism:

> I was also the victim of certain things. Little by little I began to acquire notions of justice and dignity, certain central values. So my character was moulded by the hard tests I had to pass, difficulties I had to overcome, conflicts I had to face, decisions I had to make, rebellions . . . I started to question that whole society, on my own—perfectly normal, a habit of thinking with a certain logic, analyzing things. With no one to help me, really. . . . all those experiences led me to see abuses, injustice, or the simple humiliation of another person, as

> inconceivable wrongs. I acquired a profound sense of justice, ethics, a sense of equality. All that in addition to a temperament that was unquestionably rebellious, must have exerted a strong influence on my political and revolutionary vocation.[29]

Unlike his anecdote concerning the lack of tutoring in Santiago, these remarks proffer a more characteristic Castro trait. Gone is the plaintive cry of abandonment and in its place we hear how Castro triumphed adversity with no help from anyone—*really!*—and in so doing, became the revolutionary Maximum Leader, champion of social justice. Psychologically, the pieces fit together well. Fidel Castro does indeed possess a unique gift for overcoming adversity. A strong ego, stemming from his mother's belief in her children's greatness and the high self-esteem he achieved from sports, helped him turn his sorrow of separation and neglect as a child into anger. He then used that anger as a weapon, just as he had against the monk who hit him at the La Salle School. Consequently, much of what he assumes to be rebellion from perceived injustices perpetrated against *him* are actually no more than the setbacks and tribulations that plague many people across the world—including hunger. But to an ego like Fidel Castro's, personal humiliation is an outrage merely masquerading as injustice. For example, Fidel claims another of his earliest "rebellions" was against the local teacher who sent him and his siblings to their erstwhile tutors in Santiago, and the abuses they suffered under her family's tutelage. Yet, he describes his actions as "an act of vengeance."[30] The situation had been corrected; the children had returned home, and thus, no rebellion was required. Revenge is not the arsenal of social advocacy; it is the tool of a humiliated ego. To a personality archetype like Fidel Castro's, any humiliation or personal slight is compounded by the belief that his superiority should have rendered him immune from such "abuse." So Fidel translated his personal anger into the more noble cause for *justice, ethics,* and *equality.* The great irony is that in Fidel's mind, his sense of personal efficacy and greatness makes him anything but equal. Herein lies the genesis of the authoritarian archetype in Krasno's theory: ego-defensiveness, megalomania, and a narcissistic self-aggrandizement.

Fidel's predilection for authoritarianism had shown itself in high school at Belén. It fit the Jesuits' soldier-monk sensibilities and they "encouraged him to read . . . the young Spaniard José Antonio Primo de Rivera, the founder of falangism—a fascist movement that called for the use of force to maintain a Spanish 'way of life' in the face of capitalism, socialism, and liberalism."[31] For the majority of Castro's life at this point, national politics in Cuba had been marked by one violent dictatorship after another. The repressive Machado regime had been overthrown in 1933—when Fidel was six—by the equally corrupt and tyrannical Batista government. Among Cubans, the reality of political violence, where "murder could . . . be a way of wielding political power" led to the belief that "power was an end in itself; it was the acquisition of power ... that mattered. The exercise of power was ... the potential for inflicting violence."[32] In 1944, Ramón Grau assumed the presidency, ousting Batista. Any hope for a new liberal democracy in Cuba was short-lived.

THE YOUNG POLITICIAN

Fidel entered the University of Havana in September 1945 and, by his own account, was a "dreadful, terrible example of a student because [he] never went to class."[33] The university had no athletic teams and Castro, like many students, used university politics as a means of making an impression on students and professors and to build a political following. Anyone with national political aspirations would first need to become a force within campus politics. The university was not a political training ground, as such, but rather the "anteroom to power. There was a continuum between university and national politics, so that a position in the student leadership assured a subsequent position in the national leadership."[34] Since he already considered himself a leader, Castro turned his attention to running for representative of his law class in the student government. His father had bought him a new Ford automobile, which Fidel used to obscure his humble background amid the wealthy and upper middle-class student body. In order to win over the more polished students of aristocratic parentage, "he dressed in pinstripe suits with garish ties that were always askew." Upperclassmen were not impressed. His unkempt appearance earned him epithets like "greaseball" or "dirtball."[35] Fidel was nonetheless successful in his election bid to represent the freshman class with "181 votes in favor and 33 opposed."[36]

Earlier education reforms had granted students the right to govern the university. These reforms also granted the university a form of political and legal autonomy. Police were forbidden to enter the campus, which meant that students ran it as a political fiefdom. Under the guise of social reform, student groups "employed terrorist methods against their enemies on and off campus."[37] Two action groups, the Socialist Revolutionary Movement (MSR) and the Insurrectional Revolutionary Union (UIR), dominated the university, fixing grades and racketeering textbooks. Both vied for Fidel to join and he recognized the power they wielded plus the benefits they could bestow on his later political career. Furthermore, he was undeterred by their violent methods. Rather than commit to one, he initially sought to garner support from both.[38] He began to run afoul of the MSR in his sophomore year, during his attempt to run for president of the Federación Estudiantil Universitaria (University Student Federation). The Grau government, through its control of the MSR, put forward its own candidate. Perhaps a bit naively, Fidel spoke out against the candidate and the Grau administration in general, which he saw as corrupt. The MSR quickly tired of his public criticisms, especially since he was playing against both action groups. An MSR strongman, Mario Salabarria Aguilar, used the MSR's ubiquitous intimidation tactics to silence Castro by forbidding him to enter the university under penalty of death. Clearly rattled, young Fidel fled to a beach and "at the ripe old age of twenty, lay face down and cried."[39]

Up to this point, all of Fidel's "rebellions" had been benign transgressions against authority. This time his life was actually in danger and the authority against which he took his stand made and summarily violated its own rules at will. Castro opted to go back to the university in defiance, though he admits that he was frightened. He recognized that the university police would do Grau's bidding; they could kill him and make it look like an inter-gang rivalry. A friend found him a small Browning pistol. Though the weapon gave him some security, it also increased the risk. If found with a firearm, he could be arrested and sent for a swift "emergency trial." Five young men, similarly armed, recognized the courage in his decision and accompanied him back to campus. Castro claims this single act of defiance "began my first, very idiosyncratic armed struggle against the government and the powers of the state."[40]

The episode also pushed him to join the UIR. As chairman of the Committee for Dominican Democracy within the Student Federation, Castro and other idealists decried the violence and corruption of Rafael Trujillo, the U.S.-supported dictator of the Dominican Republic. He joined an ill-fated expedition of 1,200 men during the summer of 1947 to oust Trujillo. Castro knew that the ragtag Cuban forces embarking on the journey would find themselves unprepared to face Trujillo's professional military. Drawing from his studies of the Cuban war of independence, he began formulating the strategy of using guerilla tactics with his troops based in the mountains of the Dominican Republic. Placing his company in the mountains would obviate the government's naval advantage.[41] He did not get the chance to put his ideas into practice until many years later, when he launched his revolution from the Sierra Maestra. The Cuban navy, under orders from Grau, intercepted the ship carrying the young mercenaries and captured most on board. Castro jumped ship, swam the 10 miles to shore, and walked to his parents' house.

THE POLITICIAN BECOMES A REVOLUTIONARY

In April 1948, a meeting of foreign ministers from across the Americas took place in Bogotá to lay the foundations for the Organization of American States. Fidel organized a conference of Latin American student organizations to coincide with it. Their goal was the diminishment of U.S. influence and the end of colonialism in Latin America. Colombia had shed a great deal of blood throughout a two-year civil war that pit conservatives against liberals. Fidel and his friend, Alfredo Guevara, arrived into this potential powder keg. The head of the liberals was the Opposition Leader, Jorge Gaitán. To Castro's great delight, Gaitán met him and the student delegation and promised to support their congress's goals. Two days later, he was assassinated on the street in front of his office. The perpetrator was caught red-handed and lynched by an angry mob of Gaitán supporters. The unfortunate incident sparked an "orgy of violence."[42] In all, about 3,500 people had been killed or wounded by morning. For Fidel, the death of Gaitán was a crime that required avenging. He later lamented the indiscriminate frenzy with no sense of organization. The following day, Colombian security forces denounced communist agitators from Cuba as the culprits. Castro remarked later in his life, "the truth is, that we had nothing to do with [starting] it. We simply took part as idealistic, Don Quixote-like students."[43] Castro may have arrived in Bogotá as an idealistic undergraduate but the incident served as an initiation into the "netherworld of political violence."[44]

Havana was already a violent place when he entered the university and the UIR and MSR bore a large portion of the responsibility. Both the organizations carried out 64 political assassinations during Grau's four-year term.[45] But during the Bogotá incident, Castro was "fascinated by the violence." He and another fellow Cuban, Rafeal del Pino, grabbed weapons as they joined in an attack on a police station. Later as armed troops dispersed the rioters, del Pino returned to the hotel. Castro decided to go to the university "in a state of exaltation ... and was disappointed to find that Colombian students had no stomach for dangerous adventures."[46] Later in his life, he commented that he had been consumed with revolutionary fervor and had tried to convince as many people as possible to join the revolutionary movement.[47]

Most striking, however, is that Castro showed no inclination toward communist ideology or communist organizations. Furthermore, he insisted that his grasp of Marxist literature at that point had been perfunctory at best. He referred to himself as a "utopian communist ... someone whose ideas don't have any basis in science or history, but ... who sees poverty, injustice, inequality, an insuperable contradiction between society and true development."[48] On the one hand, Castro seemed driven by poverty and social justice, having witnessed so much of both personally. On the other hand, he not only tolerated violence as a necessary means of political expression (having witnessed so much personally), but also seemed excited by it. He did not regret taking part in the Bogotá melee; he only regretted having been accused of starting it. He recounted that what bothered him about the violence during that long night was its indiscriminate lack of organization.[49] This leads one to wonder exactly what type of "revolution" young Fidel thought he was inviting all to join in Bogotá.

It seems that Castro's tolerance for violence relies upon its use in overthrowing tyranny and injustice—or preventing a return to tyranny and injustice. Yet he is incapable of seeing his own culpability in the same crimes. In addition to social justice, the tropes of honesty and integrity are fundamental to Castro's political philosophy. His growing rage toward the Grau administration was largely based on the graft and corruption so endemic in the Cuban government, while poor people starved:

> because I had been born on a *latifundio* (plantation), . . . I knew what life was like there for those people. I'd had the experience, at first hand, of what imperialism was, domination, one government subservient to another government that was corrupt and repressive. The Orthodox Party (Ortodoxos) denounced those abuses, that corruption. But I was already to the left of that party. . . . Within me, certain sentiments of justice and certain ethical values were already deeply rooted. I had an abhorrence of inequalities, of abuses.[50]

Another turning point occurred for Fidel in the autumn of 1948. He married his college girl friend, Mirtha Diaz Balart, to the delight of his parents and the consternation of hers. Mirtha's brother was a classmate of Castro's. The wealthy Balart family had ties to Fulgencio Batista. Fidel had already garnered a reputation as one of the student gangsters, especially after he participated in riots over bus fare increases. Angel Castro paid for a lavish wedding and sent the couple for an extended stay in New York City for their honeymoon. Once in the United States, Fidel took an apartment and worked on improving his English language skills. He thought about enrolling at Columbia University and his father offered more money to enable him to do so.[51] His stay in New York was a watershed moment because, despite three years of carrying weapons around campus and embarking on various idealist missions, he could have returned to his bourgeois roots. He had married into a wealthy, well-connected family; he had planted the seeds for an Ivy League education, and got a glimpse of the possibilities such a lifestyle would offer. He also had the full backing of his father and, more importantly, had the approval of his father, perhaps for the first time. But Fidel chose in the end to return to Cuba, where he became a member of a new political party, the Ortodoxos.

Castro's political mentor was Eduardo Chibás, a member of Grau's Autenticos party. He hosted a radio show, which he used as a bully pulpit against politicians he felt were corrupt. Chibás and his following of idealistic professors and students expected that he would be chosen as the party's candidate to succeed Grau in the 1948 election. When Grau and the party stalwarts selected Carlos Prío Socarrás, Chibás broke away and formed the Ortodoxos. Castro had become disillusioned already by the inherent corruption in politics. Like many Cubans, he believed that elections were rigged; especially since young Fidel had personally "witnessed payoffs with which his father was involved to fix elections."[52] Castro's thuggish reputation did not endear him initially to Chibás, who snubbed him as a gangster. During a July broadcast in 1951, Chibás accused Aureliano Arango, minister of education in the Prío government, of having embezzled public funds. The following week, he was unable to offer proof and shot himself at the end of his broadcast.

Fidel took up the crusade against the corruption endemic within the Cuban government and attempted to fill Chibás's role as the voice of shaming the government. He also thought that he could fill the leadership vacuum as a candidate within the Ortodoxos. In order to create a public persona for himself and presumably to distance himself from his "gangster" past, he spent weeks tracking down any hint of government scandal. When he discovered that Prío had pardoned a wealthy friend convicted of raping a nine-year-old girl, he published his findings in *Alerta.* His writings conveyed only his passion for a corruption-free government; he indicated no sense of political ideology or dogma.[53] Castro sought to use the momentum from his revelations and the political backlash against the Autenticos following Chibás's death to run for a seat in the House of Representatives. A victory would not have yielded him great power or authority but it would have been the beginning of a political career.[54] It seems clear that Castro saw politics as his true vocation, having put all of his considerable drive and energy into crafting a win and garnering a place within the Ortodoxos leadership. The elections never happened. In March 1952, former dictator Fulgencio Batista returned from exile in the United States and captured the Cuban government in a coup led by junior officers in the military. The junta became the third major turning point for Castro within a two-year period. Batista correctly deduced that a large swath of voters was unconvinced by either the Autenticos or Ortodoxos, which created an opportunity to sweep both aside.

In theory, Fidel might have taken a more opportunistic view of the political landscape. It was certainly true that Batista had run a brutal authoritarian government until Grau deposed him. But Fidel was in high school at the time, and by his own words, he was not politically astute until he reached university. Furthermore, Castro did not espouse any particular political theory other than legitimacy and transparency, and Batista promised to rid the country of Prío's gangster politics. He invoked national hero Martí and Cuban patriotism, just as Fidel often did in his speeches. He assured the labor federation that his government would heed their demands.[55] Lastly, he was politically and financially tied to Castro's in-laws. In short, if Fidel wanted a career in politics and a chance to clean up after the Autenticos, he might have sought a pragmatic alliance. Instead, he fomented a revolutionary action against the coup by attacking the Moncada Barracks—an action that ultimately sent him to prison. His decision is entirely consistent with the authoritarian leader, who will typically find no space for pragmatism and compromise. It also fits the psychological pattern Castro exhibited since his youth. He had always responded to personal affronts with anger. His anger then turned into a weapon against his "enemies." Given Batista's willingness to embrace some social reforms (albeit disingenuously), Castro's response to the coup was less about constitutionality and more about vengeance for derailing his political career and his personal sense of loss.[56] In his later years, he maintained that he had already become a Marxist, even before the attack on the Moncada Barracks:

> By 10 March 1952, the day of Batista's coup d'état, I'd already been a convinced Marxist-Leninist for several years. I say that because of the values I'd acquired, because of what I'd learned in all those years at the university. Without those lessons, I wouldn't have been able to play any role at all.[57]

Castro had clearly begun an acquaintance with Marx but neither his writings from the period nor his speeches bore any hint of Marxist thought. However, Castro also contradicts himself depending on the point he wishes to make. When speaking of Batista's coup, he claims, even as the events took place, to have already formulated a plan "to launch a revolutionary program and organize a popular uprising."[58] But when discussing the attack on the Moncada Barracks—which occurred 16 months later—he stated that his only intent was to oust Batista and restore the Constitution:

> at the beginning, we began to recruit and train men not in order to make a revolution, but rather to engage—this seemed perfectly elementary—in a struggle, along with others, to reestablish the constitutional status quo of 1952.[59]

Castro's rhetoric claiming to have planned a revolution even before the coup seems especially contrived, considering that the manifesto he delivered on the eve of the attack espoused modest ideas on development, both agriculture and industrial. It contained "nothing about social change or agrarian reform or the nationalization of large properties . . . he was more concerned with winning a position of power for himself than with formulating an ideological position."[60] The length of time between the coup and the attack supports Castro's latter commentary; he did not intend to establish a new form of government, he only wanted to wind the clock back to March 1952, let the elections take their course, and let his inevitable electoral victory come to fruition.

Castro's entire upbringing had conditioned him to win—at sports, at academics, at politics. When he began in earnest to raise men and funds for the attack, he asked his father for $3,000. Angel gave him a mere $140 and a rebuke: "It's really stupid to think that you and that group of starving ragamuffins could bring down Batista, with all his tanks, cannons, and airplanes."[61] These remarks bring to light the characteristic lack of his father's approval, not over ideological grounds but because he could not win. Fidel's entire reason for pursuing this ill-fated course of action was to regain his career, to reclaim his political win.

Since he ran for class representative, he had effectively had no successes; Castro has always been a sore loser. When he ran for president of the student body at university, he lost to Grau's candidate. He subsequently organized an assembly to impeach the winning candidate on specious grounds. His eloquence was sufficient to convince enough of his fellow students and he was elected by acclamation. His action split the student body while the other candidate appealed. Ultimately, the impeachment was overturned and Fidel's election was declared invalid "because it had violated the constitutional procedures for electing students."[62] The episode illustrates that Castro's sense of justice and fairness goes only so far when his own success hangs in the balance. He is perfectly willing to abrogate constitutional norms for the sake of his own power and prestige.

It also illustrates Castro's formidable rhetorical prowess, a skill he put to good use in defending himself at his trial. At the conclusion, he delivered his famous "History Will Absolve Me" speech. Speaking with a well-rehearsed eloquence, he invoked the suffering of most of the population at the hands of an indifferent, repressive regime. The speech lasted approximately two hours and stunned the courtroom as much for the audacity of the delivery as for the content. At the conclusion, as Fidel resumed his place next to the lawyer, the "flustered judge rang his bell and called, 'Order! Order!' even though there was silence."[63] Whatever his motivations may have been in starting the attack, his oratory clearly spoke to deep-held beliefs of social justice and ethics.

THE PHILOSOPHICAL REVOLUTIONARY TURNED DICTATOR

Fidel Castro effectively came to power on January 1, 1959. Most heads of state do not come to power before the age of 40 and often much later. Castro, however, had just turned 32 years the preceding August—an age at which his contemporaries in the United States were barely old enough to run for election to the U.S. Senate, and still too young to run for president. That he accomplished the feat so young speaks to two points: his particular gifts of tenacity and leadership and the lack of maturity and seasoning that governing requires. Herein lies a particular pitfall of Castro's overnight success: our psychological patterns grow and change with our maturity. Failures lead to introspection from which we learn. By coming to power so young, he adopted the same authoritarian leadership style his father had exhibited in the home and on the latifundio. Because Castro became an autocratic head of state, he remained in a de facto isolation where he was never wrong. Fidel's psychological growth was thus effectively stunted, resulting in a condition of *situational narcissism.* This mimics clinical narcissism, and occurs when power or celebrity combines with sycophantic subordinates. In Castro's case, it would explain why he always believed that every decision he made was correct and would benefit his people.[64] It also explains his often-tyrannical treatment of dissent—not because it threatened his grip on power, but because dissent threatened what he knew to be a correct action.

Our youthful selves influence whom we become later in life. As children, this influence is largely predicated on parents' approval or disapproval. In young adulthood we add to it triumphs over adversity, defeats at the hands of others, and the wounding unfairness of the world. For most of us, the youthful influence is mitigated by the seasoning and personal growth we endure into middle age. For Fidel Castro, this mitigating process never took place. He was not merely influenced by his youth—he was forged and cast in iron by it.

Castro created his own isolation by surrounding himself with men who would not challenge his decisions or question his actions. This pattern was born in his late adolescence. When he arrived at university, he desperately wanted to impress the more sophisticated, urbane students. Into adulthood, he continued to "mistrust those who were highly educated, polished, worldly. He preferred to work with men who were his intellectual inferiors."[65] His ascendance to power was not a consequence of his narcissism, or of his control of the military. Fidel Castro possesses a natural leadership that transcends charisma. During his visit to the United States in 1959, Nixon wrote a confidential memo to President Eisenhower that Castro "possessed 'those indefinable qualities' that made him leader of men."[66] As he departed on his way to Argentina, a State Department assessment concluded, "It would be a serious mistake to underestimate this man."[67]

To be clear, situational narcissism in Castro does not indicate pathology. The phenomenon simply duplicates the symptoms. It does, however, place him unquestionably into the authoritarian leadership style, but with some caveats. Though Castro certainly clings to power with his last remaining strength, I would argue that he does not see power as an end in itself. I have already pointed out that his commitment to social justice was sincere—it began too early for it to be a political contrivance. Therefore, his incessant grip on power is merely the narcissistic tendency manifesting itself in the equally strong conviction that only he can bring about the desired reforms without devolving into personal corruption. Furthermore, he has always emphatically maintained that:

> by nature, I'm against anything that might appear to be a cult of personality, and you see for yourself, as I've said, that in Cuba there's not a single school, factory, hospital, or building that's named for me. Nor are there statues, or practically any portraits of me.[68]

Whereas Castro's narcissism is not necessarily pathological, his penchant for violent response may be. During the bloody night in Bogotá following Gaitán's death, Fidel had been fascinated almost to the point of euphoria by the bloodshed. As a psychiatrist, Peter Bourne concedes "violence seemed to have a certain appeal" for Fidel, but argues that his ruthless response to threats lies in the "political baptism" of organized violence within the MSR and UIR at university.[69] If Bourne were correct, we would expect to find no discernable pattern of violence outside the politics of insurrection. Two men from Castro's youth, Rolando Amador and Rafael Díaz-Balart, recalled driving through the countryside en route to a meeting. Cows grazed in the field bordering the road and Castro insisted on stopping the car. Brandishing a .45 caliber pistol, he began to shoot the animals. When asked what he was doing, Castro replied that he was just getting some target practice. Díaz-Balart contends this needless use of violence on defenseless animals speaks to "how easily he could later shoot informers."[70]

Castro's propensity toward lengthy oratory presents another manifestation of his narcissism. He can be passionate and eloquent, two gifts that helped him form a following despite his bucolic upbringing. His most impassioned speech, "History Will Absolve Me," flustered the trial judge and inscribed a degree of dignity and martyrdom onto Fidel as he went to prison. It likely played a role in the commutation of his sentence after only two years. On the other hand, he does not always deliver lengthy, impassioned political poetry; he sometimes just lectures. For hours. But perhaps the most indicative element is the fact that Fidel really believes his own success. To be fair, his revolution did engage reforms within the first six months that benefited the Cuban people: he lowered petroleum prices, scaled back mortgage rates, lowered pharmaceutical prices, "and installed, for the first time in Cuban history, an honest and sound fiscal system."[71] However, he also jailed and executed political prisoners for disagreeing with him. His youthful lack of introspection —now permanently frozen in time—allows him to maintain contradictory positions. During his tour of the United States, he was a guest on *Meet the Press.* When asked about the prospect of free elections, he replied, "Don't worry about elections. . . . I'm not interested in being in power one minute more than necessary."[72] Yet, when he met with Nixon, he insisted that Cubans were uninterested in free elections because they had only produced corrupt regimes.[73] He claims to have fostered within his society, a "critical spirit" because "it's fundamental to perfecting our system." Yet, when questioned whether the critical spirit includes a free press, he stated:

> If what you call freedom of the press is the right to mount a counter-revolution and allowing Cuba's enemies to speak and write freely against Socialism and against the Revolution, to write slanders and lies and create conditioned reflexes, I'd have to say that we are not in favor of that "freedom."[74]

Though this response was published in 2006, Fidel still employs the ideological language of socialist dogma he espoused in 1959. Yet within the same series of conversations, he claims "I'm anti-dogma; I'm profoundly anti-dogmatic ... that's where our faith lies, in the tremendous strength of ideas,"[75] as long as the ideas in question do not contravene his dogma.

The conflicting nature of Fidel Castro fits perfectly within the authoritarian archetype. He is unable to accept defeat in any capacity; so he simply never loses and no decision is ever incorrect, notwithstanding the empirical evidence to the contrary. Consequently, he never learns from failures because he never has any. To an even greater degree, this apparent duality reflects Castro's particular psychology. His lack of introspection means that he cannot see the contradictions. He is unaware that he is the anti-dogmatic dogmatic; that he is the supreme authority who hates authority; that he cries for social justice while imprisoning people who speak against the government; and that he fomented a revolution against a brutal regime while he brutalizes in the name of his revolution. One further distinction ties his personal psychology with the authoritarian model. He assumes his personal experience and observation to be an immutable norm. For instance, he hates authority and, in fact, overthrew the authority he hated. So he rules with an iron fist because he assumes everyone hates authority. His ruthlessness "against those who pose a threat to him ... often have a paranoid quality to it ... [because] ... he learned how easily the unwary could become the victims of duplicity and violence."[76] We all draw from our experiences but Fidel's overnight ascension to power and the resulting narcissism deny him the psychological maturity to move beyond his most puerile impressions.

Unsurprisingly, the collapse of the Soviet Union has taken a devastating toll on the Cuban economy and, with it, the demise of Castro's utopian dream. Fidel still trumpets free education and medical care, but the economic stagnation has created a shortage of teachers, dilapidated hospitals, and scarce medical supplies. Young Cubans have failed to embrace the revolutionary mantra.[77] Chronic housing and transport shortages have plagued an already faltering economy. With low wages in every sector, Cubans have resorted to a shadow, informal economy.[78] Characteristically, Castro remains intractably committed to his vision of reality. In a similar vein, he waxes nostalgically about his fortitude in the Sierra Maestra, his attack on the Moncada Barracks, and the heroes of the revolution; "and through the years, as he came to believe what he had imagined, he wove a mythic tapestry that superseded and magnified the real episodes that were often, after all, only ordinary and thoroughly unheroic occurrences."[79] Thus, the Maximum Leader remains trapped in a psychological resin of his own making—the impetuousness of an idealistic young man sealed in the body of an octogenarian.

CONCLUSION

Writing about Fidel Castro presents several challenges. Most of all, because he is a much more complex politician than his many detractors in the industrialized world would probably care to admit. He sometimes comes across as a caricature of himself, in part due to his temperament and his unequivocal response to dissent, and in part due to his portrayal by Western media. That he is an authoritarian leader must be beyond dispute. While he may not exhibit every trait within that archetype, he has never shown any behavior that would be consistent with a different one. Despite his penchant for working very long hours with little sleep and alternating fasting with gorging, there is nothing *chaotic* about Castro. His prodigious energy level and legendary appetite were character traits he developed as a student.[80] Neither flexibility nor pragmatism is a trait associable with Castro. Some observers have called attention to his halting of executions after his meeting with Nixon as a measure of pragmatism, given his bid to gain funding from the United States. I find that analysis unpersuasive. A more likely explanation would be his having reached the conclusion himself that the executions had become egregious.

With Castro's ego-defensiveness, he has tended to lash back at criticism, even when a degree of pragmatism would have worked in his favor. For example, after the Bay of Pigs, he paraded the "mercenaries" in front of television cameras and questioned them personally. At one point, a prisoner asked him if his revolutionary government was communist. Castro, who had not yet embraced communism, responded testily, "What if it is?" No one would dictate to the Cubans what form their sovereign government should take. He then insisted it was socialist and not communist, as many private farms still operated.[81] In 1962—having subsequently become a communist—Castro was courting the Soviet Union as a benefactor. Khrushchev sent two journalists to ascertain Castro's reliability. He assured them that his foreign policy mirrored the Kremlin's policy of "peaceful coexistence"—except in Latin America, where Castro insisted on the primacy of his own policy against (presumably American) exploiters.[82] A touch of flexibility might have kept him in the decision making loop on the question of Soviet nuclear weapons on Cuban soil. Fidel's petulance simply rendered those later discussions above his head.

A final point solidifying Castro as an authoritarian leader is his obsession with details. However, this particular personality trait speaks as much to his management style as to his leadership. We typically find a correlation between authoritarian leadership and the hierarchical management style. But this suggests that advisers and department heads report directly to the chief executive (or a chief of staff). In addition to the strange hours he keeps, by all accounts "Castro is an obsessive micro-manager."[83] In other words, he does not manage subordinates; he effectively does their jobs for them. Though this would seem to obviate the concept of a management style, I find it entirely consistent with his personality. He manages everything personally for the same reason he clings to power; no one else could possibly do a better job.

The complexity of Castro as a personality, a leader, and a theoretical test case made an inductive methodology the best chance to broaden the focus and pose somewhat different questions. I began this chapter by asking how a wealthy landowner's son became a Marxist revolutionary. The recipe is quite simple: Take a small boy sensitive enough to notice the vast inequality between himself and his playmates. Add uncritical maternal praise until ego becomes enlarged. Set aside in a dark boarding school then stir in unwavering paternal authority until angry. In concise, albeit simplistic terms, this is how a wealthy young man became a revolutionary Marxist dictator. As I argued previously, anger is Castro's inherent response to authority and humiliation—which for him are one and the same. When his anger comes to a boil, he lashes out in violence. The first turning point came when the MSR threatened him at university. Fear turned to anger and he defied the aggressors, learning the power of violence in the process. The excesses of foreign corporate interests juxtaposed against the abject poverty of his countrymen stirred greater anger and sowed the seeds of social change. Had he been elected to office, he likely would have worked within the system as a politician, lawyer, and advocate for social justice. That the election was stolen—in his mind, from him—changed his path once again. By the time of his failed attack on the Moncada Barracks, his course was set. Since he cannot accept defeat, he viewed his incarceration as a set back to real revolution.

Castro views the world and assesses other people by the same parameters of his own actions. He does not posture for political gain because he does not believe he needs to. So he assumes any rhetoric that disparages him or otherwise collides with his own sensibility is as immutable a truth as he sees in his reality. Herein are the seeds of miscues that have rendered relations with the United States so tenuous for more than half a century. To compound the lack of common ground, the United States makes the same tactical error. Successive administrations have lumped Castro with other despotic leaders who fail to conform to the Western notion of democracy and good governance. In turn, Castro sees Cuban émigrés as traitors to his rather narrow revolution, and America's pandering to them another form of oppression. If he had been able to understand the nuances of electoral politics—and summoned a modicum of flexibility—Cuba might now be a trading partner, as are Venezuela and China. Castro's violent overthrow of Batista, his ruthless repression of dissent, and his outrage at perceived slights are hyperbolic expressions of his anger—an anger born from a child's sense of rejection by being sent away to a place where no one really cared.

NOTES

1. Peter G. Bourne, *Fidel: A Biography of Fidel Castro* (New York: Dodd, Mead, 1986), 15.
2. Ibid., 17.
3. Bourne, *Fidel,* 16
4. Ibid., 18.
5. Fidel Castro and Ignacio Ramonet, *Fidel Castro: My Life* (New York: Scribner, 2006), 26.
6. Ibid., 53.
7. Bourne, *Fidel,* 16–17.
8. Ibid., 18
9. Bourne, *Fidel,* 20.
10. Castro and Ramonet, *Fidel Castro,* 44–45.
11. Bourne, *Fidel,* 21.
12. Castro and Ramonet, *Fidel Castro,* 52.
13. Robert E. Quirk, *Fidel Castro* (New York: W.W. Norton, 1993), 6. See also Bourne, *Fidel,* 21. Though both biographers include the bed-wetting episode, Fidel does not mention it himself when recounting his experience in Santiago in the autobiography.
14. Castro and Ramonet, *Fidel Castro,* 54–55.
15. Ibid., 58–59.
16. Bourne, *Fidel,* 22.
17. Castro and Ramonet, *Fidel Castro,* 64.
18. Ibid., 69.
19. Ibid., 72.
20. Castro and Ramonet, *Fidel Castro,* 74–75.
21. Bourne, *Fidel,* 26–27.
22. Castro and Ramonet, *Fidel Castro,* 67.
23. Bourne, *Fidel,* 20.
24. Ibid., 29.
25. Castro and Ramonet, *Fidel,* 66–67.
26. Ibid., 66.
27. Bourne, *Fidel,* 30.
28. Castro and Ramonet, *Fidel Castro,* 81.
29. Ibid.
30. Ibid., 57.
31. Quirk, *Fidel Castro,* 21–22.
32. Bourne, *Fidel,* 34.
33. Castro and Ramonet, *Fidel Castro,* 93.
34. Bourne, *Fidel,* 35.
35. Quirk, *Fidel Castro,* 20.
36. Castro and Ramonet, *Fidel Castro,* 94.
37. Quirk, *Fidel Castro,* 22.
38. Bourne, *Fidel,* 36.
39. Castro and Ramonet, *Fidel Castro,* 94–95. See also Bourne, *Fidel,* 36.
40. Castro and Ramonet, *Fidel Castro,* 95.
41. Castro and Ramonet, *Fidel Castro,* 97.
42. Volker Skierka, *Fidel Castro: Eine Biographie* (Hamburg: Rowohlt Taschenbuch Verlag, 2008), 41.
43. Ibid., 42.

44. Quirk, *Fidel Castro*, 26.
45. Ibid., 23.
46. Quirk, *Fidel Castro*, 26.
47. Skierka, *Fidel Castro*, 42.
48. Castro and Ramonet, *Fidel Castro*, 99–100.
49. Skierka, *Fidel Castro*, 42.
50. Castro and Ramonet, *Fidel Castro*, 100.
51. Quirk, *Fidel Castro*, 27.
52. Bourne, *Fidel*, 53.
53. Quirk, *Fidel Castro*, 32–34.
54. Bourne, *Fidel*, 60.
55. Quirk, *Fidel Castro*, 39. See also Castro and Ramonet, *Fidel Castro*, 111. Fidel states that he was never a member of the Communist Party.
56. Bourne, *Fidel*, 60.
57. Castro and Ramonet, *Fidel Castro*, 103.
58. Ibid.
59. Ibid., 106.
60. Quirk, *Fidel Castro*, 53–54.
61. Ibid., 46.
62. Bourne, *Fidel*, 38.
63. Ibid., 93.
64. Kevin C. Davis (licensed psychotherapist), in a personal interview with the author, October 2, 2013.
65. Quirk, *Fidel Castro*, 356.
66. Ibid., 241.
67. Quirk, *Fidel Castro*, 243.
68. Castro and Ramonet, *Fidel Castro*, 550.
69. Bourne, *Fidel*, 33–34.
70. Georgie Anne Geyer, *Guerilla Prince: The Untold Story of Fidel Castro* (Boston: Little, Brown, 1991), 72. Amador had been a childhood friend of Castro's and Díaz-Balart was his brother-in-law, whose family had strong ties to Fulgencio Batista. Both men ultimately became enemies of Castro and fled to the United States.
71. Quirk, *Fidel Castro*, 246.
72. Ibid., 240.
73. Ibid.
74. Castro and Ramonet, *Fidel Castro*, 546.
75. Ibid., 391.
76. Bourne, *Fidel*, 34.
77. "Cuba: The Comandante's Last Move," *Economist*, February 21, 2008, www.economist.com/node/10727899/print.
78. "Cuba after Castro: The Comandante Retires—Sort Of," *Economist*, February 19, 2008, www.economist.com/node/10715023/print.
79. Quirk, *Fidel Castro*, 353.
80. Bourne, *Fidel*, 32.
81. Quirk, *Fidel Castro*, 377.
82. Ibid., 396–397.
83. "Cuba: The Comandante's Last Move."

5

Gamal Abdel Nasser: Legacy in the Arab World

Jean Krasno and Emad Abdel Karim Baniyounes

In this book, we are examining leaders along a full spectrum from those whose tactics we may despise like Saddam Hussein of Iraq to those whom we most admire, as South Africa's Nelson Mandela or Ellen Johnson Sirleaf of Liberia. The focus of this chapter is the leadership of Gamal Abdel Nasser, who even today remains a historic figure in Middle Eastern politics. Nasser's legacy endures as a symbol of defiant confrontation toward the West by the Arab world, which has greatly influenced other leaders in the region. The conundrum that plagued Nasser, however, was his passion for Egyptian independence from colonial domination coupled with his admiration for Western culture and modernization.

Leadership connotes the recognition of respect for one person as someone whom others trust to guide and direct them toward the accomplishment of certain objectives or missions. In the case of Nasser, his desire to end colonial occupation merged with the sentiments of the Egyptian people. He wedded their passion with his own through the power of a common goal. Yet, charismatic leaders may also use their oratory skills to motivate followers by tapping into their fears and sense of pride, a strategy that Nasser also used in his rise to power.

Gamal Abdel Nasser, born January 15, 1918, became president of Egypt in 1956 and retained this leadership position for some 15 years until his death in 1970. The July 1952 military coup had forced Egypt's King Farouk into exile and the "Free Officers" who had led the overthrow named Muhammad Naguib as their first president. However four years later, Nasser assumed the presidency, having manipulated Naguib from power. Even though Egyptian nationalist forces had wrested the country's independence from British occupation 30 years earlier in 1922, the king had maintained close ties with the former colonial power and allowed the British, who considered Egypt a strategic asset,[1] to retain military bases inside its borders. The 1952 coup and revolution that followed had evolved after months of internal chaos and the military appeared to provide the needed stability.[2] The revolution brought with it not only a sense of nationalism but also pride that finally "the Muslim world could rid itself of foreign domination."[3] Nasser's charismatic leadership elicited attention not only at home but also internationally. "Gamal Abdel Nasser was the first secular, modern, and revolutionary Arab leader the West encountered in the postwar era."[4] Western media struggled with how to classify or depict this new leader. Was he a modern Ataturk dressed in a suit and tie, a neutral who created the Non-Aligned Movement (NAM) in 1961 with others like India's Nehru and Yugoslavia's Tito, or was he a dangerous enemy of Israel? These questions in the press brought Nasser even greater popularity in the Arab world. Egypt's nationalist movement spread across the region and a greater Arab-centered identity and unity began to emerge, focused on Cairo. Even Egypt's dramatic defeat in the 1967 Six-Day War did not permanently spoil Nasser's image as a symbol of Arab dignity. As biographer Robert Stephens states, "Nasser left his mark on nearly two decades of Egyptian, Arab and world history."[5]

Nasser, his parents' first child, was born in Alexandria, Egypt's second largest city. His father at the time worked as a post-office clerk in Alexandria but was from a village called Beni Murr, which stands in the Assuit Province of Upper Egypt, about 500 miles up the Nile River from Alexandria. Nasser's father, Abdel-Nasser Hussein, made very little money but being the postmaster earned him a certain amount of respect in the community. Gamal's mother, Fahima, was the daughter of a successful merchant in Alexandria, Mohammed Hammad, who made a substantial living, transporting goods along the canals in the area. "Nasser's mother, who seems to have had a stronger influence on him than his father, perhaps transmitted to him some of her family's shrewd business acumen."[6] Fahima may have had a more sophisticated worldly view than Nasser's father who grew up in a poor village.

Nasser's father retained close ties to his family in Beni Murr and Nasser spent many holidays there as a child.[7] A town of some 6,000 inhabitants in the 1960s, life in Beni Murr was difficult and the town had little money. The streets were unpaved and most houses were made of mud brick. People and animals packed the narrow streets, running along a small canal through palm groves. The village appears to have gotten its name from the Beni Murr tribal group that came from Arabia and settled in the area along the Nile. Nasser's father's family was one of the large family clans but pressure brought by the scarcity of land meant that his father had to leave the region to take a job. However, as a post office clerk, his father was a government official and thus gained a certain level of prestige.[8] The family clans of Upper Egypt had a reputation for hard work, manliness, and pride with a deep concern for honor, which could spill over into acts of revenge.[9]

At the time of Nasser's youth, Egypt was still a British Protectorate. British officials controlled all aspects of the government as "advisers," and commanded the army and police. Sultan Fuad served under British rule and was brought up and educated in Europe. Under the sultan those who controlled the social and economic affairs of Egypt were the upper class of landowners and businessmen, frequently of Turkish decent, left over from the Ottoman Empire, who collaborated closely with foreign business communities.[10] This business class in Alexandria was intermixed with masses of city workers and migrants from poor villages. Nasser was born in the Bacos Quarter of the city, a fairly quiet lower- to middle-class neighborhood.

When Nasser was two years old, his father's brother who had been living with them, Khalil Hussein, disappeared. Later, the family learned that he had been arrested for organizing anti-British demonstrations. Nasser's father was terrified that his brother's actions would cost him his job and he decided then that no other member of his family would ever get mixed up in politics.[11] Nasser as a child was living in troubled times, both politically and economically, and his own family had to move frequently as his father took different jobs with the post office. By the time Nasser was six years old, his family had moved to Khatatba, a small village 40 miles from Cairo. Nasser now had two younger brothers. He went to kindergarten in Khatatba, where only the children of government employees could attend. However, when he turned seven years old, his father sent him to live with his uncle Khalil, now out of prison, in Cairo where he was enrolled in the el-Nahassin school, in the commercial center of Cairo.

> Religious devotion and business mingled intriguingly with history and the struggle for daily subsistence. This was the quarter of the cauldron-makers and coppersmiths—half alchemists, half successors to the old fire-worshipping cults. What better school to study the Egypt of the *medinas*, of the city life—after years in the village and field—than this quarter of deepest Cairo.[12]

This was the boy's first experience with city life. He liked the variety of people and the constant activity. He was disgusted by the filth, however, and the poor living conditions. His uncle often worked late and Nasser was left to look after himself. This forced him to become fiercely independent and he learned to enjoy keeping secrets.

When he was eight, having lived in Cairo for one year, Nasser arrived home in Khatatba to find that his mother had died in Alexandria two months earlier. Keeping her death a secret, the family had apparently kept up the appearance that she had been away on a visit to her parents in Alexandria. The shock of this secretiveness accentuated the natural grief of losing his mother and added to his demeanor of serious reserve.[13]

> Gamal was to remain deeply wounded by this disappearance. It was one of the most frequent subjects in his conversations with his friends, who were struck by his precocious gravity. Things became even worse when less than two years after the death of Fahima his father remarried. He would never really forgive the postal clerk for having begun a new life so fast; and never again would re-establish a real family life with his father and his three brothers at home.[14]

Nasser described it as "a cruel blow that was imprinted indelibly on my mind."[15]

Following his mother's death, Nasser was sent to live with his maternal grandparents and attended the Attarene Primary School in Alexandria, where he did not do very well. When Nasser was still a young boy in Alexandria, he happened upon a protest against the British, and he joined the group. He was hit in the face by the police and wound up in jail with the other rioters. His father, who rescued him the next day, was horrified and reacted harshly by sending Nasser to a boarding school in Helwan.[16] At the time, the Egyptian government, under the dictatorial rule of King Fuad and Ismail Sidky Pasha, had become ruthless in suppressing the opposition and hundreds of protesters ended up dead or wounded. The regime outlawed political meetings and placed limits on both the parliament and suffrage.[17]

By 1933, when Nasser was 15, his father was posted to Cairo and Nasser continued his secondary school education there at the El Nahda al Misria school, living with his father and his family. In 1934, Nasser turned 16 and tensions with his father grew. Nasser loved literature, history, and drama, and read voraciously but did not do well in mathematics or science. This displeased his father, and Nasser spent more and more time away from home. The El Nahda school had a reputation for taking part in student demonstrations and Nasser became so involved in political work that during his last year at school there, he only spent 45 days in school.[18] During the same period, 1934–1935, Nasser was elected chairman of a committee of Cairo secondary school students interested in Egyptian political reform, demonstrating that even in these early years he was emerging as a leader. In 1935, Nasser wrote in a letter to his friend:

> Today the situation is critical and Egypt is in an impasse. It seems to me that the country is dying. Despair is great. Who can end it? . . . Where are the men ready to give their lives for the independence of the country? Where is the man who can rebuild the country so that the weak and humiliated Egyptian can stand up again and live free and independent? Where is dignity? Where is nationalism?[19]

In this letter, he seems to be testing the idea that perhaps he might fill that leadership role. In November of that year, Nasser organized three days of protest with other secondary schools as well as university students. The police opened fire on the students, killing two and wounding Nasser in the forehead. He refused to go to the hospital, afraid that he would be arrested. The wound left a permanent three-inch crescent scar. The newspapers mentioned the protest and Nasser by name.[20] Also, by 1935, Nasser had joined Misr al Fatat, the Young Egypt Party. This was the same extreme, ultranationalist group that had run the protest he had joined in Alexandria, which had landed him in jail. When the school year started again, he began organizing demonstrations, both in his own school and in others. However, the party leaders disgusted Nasser. He considered them more interested in profit than ideals, so by the end of the year, he had quit the Young Egypt Party.[21] Nevertheless, the demonstrations made an impact on the British and were taken as an indication of how serious Egypt was about gaining its independence. New treaty discussions began but were delayed somewhat by the death of King Fuad, who was then replaced by his young son, Farouk. By August 1936, the new treaty was signed, which replaced the British occupation by a military alliance, allowing the British to station 10,000 troops inside Egypt. While Nasser was not pleased with the results that allowed the British troops to stay, he had to stop his political activities in order to complete his secondary school studies and graduate.[22]

Nasser was an avid reader and spent many hours pouring over books, especially when he lived near the National Library. Not only did he read the Qur'an, but was also fascinated by the biographies of leaders such as Napoleon, Ataturk, Otto von Bismarck, and Winston Churchill. The stories of these leaders inspired his own leadership ambitions. He was also deeply influenced by Egyptian nationalists Mustafa Kamel, Ahmed Shawqi, and Aziz al-Masri, and Tawfiq al-Hakim, whose novel called for a man to lead the Egyptian people. "Nasser later credited the novel as his inspiration to launch the 1952 revolution."[23] In an article in his school's magazine on "Voltaire, Man of Liberty," Nasser wrote of his approval of "Voltaire's opposition to the abuse of power and to the Church. He also admired Voltaire because 'he was a calm man and not cruel.' "[24] Charles Dickens's *The Tale of Two Cities* also influenced Nasser when "he opposed shedding the blood of political enemies, since the book had left him with the lesson that violence breeds violence."[25] These men became the authority figures that shaped his belief system as he searched to put together his own worldview.

After graduating from El-Nahda, Nasser studied law at Fuad I University. Even then, Nasser had dreams of changing and reforming Egypt. He chose law because he hoped to better understand the rules that kept so many people poor and unhappy. Without understanding such laws, it would be impossible to change them. Law was also a prestigious profession. Unfortunately, that meant that many young men studied law, far more than could ever find jobs as lawyers. After a few months, he left the university. While Nasser had tried to join the military earlier, he had been turned away; but following the 1936 treaty with Britain, the Egyptian military was expanding and more officers were needed. He was able to enter the Military Academy in March 1937, and there he found his home. "He was an educated revolutionary who merged a sense of tribal honor with teachings on equality and freedom."[26] He was an avid reader of von Clausewitz and the laws of war and now could put these theories to work to liberate Egypt. At the military college he met Abdel Hakim Amer and Anwar Sadat who became his close collaborators. Sadat later succeeded Nasser as president in 1970. Nasser's first military post was in the town of Mankabad, not far from his native town Beni Murr, and it was there during 1938–39 that these men began to talk about the problems of state corruption and their desire to overthrow the monarchy.[27]

In February 1942, Lord Lampson, the British ambassador to Egypt, forced King Farouk to accept a more pro-British government and backed his demand by surrounding the palace with a battalion of British troops. After the 1922 independence of Egypt, this act was an audacious disregard for Egypt's sovereignty, but the British were concerned with the growing support for the Nazis in Egypt in the midst of World War II.[28] Nasser felt that the British action had humiliated Egypt's dignity and the military should have defended the nation's honor, but others knew that they would have been swiftly defeated and acquiesced.[29] When later that year Nasser was admitted to the military staff college, he continued to persuade other officers that they must ultimately drive the British out of Egypt.[30] The period of time he spent at the staff college offered Nasser direct access to younger officers who listened to his views.[31]

Nevertheless, Nasser exercised some caution in his relationship with different groups whose origins and purpose were often hard to ascertain, such as certain militias like the Blue Shirts and, a counter movement, the Green Shirts.[32] By 1949, after the war ended with the creation of the State of Israel, Nasser went to work creating what had been a loose group of like-minded officers into a more formal organization called the "Association of Free Officers."[33] This group of officers, eventually numbering about 13 men, had secretly formed an alliance that broke from the traditional, loyalist military and Nasser emerged not only as a leader but as an instigator. The group's main goals were to rid Egypt of the British and to address the problem of government corruption.[34] At one point, Nasser considered forging an alliance with the Muslim Brotherhood but then considered the group incompatible with his goals of nationalism. Nasser's organizational skills grew during this period and his astute political sense became clear in his writings that appeared in the underground leaflets distributed by the secret society.[35] Nasser understood that to push the British out of Egypt, the military would have to end the tight relationship between the government of the king and the colonial power. The Free Officers' plot to overthrow King Farouk materialized in the bloodless coup of 1952.

Nasser demonstrated his political acumen by utilizing the basic Islamic/Arab traditional cultural norms of forming consensus and consultation, which he used to build public opinion in support of his positions and connect with the people. He used religious symbolism to paint a portrait of himself as a messiah who was a savior of his people. This approach today may appear to lack cultural depth, but it was effective in creating support among the uneducated people of Egypt, something he may have learned from his early village experiences in Beni Murr. Thus he cleverly intertwined religion with politics. He appealed to the emotions of the people in building up their identity and honor, while manipulating his own political space.

Nasser had fought in the 1948 war and the humiliating defeat strongly affected Nasser, especially because the Egyptian Army was forced to fight with dysfunctional weaponry, a factor that was blamed on misappropriation of funding and corruption, involving the monarchy. Nasser blamed certain members of the royal family for bringing about the devastating defeat and advocated that the army should rescue the country from this debilitating corruption.[36]

On July 23, 1952, the Free Officers overthrew the monarchy in a coup led by one of its members, General Naguib. Nasser, however, was against executing Farouk, as he explains here:

> The liberation movement should get rid of Farouk as quickly as possible in order to deal with what is more important—namely, the need to purge the country of the corruption that Farouk will leave behind him. We must pave the way towards a new era in which the people will enjoy their sovereign rights and live in dignity. Justice is one of our objectives. We cannot execute Farouk without a trial. Neither can we afford to keep him in jail and preoccupy ourselves with the rights and wrongs of his case at the risk of neglecting the other purposes of the revolution. Let us spare Farouk and send him into exile. History will sentence him to death.[37]

In this quote, we can see the influence of thinkers and writers Nasser was so engrossed in reading, like Dickens and Voltaire, who shaped his belief system and the formation of his policies against violence. Shortly thereafter, Farouk fled to Italy and Naguib took over the leadership of the nation.

Nasser's charisma and leadership skills at power manipulation enabled him to control most of the internal power struggles as events unfolded. The military junta that took over the country after the nonviolent coup was made up of the 13-member executive committee of the Free Officers that became known as the Revolutionary Command Council (RCC), of which

Nasser had become a key member. According to Nasser in 1953, the goals of the coup were deliberately general in nature:

> The political ideas of the Free Officers differed, according to their temperaments and the family of social milieu from which they came. . . . What we all wanted was to purge the army, rid the country of foreign occupation and establish a clean, fair government which would work sincerely for the good of the people. Once in power, we found ourselves faced with the difficult problem of establishing a political, social and economic programme. It was necessary to improvise. We did our best. The divergence of political ideas then obliged us to separate from those who did not agree to apply the majority decisions of the Council of the Revolution and then those of the Government we set up.[38]

One of the first reforms the Free Officers initiated was land distribution that would grant small farmers larger plots to grow their food and other products. By mid-1953, with land reform fully under way, the Free Officers announced the official abolition of the Egyptian monarchy and proclaimed General Mohammed Naguib, who had informally held the presidential position since the coup, as president of the Republic of Egypt.[39] However, after the establishment of the Republic, Naguib and Nasser became embroiled in a series of personal and political conflicts. The bitter divide resulted in Naguib's resignation from his posts as both president and prime minister on February 23, 1954, and the RCC placed Naguib under house arrest.[40] However, the council soon discovered that it had overstepped its popular support in dealing with Naguib as masses of Egyptians took to the streets, demanding that he be reinstated. As a result of these demonstrations, Nasser was forced to allow Naguib to return to the presidency and Nasser stepped down in favor of Naguib. Although he did not hold onto the position, Nasser did use his brief time as prime minister to purge pro-Naguib elements in the army.

Nevertheless, Nasser's heroic image was made permanent following an unsuccessful assassination attempt on October 26, 1954. Particularly poignant was his defiant response to the attempt in the immediate aftermath. While he was delivering a speech in Manshia Square in Alexandria, a series of shots pierced the air. Unharmed, instead of leaving the podium, Nasser shouted his defiance over the horrified screams of the crowd:

> My countrymen, my blood spills for you and for Egypt. I will live for your sake and die for the sake of your freedom and honor. Let them kill me; it does not concern me so long as I have instilled pride, honor, and freedom in you. If Gamal Abdel Nasser should die, each of you shall be Gamal Abdel Nasser . . . Gamal Abdel Nasser is of you and from you and he is willing to sacrifice his life for the nation.[41]

In this speech, Nasser evoked the sense of pride and honor held so dear by his village ancestors. He also appealed to the public, using phrases and language much like a religious prophet and martyr. A member of the Muslim Brotherhood, Mahmoud Abdul Latif, was accused of firing the eight shots at Nasser on that day. The assassination attempt provided the pro-Nasser faction of the Free Officers' movement the opportunity to remove Naguib from the leadership because of his close relationship and support for the Muslim Brotherhood.[42] Nasser did not agree with the Brotherhood's goal of an Islamic state and he also did not believe that the communist movement in Egypt supported his vision for the country. This became a strategic opportunity to move both these movements out of any powerful positions. Within a few hours of the October 26 event, some 4,000 members of the Brotherhood along with its leaders were arrested. Undergoing intensive interrogation, many pleaded guilty to charges of subversive organizational activity and implicated Naguib. Key members were brought before a special tribunal made up of Nasser loyalists within the Officers' movement. Six were executed. However Naguib was placed under house arrest.[43] There were claims that the whole event was stage-managed by Nasser and his supporters, which is entirely possible, but no proof has emerged.

> Naguib was unable to muster the political forces necessary to confront the Officers. Exhausted from the stress of the near-constant political struggle, the president was hospitalized and remained a non-factor in politics until he was formally deposed that following November.[44]

Naguib continued under house arrest through the first years of Sadat's presidency but was released by the end of Sadat's time in power. Importantly, Nasser did not call for Naguib's death, but nevertheless effectively removed Naguib from posing any threat to Nasser's claim on power.

The Free Officers became the "guardians" of the people and governed as the RCC. In January 1955, the RCC named Nasser as its president and announced national elections the coming year.[45] With Naguib out of the picture, Nasser was elected president in 1956 and held that position for the next 15 years until his death in 1970. It was only in 1956 when Nasser became president that the 1952 military coup materialized into a real social and political revolution, now referred to as the "1952 Revolution." Nasser has been credited for modernizing Egypt and highly praised for his nationalization of the Suez Canal, his agrarian reform, and his socialist policies that attempted to bring a majority of Egyptians out of poverty. He envisioned Egypt becoming a major world player and embraced modern Western architecture as a symbol of Egypt's arrival on the world stage. Nasser developed Tahrir Square into a model of Egypt's new look. He ordered the modern design of government buildings around the square, including the building that became the seat of the League of Arab States. The Nile Hilton Hotel, facing the square, symbolized Nasser's admiration for the West, even though he despised its colonial history.

> An archival image from the opening of the hotel, showing Conrad Hilton (founder of the Hilton Hotels) and Nasser as well as Tito (former president of what was then known as Yugoslavia) is telling of the changes taking place in Egypt and the extent of its alignment with the outside world.[46]

On July 23, 1956, Nasser announced his decision to nationalize the Suez Canal. The decision was a direct result of the denial by the United States a few days before to assist Egypt in building the Aswan Dam, a project Nasser considered highly important to Egypt's modernization. Nasser decided he could then use the revenue from the Suez Canal to finance the building of the dam. He immediately put plans in place to take control of the Canal Company, primarily run by the British and French. Nasser ordered the takeover of "the company's headquarters in Ismalia and the other two chief control points of the Canal in Port Said at the northern end and Port Tewfik at the south."[47] When later that year, the United Kingdom and France colluded with Israel to take back the canal, the United States and the United Nations backed the sovereign rights of Nasser's Egypt, thus boosting Nasser's prestige as an Arab leader.

Nasser cemented his prestige as a nationalist in the Arab world by bringing about the removal of the British as the colonial power in Egypt, overthrowing the monarchy of King Farouk, and thwarting the former colonial power's attempt to take back the canal. Nevertheless, the experience of the 1956 invasion forced Nasser to think about strengthening his power position in the region in order to deter any future attempts. Syria welcomed his ideas of Pan-Arabism, and plans to create the United Arab Republic took hold.

> Nasser's primary interest in Arab unity was the creation of a common front to preserve the independence of Egypt and the Arab area against outside Powers. His secondary interest was to advance Egypt's economic development. The Arab world offered a wider market for the products of Egypt's industrialization. There were mutual benefits to be gained from a large regional economy, as in the case of the European Common Market, including the hope of obtaining investment funds from the Arab oil states.[48]

On the other hand, Nasser's goal of Pan-Arabism began to rattle the remaining Arab monarchies and Nasser experienced increasing isolation in the region. Therefore, when a group of pro-Nasser army officers seized power in Yemen, removing the ancient theocratic monarchy, Nasser offered his full support.[49] Saudi Arabia supported the monarchy and Nasser saw an opportunity in Yemen to take revenge on the Saudi royal family, who had undermined Nasser's union with Syria, which early on had also included Yemen. However, Yemen became uncontrollable as tribes would shift sides with no sense of loyalty.[50] In addition, the British supported and armed the royalists. Nevertheless, Nasser was adamant about the need to protect the Arab nationalist pro-Nasser movement in Yemen, using Egyptian forces.[51]

Nasser believed Egyptian troops could secure the stability of the new Yemeni regime. He deployed some 5,000 troops to Yemen initially. Within two months, Egypt had sent 15,000 troops. Then in late 1963, the number grew to 36,000, and eventually 55,000 troops.[52] Not only did Egypt encounter extensive casualties in Yemen, but the futility of the ongoing conflict also tarnished his image in the Arab world. Having troops tied down in Yemen also ultimately had a deleterious impact later during the Six-Day War with Israel in 1967.

In the spring of 1967, the Soviet Union warned Nasser of a planned Israeli attack on Syria after a minor cross-border skirmish occurred when Israel's air force shot down six Syrian MiG-21s.[53] Nasser had to weigh his options: do nothing and appear weak, or threaten Israel. Given the number of troops out of theater in Yemen, he was completely unprepared for war. Unwilling to appear weak, he decided on a series of steps intended to augment his image of strong leadership. By May, Nasser's chief of staff, General Fawzi, demanded that the United Nations Emergency Force be removed from the buffer zone it had occupied since the 1956 Suez crisis.[54] UN Secretary-General U Thant honored Nasser's request, acknowledging that the United Nations no longer had the consent of the host country, Egypt. In addition to remilitarizing the Sinai, on May 23, 1967, Nasser prohibited Israeli ships from passing through the Straits of Tiran.[55] Israel had gained access to the straits after the 1956 war and considered the closing an act of war. It meant blocking a key Israeli port and the country's single access to the Indian Ocean. Nasser intensified his position and became increasingly aggressive. Radio Cairo broadcasted persistent threats that Egypt would destroy Israel.[56] Yet despite these threatening pronouncements, Nasser had not declared war on Israel. He continued to insist that he would welcome a war should the Zionist state choose to start one.[57] Hrair Dekmejian suggests that Nasser most likely intended to engineer a political victory "by going to the brink." And his decision to send his pro-Western vice president "to Washington just prior to the Israeli attack may have been an attempt to withdraw from the brink."[58]

Israel responded to the closing of the straits and the remilitarization of the Sinai with a preemptive attack, thus initiating the Six-Day War. A war between Israel and Egypt, Jordan, and Syria began on June 5, 1967, and ended on June 10. In the war, Israel occupied the Sinai Peninsula, the Gaza Strip, the West Bank, Jerusalem, and the Golan Heights, now referred to as the Occupied Territories. Officially, no Arab country had recognized the armistice lines of 1949, mediated by the United Nations to end the 1948 war. Nor did they recognize Israel, diplomatically. Israel, according to Arab rhetoric, had no right to exist and was referred to as the Zionist entity. Defeating and destroying Israel and reversing the results of 1948 became central goals of Arab political policy. The prestige and leadership of the Arab world were based on a confrontation with Israel.

Whatever the intent of Nasser's bombastic language and actions, Israel interpreted his moves as evidence of imminent aggression and the Israeli air force conducted surprise attacks against Egypt and Syria on the morning of June 5, 1967. The first wave of attacks by the Israeli air force destroyed most of Egyptian and other allied Arab air capabilities on the ground. Within hours of the attacks, the two Arab air forces lay flattened.

Nasser's posturing had backfired. His actions and statements had provoked an Israeli attack. What lay behind Nasser's decision to concentrate his forces in the Sinai Peninsula and close the straits? It appears that he felt forced to defend his honor and the prestige of Egypt's prominence in the region and the world. His decisions to deploy troops to Yemen, again a political move to buffer the pro-Nasser factions there, and his general need to keep the military under control culminated in a set of poorly executed decisions. Nasser had always preferred a weak and highly politicized army preoccupied with infighting that would pose little or no threat to his regime.[59]

The appalling defeat in the Six-Day War was so humiliating that the Cairo regime knew there had to be a domestic political reaction. Nasser's resignation statement was broadcast live on Egyptian television and radio on the evening of June 9, 1967. Nasser declared that he was handing over the presidency to his vice president, Zakaria Mohieddin.

> I have taken a decision with which I need your help. I have decided to withdraw totally and for good from any office post or political role, and return to the ranks of the masses, performing my duty in their midst, like any other citizen. This is a time for action, not grief. . . . My whole heart is with you, and let your hearts be with me. May God be with us—hope, light and guidance in our hearts.[60]

He also repeated accusations about the United States aiding Israel and exclaimed bitterly, "The Sixth Fleet runs on Arab petroleum."[61] Immediately following the broadcast, Egyptians poured into the streets in mass demonstrations, vociferously shouting their support for Nasser and a rejection of his resignation. The mass demonstrations may have been orchestrated; nevertheless, he was called back to office. The demand for his reinstatement can be explained by "reasons that are basic to an understanding of Egyptian politics. The most fundamental of these was the high degree of residual legitimacy that Nasser possessed by virtue of his leadership performance during the fifties."[62]

After the 1967 defeat, the international community expected that Egypt and the Arab world would now want peace. Instead, Nasser led the Arab countries in rejecting UN Security Council Resolution 242, which calls for Israeli withdrawal from the newly occupied territories in return for peace.[63] Led by Nasser, the Arab states announced the "three no's" of the Khartoum summit: no peace with Israel, no negotiations, and no recognition.[64]

The Khartoum resolutions clearly did not imply a peaceful stance and nobody interpreted them to suggest that the Egyptians had any peaceful intentions. Nasser was once again using the situation to enhance his prestige through an image of defiance. Whether realistic or not, Nasser's goal was to demand an Israeli withdrawal without any concessions or a peace treaty.

Nasser died on September 28, 1970, at the age of 52. He had come from a meeting of Arab leaders in Cairo to discuss among other items the "Black September" in Jordan when the Palestine Liberation Organization had taken three planes full of passengers hostage, landing the planes at the Amman airport. Nasser had not been well and suffered a massive heart attack. "Men, women, and children wept and wailed in the streets after hearing of his death."[65] His emotional funeral was historic in its sheer size, attended by an estimated 7 million people. MiG-21 fighters flying overhead accompanied the long procession to his burial site.[66] Anwar Sadat served as interim president following Nasser's death and was officially selected to succeed him on October 5, 1970.

Nasser's legacy is complex. For some, he was a leader who rid Egypt of colonial occupation and coercion. He was even able to garner the support of the international community in 1956 and the UN General Assembly to force the United Kingdom and France to abort their plan to retake the Suez Canal. As a secular leader, Nasser modernized his country, bringing Egypt into the post–World War II global community. He initiated reforms and reestablished Arab pride both domestically and internationally. But for others, Nasser controlled a military regime that led Egypt into defeat and losses rather than peace and prosperity that included political suppression of the opposition and the massive expansion of the police and security apparatus. His leadership left a legacy of political repression, mirrored once again in the military takeover in 2013.

Charismatic leaders who thrive on a cult of personality often personally control a system devoid of other leadership voices, a method that ultimately weakens governance. The Egyptian people, "the street," were content to leave decisions to their revered leader. "A similar trend characterized the government bureaucracy. Unwilling to make decisions, bureaucrats tended to pass the buck upwards to the presidency."[67] This vacuum left Nasser without good council. Still, Nasser is a clear example of an authoritarian leader, according to our typology, who used skillful manipulation and the hierarchical structure of the military to maintain control. He also demonstrated a belief system developed in his youth that sought to avoid brutally murdering his rivals, as Saddam Hussein or Gaddafi might have done, and instead chose to exile them or put them under house arrest. That is not to say he always shunned violence; he was careful to eliminate his enemies through shrewd cunning, but with some moderation.

Nasser championed the NAM and inspired many Arab leaders and nationalists such as Muammar al-Gaddafi of Libya, Saddam Hussein of Iraq, Ahmad Ben Bella of Algeria, and George Habbash of the Arab Nationalist Movement to seek independence from colonial domination. Some of these leaders have met tragic ends brought about by their own hubris, but nationalism itself was a legitimate means of ridding these Arab countries of colonial occupation and exploitation. "Nasserism" as a revolutionary Arab nationalist and pan-Arab ideology combined with a vaguely defined socialism lives on as an ideology that challenges the West and modern imperialism.

NOTES

1. Steven Cook, *The Struggle for Egypt: From Nasser to Tahrir Square* (Oxford: Oxford University Press, 2012), 12.
2. Hrair Dekmejian, *Egypt under Nasir: A Study in Political Dynamics* (Albany, NY: State University of New York Press, 1971), 23.
3. Cook, *The Struggle for Egypt*, 41.
4. Richard J. McAlexander, "Couscous Mussolini: US Perceptions of Gamal Abdel Nasser, the 1958 Intervention in Lebanon and the Origins of the US–Israeli Special Relationship," in *Cold War History*, Vol. 11, No. 3 (August 2011), 380.
5. Robert Stephens, *Nasser: A Political Biography* (New York: Simon and Schuster, 1971), 580.
6. Ibid., 23.
7. Ibid., 22.
8. Ibid., 23.
9. Ibid., 24.
10. Ibid., 25.
11. Ibid., 26.
12. Jean Lacouture, *Nasser: A Biography* (London: Alfred A. Knopf, 1973), 25.
13. Anwar Sadat, *Revolt on the Nile* (New York: J. Day, 1957), 13.
14. Ibid., 26.
15. Interview with Gamal Abdel Nasser, *Sunday Times*, June 17, 1962.
16. Stephens, *Nasser*, 31.
17. Ibid.
18. Ibid., 32.
19. Ibid., 34–35.
20. Joachim Joesten, *Nasser: The Rise to Power* (London: Odhams Press, 1974).
21. Lacouture, *Nasser*, 31.

22. Stephens, *Nasser*, 36–37.
23. Anne Alexander, *Nasser: His Life and Times* (London: Haus Publishing, 2005), 16.
24. Stephens, *Nasser*, 33.
25. Ibid.
26. Said K. Aburish, *Nasser: The Last Arab* (New York: St. Martin's Press, 2004), 14.
27. Ibid., 15–17.
28. Ibid., 18.
29. Ibid., 18–19.
30. Ibid., 19–21.
31. Stephens, *Nasser*, 61.
32. Cook, *The Struggle for Egypt*, 26.
33. Aburish, *Nasser: The Last Arab*, 28.
34. Ibid.
35. Ibid.
36. Walid Khalidi, *Nasser's Memoirs of the First Palestine War*, translated by Walid Khalidi and published in the *Journal of Palestine Studies* in 1973; these memoirs were written by Gamal Abdel Nasser in 1955 and first appeared in Arabic in the Egyptian weekly *Akher Sa'a*, 4–32.
37. Stephens, *Nasser*, 107.
38. Ibid., 112–113.
39. Cook, *The Struggle for Egypt*, 48–52.
40. Stephens, *Nasser*, 124–130.
41. Eugene Rogan, *The Arabs: A History* (New York: Basic Books, 2011), 228.
42. Dekmejian, *Egypt under Nasir*, 33.
43. Ibid., 33–34.
44. Cook, *The Struggle for Egypt*, 57.
45. James P. Jankowski, *Nasser's Egypt, Arab Nationalism, and the United Arab Republic* (Boulder, CO: Lynne Rienner, 2001), 67.
46. Yasser Elsheshtawy, "City Interrupted: Modernity and Architecture in Nasser's Post-1952 Cairo," *Planning Perspectives*, 28, no. 3 (2013), 347.
47. Stephens, *Nasser*, 194.
48. Ibid., 270.
49. Aburish, *Nasser: The Last Arab*, 208.
50. Ibid., 208–209.
51. Stephens, *Nasser*, 380–382.
52. Ibid., 390–391.
53. Cook, *The Struggle for Egypt*, 96.
54. Ibid., 97.
55. Ibid.
56. Dekmejian, *Egypt under Nasir*, 242.
57. Stephens, *Nasser*, 470.
58. Dekmejian, *Egypt under Nasir*, 242–243.
59. Aburish, *Nasser: The Last Arab*, 252–257.
60. Hiltrud Awad, Hilmi S. Salem, and Suhail Khalilieh, *40 Years of Israeli Occupation 1967–2007*, a publication of the Applied Research Institute Jerusalem, ARIJ (Bethlehem: ARIJ, 2007), chapter one.
61. Nasser's speech following the Khartoum Agreement that ended the 1967 War, accessed at www.mideastweb.org/Khartoum.html.

62. Dekmejian, *Egypt under Nasir*, 245.
63. Aburish, *Nasser: The Last Arab*, 260.
64. *The Six-Day War: Immediate Aftermath, The 3 "No"s of Khartoum*, www.sixdaywar.org/content/khartoum.asp.
65. Nesma ElMeligy, 2014, "Gamal Abdel Nasser 4," www.bubblews.com/news.
66. Ibid.
67. Dekmejian, *Egypt under Nasir*, 304–305.

6

Hugo Chávez: A Quintessential Political Personality

James Suggett

It is difficult to categorize Venezuela as democratic or nondemocratic. Nevertheless, we decided to place the study of Hugo Chávez within this section of nondemocratic states based on the Freedom House Democracy Index, which names Venezuela under Chavez as only "Partly Free," weak on democratic principles. Freedom House in its 2014 report gives Venezuela a downward trend with a rating of 5 across its three categories: freedom, civil liberties, and political rights, where a rating of 1 is best and 7 is worst.[1] Therefore, Chávez was not a comfortable fit in our next section on authoritarian types in democratic states. His personality and leadership style fit better with the types in this section of nondemocratic states.

INTRODUCTION

Hugo Chávez, the late president of Venezuela, was a quintessential political personality.[2] He believed that his life and his leadership filled a historical mandate ingrained in Venezuela's perennial process of defining and developing itself as a nation. He often characterized his political struggles with metaphors drawn from his personal background as a soldier, a baseball player, a painter, and a multiracial man of poor, rural origin. Millions of his supporters saw him as an incarnation of their struggles and hopes. People commonly attributed the country's strengths, flaws, and changes over the past 14 years directly to him. The government seemed to wake up and go to sleep with Chávez. When the president was absent for several months prior to his death from cancer on March 5, 2013, many of his government's programs stalled or lost direction, at least temporarily.

This study's purpose is to examine the political psychology of this larger-than-life, profoundly powerful, loved and hated leader. How did this man's inner script, his personal story, and his personality manifest in his managerial and leadership style? Answering this question serves several purposes. It can enhance our academic understanding of political psychology and organizational leadership. It can also help policy makers to weigh and select policy options as they engage in international relations.[3] In the same way that U.S. President Jimmy Carter studied psychological profiles of Menachem Begin and Anwar Sadat to strengthen the peace process at Camp David, policy makers can use this study to promote political reconciliation, global development goals, and international governance.[4] Moreover, this study can contribute constructively to the debate about Chávez's policies, methods, and general legacy. In this respect, its goal is to challenge readers to suspend judgment, look beyond the superficial and simplistic assessments of Chávez, and forge nuanced interpretations of the Chávez phenomenon.

Political psychologist Stanley Renshon suggests that authors explicate their potential biases and clearly outline their methods of inference in order to improve the validity of their study. This is especially important when analyzing contemporary political leaders.[5] I spent several years in Venezuela during Chávez's second term as president. I organized study-abroad groups, taught English, volunteered in the local community, and wrote about what I was learning. I lived in a poor neighborhood and observed firsthand the way the Chávez presidency worked directly with the marginalized poor to improve their material conditions, increase their political participation, and inspire them to love their country and value themselves. I heard ample testimony about the disintegration of Venezuela's democratic institutions and economy during the 1980s and 1990s. In this context, I thought it was understandable and positive that a leader from outside the political establishment used elections to take office, address poverty, and reform the country's institutions. But I also observed within and outside the government many worrying trends that I thought undermined basic democratic ideals and many of the ideals that the Chávez government espoused.

A methodological precept of this study is that political personality lies in the nebulous realm between nature and nurture. History may impose conditions and limit the impact of any given individual, but individuals can make autonomous decisions and take actions that influence and shape history. Deterministic theories of social behavior cannot emulate the precision and predictability of the physical sciences because environmental factors cannot fully penetrate the deep and complex psychology of individual choice.[6] In addition, this study follows the functionalist conceptual map that places political behavior in a dynamic, mutually influential relationship with the individual personality, the immediate political situation, the social environment (neighborhood, church, school, family, peers), and historical context.[7]

This chapter contains six parts. The first part introduces the study. The second part highlights aspects of Venezuela's history, political system, and national identity that are pertinent to Chávez's political personality. The third part describes how Chávez's upbringing and social environment produced personality traits that reflected Venezuela's broader transition. The fourth part shows how these personality traits took shape in the form of a belief–disbelief system. The fifth part delves into a variety of concrete practices that manifest Chávez's heterogeneous management and leadership style. The sixth part summarizes and presents several important points of caution, emphasizing the limits of this examination.

HISTORICAL CONTEXT: VENEZUELA'S INCHOATE NATIONAL IDENTITY

Chávez was not an anomaly; he was a product of Venezuelan history. His psychology, political personality, and leadership reflected deeply rooted underlying trends in Venezuelan society. The first and most transcendental trend was Venezuela's postcolonial quest for national unification and sovereignty. The second was the overwhelming predominance of violent and autocratic regimes throughout the nation's history; civilian governments ruled intermittently for only nine and a half years during the period 1826–1958.[8] The third was the pervasive effect of oil in the economy, political structure, and culture. The fourth, a more recent trend, was people's sense that their leaders had betrayed them as the post-1958 democratic order unraveled. The fifth was a series of identity paradoxes that many Venezuelans confront and that Chávez injected into the public discourse.

The fall of the Spanish Empire in the early nineteenth century destroyed all centralized institutions and left Venezuela politically disintegrated. Against this backdrop, two types of violent and autocratic regimes dominated the country. The first type, the *caudillo*, was a strongman who ruled through personal charisma, arbitrary violence, and conquest of rivals.[9] Many legendary caudillos were said to have magnetic appeal and a psychological command of a multitude.[10] These local bosses aligned with large estate owners to regulate political patronage in a network of local and regional power hubs and familial ties. This was the primary means for political organization in Venezuela after the independence struggle, indicative of a "profound crisis of a quasi-national community struggling to achieve its definition as a society [. . .] an inchoate, almost instinctive process of social formation."[11] The second type of regime was the modern military dictatorship, which arose in the twentieth century and spurred the unification of Venezuela into a modern nation. The modern dictators began to build a professionally trained military loyal to the country as a whole rather than to regional elites. They made public investments in large infrastructure projects and economic development, largely oriented toward raw material exports. Despite the differences between caudillos and modern dictators, several factors characterized both: power changed hands either through brute force or by pacts among elites. The economy remained highly stratified, with social authority and wealth concentrated in the elite. And, the illiterate and politically marginalized majority labored in agriculture, the extractive industries, or the margins of urban service industries and informal economy.[12]

The expansion of Venezuela's oil industry, which began in the 1920s, exacerbated the process of national unification under modern military dictatorship. It also had five other effects. First, it created a pool of money of which Venezuela's national government took a growing share. As oil profits rose as a percentage of government revenue—a trend that continued throughout Chávez's childhood and adolescence—Venezuelans latched onto the idea that oil profits should be invested in the domestic economy. Venezuelans developed a feeling of entitlement to a share of the nation's wealth and an expectation that Venezuela's oil would allow them to lead a middle-class consumer life. Second, political power coalesced into interest groups common to modern industrial societies, including the national state, the professional military, private industry, unions, the Church, modern political parties, and civil society. Third, the oil industry fueled domestic migration from the countryside to the cities. The dominance of oil exports weakened agricultural exports by putting upward pressure on the currency, while the government invested in large urban infrastructure projects. Fourth, oil fueled international migration, which inflamed racial tensions and labor disputes. U.S. and European immigrants held management positions in the oil companies, lived relatively wealthy lives, and employed dark-skinned natives as domestic workers. Venezuelan workers competed directly with immigrants from China and the Caribbean, and racial stereotypes abounded. And fifth, the oil industry changed the structure of society in many ways. It replaced traditional Venezuelan communities with modern housing complexes that reflected the U.S. and European social orders. It introduced middle class gender roles. Modern indoor supermarkets competed with traditional outdoor farmers' markets. Country clubs, corporate culture, recreational consumption, and the rhetoric of meritocracy established a presence. The "Spanglish" lingo of the oil industry managers infused Venezuelan Spanish.[13]

In 1958, when Chávez was a young child, a civilian-military coalition that included center-right, center-left, and radical organizations successfully overthrew Venezuela's last military dictator, Marcos Pérez Jiménez. The subsequent regime sought to channel Venezuelans' ambitions and interests through a new, modern constitution based on representative democracy and economic liberalism. This constitution featured basic liberties, division of power with checks and balances among three branches of national government, and popular elections for national political offices. But it was flawed from the beginning because two political parties, Acción Democrática (AD) and the Social Christian party (COPEI), made an explicit agreement to exclude the radicals and communists who had helped bring down the dictatorship. These leftists initiated guerrilla warfare and endured heavy persecution during the 1960s and 1970s. They fought in the name of the poor and politically alienated but failed to grow in number or in power and were ultimately killed or forced back into civilian life. Nonetheless, they played a fundamental role in Chávez's political socialization as a young military cadet.[14]

By 1993, Venezuela's constitutional order had unraveled and lost legitimacy. Political scientists Jennifer L. McCoy and David J. Myers outline four main failures of the post-1958 regime. First, it failed to diversify Venezuela's economy and lessen its dependence on oil revenue. Second, the state's regulative capacity deteriorated, leading to the declining provision of basic services. Third, AD and COPEI became a centralized and exclusive duopoly. Corruption grew within its paternalistic, tutelary, and distributive culture. The two parties were so unpopular by 1993 that President Rafael Caldera was elected that year on a brand new party platform. Fourth, the state failed to respond to rising political constituencies in an increasingly complex political arena: the middle class, civil society, the marginalized urban poor, the junior ranks of the military, and the intellectuals.[15]

These failures occurred amid a drastic deterioration of the economy after 1978. The economy boomed in the 1970s due to high global oil prices and Venezuela's oil industry nationalization. But by 1998, income per capita was the same as it was in 1962, and the purchasing power of the average salary was 33 percent of what it was in 1978. Inflation accelerated to around 80 percent in the late 1980s and between 60 percent and 100 percent annually during the mid-1990s. Consumers suffered a sustained depreciation of the value of the bolivar. The oil industry was gradually opened to volatile foreign investment, reducing the state's share of the oil revenue. And finally, the government of Carlos Andres Pérez, newly elected in 1988, agreed to a set of economic reforms recommended by the International Monetary Fund in exchange for loans. Not only did this cause great hardship for the most vulnerable Venezuelans, but it also seemed like a betrayal of the nationalist economic platform that got Pérez elected.[16]

The public outcry against Pérez's economic policies produced one of the defining moments in contemporary Venezuelan history. The poor spontaneously filled the streets of Caracas to raucously demonstrate their disapproval. People pillaged and set fire to buildings. The massive, chaotic, leaderless, rage-driven movement of people shocked government authorities, who responded by ordering state security forces to shoot to kill.

Official figures estimate the death toll in the hundreds; unofficial studies alleged thousands. Bodies were dropped in mass, unmarked graves. This massacre of late February 1989, known as the *Caracazo*, proved to the nation's poor that the government was not on their side. Chávez, who was already plotting a coup d'état, and other soldiers were ordered to repress the uprising, but they chose not to fire on the people. President Chávez would later invoke this incident frequently to arouse political support and demonize previous regimes.

All of this left Venezuela's national identity in a paradoxical state. The country was conspicuously rich in wealth and natural resources but devastatingly poor in human terms.[17] It was a country of great optimism that went from dictatorship to democracy, but it was engulfed in pessimism, distrust, and betrayal. The myth of oil-driven progress led to a paradoxical sense of sovereignty: the oil industry was the source of national economic strength, but it made the country dependent on imports and vulnerable to international market fluctuations. Venezuela seemed to harbor a visceral rejection of foreign encroachment and a disparaging self-hatred that posited U.S. and Western European cultures to be superior. Venezuelans identified proudly as the tough, humble, and downtrodden, but they desperately sought economic development that would bring accumulated wealth and middle-class status. The national hero, Simón Bolívar, who is the namesake of Chávez's movement, embodies these paradoxes. Bolívar was an aristocrat of Spanish origin who heralded the ideas of the European Enlightenment; but he was also a fierce advocate of South American unity and pride.

CHÁVEZ'S BACKGROUND AND SOCIAL ENVIRONMENT

Chávez's social environment and personal journey reflected Venezuela's broader political and economic transition. He psychologically internalized the social volatility of the time period. In his early life, Chávez experienced a separation from his parents, but he also developed a profound feeling of connection to maternal caretakers and to the humble, poor people of his rural community. He was never without a dream of becoming great, and his ambition compelled him to leave his home town. His identity was deeply important to him, and he grew to identify strongly as both a rebel and a nationalist soldier. This led him to have a complex relationship with authority.

Chávez grew up in a poor, rural village on the hot, fertile plains of central Venezuela. His house was made of mud walls with a dirt floor and a roof of palm leaves. There was no hospital, and little infrastructure. Chávez sometimes tells the story about his first day of school in the nearby town. He wore worn-out *alpargatas*, which are traditional sandals made of woven cloth.

The school master sent him home until he could find the money to buy a new pair of black, closed-toed shoes to fit the dress code. Throughout primary and secondary school, Chávez brought sacks of his grandmother's sweet fruit treats to sell to neighbors, classmates, and anyone else along the way.[18]

Chávez and his brother, Adán, lived with their paternal grandmother, Rosa Figueredo, for their entire childhood and adolescence. Rosa was extremely poor, but very formal. She was humble and respectful of tradition. She cared for her neighbors. Chávez later wrote of her:

> At Rosa's side I came to know humility, poverty, pain, sometimes not having enough to eat; I learned about the injustices of this world. I learned to work and harvest. I learned solidarity . . . it was my task to go around, in her name, distributing little bits of food to our friends who had nothing, or almost nothing, like us. And I always came back with other things that they sent . . . I learned from her the principles and the values of the humble Venezuelans, those who never had anything and who make up my country's soul.[19]

Sometimes a young woman named Sara came to the house to look after Rosa, Hugo, and Adán. In Chávez's words: "I have three mothers: Mother Elena, who gave birth to me, my mother who I love very much; Mother Rosa, my grandmother, who raised Adán and me; and Mother Sara." Chávez recounts his sadness when Sara died of tuberculosis at the age of 27.[20] However great his love and appreciation for his three mothers, Chávez demonstrated the greatest reverence for grandmother Rosa.

Chávez's parents lived nearby. They were elementary school teachers, and at one point Chávez attended the school where they taught. As Chávez's parents tell the story, they wanted their sons to live with Rosa in order to keep her company; she was alone and would not survive without someone to care for her. Other accounts suggest the family lacked the means to care for the boys, and that Chávez's parents moved into a home with a cement floor and asbestos roof—a nicer abode—but left him with his grandmother.[21]

Chávez must have questioned and perhaps resented being separated from his parents at an early age. One can imagine that a child raised in this situation would feel a lack of control over his life and a sense of loss, deprivation, and confusion; later, he may compensate with a need for control in adult life. Psychological and anthropological theories of attitude formation and political socialization show that early life experiences, whether political or seemingly nonpolitical, remain latent and later reemerge in political settings. For example, the phenomenon known as "externalization" occurs when a person, perhaps subconsciously, draws an analogy between a present event and a past event that caused unresolved inner turmoil, and reacts to the present event in a way that serves the need to address this inner turmoil.[22]

Chávez's family members and teachers describe him as studious, responsible, a little rowdy with his friends, very tender with his teachers and family members, and prone to childish infatuation with girls he liked.[23] From a young age, Chávez displayed a talent for painting and drawing. His first dream was to be a painter. Then, a neighbor taught Chávez and his friends to play baseball. He played on dirt clearings, using trees as the bases, and dreamed of becoming a professional baseball player. He greatly admired and tried to emulate Venezuelan pitcher Nestor Chávez. This pitcher died in a plane crash, an event that Chávez recalls as emotionally traumatic.

Chávez and his brother knew that in order to pursue their ambitions, they had to leave their rural town and gain a foothold in one of the cities. When Chávez was finishing secondary school, his father encouraged him to go to the University of the Andes in Mérida State to study education, as his brother had already done. Chávez refused because there was no major baseball team in Mérida. When an army recruiter came to his school, Chávez signed up for the military academy, considering it a ticket to Caracas to pursue his baseball dream.[24] Although Chávez chose to leave his home town, he said he did so because it was the only way to find opportunities to advance: "This is something that I have felt ever since I was a child; I never wanted to move away from my home village, but I had to go; I was drawn into the city by a centripetal force."[25] He was swept up in the tide of modernization that drew the masses to the cities as the oil industry expanded. Here, one notices a recurring theme: Chávez felt uprooted by forces beyond his control, first as a child separated from his parents and later as a young man pressured to leave his home town.

As he grappled to reestablish his roots, Chávez deeply questioned his identity and showed intense interest in discovering his past. His parents and grandparents spoke little of their heritage. All Chávez knew of his maternal grandfather was that he was a poor cattle rancher who was absent from his mother's life. Grandmother Rosa told him that her grandfather, Pedro Pérez Delgado, was a murderer and a thief—that was how local authorities described him, as well. Chávez later learned that Pérez, known as Maisanta, was a caudillo and rebel fighter who joined Ezequiel Zamora, the famous peasant leader who led an ill-fated uprising against the dictatorship of Juan Vicente Gómez in the early twentieth century. All Maisanta's lands and property were confiscated after his death. Chávez's ancestors did not carry Maisanta's name because Maisanta's children were born of different mothers out of wedlock. Chávez felt pride in being the descendent of this legendary rebel. When he was in the military academy, he traveled to meet other descendants of Maisanta to whom he felt a significant connection.[26] He deeply resented those who had tarnished Maisanta's reputation.[27] He later projected this internal identity script onto the national political scene: he framed his presidency as a triumph in the never-ending rebellion against the oligarchy, and he vehemently accused his political opponents of spreading lies about him.

Chávez's political socialization resulted from a combination of factors. One was group influence in the family. His father was involved with left-wing organizations in Barinas. His brother, Adán, became involved with the Movement of the Revolutionary Left and the Party of the Venezuelan Revolution as a university student.[28] Chávez would later interact extensively with these leftist groups while building his subversive movement within the military in the 1980s.

A second factor was his training at the military academy. Chávez said he felt like a soldier from the beginning; the first time he put on a uniform, he knew he had found his calling. Chávez was part of a new generation of soldiers who entered a formal, competitive program of military studies and earned postsecondary degrees. This was a concerted government effort during the 1970s to professionalize the military and promote nationalism among the soldiers.[29] At the academy, he studied constitutional law, military history, and national history. He said his military training inspired an emotional connection to his country, and this went hand in hand with his growing political aspirations.[30] Also, the military's strict, authoritarian structure may have appealed to Chávez as he struggled with the lingering feeling of lack of control during his youth.

A third factor was his own reasoning and learning process.[31] As a young officer, Chávez read avidly outside of his regular studies at the academy. He read books on Venezuelan history, political theory, and military strategy. He contemplated questions of nationalism and the purpose of being a soldier. Chávez also conferred with soldiers from the left-wing nationalist military regimes of Omar Torrijos in Panama and Juan Velasco in Peru. He recounted that Allende's overthrow in 1973 fueled his disdain for right-wing authoritarian military juntas that ruled much of South America at the time.[32]

Chávez was deeply nationalist, but he longed for vengeance against national leaders who, from his view, deprived people of his background from dignified membership in the national community. This demonstrated his complex relationship to authority. He sought to have control, which inspired respect for authority (especially his own). But he identified as a rebel, which inspired disrespect for authority. At the military academy, he was extremely loyal and reverent toward authority that he considered honorable and legitimate, but he was irreverent toward officers and leaders he considered unprincipled and abusive. His superiors sometimes referred to him pejoratively as a "lawyer" or a "politician" because he talked back to them. He recalled that when he was a low-level officer, his superiors asked him to speak during a ceremony to commemorate the anniversary of Simón Bolívar's death. Military protocol required Chávez to submit his speech for review before the ceremony, but Chávez refused. He improvised his speech, speaking with a colloquial tone and vocabulary (this was his style of public speaking throughout his presidency, as well). Senior officers wanted to discipline him, but they could not because his words resonated so strongly with the troops, according to Chávez. He also recalled the time he disobeyed orders to chase and capture indigenous people who had allegedly stolen landowners' property.[33] And he resisted the government's anticommunist tactics, especially the torture of peasants to acquire information about the guerrillas.[34] Because of these acts of willful disobedience, higher military officers flagged him as a potential subversive and on multiple occasions transferred him to remote, unpleasant outposts to stymie his schemes.

BELIEF SYSTEM AND DISBELIEF SYSTEM

People's cognitive systems develop in relation to their personal experiences, historical context, and social environment. The building blocks of the cognitive system are beliefs, attitudes, and core values, which present themselves in the form of opinions, behaviors, expressed emotions, and other mediators between the cognitive and social worlds.[35] In the context outlined earlier—his uprooted childhood, distant maternal connection, lack of control over the present or future, paradoxical identities, thwarted ambitions, and anger at corrupt national leaders—what did Chávez grow to believe and value?

A tool for assessing this question is the belief–disbelief continuum, developed by social psychologist Milton Rokeach in 1960.[36] His method was to define his subject's belief system, which included all conscious and unconscious beliefs, expectancies, and hypotheses about the world. Then he defined the subject's disbelief system, which included beliefs the person rejects as false, arranged in order according to their degree of difference from the belief system. Then, he analyzed the degree of differentiation, compartmentalization, and comprehensiveness within and between the two systems. The result was an assessment of the degree of dogmatism, which Rokeach defined as "resistance to change of a total system of beliefs."[37] Rokeach posited that the structure, not the content, of the belief and disbelief systems was the indicator of open- or closed-mindedness. Thus, people with radically different beliefs (e.g., fascists and communists) could be equally open- or closed-minded due to the structure of their beliefs[38] at opposing ends of the spectrum.

The content of Chávez's belief system focused on Venezuela's socioeconomic inequality and political corruption. Chávez believed that Venezuela needed a new political regime that would wrench political control away from the elites, empower the poor and marginalized, and alleviate poverty. He wanted Latin American countries to unite in solidarity, oppose U.S. hegemony, and overcome their economic dependence on raw material exports. He wove these into religious beliefs with Christianity, often quoting biblical passages related to social justice and hailing Christ as the redeemer for the poor.[39] He also believed the military should play an important role in politics, and he viewed society as three battlefronts: the political and legal front, the socioeconomic front, and the ideological front. He said one must attack the opponent on whichever front the opponent is weakest.[40] He called his belief system "Bolivarianism." This was neither communist nor anticommunist; Chávez believed that Marxism did not mesh well with the mentality of the military, where his movement was based.[41] And, he was disillusioned with the older Marxist guerrillas who, he thought, failed to adapt to the new conditions in the country, leaving a leadership vacuum on the left.[42] Bolivarianism filled the ideological void by splicing Bolívar's ideas with those of other Venezuelan forefathers, the Bible, various foreign and domestic communist leaders, historical structuralism, military strategists, and contemporary critical theorists. Bolívar, Chávez emphasized, predicted that if South America divided into fractious regions, the United States would dominate it militarily, economically, and politically. But Bolívar also supported a liberal market economy and meritocratic system of representative democracy based on the rational humanist philosophers of the West, a point that Chávez de-emphasized.

The content of Chávez's disbelief system encompassed Venezuela's established political system. He rejected the 1961 Constitution and the main political parties that drafted it. He deemed the major media outlets of the country unworthy of the public trust. He framed Venezuela as a battleground between good and evil in which the country itself was at stake. During the campaign for the 1998 presidential election, he described the situation as a struggle between his own "Patriotic Pole" and his opponents' "Pole of Destruction."[43] Later in his presidency, he wrote in his presidential opinion column that his opponents:

> want to convert Venezuela once again into a colony, into an imperial subordinate, a sub-republic. [. . .] They represent what is contrary to the homeland, they are the anti-flag, they are the anti-Venezuela, they are anti-Bolívar. They are the negation. They are the no-homeland.[44]

He prolifically disseminated the message that the country needed him to remain in the presidency in order to defend against his opponents, who were lackeys of the U.S. "empire." Needless to say, Chávez's political world was an extremely polarized place, and bitter conflict was the essence of politics.

The structure of Chávez's belief and disbelief systems was essentially closed. He rejected every part of his disbelief system; this rejection became more absolute over the course of his presidency. He tolerated only a small degree of differentiation within his belief system. Although his governing coalition included a spectrum of left-leaning groups, he vehemently condemned allies who questioned his authority, including communists and anarchists to his left and reformist social democrats to his right.[45] He also appeared to isolate different parts of his belief system. For example, his belief in democracy and popular participation contradicted his militaristic and ideologically conformist approach to management (to be examined in more detail later). The discrepancy between his belief system and his disbelief system was like night and day. He attributed flaws in his movement and his government to the "poison" of U.S. imperialism and capitalism.[46] He admitted some errors, but most were attributed to insufficient radicalization: not moving fast enough away from the decrepit past and toward revolutionary goals.[47] Chávez showed very little differentiation in his disbelief system. Literally everything about the regime that preceded his presidency had to be discarded, and his opponents had to be completely isolated from power, regardless of their differing degrees of ideology.[48]

Chávez lacked integrative complexity in his cognitive style. This is another way of saying he differentiated little within and between his belief and disbelief systems, and he had high degrees of isolation of ideas and rejection of his disbelief system. Chávez saw the political landscape as a juxtaposition of fundamentally incompatible beliefs, not a plurality of different, overlapping, and ultimately compatible beliefs. This served his objectives well in some cases, but it detracted from his efforts in other cases. Leaders are most effective when their level of integrative complexity matches their task at hand. For example, Neville Chamberlain, an integratively complex thinker, was diplomatically outmaneuvered by the Nazis, who were integratively simple in cognitive style (meaning, dogmatic). As another example, nineteenth-century abolitionists were guided by an integratively simplistic belief system that posited slavery as a quintessential evil, and their movement succeeded.[49]

Leaders' belief systems also include their level of optimism and their belief in their ability to control and influence the course of history.[50] Chávez was extremely self-confident; he had a strong belief in his own influence, and he was optimistic about the prospects of realizing his political goals. His interviews, writings, and speeches are rife with references to his role in history. He frequently compared his lifelong political struggle to processes that occur in nature. For example, he likened the endemic political corruption of the old regime to ice that melted and gradually weakened its grip on a mountainside; his movement was the rock that fell and caused an avalanche.[51] He believed his purpose was to wake up the people and get them to participate in the construction of their own destiny, and he was sure success would eventually come:

> Chávez may go, but Chávez is not only Chávez . . . Beyond my structural and political concerns and errors, I'm certain that this process is irreversible. This movement of change, of restructuring, of revolution, will not be stopped.

> [. . .] Now, I'm convinced that if we were to fail in this effort of making profound political, economic, and social changes in this way, other paths will open. [. . .] Perhaps violent ways, perhaps military ways, or perhaps civilian-military ways. But this process has assumed its own strength. I'd make an analogy to a river, a river you can dam but not detain. If you don't give it the possibility to flow, it will tear down the dam or find its own course, but it will always flow toward the sea.[52]

It was unclear, however, where Chávez thought his role stopped and where the people were to take over as protagonists on their own stage.[53] He repeatedly disavowed the notion that a revolutionary process of change should depend on him. "This is not just about me, this is a collective effort," he told Aleida Guevara in an interview in 2005. "A leader is partly a prisoner of history itself, of historical conditions."[54] In another interview in 2005, he described himself as a "natural leader":

> I believe in natural leaders, not those who are imposed. And if I ever believe that my leadership has weakened so much as to put the process at risk, and another leader arises, I will not have any problem supporting that person.[55]

His analogies to nature and history also reflected some pessimism: they implied that the struggle for justice would never end because his eternal antagonists were also ingrained in history. And, despite his verbal recognition that his role was limited, his self-adulation bordered on messianic. His notion of "natural leaders" implied not so much that leaders possess natural traits that make them effective, but that leaders are the chosen ones put in position by forces beyond any individual's control. This messianic tendency was also evident in the way Chávez compared himself to Bolívar. He had an ironic way of de-emphasizing his role in the revolution by aggrandizing himself in the image of Bolívar, using quotes such as, "I am but a light feather dragged along by the revolutionary hurricane." By identifying with Bolívar, he also crafted a father figure image for himself in the popular psyche. This image served as a fervent symbol to unite and compel his followers.

The analysis thus far has taken a trait-based approach. A psychoanalytical approach digs deeper by presuming that subconscious feelings and thoughts drive behavior. Psychoanalysis offers two analytical concepts that help to interpret Chávez's belief system. The first concept addresses the drive to cleanse the nation of impurities by eradicating a class of people identified as the source of badness, a theme common in nationalist and racist movements. Chávez may be subconsciously identifying the nation as an ailing mother. And he may be projecting onto public life an "infantile narcissistic ego," which takes the form of "a people's belief in its own greatness, power, and beauty."[56] This seems to resonate with evidence in Chávez's background that he strongly identified grandmother Rosa as the "soul" of Venezuela, and he was given the responsibility to take care of her. He also felt that he was the caretaker of the nation and that he—and his nation—were great in essence, but were being held back by nefarious elitists. But if this concept resonates so strongly in observable traits, perhaps it is the material of trait analysis rather than psychoanalysis.

The second psychoanalytical concept addresses nationalism in the context of urbanization. In a rural or provincial setting, community is based on person-to-person relationships and strong social controls. Urbanization brings individuation and loosening of social controls. This leads to a contradictory feeling of being liberated from the community while also yearning to reconnect to it. Like others, Chávez felt he had to leave his village to seek his own identity. To deal with this crisis, people feel connected to the nation without actually having relationships with one another. Nationalism in this identity conflict serves "to alleviate anxiety associated with separation from the intimate community."[57] This resonates strongly in Chávez's personal history of upheaval and his search for identity. And it is notable that Chávez promoted nationalism with reference not only to the territorial nation of Venezuela, but also to his ideological and socioeconomic in-group, Bolivarian Venezuela. Both forms of nationalism seemed to fit the psychoanalytical description outlined here.

MANAGEMENT STYLE AND LEADERSHIP STYLE

> Most of them [heads of state] have a laconic style and keep a low profile, Chavez is quite the opposite: he accepts a challenge in any area; he really enjoys permanent confrontation; he is an extrovert and an excellent communicator, and he likes polemic and seeks it out . . . he is a pragmatic romantic, a mixture of passion with calculation.[58]
>
> —José Vicente Rangel, Chávez's defense minister and later vice president

Chávez's leadership style was heterogeneous. Two key factors contributed to this heterogeneity: First, his closed and dualistic belief system allowed him to apply different leadership styles to his in-group and his out-group. Second, he led his nation through a period of massive organizational crisis and change. This required constant realignment of power, vision-making, communication, building of new organizational structures, and institutionalization.[59] As leaders of change initiatives commonly do, Chávez employed a diverse array of leadership methods and management strategies.[60] These included participatory democratic techniques (primarily oriented toward his in-group) as well as highly coercive and authoritarian tactics (mainly but not entirely oriented toward his out-group). He was also a pacesetter and a vanguardist who was extremely demanding of the "revolutionaries" on his management teams. This led to the high-speed production of tangible results, but it also set the conditions for groupthink. His psychological makeup contributed significantly to each of his approaches to management and leadership. His political personality had strong elements of flexibility and empowerment as well as elements of paranoia, obsessive-compulsiveness, and narcissism.

Chávez's beliefs about the role of the military in politics reflected his hybrid leadership style. For him, violent uprising was as legitimate as constitutional means to take power. In 1977, Chávez and other officers formed a subversive force named the Army for the Liberation of the People of Venezuela. This grew into the Bolivarian Revolutionary Movement (MBR-200) in 1982. (The number 200 represents the two hundred years since Venezuela's independence.) The group was fundamentally different from the communist guerrilla groups of the 1960s because it was based in the military.[61] The MBR-200 debated extensively whether its rebellion against the government should be led by the military or through civilian street demonstrations, strikes, and the media. Chávez believed that massive civilian participation was crucial for the legitimacy and success of his movement.[62] But he also believed the military had a crucial role to play in society. He quoted Mao Zedong: "The people are to the army what the water is to the fish." He concluded that the military should take over the government first, and then convoke the civilian population to join the rebellion.[63] The MBR-200's unsuccessful military coup against the Carlos Andres Pérez presidency in 1992 failed in part because of the lack of support from civilian leftist organizations. In the years leading up to Chávez's electoral campaign, which began in 1997, his movement did not rule out reverting to armed struggle; they chose the electoral route because civilian leftist leaders convinced them it was the path most likely to lead to their goal of a new constitutional assembly.[64]

Early in his presidency, the military deployed soldiers to provide urgent, short-term services, including immediate food assistance, emergency response to mudslides caused by storms, and housing construction to poor and marginalized communities nationwide. In Chávez's view, the nation faced an immediate crisis of poverty and basic dignity for millions of Venezuelans. The military was the most efficient way to respond. The deployment also had a pedagogical purpose: the soldiers were to learn, through service to the people, that they were part of the people and should not be used to repress the people in the name of the ruling class:

> After the February 27 massacre, for instance, to go to a poor neighborhood a soldier had to dress as a civilian. He was taking a risk because the army had massacred the people. Today, when a soldier shows up, people greet him with enthusiasm and happiness.[65]

Nevertheless, the unprecedented use of the military in nationwide social projects drew criticism from opponents, who claimed Chávez wanted to set up a military dictatorship. It also brought wariness among some

Chavistas, who wondered if the hierarchical military structure was not antithetical to the participatory democracy that Chávez espoused.

Although the Bolivarian movement was based in the military, the central tenet of its political program was a new constitution for Venezuela. And the basis of that constitution was the sovereignty of the people. An elected constitutional assembly drafted the constitution, which voters approved in a national referendum. Chávez widely disseminated copies of the new constitution and ubiquitously referred to it in public speeches, often emphasizing how the constitution empowered the people to change their government:

> [The constitution] stabilizes the structures that prevent the constituents' power from being expropriated from the people. In the case of an institutional political crisis with no apparent solution, there is always one last resort: that the people, collecting enough signatures, or the National Assembly, or the president of the republic can call for a referendum to reform, amend, restructure, or even reframe the constitution.[66]

The Constitution also allowed citizens to collect signatures and invoke a national referendum on the presidency; it gave the citizenry the power to impeach. When the opposition exercised this power in 2004, Chávez welcomed it, and he won the referendum in a landslide. He had faith in his charismatic public appeal.

Chávez also denounced clientelism in politics, where politicians essentially purchase political support with money and favors. He advocated a new form of social programming and political decision making that delegated more power and authority to community organizers and low-income entrepreneurs. The National Assembly, controlled by Chávez's governing coalition, passed a Communal Council Law that allocated community development grants to neighborhoods on the condition that they organize democratic assemblies and elect community representatives. Grants went to housing construction, infrastructure, education, culture, and health projects according to the priorities set by the communities. Chávez also set up a program, based on a new law, to train small groups of unemployed workers in a new skill, teach them how to organize and administer a cooperative business, and then give them a low-interest loan to launch their small cooperative enterprise. Together, these two initiatives spurred massive community participation and the creation of tens of thousands of small-scale organizations and businesses. It delegated resources, attention, and power to a previously marginalized sector of the population. And it clearly set new priorities and infused the public discourse with new ideas and new vocabulary.

Chávez's weekly talk show, "Aló Presidente," was empowering to his followers but coercive toward his management team and his opponents.

Many people interpreted the Sunday program as a positive step toward restoring communication between the government and the people. The poor felt empowered to see someone of their background on television speaking in a colloquial language about issues relevant to their lives. It also represented an effort to ensure accountability and project an image of responsible government. But this effort led to coercion. The president demanded that all his ministers attend the lengthy talk shows, "Aló, Presidente." Frequently during the show, he asked his ministers detailed questions about the funding and performance of their programs, and reprimanded them on national television if they did not come up with complete answers on the spot.[67] On several occasions Chávez harshly lashed out against even the most timid and seemingly nonthreatening critiques of his administration. The result was an implicit demand for loyalty, obedience, and control.

Indeed, Chávez demanded a great degree of loyalty and moral rectitude in his administration. He set extremely high performance standards, which he exemplified with his fervent work pace. He often accused allies and subordinates of being undisciplined if they did not follow his directives. For example, during National Assembly elections, the leaders of the left-leaning Homeland for All (PPT) ran its own PPT candidates in some local elections independently of Chávez's MVR electoral coalition. Chávez said he never agreed to this and he turned out an MVR rally to support a candidate running against the PPT. Chávez said this conflict was the result of the PPT's "undisciplined attitude and sabotage." He referred to the PPT as having "weak political and ideological fiber" because it is "willing to compromise on anything."[68] He blamed the PPT and other internal dissenters for allowing the opposition parties to retain some influence in the government:

> We went to the National Assembly with a very narrow majority. And, in order to get the two-thirds of the assembly required to appoint members of the Supreme Court and the rest of the government positions, we had to compromise all the time—with the AD, COPEI, and the Venezuelan Project. They put forward unqualified candidates for various government positions. That is why in the Supreme Court today you see a group that is not qualified to honorably fulfill their duty and who are manipulated politically because of their historic ties to the AD, to COPEI, or other counterrevolutionary sectors.[69]

Chávez also directly intimidated and coerced his opponents. In 2004, a pro-Chávez deputy of the National Assembly released a list of those who had signed the petition for an impeachment referendum against Chávez, causing a significant number to lose their jobs in the government.

Also, Chávez was sometimes willing to circumvent democratic deliberation not only for the sake of celerity, but also to maintain control. For example, he insisted (against advice from advisers) on simple majority voting rather than proportional voting for the election of the constitutional assembly, ensuring minimal representation of his opponents among those who drafted the Constitution.[70] The president also insisted the Constitution be subject to an all-or-nothing vote, rather than article-by-article voting, which would have assured that the people understood and consented to each article. Furthermore, the Constitution permitted the National Assembly once per presidential term to grant the president the power to pass laws by decree for 18 months. Chávez used this power in 2001 and again in his second term to pass dozens of laws that deeply altered the way the country was to operate.

Chávez was frustrated by constraints on his power. He resisted compromise and deemed opposition to be a capricious limit to his forward momentum. He was eager to shed the pre-1999 state apparatus and produce a new state that would be an engine for the Bolivarian project:

> Sometimes it is necessary to sacrifice some important things for the sake of expediency, and at that time it was urgently necessary to transform the political map, to be able to continue moving the revolutionary project forward. [. . .] to be realistic—we must connect ideas with reality—in this case I am referring to the speed of the political process.[71]

Usually in personality assessment, the narcissist, obsessive-compulsive, and paranoid personality types are considered to be different in the ways they individually react to their belief systems and make decisions.[72] Chávez does not fit fully into any of these personality types, but he bears characteristics of all three.

Chávez resembled the narcissist in his charm, his immense sense of self-importance, his exhibitionism, and his conflation with the nation and himself. But he does not share the narcissist's ideological flimsiness or resistance to learning. Nevertheless, pro-Chávez propaganda promoted the idea that the president would solve people's problems by using the levers of the state to distribute oil funds.[73] This reinforced the preexisting tendency among the poor Venezuelans to view the state as quasi-supernatural, omnipotent entity that operated in an ethereal sphere to magically protect and structure the lives of the people. As a natural extension of this, Chávez's supporters treated him like a Jesus figure who could perform miracles. Elderly women adored him; mothers placed their babies in his arms; and masses of men and women sent him letters pleading for help to find food, repair a roof, heal a wound, or purchase a badly needed item. This attested to the strong narcissistic tendencies in Chávez's political personality.[74]

Obsessive-compulsive leaders commonly express a strong need for control, an impulse to work incessantly, and a tendency to impose their methods on groups. Chávez certainly had these three traits. Diosdado Cabello, who was a member of the MBR-200 and held top posts in Chávez's government, recalled that as an officer Chávez was "very refined in the national symbols. For example, if he was on guard on a Sunday, the raising of the flag had to turn out perfectly, and one error in the ceremony meant you had to stay up and practice all night."[75] This extended beyond the armed forces. Chávez admitted that he lost patience easily, offended his collaborators, and found it difficult working in a team. He had a very erratic schedule to which he expected his top management team to adapt, even if it meant waking up unexpectedly at two o'clock in the morning to work after a phone call from Chávez.[76] However, obsessive-compulsive leaders also tend to avoid political conflict and military escalation, pay close attention to rigid procedural guidelines, obsess over details, and lose the big picture. Chávez had a goal to reform the Venezuelan political system and did not lose sight of that, but he believed that he needed to maintain control in order to achieve this end. Therefore it would be inaccurate to call him fully an obsessive-compulsive leader[77] though he exhibited some of these traits.

Paranoid leaders live in a world shaped by the friend–enemy distinction, constant external threats from evil and increasingly powerful adversaries, and pervasive suspicion. They think in historical analogies more than contextual facts and seek information to confirm their preconceived theories. Chávez bore more signs of paranoia than narcissism or obsessive-compulsiveness. But he was not always so; it seems his paranoia was learned through historical conditioning. His mother once said of him, "My son's biggest flaw is he is sort of Franciscan; he confides a lot and thinks that everyone is like him and cherishes friendship, trust, and loyalty."[78] But throughout his life, Chávez confronted a barrage of lies: lies about his ancestors, lies told by national politicians, and lies told about him by media outlets unabashedly aligned with his opponents. In 2002, Chávez endured a coup d'état led by disloyal military generals and the most powerful private business association. The national oil company, PDVSA, went on strike in a second attempt to take him out of office. The U.S. government supported these overthrow efforts, as it had done in so many other cases in Latin American history.[79] Chávez focused his paranoia on the United States. In a speech to the General Assembly of the United Nations, Chávez called U.S. President George W. Bush "the devil." He frequently sounded the alarm about secret CIA assassination plots against him, and he justified many of his government's military purchases by referring to an imminent threat from the North.[80]

Paranoia about the United States drove Chávez to shape his foreign policy significantly, though by no means entirely, around opposition to the United States. He worked to derail the U.S.-promoted Free Trade Area of the Americas, vociferously opposed Washington's wars in the Middle East, cut off collaboration with the United States on antidrug efforts, and worked to construct a "multi-polar" world order to supplant the unipolar order of the United States. Among Chávez's most controversial foreign policy decisions were his alliances with autocratic regimes that comprised the polar opposite to the United States in the global balance of power. This included Russia, China, Syria, Belarus, Libya (before Gaddafi's downfall), Iran, and the nations of the Organization of Petroleum Exporting Countries. Also, he antagonized a key intergovernmental organization in the Western Hemisphere, the Organization of American States (OAS), by accusing the United States of manipulating the OAS like a puppet.[81] Some of these policies, like befriending Iranian leader Ahmadinejad, who has denied the Holocaust, appeared to be simply symbolic, as acts of spite against the "bullies" of the North.

As mentioned earlier, Chávez expressed his dualistic belief–disbelief system by varying his leadership style to adapt to his in-group and his out-group. Beyond his U.S.-oriented policies, Chávez had a nuanced and forward-thinking foreign policy that garnered widespread respect and support across Latin America and the Caribbean. Its premise was respect for national sovereignty. It was guided by the concept that countries of the Global South should form alliances and support each other's development. Its initial expression was humanitarian aid in the form of food supply shipments following a natural disaster, discounted oil, or gifts of free health services such as eye surgery. And its end goal was greater regional integration among Latin American countries. This took the form of at least four major new regional organizations, including the Community of Latin American and Caribbean States, which includes 33 countries with an array of political ideologies. The nine-member Bolivarian Alliance for the Americas (ALBA) worked to create a model for trade deals in which leader states negotiate deals based on the principle of fairness and respect for sovereignty.

Chávez's political behavior appears to reflect a combination of motives, including achievement, affiliation, and power. These followed the same dualistic framework arising from his in-group–out-group psychology. His achievement motive was embodied in the immense clarity of his political project and his indefatigable drive to surmount all obstacles, including all opponents and some normative democratic checks and balances, to solve the nation's enormous problems. His affiliation motive was nonexistent with respect to his opponents; he included virtually no opponents in his government and placed minimal value on cultivating relationships with them. But he was driven by a profound, almost spiritual desire for interrelations with his in-group, which were those Venezuelans who were deprived of national identity and left out of the national project throughout history. However, this need for affiliation is not in the generally understood definition of the term, which refers to the desire to work with a group of trusted friends and colleagues as a team in creating policy. His identification with the poor of Venezuela was more in an abstract sense. His power motive was very strong on all accounts. He seemed never to question his own legitimacy and authority as the nation's supreme leader. He was unsatisfied with merely taking the presidency; he sought to use every constitutional means available to him to rid the government of oppositionists altogether. Power was his indispensable tool for propelling the country down the revolutionary path he envisioned.

Was Chávez obsessed with power as an end in itself? On the one hand, it appeared that he always sought power with an eye on end results, which took the form of social projects and political achievements such as the reduction of poverty, the massive expansion of public education and public health care, and infrastructure improvements. This would suggest his power motive never overstepped his achievement motive; power was always a means to an end. On the other hand, as this study has highlighted, his drive to power seemed to project a personal script onto the public sphere. This script came from his early childhood experiences and from adult learning. Sometimes his narcissistic and paranoid tendencies led him to reach for power in a way that was unaligned with normal human ambitions and need for competence and mastery of the environment. At these times, his power motive was inflated and much stronger than his achievement and affiliation motives.[82]

SUMMARY

Chávez was raised during a significant historical period marked by rapid political, economic, and cultural change in Venezuela. His social environment reflected this broader context. Personally, he felt uprooted, unable to live with his parents, and scorned for being poor. Yet he formed a strong identity as a rebel and as a nationalist. He felt a connection with the poor, identified with their lack of control and anger at broad injustices. He became a soldier and identified strongly with the military hierarchical lifestyle and with the soldier's mentality. From this emerged a dogmatic and closed belief system characterized by a unique and closed ideology and the utter negation of his political opponents. Upon this basis, he built a record of heterogeneous management and leadership styles. He promoted democratic reforms and the empowerment of his in-group. But his approach to his out-group was formalistic, hierarchical, and authoritarian. This approach was also used toward his in-group at times when they disagreed with him. His most powerful motive was power, followed very closely by achievement, and his affiliation motive was reserved for his emotional (not directly relational) connection with his followers.

It is important to distinguish between Chávez's leadership style and his government. He managed and led in the formalist/authoritarian type set out in the typology posited in the opening chapter of this book. However, this was not close to the type of authoritarian dictatorship that ruled Venezuela and much of Latin America throughout much of postcolonial history. Although Chávez made it clear he was willing to use extra-constitutional means to achieve his revolutionary goals, as president he generally remained within the boundaries of democratic constitutional legitimacy, using his constitutional right to announce presidential edicts when he saw fit. Nevertheless, his incorporation of the formerly marginalized into the political process was a concrete step forward for Venezuelan democracy.

NOTES

1. Freedom House Democracy Index 2014, found at freedomhouse.org/report.

2. Harold Lasswell, who was one of the first to apply psychoanalysis to politics, defined the political personality as the projection of private issues into the public domain. Although Lasswell, very much of the Freudian school, focused mainly on sexual and aggressive subconscious impulses, Lasswell's concept of political personality is applicable beyond the Freudian framework. See William F. Stone and Paul E. Schaffner, *The Psychology of Politics*, 2nd ed. (New York: Springer-Verlag, 1988), 82–85.

3. Jerrold M. Post, Stephen G. Walker, and David Winter, "Profiling Political Leaders: An Introduction," in *The Psychological Assessment of Political Leaders with Profiles of Saddam Hussein and Bill Clinton*, ed. Jerrold M. Post (Ann Arbor, MI: University of Michigan Press, 2003), Chapter 1.

4. Jerrold M. Post, ed., *The Psychological Assessment of Political Leaders with Profiles of Saddam Hussein and Bill Clinton* (Ann Arbor, MI: University of Michigan Press, 2003), 53.

5. Stanley A. Renshon, "Psychoanalytic Assessments of Character and Performance in Presidents and Candidates: Some Observations on Theory and Method," in *Psychological Assessment of Political Leaders*, 126–127.

6. Gordon J. Direnzo, ed., *Personality and Politics* (Garden City, NY: Anchor Books, 1974), Introduction.

7. Stone and Schaffner, *Psychology of Politics*, 33–35.

8. Philip B. Taylor, *The Venezuelan Golpe de Estado of 1958: The Fall of Marcos Pérez Jiménez* (Washington, DC: Institute for the Comparative Study of Political Systems, 1968), 3.

9. Robert Gilmore, *Caudillism and Militarism in Venezuela, 1810–1910* (Athens, OH: Ohio University Press, 1964), 26.

10. Ibid., 53.

11. Ibid., 158.

12. Ibid., 19.

13. Miguel Tinker Salas, *The Enduring Legacy: Oil, Culture, and Society in Venezuela* (Durham, NC: Duke University Press, 2009).

14. Daniel Hellinger, *Venezuela: Tarnished Democracy* (San Francisco: Westview Press, 1991), 84–119.

15. Jennifer L. McCoy and David J. Myers, eds., *The Unraveling of Representative Democracy in Venezuela* (Baltimore, MD: Johns Hopkins University Press, 2004), 6–7.

16. Ibid., 206–213.

17. Ibid., 204–205.

18. Raul Padilla, Thaís Rodríguez, Henry Linares, and Sergio Arria, prod., *El Arañero de la Sabaneta* (Venezuela: Venezolana de Televisión), motion picture, http://www.youtube.com/watch?v=PrK6M6pPGz0.

19. Rosa Miriam Elizalde and Luis Báez, *Chávez Nuestro* (Havana: Casa Editora Abril, 2005), 369–370.

20. Padilla et al., *El Arañero.*

21. Alma Guillermoprieto, "Don't Cry for Me, Venezuela," New York Review of Books, October 6, 2005, http://www.nybooks.com/articles/archives/2005/oct/06/dont-cry-for-me-venezuela/?pagination=false.

22. Stone and Schaffner, *Psychology of Politics,* 65–72.

23. Elizalde and Báez, *Chávez Nuestro,* 24.

24. Padilla et al., *El Arañero.*

25. Richard Gott, *Hugo Chávez and the Bolivarian Revolution* (New York: Verso, 2005), 29–30.

26. Elizalde and Báez, *Chávez Nuestro,* 64, 19–21.

27. Aleida Guevara and Hugo Chávez, *Chávez, Venezuela, and the New Latin America: An Interview with Hugo Chavez* (New York: Ocean Press, 2005), 76–78.

28. Elizalde and Báez, *Chávez Nuestro,* 336.

29. Hugo Chávez and Marta Harnecker, *Understanding the Venezuelan Revolution: Hugo Chávez Talks to Marta Harnecker,* trans. by Chesa Boudin (New York: Monthly Review Press, 2005), 23–25.

30. Elizalde and Báez, *Chávez Nuestro,* 335.

31. See Direnzo, *Personality and Politics,* 273–275, for more on this framework.

32. Chavez and Harnecker, 26–40.

33. Elizalde and Báez, *Chávez Nuestro,* 356.

34. Chavez and Harnecker, 27–29.

35. Stone and Schaffner, *Psychology of Politics,* 60–67.

36. Milton Rokeach, *The Open and Closed Mind: Investigations into the Nature of Belief Systems and Personality Systems* (New York: Basic Books, 1960).

37. Ibid., 22.

38. Ibid., 33–39.

39. Chávez, Hugo. "Chávez's Lines #100: The Sermon on the Cerro," trans. by MINCI, December 28, 2010. Web access July 2013, http://venezuelanalysis.com/analysis/5899.

40. Harnecker, 56.

41. Elizalde and Báez, *Chávez Nuestro,* 354.

42. Gott, *Hugo Chávez,* 62.

43. Gott, *Hugo Chávez,* 129.

44. Hugo Chávez, "Las Líneas de Chávez," published by Partido Socialista Unido de Venezuela, January 22, 2009, http://www.psuv.org.ve/opiniones/lineas-chavez/lineas-chavez/#.UfVVgcWs31U, July 2013.

45. James Suggett, "Chavez Clashes with Communist Party of Venezuela over Candidacies," *Venezuelanalysis.com,* October 8, 2008, http://venezuelanalysis.com/news/3871.

46. One of many examples appears in Lowell Bergman, prod., *The Hugo Chávez Show* (November 26, 2008), Frontline Television Broadcast, minute 10:00.

47. Harnecker, 64–67.

48. To see the detailed framework on which this belief–disbelief system analysis is based, see Rokeach, *Open and Closed Mind,* 55–57.

49. Peter Suedfeld, Karen Guteri, and Philip Tetlock, "Assessing Interactive Complexity at a Distance: Archival Analysis of Thinking and Decision Making," in *Psychological Assessment of Political Leaders*, 256–258.
50. Post, *Psychological Assessment of Political Leaders*, 181–190, 218–220.
51. Chavez and Harnecker, 47.
52. Ibid., 102–103.
53. Ibid., 105–106.
54. Guevara and Chávez, *Chávez, Venezuela, and the New Latin* America, 57.
55. Chavez and Harnecker, 54.
56. Richard Koenigsberg, *The Psychoanalysis of Racism, Revolution, and Nationalism* (New York: Library of Social Science, 1977), 10–11.
57. Ibid., 36–40.
58. Gott, *Hugo Chávez*, 29.
59. For an overview of common facets of organizational change, see John P. Kotter, "Leading Change: Why Transformation Efforts Fail," *Harvard Business Review*, January 2007.
60. For more on common change strategies, see John P. Kotter, and Leanard A. Schlesinger, "Choosing Strategies for Change," *Harvard Business Review*, July–August 2008. For more on the adaptation of leadership styles to situational context, see Daniel Goleman, "Leadership That Gets Results," *Harvard Business Review*, March–April 2000, 78–90.
61. Gott, *Hugo Chávez*, 37.
62. Chavez and Harnecker, 24–33.
63. Gott, *Hugo Chávez*, 61.
64. Chavez and Harnecker, 34–43.
65. Ibid., 77–82.
66. Ibid., 71.
67. Bergman, *Hugo Chávez*, minute 36:00.
68. Chavez and Harnecker, 51–53.
69. Ibid.
70. Thomas Ponniah and Jonathan Eastwood, *The Revolution in Venezuela: Social and Political Change under Chávez* (Cambridge, MA: Harvard University Press, 2011), 70.
71. Chavez and Harnecker, 50.
72. Post, *Psychological Assessment of Political Leaders*, 81–82.
73. Chavez and Harnecker, 170–177.
74. For a full profile of the narcissist leader personality type, see Jerrold M. Post, "Assessing Leaders at a Distance: The Political Personality Profile," in *The Psychological Assessment of Political Leaders: With Profiles of Saddam Hussein and Bill Clinton*, ed. Jerrold M. Post (Ann Arbor, MI: University of Michigan Press, 2003), 83–88.
75. Elizalde and Báez, *Chávez Nuestro*, 196.
76. Chavez and Harnecker, 164–167.
77. Post, *Psychological Assessment of Political Leaders*, 89–95.
78. Elizalde and Báez, *Chávez Nuestro*, 28.
79. Stephen Kinzer, *Overthrow! America's Century of Regime Change from Hawaii to Iraq* (New York: Times Books Henry Holt, 2006).
80. For a full profile of the paranoid leader personality type, see Post, "Assessing Leaders at a Distance," 97–100.
81. Ponniah and Eastwood, *Revolution in Venezuela*, Chapter 8.
82. Margaret G. Hermann, "Assessing Leadership Style: Trait Analysis," in *Psychological Assessment of Political Leaders*, 190–198.

7

The Emperor Hirohito and the Decision to Attack Pearl Harbor

Shun Sakugawa

INTRODUCTION

In the morning of December 7, 1941, the Imperial Japanese Navy attacked the U.S. naval base at Pearl Harbor, Hawaii. This was the first time the United States had experienced a military attack on its territory, and this led the U.S. government to officially declare war with the Empire of Japan. As this attack marks a historically significant turning point, there have been a number of academic studies on how and why this attack took place. However, there has not been significant research on determining what was occurring behind the scenes, leading up to this incident. It is not possible to cover the whole spectrum of events here; therefore this chapter will focus on the leader of the Empire of Japan at that time, Emperor Hirohito, and his role in the decision making process to adopt the war plan, which led to the attack on Pearl Harbor.

On December 25, 1926, Hirohito was named Emperor, following the death of his father, Emperor Taisho. Hirohito took the 124th Chrysanthemum Throne and was given the title "Showa," which means "enlightened peace." Emperor Showa (Hirohito) was born on April 29, 1901. He was brought up as the crown prince of the Empire of Japan, and was ultimately crowned at the young age of 25, when his father passed away from a long illness. Even though Hirohito was young when he was named Emperor, he became the highest authority in the Empire of Japan. The characteristics of the power and authority given to the Emperor under the constitution at the time, the Meiji Constitution, however, had gradually changed over the years, in accordance with the gradual but significant shift in Japanese domestic politics and the changes in the international situation in the prewar period.[1] The Taisho period is known as the era when Japanese democracy prospered under the Meiji Constitution. Party politics had worked effectively over a couple of decades to bring the voice of the parliament into decision making. Unfortunately, changes in the international situation and domestic politics, especially the rise of the influence of military groups in Japan, led the political structure in the opposite direction, away from the period of Taisho democracy during the Showa period.

Previous research demonstrates diverse opinions on the role of Hirohito. For example, Herbert Bix points out in his book that "in his single-minded dedication to preserving his position, no matter what the cost to others, he was one of the most disingenuous persons ever to occupy the modern throne."[2] However, many other scholars, such as Akira Yamada, point out that there have not emerged any significant examples of Hirohito taking the leadership in making decisions during the war.[3] Peter Wetzler argues that the Emperor was not the only one to blame for the responsibility of this decision, considering the situation of the Showa period.[4] There are also several other scholarly pieces that focus on the war responsibilities of Hirohito; Hirohito was not accused of any war crimes after the Pacific War, in contrast to other political leaders in Japan, such as Tojo Hideki. These studies are important because the Emperor under the prewar Japanese political system had significant authority over different aspects of governmental structures.

Considering these different points of the debate, there are several issues worth covering when considering the role of Hirohito during the war. Thus, the focus of this chapter is the decision making process undertaken by Emperor Showa. To illustrate the significant characteristics of his role and analyze the reasons why Hirohito made the decision to enter the war, I will cover three main aspects: (1) the political system and the related debates on the role of the Emperor in prewar Japan; (2) the domestic and international situations when Japan decided to attack Pearl Harbor; and (3) the personal background of Hirohito.

The political system established by the Meiji Constitution had changed significantly over the years. There had been an ongoing discussion over the role of the Emperor, from both the scholarly and the political sides, and also on the decision making process in which the Emperor was involved. By reviewing these points, the actual role of the Emperor during the war related to the decision making process will be more clearly understood. Also, the domestic and international situations before the decision to attack Pearl Harbor must be reviewed. In the third section, I will go through what factors were taken into consideration at the time of the decision, and what the Emperor's perceptions were that led to the idea to launch the attack on Pearl Harbor and enter a war with the United States. Lastly, the personal background of Hirohito is an important aspect when we try to understand the criteria with which Hirohito made decisions on policies. Focusing on his childhood education and also the relationship between Emperor Meiji and the imperial family will shed light on the rationale behind Hirohito's decision to support the war plan to attack Pearl Harbor.

THE EMPEROR AND THE PREWAR POLITICAL SYSTEM IN JAPAN

To understand the role of the Emperor, it is important to examine the structure of the political system at that time of prewar Japan and its evolution over the years. There had been a significant shift in the political structure away from party participation in politics to a military-supported theocracy based on the Emperor.

The underlying political structure of imperial Japan was based on the Meiji Constitution (also known as the Constitution of the Empire of Japan). It was brought into effect in 1890 as a starting point of Japanese modernization. Faced with insecurity and the threat of invasion by Western countries, the main aim of the Constitution was to establish the conditions for the Japanese people to unite under clear leadership and establish strong governmental power under the Meiji Constitution.[5] Thus, learning from several Western constitutions, the Japanese government decided to write a constitution based on that of Prussia, which allows the Emperor to have significant power over many aspects of governmental authority. It is clear that the Meiji Constitution was not made by the will of the Japanese people but rather followed the interest of those supporting a strong government that could catch up with the already industrialized Western powers.[6]

The concept of the Meiji Constitution is based on both constitutionalism and theocracy. Also, the importance of the Emperor is clearly stated in the Constitution, as the first 17 articles are dedicated to the determination of the Emperor's capacities and authority. For example, Article 1 establishes the constitutional monarchy by announcing that it is the Emperor who governs the Empire of Japan. These articles also determine the status of the Emperor as the head of state, his legislative capacity in cooperation with the imperial parliament, and his supreme command over the military forces.

Considering these points, it appears that the Emperor had taken on significant political power and had a leading role in making many political decisions on his own. However, a more democratic process had gradually taken a leading role after several decades, and party politics had significantly emerged in the real decision making process. A good example of this is the so-called Taisho democracy, the time period between Meiji and Showa under Hirohito's father. During this period, Japanese participatory, party politics developed and expanded significantly. Also, the other significant contribution, popular in the Taisho period, was the introduction of the general election law and the Emperor Organ Theory.[7]

The general election law was finally brought into effect in 1925, about a half century after the imperial parliament started its work in 1880.

This movement followed the so-called freedom and people's rights movement at the beginning of the Meiji period, which was the first social and political movement in Japan to call for democracy. This movement accomplished the establishment of both the Meiji Constitution and the imperial parliament; however, the House of Representatives tended to be overshadowed by the influence of the Senate, which was formed by the aristocrats. In addition, the government itself did not respect the decisions taken by the parliament. Thus, there was a significant demand by the general public to introduce the general election law, and its establishment allowed all men the right to vote regardless of the amount of tax they paid.

The Emperor Organ Theory is also an important aspect of the Taisho democracy. According to this theory, the Emperor is one of the organs of the governmental structure and is not seen as sacred or holy. The leading scholar behind this theory is Tatsukichi Minobe, who was a professor of law at the Imperial University of Tokyo. This theory was significant in terms of causing a shift in the Japanese people's perception of the Emperor. At the beginning of the Taisho period, even though the Meiji Constitution established that sovereign power lies with the people, this was not the commonly understood by the general public. Many Japanese people considered the Emperor as the epicenter of Japanese sovereignty and that the general public should follow the orders of the Emperor.[8] In an attempt to change this perception, Minobe first explained that a state could be considered similar to the juridical person. If Japan as a state is considered as a juridical person, all of the political structures, such as the parliament, the executive government, the courts, and even the Emperor, should be considered as organs of the whole body of the state.[9] Thus the concept of a constitutional monarchy is important in a way that considers the Constitution to be a constraint on these organs and to prevent any harmful effects on the people, as sovereign powers.

From this point of view, the Taisho democracy was considered a success by expanding democracy in Japan, and in a way restricting the power of the Emperor. Thus, apolitical custom called "the way of constitutional politics (*Kensei no Jodo*)" was established. This is a custom that requires the Emperor to nominate the head of the leading party in the House of Representatives as prime minister.[10] Even though it was just a political custom and did not have any legal authority, the practice had continued until the May 15 incident in 1932 when the radical members of the Japanese Imperial Navy assassinated the then prime minister Tsuyoshi Inukai in attempt to carry out a coup d'état and expand the influence of the military in Japanese politics.[11] As well illustrated by this incident, the Japanese military gradually expanded its authority over the political decision making process in the 1930s, especially after the economic turmoil that had grown worse in the aftermath of the Great Depression. The military had an interest in territorial expansion into neighboring countries in order to gain natural resources and markets to sustain Japan's economic growth.

With this shift in Japanese politics, the conservative military personnel and other right-wing radical groups blamed the Emperor Organ Theory, which had stated that the Emperor was just one organ in the decision making process and not the supreme leader. The significant event that brought an end to this concept is the so-called Emperor Organ Theory Incident in 1935. Even though the Emperor Organ Theory had been widely accepted as the common scholarly interpretation of the Meiji Constitution during the Taisho democratic period, the right-wing politicians and military began to criticize this concept as it conflicted with the concept of a national polity, put forth by Kokutai.[12] The basic interpretation of the Kokutai theory is the idea that national sovereignty lies with the Emperor. Thus, these right-wing politicians attacked the Emperor Organ Theory in order to garner political power into their own hands. During the sessions of the imperial parliament in 1935, Senator Takeo Kikuchi, who was also a lieutenant general in the Army Reserve, claimed that Professor Minobe was against the Emperor by trying to deprive him of his role as national sovereign.[13] This caused a huge political turmoil and the books written by Minobe were even banned for the general public. In addition to that, the imperial parliament ratified two official statements related to national polity, and announced that national sovereignty lay with the Emperor, not the people. These statements destroyed the Emperor Organ Theory and at the same time ended the Taisho democratic period. Political participation, which seemed to have developed over the years, significantly waned, and the radical sentiment of the military and right-wing politicians began to account for the majority within the political sphere.[14]

As the military and right-wing political groups began to take the initiative in the decision making process, greater focus was placed on the Emperor as the political authority. The Ministry of Education published a document of national polity, which required all schools in Japan to teach national polity as the main political structure of the Empire of Japan. This meant that the Emperor's authority was imprinted on the minds of the people.

Under this increasing tension, the Empire of Japan began engaging in the war with China. Even though there was no reference to it under the Meiji Constitution, the most important decision making process relating to the war plan was the imperial conference called *Gozen Kaigi*.[15] It started right before Japan decided to enter into war with China in 1938. This became the first decision carried out in the first *Gozen Kaigi*, to launch the war with China. The members were the Emperor, the prime minister, the minister of foreign affairs, the minister of finance, the minister of war, the minister of the navy, the chief of the army general staff, and the chief of the navy general staff. The unique point of the *Gozen Kaigi* was that even though the

Emperor attended the conference, he usually did not make any comments or display his own interests. Stephen Large points out that this is because the Emperor was superior to any of the political figures in Japan at that time, and the other politicians were trying to evade their responsibility by not expressing the clear intent of the Emperor. This was a way to reduce any possibility for the Emperor to avoid taking responsibility for decisions the *Gozen Kaigi* conference made.[16] There were 15 conferences that took place between 1938 and 1945, and there were only three times when the Emperor made comments: one was before entering into the war with the United States, and the other two are before accepting the unconditional surrender to the Allied Forces. The details are illustrated in the next section, but the Emperor Showa took his decision to enter the war at the behest of the *Gozen Kaigi* in 1941. He actually did not clearly support the plan of entering into war with the United States, and even extended his regret on the disastrous situation in the region and his hope to step away from the additional war. However, he also did not clearly oppose the decision to enter into war, and with his authorization, the navy carried out the covert attack on Pearl Harbor. In this regard, it would be possible to say that the Emperor had taken some level of responsibility in the decision making process of the attack on Pearl Harbor.

As illustrated earlier, the political structure under the Meiji Constitution had shifted back and forth between a democratic system and the Emperor's theocratic system. It is important to note that the democracy, which was led by the development of participatory, party politics, was eminent in the Taisho period. However, the rise of the military forces and right-wing politicians in accordance with the global depression and the increasing uncertainty in neighboring countries resulted in strengthening the authority of the Emperor, albeit manipulated by the military, in politics and the decision making process.

THE DOMESTIC AND INTERNATIONAL POLITICAL SITUATION BEFORE THE WAR WITH THE UNITED STATES

Building upon the analysis of the political structure and debates in prewar Japan, it is also important to clarify the domestic and international political situation before the Japanese government decided to attack Pearl Harbor. Two important questions emerge: What was the main reason for the Japanese government to decide to attack the United States? What kinds of domestic considerations played a role in that decision?

In 1941, the Empire of Japan had already commenced the war with China and the situation of the war was in a stalemate. In this environment, the most necessary course of action for Japan to be able to continue the war and take the advantage was maintaining a supply of natural resources, especially oil and iron. As an island country, Japan did not have sufficient amounts of these resources within its territory, and this had been the biggest reason for the Japanese government to expand its zone of influence over other countries. Especially after finding out that Chiang Kai-Shek was supported by the United States and the United Kingdom through several routes from Southeast Asia, the leadership of the Japanese military forces argued that it was necessary to expand the battle field into Southeast Asia to keep these support routes open and at the same time secure the vast amount of natural resources coming from these territories. From the perspective of global military balance, even without the war in China, the Japanese relationship with the United States and the United Kingdom had not been going well. Japan was expanding economically and militarily, especially after World War I. Therefore, the United Kingdom and the United States were uncertain about Japan's intentions and their level of insecurity had gradually increased.[17] Also, the United Kingdom had decided to dissolve its military alliance with Japan after World War I, and both the United Kingdom and the United States shifted their policy orientations on how to handle their relationships with Japan.

With this international environment as a backdrop, the decision to attack Pearl Harbor and enter into a war with the United States and its allies was decided during four of the *Gozen Kaigi* conferences. On July 2, right after the war between Nazi Germany and the Soviet Union erupted, the Japanese government headed by Emperor Hirohito first adopted the decision to strengthen the military in the south and to seriously consider the possibility of entering into war with the United States. In the *Gozen Kaigi* on September 6, it was decided to enter into war with the United States if bilateral diplomatic negotiations did not turn out well by the end of October. After that, while still continuing negotiations with the United States, the *Gozen Kaigi* on November 5 decided to exercise military action against the United States by the beginning of December. Then on December 1, the actual war plan to attack Pearl Harbor on December 7 was finally approved. Emperor Hirohito had taken a cautious approach toward the war with the United States and favored peace talks until the *Gozen Kaigi* of September 6. However, after Prime Minister Fumimaro Konoe, who had supported peace negotiations with the United States, was forced by the military to resign on October 16, 1941, Hideki Tojo, a supporter of the war, was named as the new prime minister. Two days later, on October 18, Prime Minister Tojo gathered the Cabinet and six weeks later Japan attacked Pearl Harbor.

Konoe explained his interpretation of Hirohito's position on the war:

> Of course, His Imperial Majesty is a pacifist and he wished to avoid war. When I told him that to initiate war was a mistake, he agreed. But the next day, he would tell me: "You were worried about it yesterday but you do not have to

> worry so much." Thus gradually he began to lead to war. I felt the Emperor was telling me: "My prime minister does not understand military matters. I know much more." In short, the Emperor had absorbed the view of the army and the navy high commands.[18]

It became clear that Emperor Hirohito had changed his mind on the war. However, what were the reasons for the Emperor to change his attitude toward the war with the United States when he had previously supported peaceful settlement? There are two main reasons for his not wanting to enter the war: skepticism about the possibility of winning and the ongoing diplomatic negotiations.

Akira Yamada points out in his book that the Emperor asked the chief of staff who was in charge of the war plan a number of questions, but the chief of staff at that time was not able to offer any straight answers to his questions.[19] The plan to attack Pearl Harbor was not yet finalized even inside the military, so the chief of staff answered the Emperor's questions by giving a more general and ambiguous war plan, which aimed at gradually reducing the number of American battleships and submarines by successive attacks. However, the chief of staff was not fully confident in the plan and replied that "it would be impossible for us to win as in the Battle in the Sea of Japan during the Russo-Japanese war, and an outcome of the battle with the United States is not perceivable right now."[20] Clearly, this uncertainty made Emperor Hirohito reluctant to undertake a war with the United States.[21]

Furthermore, the Emperor was more inclined to take the alternative and avoid war with the United States, pursuing bilateral diplomatic negotiations. A day before the *Gozen Kaigi* on September 6, Prime Minister Konoe adopted the agenda for the meeting, which listed the possible actions by the Japanese government in the next couple of months:

1. Preparations to enter into war with the United States, the United Kingdom, and the Netherlands should be completed by the end of October, in order to protect the Empire.
2. While preparing for the war, the Empire will continue the effort to reach an agreement with the United States through the diplomatic channel to avoid the war.
3. If there is no achievement made by the beginning of October, the Empire will decide to enter into war with the United States, the United Kingdom, and the Netherlands.[22]

Emperor Hirohito expressed to Prime Minister Konoe his concerns that the government seemed to be too inclined to start a war with the United States, saying, "preparations for the war is listed as number one and diplomatic negotiation is listed as number two, so it seems like starting the war is the main purpose and negotiation is just the subordinate alternative."[23]

This skepticism led the Emperor to speak out in the *Gozen Kaigi* on September 6, and he cited a poem by Emperor Meiji to indicate the need to avoid entering into war with the United States, the United Kingdom, and the Netherlands.[24]

Considering these points, the Emperor was clearly reluctant on September 6 to enter into another war. Then, what were the reasons for the Emperor to change his mind to support the decision to enter the war, or at least not try to stop the decision?

As Yamada points out, the primary reason why Emperor Hirohito was skeptical about the war plan previous to September 6 was the uncertainty over the outcome of the attack and the plan's lack of clarity.[25] After the chief of staff realized this, the military tried to clarify all the Emperor's concerns, such as the probability of winning the war and the possible ending of the war once it started. It was very difficult to know the future prospects for the end of the war because it was highly dependent on other variables, such as the situation on the war front in Europe and also the situation of the other battle fronts Japan was involved in with China and Southeast Asia.[26] Within this environment, the navy proposed, with the endorsement of the new prime minister Tojo, a plan to attack Pearl Harbor and then seek a peace agreement with the United States before the war would evolve into a stalemate.[27] Considering this plan as a concrete and plausible one, the Emperor shifted his previous position and accepted the plan to enter into war with the United States and its allies.[28]

A second reason that Bix highlights was the absence of strong leadership by the Emperor who cited the constitutional monarchy as a reason for going to war. Hirohito states:

> When I look back on it now, my first thought was correct. For even at the end of the war, when the power of the army and navy was extremely weak, something resembling a coup d'état occurred in opposition to unconditional surrender. So, if I had used a "Veto" against the cabinet's decision to go to war, who knows what might have happened?
>
> If I had not granted permission to stand up and act in that time of crisis, when we had an elite army and navy troops who had trained hard for many years, then, as time passed, our oil supply would have been steadily depleted and the navy would have become immobilized. If we had tried to supply the navy with synthetic oil, almost all of Japanese industry would have had to be sacrificed for that one end. If that had happened, the country would have gone to ruin, and in the end, even if pressed by unreasonable demands, we would have had to surrender unconditionally.
>
> Such were the prospects for Japan's future at the time of the opening of the war. Let us assume that I had vetoed the decision to go to war. I think it would certainly have led to enormous civil strife at home. People close to me whom

> I trusted would have been killed, and my own life would have been endangered. I would not have minded that but, ultimately, a furious war would have developed anyway and would have brought about a tragedy far worse than this war (World War II). In the end, unable to end the war, Japan would have been destroyed.[29]

According to Bix, since the government had arrived at a unified opinion in December 1941, the Emperor—being a "constitutional monarch"—had to give approval to the attack on Pearl Harbor. Had he not done so, there would have been a coup d'état, followed by a war, and "a tragedy far worse than this" would have resulted.[30] It is interesting to note that Emperor Hirohito defined the status of the Emperor as the "constitutional monarch" and thus restrained himself from using any power and authority determined in the Constitution in order to prevent Japan from entering into the war, because the decision was made and approved by the government.

Taking into consideration the political and military situation at the time that the Empire of Japan decided to enter into war with the United States by suddenly attacking Pearl Harbor, it is clear that the attitude of the Emperor toward the decision to enter into the war shifted from skepticism to somewhat implicit support and approval. This is not because there were no other choices for Japan to take in order to survive as a sovereign state, but because of the complicated decision making process in which nobody clearly took initiative and also the absence of strong leadership by Emperor Hirohito.

THE PERSONAL HISTORY OF HIROHITO

By throwing light on the decision making process, the Emperor appeared to be involved in an important way in the manner in which decisions were made. However, even though Hirohito initially did not want to go the war with the United States, he finally supported the decision. Why did he take this decision at the end? What was his rationale behind this shift? To understand his reasoning, it is important to consider the story of his education and childhood.

As crown prince, Hirohito was born to be a future emperor and was educated throughout his youth to prepare for the coming moment. As the military institution was highly integrated into the imperial family, especially after the Meiji period, the education of all male members of the imperial family included military instruction and the males served in the military after they became adults. Also, it was common for the children of the imperial family to be educated by foster parents, not by their own parents. Following this custom, Hirohito was entrusted to foster parents just 70 days after he was born, under the care of Count Sumiyoshi Kawamura.[31] After staying with the Kawamuras for three years, Hirohito moved to the East Palace Grounds where Takamasa

Kido took charge of Hirohito's education and training. In addition to Kido, Hirohito spent his childhood with General Nogi, who was a retired general of the Imperial Army and was nominated by Emperor Meiji as principal of the Gakushuin School to take responsibility for the education of the young crown prince. As Stephen Large points out, General Nogi held significant influence over Hirohito's education. Being a national hero of the Russo-Japanese war just before Hirohito started his education, General Nogi taught Hirohito the virtues of patriotism and the samurai ethic of personal austerity and devotion to duty, which constituted part of the legacy of shogunate to the Meiji government.[32] Under the supervision of General Nogi, Hirohito followed a daily routine, such as praying in the morning to honor the Sun Goddess and Emperor Meiji. His education under the tutelage of General Nogi lasted only four years due to the fact that the general committed suicide after the death of Emperor Meiji in 1912. Nevertheless, Emperor Hirohito later stated that General Nogi was one of the most influential persons during his youth and the one who established Hirohito's basic daily discipline.[33]

After Hirohito's father became Emperor Taisho in 1912, Hirohito followed the custom of the imperial family of receiving a commission in both the army and the navy. After graduating from the Gakushuin School in 1914, he entered another educational institution called Togu Ogakumonjo in order to continue his training. There, Hirohito received military and educational training, from both military personnel and academic scholars. Admiral Heihachiro Togo, another war hero from the Russo-Japanese war, was the director of the Togu Ogakumonjo and he served as the rector until the school closed in 1921. The influence of Admiral Togo on Hirohito seems to be more difficult to ascertain than the influence of General Nogi. As Wetzler points out, on the one hand, Admiral Togo was not comparable to those who became ultranationalist in the military in the 1930s, but he had the discretion to choose any teacher he wanted for the Togu Ogakumonjo school. Thus he had a control of the climate of instruction at the institution.[34]

As both Wetzler and Large point out, Shigetake Sugiura and Kurakichi Shiratori were important figures for the education of the crown prince among numerous teachers who were selected by Admiral Togo. Sugiura was the ethics instructor and his program was characterized as "Imperial Studies" (*Teiogaku*), which aimed at instructing Hirohito on how to behave as an emperor.[35] It is interesting to know that Sugiura's class focused on imperial tradition in a wide variety, from obvious topics such as imperial regalia, Mount Fuji, the military, and shrines, to less obvious topics such as George Washington and Emperor Wilhelm II of Germany.[36] In addition to this, Sugiura taught Confucian ethics and those virtues as courage, wisdom, and benevolence, symbolized by the imperial regalia.[37] In his classes, Sugiura also emphasized the Shinto rituals and mythology and the history of the Japanese imperial family. He sometimes went back to the books from ancient Japan, such as *Nihon Shoki* (History of Ancient Japan), to explain the source of power and logical structure of authority of the Japanese modern imperial family.

Slightly different from Sugiura, Shiratori taught Hirohito Asian, Western, and Japanese history. He had studied in Germany and became a sophisticated and highly respected historian, as he established the area of historical studies called *Toyoshi* (Oriental History) in Japan. In his lectures at Togu Ogakumonjo, Shiratori placed emphasis on two areas of education: *Kokutai* and Japanese superiority as a race. He wrote a book called *Kokushi* (National History), and in the general introduction of this book, he points out,

> [T]he imperial family unified our land and people and created the Empire. Not only did it rule as the head of state, it also became integrated with the people and the head of their region. [. . .] Not once has there been a change in the race. Therefore we, descendants of the people who assisted the founder at the time of her creation of the state, have carried out the will of our ancestors and become eternally loyal subjects. [. . .] This indeed is the essence of *Kokutai*, and there is no mistake saying that we have been a homogenous race since antiquity.[38]

Also, Shiratori claimed the superiority of the Japanese race relative to the Chinese. Wetzler analyzes this point by quoting a section from Shiratori's book:

> [T]he Japanese race came to these islands and established a nation in the ancient, ancient past; one can even say it is hardly possible to acquire knowledge about these origins. This antiquity certainly is one reason for Japan's superiority. [. . .] Therefore, nothing in the world compares to the divine nature of the imperial family and likewise the majesty of our national polity. Here is one great reason for Japan's superiority.[39]

As we can see from these remarks, both Sugiura and Shiratori were ardent loyalists and nationalists, and through their lectures, Hirohito was instilled with pride in the Japanese imperial institution and in Japanese economic growth and military rise since the Meiji restoration. This pride led him to hold nationalistic sentiments and a sense of superiority over the other Asian countries. The logic of this belief system then would be that because of Japanese superiority, they would clearly win in any war. Facts that might counter that core belief would have to be rejected to protect the basic belief system. If Hirohito were to doubt Japan's ability to win, then that would mean that the Japanese Empire was not superior.

The other important aspect of the childhood of the Emperor was his relationship with Emperor Meiji. Emperor Meiji was Hirohito's grandfather, and was considered and propagandized by the government as the most powerful figure in Japan, from both a military and a nonmilitary perspective. However, Hirohito did not have much opportunity to get to know him, mainly because Meiji did not have much interest in the education of his grandchildren. Even though Hirohito was able to meet Emperor Meiji, most of the meetings lasted only a couple of minutes. Regardless of his emotional distance from him, Hirohito was educated with the notion that the Emperor was the premier authority in the country, as the other children were also taught in school. So, he idealized the image of Emperor Meiji and tried to install him as the model for his lifestyle and political beliefs. With this background, Hirohito did not cast any doubts on his potential authority over every aspect of the country when he became the Emperor. As noted in the second section of this chapter, when the radical military groups and the right-wing political parties gained more and more popularity with the people, the status of the Emperor became enshrined as a sacred embodiment and this trend continued until the end of World War II. Thus, when Hirohito ascended to the throne and became Emperor Showa, he became not only the head of both the political and military branches of the government, which were clearly determined under the Meiji Constitution, but also the head of the religious and spiritual hierarchy in Japan.

In addition, one of the main philosophical beliefs of Hirohito was Shinto. From the time he was a child, Hirohito was deeply immersed with the traditional Shinto rituals. These rituals became embedded in his daily life, such as praying everyday in a small room by bowing in the direction of *Ise Jingu* shrine. Because the history of the imperial family was said to be closely related to the history of Shintoism, for Hirohito the immersion into Shintoism meant worship of the ancestors. By continuously practicing daily Shinto rituals, Hirohito magnified his respect for his ancestors. As he grew older, his visits to shrines and imperial mausoleums deepened his sense of the importance of his ancestors. The religious identity that worked its way into his thoughts and beliefs was one of the main outcomes of his early childhood upbringing. The central component of this identity was Hirohito's strong sense of moral obligation to the imperial ancestors, who were the source of his being, his authority, his household fortune, and indeed whatever sustained both him and his nation.[40]

With this educational background, what kind of child was Hirohito? Bix points out that he was a docile child, fussed over and pampered by nurses and relatives during his kindergarten years. Like other children of his exalted class, he grew up re-enacting play based on the Russo-Japanese war. As the emperor-to-be, Hirohito had to be respected in play and could never be the recipient of anger or ill treatment. Even in make-believe war games, he always had to be the commander in chief, on the winning side. Moreover, he was a distinctly cautious child. When he played tag with children from aristocratic families who had been chosen to accompany him, Prince Hirohito always played strictly according to the rules, never employing any of the little tricks that were possible in the game.[41] In addition, Harvey argues that Hirohito was a grave and clumsy child. Harvey cites from a memoire of an aide of Hirohito saying, "Hirohito looked formal and serious in his youth, neither smiling nor laughing. He did not appear to take any joy in either exercise or play."[42] Considering these points, it seems that Hirohito did not clearly show his emotions and ideas to others due to his educational background, childhood environment, and underlying reserved personality in general.

By reviewing his personal background in education and daily life during his childhood, we can see that Hirohito formed his patriotic ideology and nationalistic sentiment resulting from the education he received under the significant influence of General Nogi, Admiral Togo, Shigetake Sugiura, and Kurakichi Shiratori. Also from his adherence to the Shinto rituals and ideologies from childhood, Hirohito's belief system also included worship of ancestors of the imperial family, as supreme beings. However, despite all the education and training he received, he was described as more of a docile child; this personality trait may have led to the weak leadership of Hirohito after he assumed the throne as Emperor Showa. From the perspective of scholar Herbert Bix, Hirohito's leadership appeared weak when compared to the leaders of other countries.

> Hirohito was rarely adequate when exceptionally strong personal leadership was needed to coordinate and control the decentralized power structure and mediate conflicts between the general staffs and their ministries. [. . .] He was never able to surmount rivalries between the military services and thereby maintain their unity of purpose and effort. What Hirohito did was provide his chiefs of staff with continuous oversight based on his strong sense of responsibility for the empire, and ultimately, the interests of the imperial family.[43]

From this analysis, it appears that Hirohito believed that protecting the longevity of the Japanese imperial family was a high priority. In his own statement, Hirohito also indicated that if he were to go against the attack at Pearl Harbor, most likely the military would have launched a coup d'état and he, and thus his family, would have been removed from a position within Japanese political culture.[44] He also concluded that the war with the United States would have gone ahead any way. However, by approving the inevitable war, he never tested this second hypothesis. Therefore, we can conclude that his belief system placed a higher priority on protecting the imperial family over saving lives. His two core beliefs—the superiority of the Japanese people and the sacred nature of the imperial House of Japan—led to his acquiescence in the face of Japanese military aggression both at home and abroad.

CONCLUSION

The purpose of this chapter is to shed light on the decision making process taken during prewar Japan, and the role of Emperor Hirohito in the decision to attack Pearl Harbor and enter into war with the United States. The Japanese political structure before World War II was unique in comparison to other major countries at the time. In response to the tumultuous international situation in the nineteenth century, Japan drastically changed its political structure from the samurai-headed shogunate government to a constitutional monarchy based on the Meiji Constitution. As it was government officials and politicians, not the Japanese people themselves, who established the Constitution, the political structure set up by the Constitution became somewhere in between a constitutional monarchy and theocratic monarchy. The political instability stems from this uncertainty in the political structure, and this changed over the years. During the Taisho democracy, it leaned more toward a constitutional monarchy, but later moved drastically to becoming a theocratic monarchy in the Showa period. This is one of the reasons why the political decision making process in prewar Japan was unclear and uncertain. Thus, even though the Emperor was the head of the government and theoretically held most of the power in both political and military affairs, it appears that Hirohito was unable to decide every matter on the table. As Hirohito stated, he feared he could be killed or overthrown in a military coup, indicating that in fact, the military held the power. A clearer explanation might be that the decision making process was a consensus of the various actors. Hirohito had the final say on the approval of the plan to attack Pearl Harbor, but this war plan was made by the navy and preapproved by the Cabinet headed by the then prime minister Tojo. Taking into consideration the political custom that the Emperor does not make any comments in the *Gozen Kaigi*, even the Emperor was not able to deny approval or change the plan already authorized by the Cabinet. Even though the Emperor was the symbolic authority of the country for the general public, there was vey little wiggle room for the Emperor to make any decisions on his own.

It is also important to consider the international situation at that time. The Empire of Japan was already in a war with China, and at first Emperor Showa was not inclined to start another war with the United States. Hirohito clearly demonstrated this sentiment in a statement in which he declared, "we should focus more on the diplomacy, and we should not consider starting another war unless the diplomatic negotiations do not turn well."[45] However, negotiations with the United States did not go well, and more and more Japanese people at that time began to support the plan to enter into war with the United States in order to maintain the supply line of the natural resources, especially in the Southeast Asia. Facing the people's support and the Cabinet's approval of the war plan, Hirohito may have thought that it was necessary, and inevitable, to enter into a war with the United States, with the slight hope of obtaining an edge in the battle by the sudden attack at Pearl Harbor.

Lastly, considering his personal background, the biggest incentive for Hirohito to enter into war with the United States by attacking Pearl Harbor was to maintain the Japanese integrity and independence as a state, and not to allow the oil embargo by the United States to go ahead with no response. He also wanted to maintain the important heritage line of the imperial family, which had continued for more than two thousand years, and consequently sustain his own identity as well. When he approved the decision to enter into war with the United States, it appears as though he may also have believed in the success of the war plan, thus protecting the imperial family from ruin and perhaps defending Japan's sovereignty.

Additionally, it is important to underscore here the nonexistence of strong leadership by Hirohito. Even though he was theoretically the head of state and symbolically had the final approval of the war plan, he did not take on a leadership role in changing the situation; he simply followed the recommendations put forth by other political figures and military personnel. He had expressed his preference for diplomatic negotiations and had the negotiations with the United States been more productive, we might have witnessed a different history.

NOTES

1. Yoichi Kato, *Shōwa Tennō to Sensō no Seiki* [Emperor Shōwa and the Century of War] (Tokyo: Kodansha, 2011).
2. Herbert P. Bix, *Hirohito and the Making of Modern Japan* (New York: Harper Collins, 2000), 5.
3. Akira Yamada, *Ososugita Seidan* [The Decision Made Too Late] (Tokyo: Showa Shuppan, 1991), 13.
4. Peter Wetzler, *Hirohito and War* (Honolulu: University of Hawai'i Press, 1998).
5. The important point to consider here is that the Emperor had not been in political power for a long time since the establishment of the Kamakura Shogunate government in 1192. The Emperor regained his political power after the collapse of the Edo Shogunate government and the establishment of the Meiji government. This regime change was due to the increasing necessity to modernize Japan, faced with the significant power difference with the Western colonial powers. This fact also explains why the Emperor tried to increase his power over the government with the Meiji Constitution.
6. Daikichi Irokawa, *The Age of Hirohito: In Search of Modern Japan* (New York: Free Press, 1995).
7. Toshiaki Kawahara, *Tennō Hirohito no Shōwashi* [The Emperor Hirohito and the History of Shōwa] (Tokyo: Bungeishunju, 1983).
8. This was the main interpretation of the Constitution at the beginning of the Meiji period. Many scholars supported this theory, including Yatsuka Hozumi, one of the professors of law at the Imperial University of Tokyo.

9. Seitaro Miyamoto, *Tennokikansetsu to Sono Shuhen: Mittsu no Tennokikansetsu to Showashi no Shogen* [Emperor Organ Theory and Related Theories: Three Types of Emperor Organ Theory and the History of the Showa Period] (Tokyo: Yuhikaku, 1980).

10. The Meiji Constitution did not clearly determine the way to choose ministers including the prime minister. Customarily, the prime minister was recommended by the head of the statesmen in the imperial parliament and then nominated by the Emperor. Thus, in a lot of cases, the leading party of the House of the Representatives is not necessarily elected as the prime minister, and it would not be possible to establish the parliamentary cabinet system.

11. Ikuhiko Hata, *Hirohito: The Shōwa Emperor in War and Peace* (Kent, UK: Global Oriental, 2007), 37–39.

12. Seiichi Chatani, *Shōwa Tennō: Sokkintachi no Senso* [The Shōwa Emperor: War from the Perspective of the Aides] (Tokyo: Yoshikawa Kobunkan, 2010), 12–14.

13. David A. Titus, *Palace and Politics in Prewar Japan* (New York: Columbia University Press, 1974), 131.

14. Kenneth J. Ruoff, *The People's Emperor: Democracy and the Japanese Monarchy, 1945–1995* (Cambridge, MA: Harvard University Press, 2001), 34.

15. The Emperor actually held the right to declare war according to the Meiji Constitution (Article 13), but no Emperor had ever explicitly done so under his sole discretion.

16. Stephen S. Large, *Emperor Hirohito and Shōwa Japan: A Political Biography* (London: Routledge, 1992).

17. This resulted in the two sets of naval treaties (London Naval Treaty and Washington Naval Treaty), which tried to balance military power by setting up a quota for the number of battleships one country could have. These treaties triggered the significant opposition from Japanese political parties and military groups, as they constrained Japanese military capabilities. The arguments by these political parties and military groups gained a certain support from Japanese citizens, and this underscores the increasing influence of the military in Japanese domestic politics. (Chatani, *Shōwa Tennō*, 41–42).

18. Akira Fujiwara, *Showa Tenno no Ju-go NenSenso* [Fifteen Years of War under Emperor Showa] (Tokyo: Aoki Shoten, 1991), 126.

19. Yamada, *Ososugita Seidan*, 16.

20. Ibid., 17.

21. Bilateral tensions had increased, especially after the Japanese Imperial Army entered French Indochina in July, and the United States reacted with the comprehensive oil embargo on Japan. Emperor Showa became more reluctant to enter into a war with the United States.

22. Akira Yamada, *Showa Tenno no Senso Shido* [The Leadership of the Emperor Showa in Wartime] (Tokyo: Showa Shuppan, 1990), 86.

23. Kanjiro Tanaka, ed., *Heiwa heno Doryoku: Konoe Fumimaro Shuki* [An Attempt to Seek Peace: The Diary of Konoe Fumimaro] (Tokyo: Nihon Denpotsushinsha, 1946), 85–86.

24. The poem of the Emperor Meiji: "All the seas, in every quarter, are as brothers to one another. Why, then, do the winds and waves of strife rage so turbulently throughout the world?" See Robert J. C. Butow, *Tojo and the Coming of the War* (Princeton, NJ: Princeton University Press, 1961), 258; and Hiroshi Takahashi, ed., *Shōwa Tennō Hatsugenroku* [Records of the Remarks by the Emperor Shōwa] (Tokyo: Shogakukan, 1989), 84.

25. Yamada, *Ososugita Seidan*, 24.

26. Paul Manning, *Hirohito: The War Years* (New York: Dodd, Mead, 1986), 40–41.

27. Roberta Wohlstetter, *Pear Harbor: Warning and Decision* (Stanford, CA: Stanford University Press, 1962), 343–350.

28. Yamada, *Ososugita Seidan*, 27–32.

29. Hidenari Terasaki, ed., *Shōwa Tennō Dokuhakuroku: Terasaki Hidenari Goyogakari Nikki*, [Records of the Self-Remarks by the Emperor Shōwa: Diary of Terasaki Hidenari] (Tokyo: Bungeishunju, 1991), 136–137.

30. Bix, *Hirohito*, 350.

31. Wetzler, *Hirohito and War*, 96.

32. Large, *Emperor Hirohito*, 15.

33. Hideaki Sasaki, *Nogi Maresuke* [General Nogi] (Tokyo: Minerva publishing, 2005), 393.

34. Wetzler, *Hirohito and War*, 86.

35. Large, *Emperor Hirohito*, 17; Wetzler, *Hirohito and War*, 87.

36. Wetzler, *Hirohito and War*, 96.

37. Shichihei Yamamoto, *Showa Tenno no Kenkyu: Sono Jitsuzowo Saguru* [The Study of the Emperor Showa: His Real Image] (Tokyo: Shodensha, 1989), 206.

38. Bix, *Hirohito*.

39. Wetzler, *Hirohito and War*, 104.

40. Bix, *Hirohito*, 38.

41. Ibid., 25.

42. Robert Harvey, *American Shogun: General MacArthur, Emperor Hirohito and the Drama of Modern Japan* (New York: Overlook Press, 2006), 80.

43. Bix, *Hirohito*, 439.

44. Terasaki, *Shōwa Tennō*..

45. Takahashi, *Shōwa Tennō Hatsugenroku*, 83.

Part II

AUTHORITARIAN LEADERS IN DEMOCRATIC SOCIETIES

8

Henry Stimson and His Influence on Harry Truman: A Victorian Conservative in the Atomic Court

Monika Adamczyk

The spring and summer of 1945 presented Henry Stimson a case unlike any he had ever encountered as a student of law or as an experienced attorney. With the surrender of Germany on May 7, World War II seemed to be drawing to a close.[1] Though the war would now shift to the Pacific, Japan was sufficiently weak and the United States adequately supported internationally, as the Soviet Union had promised to enter the war against Japan at Yalta in February. The spring had also tested Stimson's managerial and leadership abilities as secretary of war as he was the chief figure responsible for spearheading the transition of presidential leadership after Roosevelt's untimely death in April. His first action, furthermore, would be to fully brief President Harry Truman about the atomic research that he had overseen since the late 1930s. In a memo dated April 24, 1945, Stimson urged Truman to have a "very important" talk with him on a "highly secretive matter" that "has such a bearing on . . . foreign relations and has such an important effect upon all [his] thinking in the field."[2] At the briefing on April 25, Stimson discussed with President Truman a 24-page memo written by General Groves that comprehensively detailed technical information about the bomb, the history of the Manhattan Project, information about nuclear plants and security, a commentary on the UK–U.S. nuclear partnership and patent and procurement information.[3] He later recounted, in his personal diary entry on that day, that Truman "read [the memo] carefully and was very much interested in it."[4] But despite the closure of the war in Europe and seemingly smooth transition of leadership, the summer also posed more threatening and pressing questions about the atomic bomb—a weapon that, up to that point, did not have any immediate moral, ethical, or strategic protocols developed for its potential usage.

The question of whether and in what capacity to use the bomb finally became paramount after the Trinity Test—the successful detonation of a plutonium bomb at Alamogordo, New Mexico, on July 16. The bomb, whose development itself was a scientific and military milestone, was now a formidable weapon with proven results and the reality of its potential use began to overshadow debates and deliberations between high-level policy makers. The news of the Trinity Test, furthermore, came at a pivotal moment during the Potsdam Conference, which took place during July 17 through August 2, 1945, and would have direct and indirect diplomatic and political repercussions in two important ways. For one, it emboldened Truman during his negotiations with Stalin. Henry Stimson recounts in his personal diary on July 22 that "Truman was evidently much fortified by something that had happened and that he stood up to the Russians in a most emphatic and decisive manner, telling them as to certain demands that they absolutely could not have and that the United States was entirely against them."[5] Winston Churchill, who was still prime minister before Clement Atlee replaced him in the middle of the conference, also noticed the change—Stimson would recount his conversation with Churchill when he told him that Truman "told the Russians just where they got on and off and generally bossed the whole meeting."[6] Implicit in this change of attitude was the assumption that the bomb could be used not only to bring about victory in the war but also to intimidate the USSR (Union of Soviet Socialist Republics) and influence the postwar power balance, later termed "atomic diplomacy."

Second, adoption of this assumption further decreased the probability of collaboration between the United States and the USSR and planted the seeds of the imminent Cold War. On July 17, Truman still favored Soviet collaboration in invading and bringing about the surrender of Japan, stating that Stalin and Russia will "be in the Jap War on August 15th" and this will "finish the Japs when that comes about."[7] After he received a second detailed report of the unprecedented destruction that the test bomb wrought on July 18, Truman entertained the idea that the war could end without Soviet help, writing that he believes that the "Japs will fold up before Russia comes in" and reiterating that he is "sure they will when Manhattan appears over their homeland."[8] On July 25, Truman declared formally that the bomb was to be used on Japan as the "most terrible bomb in the history of the world."[9] The following day, the United States and the United Kingdom—without Soviet involvement—issued the Potsdam Declaration, calling for complete and unconditional surrender with the threat of "complete and utter destruction." Japan resisted and the United States bombed Hiroshima on August 6 and Nagasaki on August 9, 1945.[10]

Scholars have debated the merits and morality of the decision to drop the bomb since August of 1945. Traditional historians, as well as policy makers at the time, argued that the bomb was the best tool to end a war that had the potential to kill many more American soldiers. Revisionists, on the other hand, argued that the decision was haphazard and not well thought out since it ignored viable alternatives—and was motivated more by desire for preeminence in the postwar world rather than for pragmatic military purposes of saving lives. Specifically, historian John W. Dower argued that "there was no single date on which all of these issues and options [concerning the bomb] came together on the table for Truman to decide" and that other alternatives—such as allowing the Japanese to retain a constitutional monarchy, engaging with the Soviet forces, laying the ground for international control of weapons, issuing a warning, and delaying the detonation of the second bomb—were neither pursued nor considered.[11] Caught in the crossfire of the debate, furthermore, had been Henry Stimson, who, as the secretary of war under Truman and the chief insider into the Manhattan Project, was the chief policy maker responsible for advising President Truman on the atomic course of action. According to John Gaddis, a prominent Cold War historian, "no man did more to set the stage for discussions within the government on this subject than Henry L. Stimson, who, as secretary of war, had supervised the Manhattan Project from the beginning."[12]

This chapter aims to explore the early life and career of Henry Stimson and to document the circumstances, both situational and personal, that led to the decision to drop the atomic bomb by examining his role in the Interim Committee. First, I will detail Henry Stimson's early life and career and how three tenets of his moral framework developed: Victorian values, legal training, and conservatism. Second, I will explore how his approach in forming and chairing the Interim Committee eventually caused him to ignore his moral framework and influence Truman in the ultimate decision. And lastly, I will consider how one factor—accepting assumptions about the bomb in committee meetings—caused him to recommend the use of the atomic bomb against Japan.

THE MAKING OF A VICTORIAN CONSERVATIVE

When he continued his post as secretary of war under the Truman administration, Henry Stimson had a lifetime of foreign policy experience. Born in New York City in 1867 to a wealthy family, Stimson attended the prestigious Andover Academy, Yale College, and Harvard Law School. His law education afforded him both the connections and the knowledge to begin a successful career as a lawyer, which was the launching pad for other high-profile careers such as district attorney for the Southern District of New York under Theodore Roosevelt, army lieutenant colonel in World

War I, secretary of war under President Taft, governor of Philippines under Coolidge, secretary of state under Hoover, and secretary of war under Franklin Roosevelt.[13] He had already written extensively about foreign affairs (books including *American Policy in Nicaragua, Democracy and Nationalism in Europe*, and *The Far East Crisis*) and was revered as a bipartisan statesman when he decided to stay on and help Truman adapt to his new post as president of the United States.[14]

In addition to his extensive professional and career experience, however, Stimson brought to the post of secretary of war a well-defined worldview and framework. Specifically, his Victorian values, legal training, and conservatism would come to greatly affect the decisions that he would make in his different posts, including his role in bringing about the attacks on Hiroshima and Nagasaki. "The values that defined Stimson's character," writes his biographer Sean Malloy, "were those of the Victorian era—his rigid bearing and his deeply ingrained prejudices render him a distant and forbidding figure to the modern eyes."[15] Yet, "the Victorian values that appear merely narrow and petty when applied to Stimson's personal life were also responsible for shaping his many notable contributions to public life—his devotion to duty and commitment to morality in the conduct of national and international affairs inspired intense respect and loyalty from those who served under him."[16] Indeed, in his Puritan household, "religion had long played an important role in the Stimson family," even to the point of making Stimson seriously consider entering the ministry.[17] Though his father dissuaded young Henry from the ministry and encouraged him to pursue a more prestigious track by attending Harvard Law, Stimson found that his strong moral framework developed and nourished by his faith could be relevant to his study of law. After law school, he returned to New York City, "attended services at the Madison Square Presbyterian Church. . . . where he first encountered a charismatic minister on a mission to redeem the spiritual and civic life of a wicked city."[18] Dr. Charles Parkhurst, who, through a series of fire-and-brimstone sermons in 1892 targeted at immorality in New York City, instilled within Stimson a conviction that municipal reform could be compatible with strict Presbyterianism and solidified his affiliation to the Republican Party, to which he would remain faithful until his death in 1950.[19]

Though Stimson did not pursue the path of ministry as he had originally intended, he found that his concern with duty and morality could be intertwined with his study of the law and legal training. He adopted what he termed as the "law of moral progress," a law that postulated human nature as not one of passiveness but rather of active engagement to control man's surroundings. "In the short term," in turn, "this belief allowed Stimson to tolerate the more tedious aspects of his legal education and embrace the law as a tool for the gradual evolution of human society toward a more perfect moral order."[20] Further, as a lawyer, "Stimson had very clear views of right and wrong that he held throughout his life, believing in certain absolutes and correct ways of conduct, guided by tradition, morality, and, most importantly, the law."[21] This training solidified his natural leanings toward closed-minded views on right and wrong and his desire for control.

Shortly after law school, he found a colleague and law-firm partner who shared his views. Elihu Root, who was a successful corporate lawyer, would reinforce Stimson's conservative leanings and moral proclivities. "What Elihu Root brought," writes Elting Morison, a prominent Stimson biographer, "was an instinct for order and for the way power can be used, with restraint but also with assurance, to introduce order in a system."[22] He further adds that "he exerted a profound influence" on Henry Stimson, and "to no man, save his own father, Stimson frequently acknowledged, did he owe as much intellectually and morally."[23] Indeed, it was within the hallowed halls of the law firm that Stimson's international framework began to form and the theories from his law classes became to manifest themselves in more concrete and practical ways. However, in addition to reinforcing some prevalent views of Stimson, Elihu Root would expand Stimson's social circle to include the most prestigious individuals and politicians of the Republican Party and, as a result, lay the groundwork for Stimson's career in the public and political realm.

With both his Victorian upbringings and legal training, Stimson emerged from law school and his practice as a lawyer with views sympathetic to and concordant with the Republican Party. Reverend Parkhurst had led Stimson away from the "Tammany-dominated Democrats and toward the reform-minded wing of the Republican Party"; Root, on the other hand, as a staunch conservative himself, put Stimson in contact with many high-powered attorneys, executives, and politicians at the time, including Theodore Roosevelt.[24] With Roosevelt, the transformation was almost complete. Stimson met Roosevelt in the Boone and Crockett Club in 1894, and instantly "shared exaltation in the 'strenuous life'" doctrine that both subscribed to.[25] Later, Root would suggest to Roosevelt that Stimson would be indispensible in the public sphere. Shortly after, Roosevelt appointed him as district attorney. Between Root, Roosevelt and Stimson, however, a much deeper bond developed that transcended the networking prospects. These men shared a bond of privilege and conservative ideals, as illustrated by a preference for "precedent, order, and capitalism as the bedrock of American life."[26]

Despite these shared ideals between the men, the homogeneity of the group that Stimson came in contact with socially and professionally fostered a sense of superiority in Stimson that would influence his personal prejudices as well as his managerial decisions in the War Department. As an opponent of women's suffrage and a staunch elitist, Stimson "insisted that political and economic reform be directed by educated, male elite, preferably Republicans who shared his own class and social background."[27] He expressed this attitude most clearly in his management of the War Department and in choices of whom he would surround himself with when making key policy decisions. For instance, most of Stimson's chief subordinates at the War Department, including Harvey Bundy, Robert Lovett, John McCloy, George Harrison, and Robert Patterson, came straight from his exclusive social clubs at Yale and Harvard. As Godfrey Hodgson details,

> Stimson, Bundy, Lovett, [and] Harrison were all members of Skull and Bones. Only McCloy and Patterson of the inner circle were not. Stimson, Bundy, Harrison, McCloy and Patterson were all graduates of the Harvard Law School; only Lovett was not. Stimson, Harrison, Lovett, McCloy, and Patterson were all prominent on Wall Street; only Bundy was not, and he practiced law on State Street, the nearest thing to Wall Street in Boston. All six men were Republicans. The plain fact is that, during a war for democracy conducted by a Democratic President—which was also, more than any previous foreign war in American history, a democratic war in the sense that millions of men from every corner of American life fought it together—the War Department was directed by a tiny clique of wealthy Republicans, and one that was almost as narrowly based, in social and education terms, as a traditional British Tory Cabinet.[28]

Further, shortly after Franklin Roosevelt's death, Stimson himself handpicked a similarly homogenous aggregation of policy makers and scientists who would make the recommendation to President Truman about whether to use the atomic bomb against Japan. Stimson, along with this group of fairly homogenous policy makers in terms of background and education (as some scholars argue), would propagate assumptions and advance faulty information that would be directly used to influence Truman in the decision to drop the atomic bomb on Japan.

THE ATOMIC COURT: THE INTERIM COMMITTEE

The Interim Committee, composed of chief nuclear scientists and diplomatic scholars, including Stimson himself, George Harrison (chairman), James Byrnes (private citizen), Ralph Bard (undersecretary of the navy), William Clayton (assistant secretary of state), Vannevar Bush (director of the Office of Scientific Research and Development, president of the Carnegie Institution), Karl T. Compton (chief of the Office of Field Service in the Office of Scientific Research and Development, president of the Massachusetts Institute of Technology), and James B. Conant (chairman of the National Defense Research Committee, president of Harvard University),[29] was formed in order to provide an advisory role to the president about the use of atomic weapons. The committee met multiple times before and after the successful July 16 Trinity Test, but its most important recommendation came on June 1, 1945. It unanimously agreed that the bomb "should be dropped as soon as possible," that it should be used on a dual target that was "a military installation or war plant surrounded by or adjacent to houses and other buildings most susceptible to damage," and that it should be used "without prior warning."[30] Byrnes communicated these results to Truman. Stimson reassured the president of their recommendations, stating that "to extract a genuine surrender from the Emperor . . . they must administer a tremendous shock which would carry convincing proof of our power to destroy."[31]

Stimson's confidence in the Interim Committee's recommendation that he communicated to President Truman, however, contradicted his worldview and moral frameworks. Specifically, two factors—Oppenheimer's overemphasis on technical success and James Conant's recommendation for worker targets—contradicted Stimson's framework. First, J. Robert Oppenheimer, who spearheaded and oversaw the project, openly propagated a "single minded drive for technical success at all costs" and "actively endorsed use for the bomb against a city and discouraged any manifestations of dissent within the gates of Los Alamos."[32] This bred an assumption that the bomb would be utilized as a weapon without great consideration of the moral dimensions of utilizing such a weapon. And second, James Conant brought reality to Oppenheimer's emphasis by advocating and propagating this assumption in the Interim Committee's meetings. Specifically, he avidly proposed considering options outside of military targets where civilians were present in order to create profound enough psychological shock. For Stimson, a man who strongly opposed civilian targeting as secretary of war and throughout his life, this emphasis on both the military use against civilians and the single-minded strategic analysis of the bomb contradicted a doctrine that he had advocated.

Two variables explain why Stimson recommended the Interim Committee's course of action, despite contradictions with his personal beliefs: the group's structure and circumstances, and the assumptions about the bomb held by both Stimson and the group. As to its structure, the group was homogenous, and, as mentioned before, composed of mostly Republican males. The committee was also under time constraints to come up with a viable solution. Therefore, the group's overall structure detracted from its ability to introduce alternatives.

> The structure of the Committee itself made the introduction of alternatives extremely difficult: its tight organization and its crowded agenda; its wide-ranging responsibilities for atomic energy policy and its limited knowledge of the military situation; its clear mandate to recommend postwar programs and the ambiguity, at best, of its responsibility for wartime decisions.[33]

Stimson's leadership of the committee, furthermore, reinforced the structure. Specifically, Stimson's responsibility of drawing up agendas limited discussion to topics proposed by the secretary. Further, "although he did seek to create an atmosphere in which everyone felt free to discuss any problem related to atomic energy, the minutes of the meetings indicate that discussions closely adhered to the questions Stimson presented" and, as a result, the atmosphere of the group was characterized by "little inclination to pursue unscheduled issues."[34] Not only did this prevent alternatives from being voiced, furthermore, but it would also lead to the strengthening of underlying assumptions about the atomic bomb in the group as well as in Stimson's mind. The behavior of the committee appears to reflect Irving Janis's theory of "Groupthink" where group dynamics trump open discussion.

In addition to assessing the group's structure and circumstances, a second important lens for explaining why Stimson advocated the committee's recommendation despite direct contradiction to his moral framework is the assumptions that both Stimson and the group held about the bomb. Much uncertainty clouded this question as the potential decision of usage was deferred by both Stimson and Roosevelt. Within this cloud of ambiguity, the assumptions propagated by J. Robert Oppenheimer at Los Alamos—namely that the bomb was developed for strategic, military usage and that it should be used—began to permeate Interim Committee meetings. "The question of whether the bomb should be used at all," writes Sherwin, "had never actually been discussed" and Interim meetings suggest that "the committee members had come together as advocates, the responsible advisers of a new force in world affairs, convinced of the weapon's diplomatic and military potential, aware of its fantastic cost, and awed by their responsibilities."[35] Sherwin argues that the committee would be constrained by several assumptions that guided its decision and that Stimson communicated those assumptions to Truman. They include,

> First, that the bomb was a legitimate weapon that would have been used against the Allies if Germany had won the race to develop it. Second, that its use would have a profound impact upon Japan's leaders as they debated whether or not to surrender. Third, that the American public would want it used under the circumstances. And fourth, that its use ultimately would have a salutary effect on relations with the Soviet Union. These assumptions suggested, at least obliquely, that there were neither military, diplomatic, nor domestic reasons to oppose the use of the weapon.[36]

The decision to drop the atomic bomb, then, was largely crafted within the Interim Committee meetings, where "eventually the secretary of war offered a conclusion with which the rest of the group expressed 'general agreement.'"[37]

In the end, it was a combination of both the circumstances and structure of the group and accepted assumptions that led Stimson to contradict his moral framework and to recommend dropping the bomb. However, the transmittal of the assumptions of the Interim Committee was significant. Truman had only been president for a few months and knew little about the atomic venture. He was thus prone to believe and accept the committee's assumptions, which severely limited his conceptualization of the purposes of the atomic bomb. Stimson contributed to this in four ways. First, as chairman of the committee, he reinforced the structure by setting strict agendas for the meetings that prevented alternatives from being introduced. Second, he had handpicked the committee as a very homogenous crowd, which would instill consensus-seeking behavior and increase group cohesion, a prerequisite for groupthink. Though the group did not as a whole suffer from groupthink, perhaps on other issues, it did to succumb to certain antecedents and symptoms such as time constraints, group cohesion, tension constraint, limiting alternatives, not doing a broad survey, not developing a contingency plan, and rationalizing the decision.[38] Third, it was the rationalizing of the decision and silencing of his personal framework that overshadowed Stimson's moral proclivities. Malloy writes:

> A combination of self-deception and misleading information with respect to the nature of the target probably helped to seal Stimson's assent to the May 31 targeting recommendations. The self-deception came in the form of his willingness to accept that a "vital war plant employing a large number of workers and closely surrounded by workers' houses" constituted a primarily military target. Stimson's self-deception was facilitated by Groves, who apparently withheld information about the targeting of the weapon. Though insisting that "we could not concentrate on a civilian area," Stimson apparently joined in the consensus that an isolated target or military base would not allow for suitably dramatic demonstration of the bomb's power. It was [then] agreed, following Conant's suggestion, that the best target would be a "vital war plant employing a large number of workers and closely surrounded by workers' houses."[39]

And lastly, Stimson, just like the rest of the group, did not question the assumption that the bomb should be used. This lack of questioning not only reinforced the group processes but also led to his recommendation. "Nowhere in Stimson's meticulous diary," writes Sherwin, "is there any suggestion of doubt or questioning of the assumption that the bomb should be used against Germany or Japan if the weapon was ready before the end of the war."[40] "This was not simply due to an absence of reflection" he further adds, "yet this awareness of its profound implications apparently did not lead him to raise the sort of questions that might naturally seem to follow from such awareness."[41] Stimson's failure to question his selection of the group, the way that he set strict agendas, and his acceptance of the group's assumptions, in short, made him shut out his moral belief that "the same rule of sparing the civilian population should be applied as far as possible to the use of any weapon" from the decision making process.[42] After this, he would be complicit in furthering the assumptions to Truman, who readily accepted them and used them as a basis to justify his decision to drop the bombs on Hiroshima and Nagasaki. Truman's lack of experience on the job and his own military background left him susceptible to Stimson's and the committee's influence.

CONCLUSION

When Stimson wrote to the public in *Harper's* in 1947, he stated that he took full responsibility for recommending the use of the atomic bomb. "The ultimate responsibility for the recommendation to the President rested upon me" he wrote, and "the conclusions of the committee were similar to my own, although I reached mine independently."[43] This statement, intended to convey a sense of confidence to the public about the deliberations and decision making process, has not proved sufficiently true. Stimson's own biases led him to pick an exclusive and homogenous group that would exert undue influence over Truman's and Stimson's decision. Furthermore, Stimson's own narrow leadership on the committee, furthermore, would reinforce detrimental group processes that would propagate assumptions and limit alternatives. Ultimately, Stimson's disinclination to question the findings or the assumptions of the committee, despite their direct contradictions with his moral beliefs and framework, increased the unhealthy consensus among the group. All of these factors, combined, contributed to the fateful recommendation that Stimson would make to President Truman to bomb Japan—and that Truman would readily accept due to his inexperience and lack of knowledge about the project. Campbell Craig, in his review of Sean Malloy's book, wrote that Stimson was largely presented "as a Victorian figure of tragedy . . . clinging to traditional notions of honor, individual morality, and political moderation" who "found himself swept away by the tide of modern war and a logic of international politics played for highest stakes."[44]

The decision to drop the bomb took place neither in Potsdam nor in a deliberation room under the orders of Truman. Instead, it took place in the deliberation room of the Interim Committee, which would produce misguided assumptions upon which Truman would base his decision. Stimson's role, as secretary of war, was to ensure that a proper course of action was recommended and implemented. In the end, however, he advocated for a decision without properly questioning the underlying assumptions. Perhaps it was the unfamiliarity of the nuclear weapon that defied all of Stimson's conceptions of war and order. Perhaps it was his lack of preparation. In law school, Henry Stimson had become accustomed to the complete collection of facts as a proper means of executing and trying a case. In the courtroom, he had passionately advocated one side of the argument and shunned alternative explanations. Now, however, he had to make a decision with incomplete information and needed to entertain multiple options and approaches in reaching his course of action. Despite his extensive service in the public realm, Stimson to a large extent ignored his moral compass to guide his decision making and in turn shaped the history of the world.

NOTES

1. "Eyewitness History: The Surrender of Germany," http://www.eyewitnesstohistory.com/vosurrender.htm.
2. "Truman Library: Henry Stimson to Harry S. Truman," April 24, 1945, http://www.trumanlibrary.org/whistlestop/study_collections/bomb/large/documents/pdfs/914.pdf.
3. Henry Stimson Diary, Manuscripts and Archives, Yale University Library, New Haven, CT.
4. Ibid.
5. Ibid.
6. Ibid.
7. "Notes by Harry S. Truman on the Potsdam Conference," July 17, 1945, http://www.trumanlibrary.org/whistlestop/study_collections/bomb/large/documents/pdfs/63.pdf.
8. Ibid.
9. Ibid.
10. John Dower, *The Most Terrible Bomb in the World* (New York: DK Publishing Book, 2001).
11. Ibid.
12. John Gaddis, *The United States and the Origins of the Cold War, 1941–1947* (New York: Columbia University Press, 2000).
13. "Spartacus Educational: Henry Lewis Stimson," http://www.spartacus.schoolnet.co.uk/USAstimson.htm.
14. "Spartacus Educational: Henry Lewis Stimson," http://www.spartacus.schoolnet.co.uk/USAstimson.htm.
15. Sean Malloy, *Atomic Tragedy: Henry L. Stimson and the Decision to Use the Bomb against Japan* (Ithaca, NY: Cornell University Press, 2008).
16. Ibid.
17. Ibid.
18. Ibid.
19. Ibid.
20. Ibid.
21. Akira Iriye, "Henry L. Stimson: The First Wise Man (review)," *Journal of Cold War Studies* 4, no.4 (2002): 106–108, http//:muse.jhu.edu:journals:journal_of_cold_war_studies:v004:4.4iriye.html.
22. Elting Morison, *Turmoil and Tradition: A Study of the Life and Times of Henry L. Stimson, Foreign Affairs* (New York: Council on Foreign Relations, January 1961).

23. Ibid.
24. Malloy, *Atomic Tragedy.*
25. Ibid.
26. Ibid.
27. Ibid.
28. Godfrey Hodgson, *The Colonel: The Life and Wars of Henry Stimson, 1867–1950* (Lebanon, NH: University Press of New England, 1992).
29. Henry Lewis Stimson, "The Decision to Use the Atomic Bomb," *Harper's Magazine* (February 1947): 97–107.
30. Dennis Wainstock, *The Decision to Drop the Atomic Bomb* (Westport, CT: Greenwood Publishing Group, 1996).
31. Michael Gordin, *Five Days in August: How World War II Became a Nuclear War* (Princeton, NJ: Princeton University Press, 2007).
32. Malloy, *Atomic Tragedy.*
33. Martin Sherwin, *A World Destroyed* (New York: Vintage Books, 1987).
34. Ibid.
35. Ibid.
36. Sherwin, *A World Destroyed.*
37. Malloy, *Atomic Tragedy.*
38. Irving Janis, *Groupthink* (Boston: Houghton Mifflin Company, 1982).
39. Malloy, *Atomic Tragedy.*
40. Sherwin, *A World Destroyed.*
41. Ibid.
42. Ibid.
43. Stimson, "The Decision to Use the Atomic Bomb."
44. Campbell Craig, "H-Net Reviews in the Humanities and Social Sciences," http://www.hnet.org/reviews/showpdf.

9

Margaret Thatcher and the 1982 Falklands War

Helen Baxendale

INTRODUCTION

Margaret Thatcher is undoubtedly one of the most distinctive and influential political figures of the late twentieth century. Yet, while there are a great many biographical studies of Mrs. Thatcher, surprisingly few of them have sought to systematically investigate how her worldview, cognitive approach, and leadership style influenced her decision making. As Rod Rhodes attests:

> The systematic analysis of leadership influences is still in its infancy in the UK . . . There is no equivalent to the sophisticated analysis of how leadership personality transmutes into characteristic institutional and policy styles which figure large in accounts of the US presidency.[1]

This chapter thus offers a very modest contribution to this still nascent field of study. As the "clearest example of Mrs. Thatcher's ability to exercise a personal stamp on policy over and above the influence of the bureaucracy,"[2] the 1982 Falklands crisis presents an obvious case study in the influence of her belief system, personality traits, and leadership style on the conduct of British foreign policy. Mrs. Thatcher's decision making process in the lead up to confrontation over the Falklands, throughout attempted diplomatic negotiations and, finally, during eventual hostilities, thus forms the basis of this analysis.

This chapter proceeds as follows. The first section explores Mrs. Thatcher's upbringing and early influences, contending that many of the personality traits and psychological characteristics of the mature politician were manifest from an early age. The next section draws on these findings in an attempt to develop a psychological profile of Mrs. Thatcher as prime minister. Particular focus is given to her self-conception as an outsider and crusader, and her aversion to conceptual complexity in combination with her relative inexperience in international affairs and a distinctly authoritarian management style. The following section argues that these personal and psychological attributes elicited the poor decision making that directly contributed to the outbreak and escalation of the Falklands conflict. Mrs. Thatcher's sense of righteousness made the necessary compromises of international diplomacy incredibly difficult and precluded any possibility of diplomatic settlement with the Argentineans. Once at war, however, her singularity of purpose and strength of conviction became undeniable advantages of her leadership style. The next section therefore contends that Mrs. Thatcher's cognitive inflexibility and moral doggedness, which had, of course, helped to catalyze the Falklands War, were, ironically, the very same qualities that enabled her to preside over an improbable but resounding victory. The final section concludes that a psychological study of Mrs. Thatcher provides valuable insights into her decision making style, and by extension, the execution of British foreign policy during her administration.

FORMATIVE YEARS

Margaret Thatcher was born to be a politician. Her lineage and formation allowed few other possibilities.[3] Margaret Hilda Roberts was born on October 13, 1925, in Grantham, Lincolnshire, to shopkeepers Arthur and Beatrice Roberts. By all accounts, Beatrice, a cowed and colorless woman, featured little in Margaret's development. In a 1961 interview, Mrs. Thatcher said of her mother, "I loved her dearly, but after fifteen we had nothing more to say to each other. It wasn't her fault. She was weighed down by the home, always being in the home."[4] Her father, on the other hand, was a singularly influential figure in her life. Upon entering 10 Downing Street in May 1979, she asserted "I owe everything to my father."[5]

Arthur Robert's influence was particularly significant in three ways. First, he was extremely ambitious for Margaret, who, from an early age, showed more academic promise than her elder sister Muriel. Margaret was treated differently, was afforded more opportunities and attention, and was always encouraged to believe that with the necessary diligence and discipline there were no obstacles to her achieving whatever station in life she desired.[6] Arthur's Victorian passion for education as "the key to a useful life" compelled him to send her to an elementary school on the more affluent side of Grantham, some distance from the family home, because the teaching was better and her peer group would be "properly motivated."[7] Similarly, she attended secondary school at the fee-paying Kesteven and Grantham Girls School instead of several other government schools closer to home.[8] In this regard, Arthur Robert's heady aspirations for his younger daughter equipped her with an unyielding self-confidence and ambition—essential qualities for her chosen career path.

The second crucial area of Arthur's influence was his fostering of young Margaret's interest in politics. Arthur was an active local politician, serving for many years on the Grantham council. At various times he was also the president of the Chamber of Trade, president of Rotary, a director of the Grantham Building Society and the Trustee Savings Bank, chairman of the local National Savings Movement, a governor of both the local boys' and girls' grammar schools, and chairman of the Workers' Educational Association. In 1943, he was elected the town's youngest Alderman and from 1945 to 1946 served as mayor.[9] In the first volume of her autobiography, *The Path to Power*, Mrs. Thatcher recalls that she accompanied him "everywhere" on civic business, from council meetings to school inspections.[10] This early introduction "awakened an appetite for politics" and determined the kind of politician and national leader Margaret Thatcher would become.[11] She regularly proclaimed that the most important lesson she ever learned from Alderman Roberts was to have the courage of one's convictions: "Never do things just because other people do them . . . Make up your own mind what you are going to do and persuade people to go *your* way."[12] On the steps of Downing Street in May 1979, the newly anointed prime minister said of her father, "he brought me up to believe the things I do believe and they are just the values on which I fought the election."[13]

Much of her political disposition was also derived from her strict Wesleyan Methodist upbringing, the third critical legacy of Arthur Roberts. Every Sunday was almost entirely consumed by churchgoing, and during the week Arthur was a lay preacher. The Roberts' Methodism was a religion rooted in industry, discipline, and above all else, moral piety. From an early age, the difference between right and wrong was very starkly drawn: "there were certain things you just didn't do and that was that."[14] While she eventually relinquished her Methodist faith, this righteousness nevertheless remained a hallmark of Mrs. Thatcher's throughout her career, to the extent that she routinely vilified those that disagreed with her, viewing their divergence as a moral failing. As biographer John Campbell observes, "this rare moral certainty and unreflective self-righteousness was, at times, her greatest political strength in the muddy world of political expediency and compromise; it was also in the end her greatest weakness."[15]

Aside from Arthur's influence, Mrs. Thatcher's wartime upbringing in the Middle England "everytown" of Grantham was also very pertinent to the development of her worldview as a mature politician. Described by a former town clerk as "a narrow town, built on a narrow street, inhabited by narrow people," Grantham prided itself on its ordinariness.[16] Throughout her premiership, Mrs. Thatcher's detractors would often invoke this small town provincialism as an explanation for her simplistic, arguably jingoistic, attitude to international affairs.[17] Equally, her vivid adolescent experiences of World War II have also been cited as reasons for her unabashed "Little Englandism" and nostalgia for Britain's past glories.[18] Certainly, these pervasive memories seem to have informed her attitude during the Falklands crisis as she implored the House of Commons not to repeat the fatal mistake of appeasing fascist aggression.[19] The then foreign secretary, Francis Pym, tellingly commented, "it was as though Grantham had been invaded by the Germans."[20] In short, Margaret Thatcher was a leader profoundly shaped by her upbringing, and, more often than not, only too happy to admit it.

DEVELOPING A PSYCHOLOGICAL PROFILE OF PRIME MINISTER THATCHER

Margaret Thatcher departed radically from the archetypal Tory politician. She was provincial not a Londoner, petite bourgeoisie rather than upper class, attended a state-run grammar school not a great English public school, had no record of military service, was poorly traveled, and, above all else, was a woman. In a fascinating study, Anthony King contends that although her background predisposed her to be a Conservative Party outsider from the outset, Mrs. Thatcher remained a deliberate *psychological* outsider even as prime minister.[21] Her public utterances are replete with examples of this self-conception:

> I am the rebel head of an establishment government.[22]
>
> You make up your own mind. You do not do something or want to do something because your friends are doing it. You never say, well, they're doing it, that's why I want to do it.[23]
>
> In the eyes of the "wet" Tory establishment I was not only a woman, but "that woman," someone not just of a different sex, but of a different class, a person with an alarming conviction that the values and virtues of middle England should be brought to bear on the problems which the establishment consensus had created. I offended on many accounts.[24]

Mrs. Thatcher's active embrace of outsider status is vital to understanding her psychological orientation and leadership style. As King explains, outsiders bring different strengths and weaknesses to positions of leadership than more conventional figures. Outsiders are generally more daring and likely to bring an unorthodox perspective to top-level decision making. They are often innovators who will reject "standard operating procedures" that inhibit wide-ranging change,[25] and may see themselves as self-styled mavericks. On the other hand, outsiders are likely to be utterly convinced of their own rectitude, and thereby inclined to surround themselves with sycophants with a tendency toward "groupthink," a phenomenon described by Irving Janis wherein members of the group go along with a decision in order to maintain group cohesion. Moreover, these types of leaders are liable to ascribe all successes to themselves, all failures to others, and willfully ignore the considered advice of subordinates if it does not conform to their agenda.[26]

King's findings concur with Kaarbo and Hermann's psychological typology of Mrs. Thatcher. By analyzing interview responses from press conferences and Prime Minister's Questions, Kaarbo and Hermann assessed Mrs. Thatcher's leadership style according to the following variables: conceptual complexity, belief that one can control events, need for power, need for affiliation, and task orientation.[27] They discovered that Mrs. Thatcher had a lower-than-average level of conceptual complexity, routinely challenged political constraints, believing she could control events, revelled in the power of her position, and was motivated to achieve goals rather than build relationships.[28] Kaarbo and Hermann characterize this style of leadership as "crusading" and "expansionist." Expansionists are "interested in increasing their span of control over people, resources, and geographical space; having pre-dominance, empire, sphere of influence, and hegemony."[29] Crusaders "identify with their goals completely, at times becoming isomorphic with the positions of their countries and willing to risk their offices for what they believe is right." They are more likely to engage their governments in extreme "conflictual, non-diplomatic" activities than other leaders and to take principled stands in the international arena.[30] Mrs. Thatcher's comments throughout the buildup to the Falklands War amply reflected this style of leadership:

> We have been called, as so often in our Island's story, to stand for freedom and the rule of law, both challenged by the unprovoked aggression of the Argentine. The task has fallen to us but our service is to all who cherish liberty.[31]
>
> When you've spent half your political life dealing with humdrum issues like the environment, it's exciting to have a real crisis on your hands.[32]

Another important aspect of Mrs. Thatcher's political persona was her hierarchical management style. Theoretically, under the Westminster system of government, the prime minister is considered "first among equals" within the Cabinet. Decisions are made collectively following Cabinet discussion, with the prime minister the final arbiter. Margaret Thatcher imposed a decidedly different style of leadership. As Anthony King observes, "if the traditional procedures did not yield the outcome she desired, she simply invented new procedures."[33] Although derived from observations of the American presidency, George and George's formalistic management model is a useful approximation of Mrs. Thatcher's interpretation of British Cabinet government.[34] By establishing exclusive channels of communication between ministers and herself, and discouraging communication and collaboration among the Cabinet,[35] Mrs. Thatcher asserted unprecedented control. Often she made decisions without so much as consulting the responsible minister, and violently punished dissenters:

> Discussion around the Cabinet table increasingly took the form of prime ministerial monologues. Thatcher became the first PM in British history to sack cabinet ministers on a large scale, not because they were incompetent, but because they disagreed with her.[36]

Perhaps the most essential element of Mrs. Thatcher's political psychology, and one that was particularly pertinent to the Falklands affair, was her lack of conceptual complexity—what Milton Rokeach termed "closed-mindedness."[37] Mrs. Thatcher bore all the hallmarks of the closed-minded individual: authoritarianism, a dogged assertion of beliefs, and contempt for those who held a conflicting view.[38] In an illuminating study, Stephen Dyson conducts a "systematic content analysis of verbal output," in order to quantify Mrs. Thatcher's cognitive subtlety. He finds her conceptual complexity scores to be "substantially and consistently lower" than those of the average world leader and the lowest of all post-1945 British prime ministers.[39] Her colleagues often noted Mrs. Thatcher's black and white worldview. According to Foreign Secretary Francis Pym, "she [liked] everything to be clear-cut: absolutely in favour of one thing, absolutely against another."[40] Sir Bryan Cartledge, Mrs. Thatcher's private secretary for foreign affairs, concurred: "Margaret Thatcher's decisions were taken with reference to a few deeply, even passionately held personal convictions against which proposals or individuals were measured: if found wanting, the proposal or individual was discarded without further ado."[41] Observers were particularly critical of her poor grasp of foreign affairs and inability to master the necessary nuance of diplomacy:

> Upon coming to office, the prime minister, quite frankly, literally did not know where Calais was. She had a small town hostility to Europeans and a *Daily Express* understanding of foreign affairs. The only non-British people she found agreeable were Americans, but this was because she did not regard them as foreign.[42]
>
> Her experience was very, very limited, she tended to look at international problems as she looked at domestic problems, and has the approach to them of an extremely practical, down-to-earth housewife who wants to get on with the job. This isn't always easily understood overseas.[43]
>
> She doesn't think in the supple way of someone who is occupied with foreign affairs a lot of the time.[44]

From these observations, a clear picture emerges of Margaret Thatcher as a dogmatic, authoritarian, and inflexible foreign policy decision maker. In this light, one much more readily understands the fatal intersection of personality and events that catalyzed the Falklands conflict.

FOUNDATIONS OF THE FALKLANDS CONFLICT—A FAILURE OF LEADERSHIP AND DECISION MAKING

The Falkland Islands are collection of windswept, sparsely populated islands in the far South Atlantic—a truly improbable theater for a late-twentieth-century war. Since 1833 they have continuously sustained British settlement, although the title to the Islands has been disputed between Spain, France, Britain, and Argentina for centuries.[45] Since 1965, it had been the considered view of the British Foreign and Commonwealth Office that because the Falklands were militarily indefensible, the interests of the Islanders would be better served by reaching an accommodation with the Argentineans, rather than living in a continual state of siege.[46] To this end, successive British governments had been looking for a viable way to transfer the sovereignty of the Falklands to Argentina while ensuring various safeguards for the inhabitants, who almost invariably considered themselves British subjects. In 1979, Nicholas Ridley, a junior Foreign Office minister, was dispatched to the Falklands to forge a solution acceptable to the Islanders and the Argentineans. He proposed a transfer of sovereignty to Argentina, with a 99-year leaseback to Britain to ensure protection of the Islanders' way of life.[47] Mrs. Thatcher's reaction to the proposal was, according to the then foreign secretary Peter Carrington, "thermo-nuclear."[48] She recalls in *The Downing Street Years*, "I did not like the proposal at all"[49]; yet, she pursued no other solution. By refusing to entertain a pragmatic compromise, as she had been prepared to do in the case of Rhodesia and later Hong Kong, Mrs. Thatcher significantly increased the likelihood of confrontation with Argentina.

The other crucial miscalculation of the Thatcher government in the lead up to the Falklands crisis was an abject failure to provide any sort of deterrent to Argentinean invasion. As Hugo Young observes, "the logical corollary of rejecting Ridley's plan was at least to consider strengthening the Falklands' defenses in face of a mounting barrage of threats from the military government in Buenos Aires."[50] In fact, the very opposite occurred. On June 30, 1981, a Defence White Paper announced that the survey ship, HMS *Endurance*, the Falklands' sole organ of defense, would be withdrawn from Port Stanley for the sake of budget efficiency.[51] The decision was taken by Defence Secretary John Nott and ratified by Mrs. Thatcher, despite sustained objections from Foreign Secretary Carrington and junior Defence Minister Keith Speed. Speed was dismissed from his post for publicly questioning the merits of the plan, and later revealed that he had been totally excluded from the decision making behind the 1981 defense review: "I don't know how these financial decisions and air, military, and naval force directives were arrived at. . . . I was certainly not consulted in any detail about these important matters."[52] For its part, the Foreign Office repeatedly warned that Buenos Aires would view the withdrawal of HMS *Endurance* as a weakening of the British commitment to defending the Falklands.[53] While Mrs. Thatcher is right to contend that the HMS *Endurance* was effectively a "military irrelevance" (with only a few light guns and two helicopters) and therefore incapable of repelling an Argentinean invasion,[54] it was nevertheless an important listening post for gleaning Argentine intentions and, more importantly, a powerful symbol of the British presence in the Falklands. Certainly, the withdrawal of HMS *Endurance* did not go unnoticed in Buenos Aires.[55] The prime minister's open contempt for the Foreign Office probably played no small part in her overriding of Carrington's eminently reasonable objections. In all, Mrs. Thatcher and her government perilously neglected the Falklands issue until it was too late. As Young notes, "between January 1981 and April 1, 1982, there was no meeting of the Defence Committee of the Cabinet to discuss the Falklands nor was there any reference to the Falklands in full Cabinet until March 25, 1982."[56] When the Argentineans invaded on April 1, 1982, it took Mrs. Thatcher by complete surprise. It need not have. Had she heeded the advice of the Foreign Office, an invasion might have been avoided altogether.[57]

Upon learning of the seizure of the Falklands, Mrs. Thatcher immediately resolved, "we have to get them back."[58] This fierce determination remained the guiding principle of her decision making throughout the conflict. Before Cabinet had even been consulted, she had asked the chief of naval staff, Sir Henry Leach, what could be done. He replied that he could assemble a task force ready for deployment in 48 hours.[59] Mrs. Thatcher immediately gave her authority to assemble the force, then reserved for the following morning's Cabinet meeting, the decision as to whether and when the task force should sail. She was of the firm belief that "effective diplomacy was impossible without the dispatch of the task force. . . . As Frederick the Great once remarked, 'diplomacy without arms is like music without instruments.'"[60] It soon emerged that Cabinet were similarly disposed. Consequently, mid-morning, Friday, April 2, orders were given to for the task force to begin its long southward journey.

The same day, Mrs. Thatcher received a memo from the Foreign Office warning of the possible adverse outcomes of the task force mobilization. Among them were a backlash against British expatriates in Argentina, problems with getting support for British actions from the UN Security Council, the lack of reliance Britain could place on the United States (a strong ally of Argentina as well as Britain) and the European Community, the risk of the Soviets becoming involved, and the disadvantage of being viewed as a colonial power.[61] Her reaction to the document is telling, deriding the Foreign Office's advice as "characteristic of the flexibility of principle of that department"[62]:

> All of these considerations were fair enough. But when you are at war you cannot allow the difficulties to dominate your thinking, you have to set out with an iron will to overcome them. And anyway, what was the alternative? That a common or garden dictator should rule over the Queen's subjects and prevail by fraud and violence? Not while I was Prime Minister.[63]

Although Mrs. Thatcher's rhetoric may suggest otherwise, at this point, war was far from guaranteed. Sending a task force was initially intended merely to force the Argentinean junta to negotiate.

Her characteristic moral indignation and belligerence were again displayed when she addressed a rare Saturday sitting of the House of Commons the following day. For the sake of public opinion and broader legitimacy, she sought a parliamentary imprimatur for the deployment of the task force. Her oratory was more than equal to the task. As John Campbell observes, "with her instinctive ability to draw abstract principles from specific events, she immediately elevated the prospect of war for a cluster of bare rocks in the South Atlantic into a crusade of world historical proportions"[64]:

> The eyes of the world are now focussed on the Falkland Islands. Others are watching anxiously to see whether brute force or the rule of law will triumph. Wherever naked aggression occurs it must be overcome. That is why, through diplomatic, economic and if necessary, military means, we shall persevere until freedom and democracy are restored to the people of the Falklands.[65]

Having won the support of the House of Commons, Mrs. Thatcher's next step was to form a War Cabinet. Significantly, this was the only time in her first two terms that she assembled a formal working group, engaging others as colleagues rather than subordinates. She was particularly influenced in this task by the advice of the permanent secretary at the Ministry of Defence, Sir Frank Cooper. When asked by the prime minister, "How do you actually run a war?," Sir Frank replied: "First, you need a small War Cabinet; second it's got to have regular meetings come hell or high water. Thirdly, you don't want a lot of bureaucrats hanging around."[66] Mrs. Thatcher promptly assembled a core unit who, for the next 10 weeks, would meet at 9.30 a.m. every weekday morning at No. 10 and at the prime minister's country retreat, Chequers, on weekends.[67] Foreign Secretary Francis Pym and Defence Minister John Nott were automatic selections, as was Deputy Prime Minister William Whitelaw. In contrast, Cecil Parkinson, the newly appointed Conservative Party chairman and Thatcher protégé, was chosen "partly to balance Whitelaw's supposedly natural alliance with Pym, but partly as one more symbol through which the party collective could be locked into the outcome, whatever it was."[68] The most important member of the group, however, was not a politician, but the admiral of the fleet and chief of the defence staff, Sir Terence Lewin. Members of the group recall that Mrs. Thatcher "always tended towards the military's persuasion," and Lewin was soon invited to fulfill a further role as the prime minister's personal defense adviser at No. 10, sharply qualifying John Nott's authority as the departmental leader.[69] This streamlined command structure suited Mrs. Thatcher's hierarchical management style completely, but as the conflict escalated, she was always careful to cover her back by securing the support of the full Cabinet for major decisions.[70]

On Tuesday, April 6, there was a long Cabinet meeting about the crisis. It was the assumption of the vast majority of the Cabinet (though not Mrs. Thatcher) at this discussion—and for several weeks afterward—that the Argentineans would be persuaded not to fight.[71] It was also recognised that the U.S. attitude toward the conflict was imperative to Britain's position.[72] As Britain's closest ally and with key strategic interests in Latin America, the United States was eager to broker a quick settlement. To this end, U.S. Secretary of State Alexander Haig assumed the role of chief negotiator. From the beginning, however, Mrs. Thatcher was never interested in a diplomatic solution. After a week of exhausting negotiations, Secretary Haig proposed a plan he believed to be acceptable to the Argentineans and the British. The main elements were: immediate withdrawal of Argentinean forces from the islands, the halting of the task force 1,000 miles north, joint control under U.S. supervision, and negotiation of sovereignty that safeguards the wishes of the Islanders for at least five years.[73] It was a compromise neither side would accept.

The longer negotiations wore on, the more Mrs. Thatcher's attitude hardened. While Foreign Secretary Pym wanted to avoid war at any cost, "Mrs. Thatcher, under instruction from the generals, came to see it as a probable necessity in a noble cause for which she felt her nature to be supremely well equipped."[74] Alexander Haig evokes the difficulties of negotiating with Mrs. Thatcher with the following anecdote:

> After I had explained the American proposals to Mrs. Thatcher, she rapped sharply on the tabletop and recalled that this was the table at which Neville Chamberlain sat in 1938 and spoke of the Czechs as "a faraway people about whom we know so little." Recalling that this omission had led to the death of over 45 million people she identified the Argentinean challenge as a repeat performance. If they got away with taking the Falklands by force, this would "send a signal round the world with devastating consequences."[75]

It was a specious analogy but entirely characteristic of Mrs. Thatcher's self-righteous and monochromatic framing of international affairs. Her intransigence was matched by the head of Argentinean junta, General Galtieri, for whom any sort of concession would have been viewed domestically as a fatal weakness and broken his junta's tenuous hold on power. At least five variants of a peace proposal were put to Buenos Aires and London. All were rejected, and by April 30, Secretary Haig's mediation had stalled.[76]

All the while, the British task force had continued to sail south and by the beginning of May had entered the waters of the Falklands in order to enforce a 200-mile total exclusion zone (TEZ). On May 2, the British hunter-killer submarine, HMS *Conqueror,* detected the Argentine cruiser *General Belgrano* just outside the TEZ.[77] Although the *Belgrano* was moving away from the Falklands, the commander of the task force, Admiral Woodward was convinced she was engaged in a "classic pincer movement" and requested permission to sink her. Chief of the defence force, Admiral Lewin, backed his request as did Mrs. Thatcher: "It was clear to me what must be done to protect our forces in the light of Admiral Woodward's concern."[78] Observed Francis Pym, "whether it was completely necessary or completely wise were questions she declined to entertain."[79] The order was given and the *Belgrano* was sunk, taking 368 Argentine lives with her.[80] This action, more than any other, escalated the conflict and nullified any possibility of a negotiated peace. It was an emphatic indication of Mrs. Thatcher's preparedness to fight—even at the risk of alienating world opinion, which hitherto had been firmly on Britain's side.

To assuage international condemnation, the War Cabinet resolved to make a final diplomatic offer to the Argentineans. On Sunday, May 16, a full-day meeting of the War Cabinet (extended to include ambassador to the United Nations, Tony Parsons, and ambassador to the United States, Nicholas Henderson) was conducted at Chequers to determine the wording of Britain's ultimatum. No one expected it to be accepted, but ambassadors Henderson and Parsons were concerned to make as conciliatory an offer as possible to demonstrate to the world Britain's determination to avoid war. Mrs. Thatcher was having none of it:

> The problem was of course, that the PM veered the whole time towards being uncompromising, so that the rest of us, and particularly the Foreign and Commonwealth Office participants, constantly found ourselves under attack for being wet, ready to sell out, unsupportive of Britain's interests etc . . . I was in no doubt that she really preferred the idea of a fight than the accusation of compromise.[81]

Eventually the Cabinet agreed upon an offer and put it to the Argentinean government. The Argentineans had 48 hours to respond and there would be no negotiation of the terms. After this point, the offer would be withdrawn and the British task force would begin landings at San Carlos Bay on East Falkland.[82] In order to keep the United States onside, Mrs. Thatcher instructed Francis Pym to brief Secretary Haig on the contents of the proposal. Satisfied that the British had made a fair offer, Haig warned the Argentineans that the United States would side with Britain if conflict ensued.[83] The support of the Americans would prove critical.[84]

On Wednesday May 19, the Argentineans formally rejected Britain's offer and the Falklands War began. It was, ultimately, a war that could easily have been avoided. Through her dogged refusal to broker a durable arrangement for the Falklands' future and failure to provide any deterrent to Argentinean attack, Mrs. Thatcher made armed conflict the most likely outcome.

As Dyson observes, "her contribution to the crisis was the unwavering conviction that if there was any military way to do it, the islands should be reclaimed by force."[85]

MRS. THATCHER AT WAR—A TENACIOUS AND TRIUMPHANT LEADER

> Nothing remains more vividly in my mind, looking back on my years in No. 10, than the eleven weeks in the spring of 1982 when Britain fought and won the Falklands War.[86]

The great irony of the Falklands crisis is that the aspects of Mrs. Thatcher's leadership style that precipitated and escalated the conflict—crusading self-righteousness, singularity of purpose, and sheer bloody-mindedness—were the very same qualities that enabled her to resolve it definitively in Britain's favor. She knew what outcome she wanted and had no doubt she would prevail if she held her nerve. Hugo Young's analysis is particularly germane:

> Throughout the fighting, Mrs. Thatcher behaved like the best kind of soldier. She was calm and, having identified her objective, clear-sighted in separating the risks she was prepared to run from those which she rejected. The acceptable risks were always in the end, those of military action, the unacceptable, those that might flow from a settlement which fell short of a complete Argentinean surrender.[87]

The rapport Mrs. Thatcher established with the military command was crucial to the success of the war effort. The military commanders appreciated the decisiveness and courage of conviction her Cabinet colleagues and Foreign Office officials had so often resented. Chief of Defence Force Lewin could not praise her leadership highly enough, declaring, "from the military man's point of view, she was an ideal Prime Minister . . . one wanted a decision and she gave it."[88] Equally, Mrs. Thatcher was prepared to accept the advice of the military brass much more readily than she would her regular colleagues and advisers because she understood instinctively that her premiership lived and died with the task force. Consequently, "the two-month Falklands Crisis is remembered uniquely as a time when she listened more than she spoke."[89]

The other reason for Mrs. Thatcher's deference to the military command was her total ignorance of what war involved. Perversely, this proved to be another advantage of her wartime leadership. Nearly all of the men around her had direct military experience. Francis Pym, John Nott, and Willy Whitelaw were all veterans of World War II with a firsthand understanding of the bloodiness of armed conflict. In contrast, Mrs. Thatcher "had a sort of television view of war," enabling her to make crucial trade-off decisions others would have balked at.[90] According to Campbell "practically every senior politician, soldier and diplomat involved in the Falklands is convinced that no male politician, except for perhaps Churchill, would have done what she did."[91] When the first British casualties resulted from the sinking of the HMS *Sheffield,* "she probably felt them more keenly than her male colleagues," thought William Whitelaw, but in the end they only made her more determined to finish the job.[92]

Ultimately, however, it was not Mrs. Thatcher's gender or abstract understanding of war that was the decisive factor, but her unwavering clarity of purpose and unshakeable faith that because her cause was just she would eventually triumph. It was this doggedness that compelled her to brutally rebuff close friend and ally President Reagan when he called her late at night on Monday, May 31, urging a peaceful settlement before the Argentineans suffered total military humiliation[93]:

> What would have been quite wrong was to snatch diplomatic defeat out of the jaws of military victory . . . I told him that we could not contemplate a ceasefire without Argentine withdrawal. Having lost ships and lives because for seven weeks the Argentineans refused to negotiate we would not consider handing the islands over to a third party.[94]

These were truly the words of an *Iron Lady.*

On Monday, June 14, the British task force captured the capital of the Falklands, Stanley, and Mrs. Thatcher secured the victory she had so desperately desired. Addressing a Conservative Party rally shortly afterward, she was characteristically righteous and crusading in declaring the significance of the triumph:

> What has indeed happened is that now once again, Britain is not prepared to be pushed around. We have ceased to be a nation in retreat . . . Britain found herself again in the South Atlantic and will not look back from the victory she has won.[95]

At much the same time, a senior colleague sagely commented, "victory fortifies her conviction that she is right on every issue."[96]

CONCLUSION

In all, the Falklands crisis revealed the best and worst elements of Mrs. Thatcher's political character and decision making abilities. The initial Argentinean invasion was the culmination, if not the direct result, of her refusal to grasp diplomatic realities and a parallel failure to provide the Islands with adequate defense. The crisis then escalated through Mrs. Thatcher's refusal to countenance any diplomatic solution and the belligerent sinking of the *General Belgrano*. Her leadership style ensured that the Falklands conflict would be resolved militarily, but equally, her bloody-mindedness gave Britain every chance of victory. While her leadership type would fall essentially into the authoritarian classification, her decision to pick a task and go her own way may also place her within the realm of the maverick/quixotic type, discussed in the introduction to this book. Through her courage and strength of conviction, she manufactured an improbable personal and national triumph from the humiliation of the April 2 invasion.

Above all else, this chapter illustrates the centrality and utility of leadership typology and political psychology to the study of foreign policy decision making. A holistic understanding of the Falklands crisis is impossible without comprehending the mind-set of its key protagonist, Mrs. Thatcher. Without appreciating the rare moral certainty and unreflective self-righteousness she inherited from her father, an explanation of the conduct of British foreign policy during this critical period is decidedly incomplete. Similarly, the study of a number of Mrs. Thatcher's other foreign policy decisions, in particular her hostility to the European community, would doubtless benefit from a personality-and psychology-based analysis.

NOTES

1. Rod Rhodes, "From Prime Ministerial Power to Core Executive," in *Prime Minister, Cabinet and Core Executive*, ed. Rod Rhodes and Patrick Dunleavy (London: Macmillan, 1995), 23.
2. Peter Byrd, *British Foreign Policy under Thatcher* (Oxford: Philip Allan, 1988), 5.
3. Hugo Young, *One of Us* (London: Macmillan, 1989), 3.
4. Margaret Thatcher, "Interview for *Daily Express* with Godfrey Winn," *Daily Express*, April 17, 1961, http://www.margaretthatcher.org/speeches/displaydocument.asp?docid=100976.
5. Young, *One of Us*, 4.
6. Ibid., 5.
7. Ibid.

8. John Campbell, *Margaret Thatcher: The Grocer's Daughter* (London: Jonathan Cape, 2000), 37.

9. Ibid., 12.

10. Margaret Thatcher, *The Path to Power* (London: Harper Collins, 1995), 15.

11. Ibid., 15.

12. George Gardiner, *Margaret Thatcher: From Childhood to Leadership* (London: William Kimber, 1975), 20.

13. Margaret Thatcher, Remarks on the steps of Downing Street, May 4, 1979, http://www.margaretthatcher.org/speeches/displaydocument.asp?docid=104078.

14. Young, *One of Us*, 6.

15. Campbell, *The Grocer's Daughter*, 31.

16. Ibid., 3.

17. Hugo Young, "Mrs. Thatcher Serves Her Time," *Guardian*, January 2, 1988.

18. George Urban, *Diplomacy and Disillusion at the Court of Margaret Thatcher* (London: I.B. Taurus, 1996), 131–132.

19. Margaret Thatcher, House of Commons Speech, April 14, 1982, *Hansard* [21/1146–50].

20. John Campbell, *Margaret Thatcher: The Iron Lady* (London: Jonathan Cape, 2003), 131.

21. Anthony King, "The Outsider as Political Leader: The Case of Margaret Thatcher," *British Journal of Political Science* 32, no.3 (July 2002): 435–454.

22. Young, *One of Us*, 242.

23. Nicholas Wapshott and George Brock, *Thatcher* (London: MacDonald, 1983), 35.

24. Margaret Thatcher, *The Downing Street Years* (London: Harper Collins, 1993), 129–130.

25. King, "The Outsider as Political Leader," 453.

26. Ibid., 453.

27. Juliet Kaarbo and Margaret G. Hermann, "Leadership Styles of Prime Ministers: How Individual Differences Affect the Foreign Policy Making Process," *Leadership Quarterly* 9, no.3 (1998): 251.

28. Ibid., 252.

29. Ibid., 252.

30. Ibid., 252.

31. Margaret Thatcher, Speech to the Scottish Conservative Party Conference, May 14, 1982, http://www.margaretthatcher.org/speeches/displaydocument.asp?docid=104936.

32. Ibid.

33. King, "The Outsider as Political Leader," 447.

34. Alexander George and Juliette George, *Presidential Personality and Performance* (Boulder, CO: Westview, 1998), 206–207.

35. Ibid., 207.

36. King, "The Outsider as Political Leader," 447.

37. Milton Rokeach, *The Open and Closed Mind* (New York: Basic Books, 1960).

38. Ibid., 14–15.

39. Stephen Benedict Dyson, "Cognitive Style and Foreign Policy: Margaret Thatcher's Black and White Thinking," *International Political Science Review* 30, no.1 (2009): 38.

40. Francis Pym, *The Politics of Consent* (London: Hamish Hamilton, 1984), 46.
41. Bryan Cartledge, "Margaret Thatcher: Personality and Foreign Policy," in *The Political Legacy of Margaret Thatcher,* ed. S. Pugliese (London: Politicos, 2003), 58.
42. Anonymous senior minister quoted in Paul Sharp, *Thatcher's Diplomacy* (New York: St Martin's Press, 1997), 28.
43. Francis Pym, quoted in Byrd, *British Foreign Policy under Thatcher,* 61.
44. Foreign and Commonwealth Office official quoted in Young, *One of Us,* 248.
45. Campbell, *The Iron Lady,* 126–7.
46. Ibid., 127.
47. Young, *One of Us,* 259.
48. Quoted in Max Hastings and Simon Jenkins, *The Battle for the Falklands* (London: W. W. Norton, 1984), 82.
49. Thatcher, *The Downing Street Years,* 175.
50. Young, *One of Us,* 260.
51. Diana Elles, "The Foreign Policy of the Thatcher Government," in *Thatcherism: Personality and Politics,* ed. Kenneth Minogue and Michael Biddiss (Basingstoke: Macmillan, 1987), 106.
52. Quoted in Young, *One of Us,* 261.
53. Young, *One of Us,* 261.
54. Thatcher, *The Downing Street Years,* 177.
55. Campbell, *The Iron Lady,* 129.
56. Young, *One of Us,* 262.
57. Ironically, it was Foreign Secretary Peter Carrington who accepted most of the blame for the government's failure to foresee and possibly prevent the Argentinean invasion. It was evidently not his fault, but he offered his resignation to provide Mrs. Thatcher with a convenient scapegoat, thereby shoring up her own position. He was replaced by Francis Pym—a Tory "wet" who loathed and was loathed by the prime minister. Defence Secretary John Nott also offered his resignation but was rebuffed as Mrs. Thatcher was reluctant to lose two senior ministers during such a difficult period. Young, *One of Us,* 266–267.
58. Thatcher, *The Downing Street Years,* 179.
59. Ibid., 179.
60. Ibid., 191.
61. Ibid., 181.
62. Ibid., 181.
63. Ibid., 181.
64. Campbell, *The Iron Lady,* 131.
65. Margaret Thatcher, Speech to the House of Commons, April 3, 1982, *Hansard* [21/633–38].
66. Campbell, *The Iron Lady,* 135.
67. Ibid., 135.
68. Young, *One of Us,* 269.
69. Ibid., 274.
70. Campbell, *The Iron Lady,* 136.
71. Young, *One of Us,* 270.
72. Thatcher, *The Downing Street Years,* 188.
73. Young, *One of Us,* 271.
74. Ibid., 272.

75. Quoted in Young, *One of Us*, 272.
76. Thatcher, *The Downing Street Years*, 210.
77. Ibid., 214.
78. Thatcher, *The Downing Street Years*, 214.
79. Quoted in Young, *One of Us*, 277.
80. Campbell, *The Iron Lady.*, 145.
81. Ibid., 148.
82. Thatcher, *The Downing Street Years*, 222.
83. Ibid., 223.
84. Despite its aversion to the entire conflict, the United States nevertheless provided Britain with critical military assistance. According to British ambassador to the United States, Nicholas Henderson, "it is difficult to exaggerate the difference that America's support made to the military outcome. The support included everything from transport aircraft to sidewinder missiles and, most crucially, a measure of collaboration on signals and intelligence that was indispensible." Young, *One of Us*, 289.
85. Dyson, "Cognitive Style and Foreign Policy," 41.
86. Thatcher, *The Downing Street Years*, 173.
87. Young, *One of Us*, 278.
88. Campbell, *The Iron Lady*, 139.
89. Young, *One of Us*, 276.
90. Campbell, *The Iron Lady*, 139.
91. Ibid., 139.
92. Campbell, *The Iron Lady*, 140.
93. Thatcher, *The Downing Street Years*, 231.
94. Ibid., 231.
95. Margaret Thatcher, Speech to the Conservative Rally at Cheltenham, July 3, 1982, http://www.margaretthatcher.org/speeches/displaydocument.asp?docid=104989.
96. Quoted in Young, *One of Us*, 280.

10

Golda Meir: Prime Minister of Israel 1969–1974

Robert Lattin

Golda Mabovitch Meir was a teacher, kibbutz member, and politician who was elected the fourth prime minister of Israel on March 17, 1969, and the world's third female head of state, after serving as foreign minister and minister of labor. Meir had a strong personality that became an important factor in shaping her policy decisions. A theoretical debate persists in international relations theory, regarding the influence of a leader's personal characteristics on political decisions as head of state. Realists would argue that the position as head of state determines policy, no matter who or what personality type holds the position. Those arguing the opposing side of the debate hold up Prime Minister Meir as a prime example of a personality that matters; she is regarded as one of the most interesting and challenging personality figures of modern history. This chapter explores the connections between her personality, leadership style, and policy formation. The traits highlighted in this chapter are those that were often attributed to Golda Meir from childhood onward until her tenure as prime minister. I view these personality traits through the lens of her most significant political policies, specifically her handling of the Palestinian dilemma and relations with Arab states. Such policies are by and large the most defining of an Israeli prime minister, and often shaped much of her legacy.

I will address two major misconceptions concerning Golda Meir. The first is the commonly held perception that she was a genial, grandmotherly figure. Contrary to this popular belief, Golda took the stance that she was a woman in a man's world. Second, even though Meir is the only female prime minister Israel has had, she was not a global leader of feminism. Throughout her career she worked for several feminist organizations, but only at the request of her Zionist colleagues, not due to an undying belief in feminist ideology. In her autobiography she says, "I am not a great admirer of the kind of feminism that gives rise to bra burning, hatred of men or a campaign against motherhood."[1] Meir was a member of socialist Zionism, an ideology where men and women were treated equally. Though she acknowledged that women had an extra burden as child bearers, she never felt overtly unequal. In her memoir she stated, "I have lived and worked with men all my life, but being a woman has never hindered me in any way at all. It has never cause[d] me unease or given me an inferiority complex or made me think that men are better off than women."[2] Recognizing Golda's views on gender equality is important to fully appreciating her personality.

GOLDA'S PERSONALITY

Golda displayed two traits of an "exaggerated dominant" personality; she was both controlling and outspoken.[3] Born in Kiev—then part of the Russian Empire—in 1898, her need for control developed at a young age and was strongly influenced by her older sister, Sheyna. For several years as a child, Golda and her family lived without her father, who moved to the United States in search of a better life. In his absence, Sheyna began disobeying her mother by taking part in illegal Zionist political activities. The family eventually moved to Milwaukee, Wisconsin, to join their father. This devastated Sheyna, as she was forced to leave behind everything she cared for, specifically her Zionist boyfriend. Reuniting with her father after many years of separation caused Sheyna to feel repressed and embittered, as he was still tied to certain aspects of traditional Russian culture, namely appropriate social roles for women. He continued to try and raise his daughters to be simple, domestic housewives, but in protest to the move and her father's strict mentality, Sheyna left home and moved to Denver, Colorado.[4]

Sheyna's escape significantly impacted Golda's view of the world. When she grew older, she too did not accept her predetermined fate and instead was determined to take control of her own life. She wanted to finish high school and become a teacher. Her parents disapproved of her goals, particularly since Wisconsin law at the time did not allow female teachers to have husbands. So in February 1913, after months of arguing, Golda decided to take control of her life and ran away from home to live with her sister Sheyna in Denver. After some time, Golda returned home to Milwaukee, with the stipulation that her parents respect her independence. As this episode of her early life illustrates, her sister was a greater role model than her parents and became her ally against the authority of her more traditional father.

From a young age Meir had a sense of responsibility to the greater good, which continued to shape her character throughout her entire life. When Golda was in fourth grade, education in Milwaukee was free. However, there was a fee for textbooks that she and many others were unable to pay. Feeling that this was unfair, she decided to organize a fund-raising campaign for the Wisconsin school district, in order to raise the necessary funds to purchase books for those who could not afford them.[5]

This "can do" attitude came out most when Golda observed an injustice against the Jewish community. One of Golda's only memories of living in Russia was hearing of a planned pogrom in her hometown of Kiev. Pogroms were frequent and spontaneous against Jews. She said, "I remember being aware that this was happening to me because I was Jewish . . . [and] that if one wanted to survive, one had to take effective action about it personally."[6] Memories like this instilled Meir's sense of responsibility to the Jewish people, which shaped and consumed her life. Almost everything she did as an adult came from her strong sense of responsibility to the Jewish people. Unfortunately, this sense of responsibility forced her to make personal trade-offs. As a mother of two, Golda was constantly traveling and her family suffered for it. Her son Menachem was especially affected. When asked to speak about his life in the 1930s and 1940s, Menachem spoke with ease about his father, but recalled that his mother was just a woman on the run.[7] Her unending dedication to Jewish and Israeli causes eventually led to the end of her marriage.

In 1917, Golda married a fellow socialist she had met while living in Denver, Morris Meyerson. Her marriage to Meyerson clearly exhibited her dominant character and desire for control. She only agreed to marry him if he would be willing to move and live permanently in Palestine with her. Control was a defining, life-long characteristic of Meir's. Levi Eshkol, Golda's predecessor to the premiership, once stated, "Golda intervenes in everything. It is impossible to know who is responsible for what."[8]

Dominant personalities also tend to be outspoken.[9] In her autobiography Golda recalls a story from her time in Milwaukee when she attempted to campaign during the American Jewish Congress election. She wanted to speak at synagogues; but, at the time only men were allowed to address the congregations. Against her father's wishes, she decided to stand on a box outside of various synagogues, leaving those who passed by no choice but to listen to her views on the campaign.[10]

Meir's outspoken ways led to one of her greatest, and most important, contributions to the state of Israel. During the 1948 War of Independence, Israel was severely lacking in weapons and funds. Israel needed to replenish the Haganah, Israel's official military, to stave off defeat by the Arab armies. Meir was picked to go to the United States to attempt to raise $25 million. She made her powers of persuasion evident and successfully raised an unprecedented $50 million.[11]

In addition to having an exaggerated dominant personality, a sense of conscientiousness was deeply embedded into Meir's personality. Specifically, she had an inherent belief in being morally right, the tendency to view complex matters in black-and-white terms, and a strong sense of responsibility to the greater good—on her terms. Her firsthand experience with anti-Semitism, which started with the spontaneous pogroms she experienced as a young child in Kiev, affected Golda psychologically. It established in her a sense that she knew what was best for the Jewish people in Israel.

Golda's active role in building the state of Israel increased her confidence in the mission, and as such significantly increased her sense of a moral mission. In her autobiography, Meir speaks about the moral conviction she felt to place immigrant housing as the highest priority for the new state of Israel.

> There had to be priorities, and for me, at least, housing and jobs for immigrants headed the list. Not all my colleagues agreed with me. A barrage of experts explained to me in details with charts and graphs, why a housing program of the kind I envisaged was not a good idea. It would lead only to inflation, they said. It would be far wiser to put the little money at our disposal into factories or streamlined methods of agriculture. But I couldn't accept or support any recommendation that didn't deal with the absorption of immigrants, first and foremost, from the human point of view.[12]

Despite the advice of experts whose recommendations were supported by empirical evidence, Golda was absolutely certain her vision was the right policy decision. The future prime minister and president of Israel, Shimon Peres, said that Golda "was motivated not so much by the desire for power, but for the self-expression of views she held as incontrovertible truths."[13] However, Golda's absolute convictions were not well received by everyone. Abba Eban, a famous Israeli diplomat and politician who worked under Meir at the foreign ministry said, "[w]hat made people so negative about Golda was her certitude. She knew everything. She was once asked by one of her colleagues to put herself in [Egyptian President] Nasser's shoes. Her response was 'I won't.' "[14]

While Golda Meir was an incredibly intelligent and versatile woman, she had a tendency to view most matters in black-and-white terms. Meir spent a significant amount of time on a kibbutz, a collective farming community, in Merhavia. A kibbutz generally distributes work among men and women equally and without gender lines. Golda recalls that the women on her kibbutz hated doing kitchen work, not because it was hard, but because they thought it was demeaning. She did not share their feelings. She said, "I didn't feel that way about working in the kitchen, I couldn't for the life of me understand what all the fuss was about and said so. 'Why is it so much better,' I asked the girls who were moping (or storming) about kitchen duty, 'to work in the barn and feed the cows, rather than in the kitchen and feed your comrades?' "[15]

This thought process was consistent throughout her political career as well. A member of the Israeli diplomatic corps who served under Meir at the United Nations said, "there was little that was nuanced about her thinking. Hers was very much a black and white orientation. She was not a conceptual thinker. She relied on her guts."[16]

PRIME MINISTER GOLDA MEIR: 1969–1974

Golda's leadership style was authoritarian and centered on control. She surrounded herself with an insulated group of like-minded people who she knew would agree with her views. The group was called "Golda's Kitchen." There were mainstays such as Defense Minister Moshe Dayan, adviser Yisrael Galili, and Deputy Prime Minister Yigal Allon, as well as individuals who rotated in and out. The name "Golda's Kitchen" came from the group's regular meetings around Golda's dinner table, where she served tea and snacks. They typically held the meetings on Saturday, the day before the regularly scheduled Knesset meeting, and more often than not, the Knesset meetings would be a mere formality for what "Golda's Kitchen" had decided the night before.[17] Whatever issues "Golda's Kitchen" deemed important became the focus of the state, usually national security and defense.[18] In terms of Golda's management style, it was authoritarian, but also mixed with the inclusion of a small, tightly knit and loyal group of advisers with whom she discussed ideas.

Being outspoken was also a defining characteristic not only of her personal life but also of her leadership. Golda was never afraid to give her opinion or make a public statement, even if it may have been controversial. One example of this defiant outspoken attitude came about when she was asked about Israel's image problem. She responded, "other people just didn't like Jews except when they could pity them, and Israel must pursue her policies without constantly wanting to be 'liked.' "[19]

One of the most defining issues of Meir's premiership was her response to the Palestinian dilemma. She was the first prime minister faced with the public task of figuring out what to do with the Palestinian territories. Levi Eshkol, her predecessor, realized the enormity of the situation, but died just two years after Israel absorbed the conquered land. It was not until Golda took over as prime minister that the question of "What to do?" became a major part of Israeli politics. Both morality and control offer relevant explanations for Meir's policy of indecision and ambiguity.

The Palestinian territories presented a rare situation, under which Golda could not maintain her inherent sense of moral certitude. She was unsure how to handle the dilemma and made ambiguous and contradicting statements to the public about how she felt. At times she would allude to annexing the territories by saying things like the "inhabitants"—she never referred to them as "Palestinians"—might find that "it is not so terrible to live together with us."[20] The Zionist dream was for the greater Israel, which included the West Bank and Gaza Strip. It was a romantic ideal to be able to reunite the Holy Land in its entirety. Many also believed that giving up the occupied territories would make Israel look weak in the eyes of their Arab neighbors, and would jeopardize the country's security.

There were other times when Golda publicly rejected annexation. She explained, "I want a Jewish state . . . without me having to count the Jewish and non-Jewish population every morning, for fear the figures have changed."[21] Her inability to decide what was morally right, or what was best for her nation, prevented her from fulfilling her sense of responsibility to the Jewish people. She was trapped in a cyclical dilemma; she wanted to do what was right for her people, but she did not know which choice would be best for the country's future success. Her indecisiveness allowed for rapid and unregulated settlement construction within the occupied territories.[22] Some claim that her indecision was unspoken approval of these developments, but that theory is arguable. Her tendency to see issues in black and white, right or wrong, appears to have seriously inhibited her ability to find a middle ground or a compromise solution.

Golda's struggles with the Palestinian issue resulted from this moral dilemma and in addition what Irving Janis calls "affiliative constraints." These are pressures and influences on a decision maker from his or her affiliation with a particular organization, individual, or group.[23] In Meir's case, her affiliations were crucial to her control. Meir's unified Labor Party, which she coalesced—one of her greatest achievements—was made up of both politicians from the left and right. She feared that any decision she made concerning the territories would cause her party to splinter and fall apart.[24] Keeping the coalition together was the only way Golda would maintain her control over the government and state affairs.

Meir dealt with the same affiliative constraints within her inner circle. Two of Meir's closest confidants in the group, Dayan and Galili, were leaders of the Labor party's smaller, right hawkish factions, *Rafi* and *Ahdut Ha'avodah*. These two leaders lobbied Meir to hold onto the territories, or at least insisted on her refraining from making any quick decisions. For them indecision was a way to retain the newly acquired territories.[25] More importantly to Meir, Dayan had followers who believed he should either take over as party leader or split from the party altogether. This constituted a potential threat to Golda's premiership, and was enough to justify her policy of indecision. Therefore, holding onto power may have been a primary motivation.

Meir's policy toward peace with the Arab countries was quite simple: she believed if and when the Arab countries were ready to discuss peace as a reality, they would engage Israel. In her "Attainment of Peace" address to the Knesset she said, "[I am] . . . prepared to go to Cairo to hold discussions with President Abdul Nasser but, to [my] sorrow, [have] not been invited."[26]

This does not suggest that Golda did not want peace. She simply believed Israel should not be the only state responsible for the initiation of peaceful collaboration. Throughout her tenure as prime minster, Golda was outspoken about her desire for peace. In the same speech she was quoted in earlier, she also expressed, "[o]ur region is now at a crossroads: let us sit down together, not as victors and conquered, but as equals; let us negotiate, let us determine secure and agreed boundaries, let us write a new page of peace, good-neighborliness and cooperation for the profit of all the nations of the Middle East."[27] Unlike her stance on the Palestinian territories, Golda's policy on peace with the Arab states was tremendously reflective of her personality. She had a clear view that peace was needed, but would not make a move until she had a trusted partner with whom to negotiate.

After Israel's miraculous victory in the 1967 Six-Day War, there was a feeling of pride, invincibility, and a new sense of regional control emanating from the country. Meir took advantage of this newfound control. She suddenly lacked the urgency to meet with her shamed and defeated counterparts. Her sense of control was so strong she declined to engage in the suggested four-power talks on the Middle East, and made a public declaration that foreign entities would not dictate how Israel would handle its problems.[28] Israel's territory was, for the time being, secure, and if the Arabs wanted peace she believed they should come to her. Golda's sense of responsibility to the Jews was their security and survival, and as far as she could see, both were ensured.

Meir's black-and-white view of the world, coupled with her inherent sense of moral righteousness played a large role in her policy toward the Arabs. Golda believed that the Arab states were Israel's villains and Israel was the force of good. The Arabs were weak, and Israel was in a position of power. If the Arab states wanted peace they would need to initiate talks; otherwise there was nothing left for discussion.[29]

Golda was well within her rights to view the conflict in such a manner. The Arab states had never before shown any great desire to make peace. This was institutionalized at the conference in Khartoum, Sudan, that took place immediately after the Arab defeat in the Six-Day War, where the Arab countries agreed on the "three 'no's": no peace with Israel, no recognition of Israel, and no negotiation with Israel.[30] Additionally, the Holocaust was still fresh in the collective memory of Israel's public and leaders. Though Golda's mind-set toward peace with the Arabs is understandable, policy requires a certain level of flexibility to be successful. Meir's personality traits and her overconfidence in Israel's perception of power appeared to render her inflexible on her stance in this particular case, and it is widely seen as a reason for the 1973 Yom Kippur War.

Golda's peace strategy suggests irrational policy making. Janis states that defective policy making has three levels—low, medium, and high—and has seven qualities.[31] Of those seven qualities, at least three are present in Golda's decision to wait for the Arabs, designating her policy as one of low-level irrationality. First, because she viewed the situation in such black-and-white terms, for example, Israel was powerful and the Arab states were weak, she failed to examine with sincerity all of the risks of her preferred policy, as well as the values attached to them. If she had, she would have realized her unwavering position was patronizing and humiliating to the Arab countries, and as a consequence it engendered a need for vengeance. But, Golda's inherent high moral certitude that she was on the right side of the issue shaped her perception of the situation so firmly that she was unable to see the Arab nations as anything other than Israel's weak enemy. As a result, she was convinced the Arabs would not attempt another invasion after their 1967 defeat.

Second, this resolute manner also affected Meir's ability to process new information. There were several instances when Golda failed to address information about the alleged interest of Arab leaders to begin peace negotiations. Her response was most notably absent when Egyptian president Anwar Sadat suggested, via both the Nixon administration and Romanian president Nicolae Ceausescu, that he was interested in peace discussions. However, Meir never truly took his overture seriously.[32] Her long-standing beliefs that the Arabs did not sincerely value peace, mixed with the complacency she felt from Israel's perceived security, caused her to ignore the hopeful signs from Sadat.

Third, Golda did not prepare provisions or contingency plans should unexpected risks or variables occur. Perhaps Golda's decision to ignore Sadat's offer was due to her inability to envision such an alliance. It similarly follows that her failure to perceive a regional change also left her unprepared with a proper response to violent attack or invasion by the Arabs. This process of rationalizing called "moralization" manifests itself when leaders interpret events as if they were in accord with moral beliefs, when in reality circumstances are the opposite of that perception.[33]

In 1973, Israel was caught off guard by the Egyptian-Syrian attacks. The state was forced to improvise. Fortunately for Golda and her cabinet, the Israeli Defense Force was experienced at mobilizing quickly and efficiently. Under other circumstances, the outcome of the Yom Kippur War may have been quite different. Because "Golda's Kitchen" was where most of the country's policies were formulated, it is easy to blame this insular, cohesive group for their overconfidence that led to a policy resulting in the 1973 Yom Kippur War. Some of this poor decision making is a result of "groupthink," which occurs when a group of people makes faulty decisions because group pressures lead to a deterioration of mental efficiency, reality testing, and moral judgment.[34] Based on preliminary research, four of the eight groupthink symptoms were definitively present.

First there was an unquestioned belief in the group's inherent morality, led by Golda. Gershom Gorenberg states, "the three central figures [of "Golda's Kitchen"]—Meir herself, Dayan, and Galili—were profoundly pessimistic about peace, an emotional stance that preceded and shaped their analysis."[35] Second, there were collective efforts to rationalize actions even in the face of contradicting information. Despite the Jordanian King's warnings that Israel was facing a likely war from both Egypt and Syria, and a report that both countries had conducted militaries maneuvers, Meir and her advisers still determined that Israel was not in danger from an invasion. Third, there was self-censorship of deviations once it appeared that the group had reached a consensus. Fourth, they also suffered from a collective stereotype of the enemy as weak. When Golda, as the leader, thought the group had come to an agreement "few disputed her conclusions."[36]

Ultimately, Golda Meir resigned on June 3, 1974, after the Yom Kippur War. She died in 1978 of lymphoma, after living 80 very full years.

CONCLUSION

The mission of this study was to explore Golda Meir's major personality traits, leadership style, important policy decisions and how they may or may not have been connected. The results are not surprising. The link between the three is situational, and other constraints independent of personality affect the way individuals conducted themselves and perceived certain situations. Golda was a controlling, self-righteous, and outspoken person, and her management style was primarily hierarchical. Those traits speak to her authoritarian leadership in her relations with the Knesset and the way she constructed policies with the Arab states. However, the same was not true with respect to the Palestinian territories. In that case, internal party politics, external pressures, and her black-and-white thinking rendered her ambivalent and unable to make decisions at all. Nevertheless, while it appears that Golda Meir's motivations were to hold onto power, this power was less sought for her own self-aggrandizement, and more to control what she saw as the best interests for her people.

Overall, Golda Meir was an extraordinary woman who defied the odds of her time. She spent her life overcoming adversity and rose to become one of the most iconic and controversial leaders of the twentieth century. This small glimpse into her psycho-biography is not meant to explore the full depth of her character, but should be viewed as a sketch and an invitation to paint a more complete portrait.

NOTES

1. Golda Meir, *My Life* (New York: Putnam, 1975), 113.
2. Ibid., 114.
3. Blema S. Steinberg, *Women in Power: The Personalities and Leadership Styles of Indira Gandhi, Golda Meir, and Margaret Thatcher* (Montreal: McGill-Queen's UP, 2008), 147.

4. Ibid., 40–41.
5. Meir, *My Life*, 38–39.
6. Ibid., 14.
7. Robert Slater, *Golda, the Uncrowned Queen of Israel: A Pictorial Biography* (Middle Village, NY: J. David, 1981), 38.
8. Steinberg. *Women in Power*, 149.
9. Ibid., 151.
10. Meir, *My Life*, 60.
11. Letty Cottin Pogrebin, "Golda Meir," *Jewish Women's Archive*, http://jwa.org/encyclopedia/article/meir-golda.
12. Meir, *My Life*, 264.
13. Steinberg, *Women in Power*, 152.
14. Ibid.
15. Meir, *My Life*, 88.
16. Steinberg, *Women in Power*, 153.
17. Michael A. Genovese, *Women as National Leaders* (Newbury Park, CA: Sage Publications, 1993), 152.
18. Steinberg, *Women in Power*, 184.
19. Gershom Gorenberg, *The Accidental Empire: Israel and the Birth of the Settlements, 1967–1977* (New York: Times, 2006), 179.
20. Ibid. 190.
21. Ibid.
22. Ibid., 191.
23. Irving L. Janis, *Crucial Decisions: Leadership in Policymaking and Crisis Management* (New York: Free Press, 1989), 17.
24. Gorenberg, *The Accidental Empire*, 190–191.
25. Ibid., 191.
26. Golda Meir, "Attainment of Peace" (Address to the Knesset. Jerusalem, Israel. May, 26, 1970), http://www.thespeeches.com/golda_meir3.html.
27. Ibid.
28. Gorenberg, *The Accidental Empire*, 199.
29. Slater, *Golda, the Uncrowned Queen of Israel*, 185.
30. Yoram Meital, "The Khartoum Conference and Egyptian Policy after the 1967 War: A Reexamination," *Middle East Journal* 54, no.1 (2000): 64.
31. Irving L. Janis, *Groupthink: Psychological Studies of Policy Decisions and Fiascoes* (Boston: Houghton Mifflin, 1982), 175.
32. Steinberg, *Women in Power*, 139.
33. Alexander L George and Juliette L. George, *Presidential Personality and Performance* (Boulder, CO: Westview, 1998), 43–44.
34. Janis, *Groupthink*, 9.
35. Gorenberg, *The Accidental Empire*, 191.
36. Steinberg, *Women in Power*, 185.

Part III

AUTHORITARIAN MIXED TYPES

11

Silvio Berlusconi: "I am the Jesus Christ of politics."[1]

John Tumminia

> If we know something about the way a person believes, it is possible to predict how he will go about solving problems that have nothing to do with his ideology.[2]

Silvio Berlusconi—the name conjures images of a dogmatic, opinionated, megalomaniac with a penchant for gaffs and controversy, and on the other hand, a wealthy and successful businessman and politician with a penchant for survival. How did the son of a bank clerk, born during some of the most difficult years in Italy's modern history, overcome considerable odds to build a business empire, amass a fortune of over $6 billion,[3] win several elections, and lead a nation with one of the world's largest economies? What do we know about his belief systems and childhood that can point to his personality type?

Given that belief systems are in large part formed in childhood, it is appropriate to take a look at Berlusconi's childhood to explore any territory that may give some insight into his belief systems and subsequent actions as an adult. The fact and fiction of Berlusconi's early years are muddied by his often embellished accounts of that period in his life. However, there are some common themes that point to the raw materials instrumental in building his personality.

Silvio Berlusconi was born on September 29, 1936, near Milan,[4] on the eve of some of Italy's more difficult days. His father Luigi was 28 and a clerk in a local bank. His mother Rosella Bossi was 25 and a housewife from a "lower middle class" family, and was the "dominant force" in the family. Berlusconi was the oldest of three with a sister Antonietta (born 1943) and a brother Paolo (born 1949).[5] At the time of Berlusconi's birth, Italy was under the control of the Fascist government of Benito Mussolini, who would remain in power until his death by execution in 1945 when Berlusconi was just eight years old. During Berlusconi's early years, Mussolini's government increasingly gained power over all facets of Italian public life in an attempt to create an Italian empire, forcibly led by a totalitarian dictator. The Mussolini regime completed the process of totalitarian transformation by legal and extra-legal means. This was a period in modern Italian history rife with violence, uncertainty, and economic chaos—a period that defined Italy by Mussolini and Mussolini by Italy. Mussolini was a genius at propaganda, guided by principles such as an awareness of "the absurd conventional lie of political equalitarianism."[6] These are characteristics that Berlusconi would later emulate (whether consciously or not), and the quasi-legal tactics were something Berlusconi would later successfully utilize to his political and personal advantage.

The Mussolini era was a period when "all the country's inadequacies, unsolved problems, shortcomings, and liabilities (of which there were many) coalesced and found expression in fascism. Mussolini's personality passionately embodied all of those traits."[7] While it is unknown whether Berlusconi was deliberately emulating these aspects of Mussolini's personality and style, some insight may be gained from Berlusconi's two most famous comments on the subject of Mussolini: "Mussolini never killed anyone . . . [he] used to send people on vacation in internal exile," and "The racial laws were the worst fault of Mussolini as a leader, who in so many other ways did well."[8]

Postwar and post-Mussolini Italy faced an array of uncertainties and many Italians looked back fondly on the Italy that had been, despite a plethora of problems, much in the same way that many Russian citizens lamented the breakup of the Soviet Union during the difficult economic years following its collapse. Undoubtedly Berlusconi's family experienced hardships due to the interposition and realities of the war, but it is in attempting to uncover specific information about his childhood that it becomes increasingly difficult to separate fact from myth. Berlusconi's own personal reflections on his early childhood have been described as having "much in common with the more sentimental Italian neorealist films, like Vittorio De Sica's *Miracle in Milan* and *The Bicycle Thief* except with a happy ending."[9]

Nevertheless, one event in particular would strongly impact Berlusconi's childhood. All accounts point to him having a close relationship with his parents. He bonded with his father in particular over Italian football.[10] A.C. Milan was the focus of their mutual sports affection, a team in adulthood Berlusconi would eventually purchase and whose slogan *Forza Italia* he would later co-opt to propel his political career.[11] In 1943 when Berlusconi was seven, the Allied forces were in the throes of a carpet-bombing campaign on Milan, and young Silvio and his mother were evacuated outside the city to escape the air raids by the Allied forces. His father had served in the military under the Mussolini government, but in 1943 when Mussolini's government fell and was replaced by a German-led fascist regime, Silvio's father fled to Switzerland rather than continue to serve in the army. This decision resulted in Silvio not seeing his father for two years, and as a result, Berlusconi is said to have "suffered this absence very much."[12] In his *Una Storia Italiana* (An Italian Story), an autobiographical account of his life, which was sent to 12 million Italian voters prior to the 2001 election, he comments that his father was in the military at the time of the fall of fascism, and that his father's being in Switzerland made his father and mother "suffer very much." He says further that for him as a young boy it was "devastating" and that he was obsessed with the thoughts of "dad, my dad."[13]

During his father's absence, his mother worked at the Pirelli Tire company in support of "two children, her mother-in-law and her father," waking up at 5 a.m. every day to begin the long journey to work.[14] As for young Berlusconi, it is said that during the period of his father's two-year absence he frequented the train station to wait and see if his father was on one of the trains coming from Como, in hopes that he would be one of the many Italians returning from Switzerland. " 'So many were coming back, but not my father. I went there every day for a month,' he remembered."[15] In *Una Storia Italiana*, he comments, "it was disappointment, it was pain. I wanted to cry without giving anyone the sight of my tears because the train went away and my father was not there." During this time, Berlusconi portrays his mother as a selfless saint, and during one particularly bad episode in which German soldiers were pointing a gun at his then pregnant mother, he recounts "all were paralyzed by fear, but not my mother . . . I was proud of her and I learned that if you overcome fear, if you have courage, in the end you will win." Then one day a train arrived and young Berlusconi recognized his father from a distance, at which time he ran and "fell into his arms." Berlusconi recounts this as a lucky moment, one that remains in his memory as "the most harrowing and happiest of my life."[16]

Further, he describes his mother Rosella as "petite . . . organized, caring, but also combative," a woman who always said exactly what was on her mind, especially to her son Silvio. She even fought him when he told her he wanted to enter politics. After a long conversation, she remarked "If you feel the duty to do so, you must find the courage to do it." In 1994 during a particularly trying political period for Berlusconi, Rosella, after finding Silvio depressed about what was happening, stated, "Silvio . . . you can't disappoint those who have confidence in you. You have to go forward . . . find your courage, your energy, your enthusiasm and your faith and you will always return a fighter."[17] From Berlusconi we get a picture of his mother Rosella as a supportive yet strict woman of faith, fiercely loyal and protective of her family and with clear opinions that she readily shared. In regard to his father,

Berlusconi's purchase of A.C. Milan was seen as something of an action of "extreme filial piety, of giving his father the victories he only dreamed of in those hard, meager years of the postwar period." On the occasion of his mother's 70th birthday, he presented her with a sculpture of the Blessed Mother being handed a flower from a child. Berlusconi was reported to have said "This is you . . . and the boy giving you the rose is me."[18]

Berlusconi's father's long absence of two years can be considered an example of something Berlusconi could not control. According to political psychologist Fred Greenstein, this fear of loss would represent:

> deeper anxiety-producing conflicts that have their source in the need to manage impulse to express unacceptable primitive desires that were suppressed or repressed during the course of development. When an attitude is influenced by the need to accommodate to inner conflicts, when it is an outer manifestation of inner psychic tensions, it is said to serve the function of *externalization and ego defense.*[19]

Therefore, these events can theoretically be linked to later behavioral patterns and point to ego-defensive responses to external stimuli. A young child who cannot completely understand external events may often blame himself for his father's leaving or his prolonged absence, or prompt a fear that his father did not love him enough to stay and take care of him. This can lead to a sense of abandonment, and again a lack of control of events or people.

When the war was over, Berlusconi was sent to Catholic boarding college (Salesian order), apparently an unorthodox yet "ambitious" choice for Italian families of the time. A relatively strict institution, students were generally not permitted to go home much during the school year, continuing the narrative of the separation from his father he experienced earlier in his life. Young Berlusconi attended for seven years, and was a good student, save his reported "lack of profound religious conviction." An often-repeated story about his early days in school is "that of him selling his rapidly completed homework to his companions for sweets or little objects, but preferably for money."[20] Recollections of school friends include indications that young Silvio was an attention-getter, due to his "bubbling and extrovert vitality . . . taste in clothes, easy way with words and success with girls."[21]

A desire for acceptance and attention continued through to adulthood, as in his teens Berlusconi was involved in music, and later entertained on Mediterranean cruise ships, often taking the role of master of ceremonies. He recounts that he had to "keep large groups entertained all evening with jokes, songs and so on."[22] This desire to entertain apparently continued, as staff working for him have commented about his penchant for entertaining them with his singing at social events. As recently as 2002, he cowrote songs for a CD with a popular Neapolitan musician.[23] In addition, he worked selling vacuum cleaners,[24] another job that requires a type of showmanship. In sum, Berlusconi's early life has shown the genesis of three major themes: (1) the potential need for acceptance from which ego-defensive traits grow; (2) the potential need for attention and adulation; and (3) the potential need to control situations to compensate for a lack of control he felt in childhood.

In his adult life, power and control became common threads initially connected to business and later to politics. Two years after graduating with a law degree in 1961, he set up a construction company, Edilnord, with the intent to build residential housing around his native Milan. Later he began Telemilano, a locally based cable station that would later morph into one of the biggest media empires in Italy. After Berlusconi's founding of the political party Forza Italia in 1993, he became prime minister in 1994, having built a coalition with the Northern League and the National Alliance and promising to create a government free of scandal. The hope was that what Berlusconi had done for his businesses he could do for Italy itself. Berlusconi "would use his entrepreneurial skills to get Italy moving again, and he would inspire by his own example: the hard-working boy who excelled at his legal studies and built a commercial empire, proving that the American dream could come true in Italy."[25] Unfortunately, this hope never materialized when the coalition he supported fell apart only seven months into his term. Attempting a political comeback in 1996, Berlusconi lost the election to Romano Prodi, a center-left adversary.

Through Berlusconi's persistence, he became prime minister again in 2001. During this term, which extended to 2006, Berlusconi identified among his highest priorities: combating high levels of public debt, poor economic growth, public administration inefficiency, high youth unemployment, low investment in research and development (R&D), declining levels of foreign investment, high company taxes, and a declining level of competitiveness. Unfortunately, Italy's economic growth while he was in power was relatively nonexistent. The data shows that "the first two quarters of 2005 resulted in less than zero growth, producing technically the equivalent of a recession," which was among the worst in Europe. Despite his promise of lower taxes, "taxation over the 5 years of his government increased by 11.1%, an annual increase of 2.8%, and as a result much higher than declared official inflation." Levels of foreign investment remained flat, and this was coupled with a sharp decline in economic and business confidence. One area in which it is possible, albeit weakly, to suggest a positive impact of a Berlusconi government was in the unemployment rate. During the first years of the millennium, Italy's unemployment rate was 8 percent, the lowest rate seen in almost a decade. However, despite the fact that it was below the rates of both France and Germany, there is data that suggest that "half of the new jobs created between 2001 and 2005 were due to immigrants regularizing their legal status, declaring their residency and, therefore, their employment."[26] In addition, during the first decade of the twenty-first century, only countries such as Madagascar, the Central African Republic, Liberia, Haiti, Côte d'Ivoire, and Eritrea had done worse than Italy in terms of economic growth per person.[27]

Scandal has continued to dog Berlusconi, and in 1996, he faced a triptych of legal troubles, convicted of making illegal political donations, bribes, and accounting fraud. Through all of these convictions Berlusconi maintained his innocence, and had considerable skill in gaining acquittal through the appeals process. In 2001, he was again elected prime minister. A year later he was convicted—and again acquitted—of a charge related to his earlier business dealings, this time false accounting.[28]

Another defeat in 2006, again to Romano Prodi, was followed by an increase in personal scandals, particularly in regard to Berlusconi's well-known philandering. During this same period, to many in the Italian business community it seemed Berlusconi had "cornered the market in cornering the market."[29] He had amassed a broad empire of holdings in areas as diverse as construction, media, and insurance. Among other businesses, he owns the Italian football team A.C. Milan, the Mondadori publishing house, the newspaper *Il Giornale*, and the Mediolanum bank—all four at the top of their game in Italy.[30] As of 2006, Berlusconi had an approximate 90 percent control (direct and indirect) over Italian broadcast media.[31] This type of "control" is present in the personalities of many successful businessmen and women, so in itself it does not necessarily indicate an obsessive-behavioral control issue. However, the evidence, particularly the details of questionable financial deals related to his businesses that would later come to haunt him, suggests that Berlusconi has a marked reluctance in business and political interactions to delegate power or to modify or bring new players into the inner sanctum of his closest circle of advisers and business partners.[32] This is important vis-à-vis the recognition of a behavioral need for control and an authoritarian management style can be found in both his business and political dealings. Nevertheless, it is clear that he would not have been able to amass such holdings if he were not, let us say, "aggressively assertive" and competitive in his interactions. His fortunes grew exponentially as a result.

> With cash from television and advertising, he bought publishing houses, film-production companies, supermarkets. The old business establishment looked on with surprise and suspicion. He was determined to get the better of it. The Fiat-owning Agnellis owned Turin's mighty Juventus football team; well, he would buy AC Milan. They owned a national newspaper, *La Stampa*; so he took control of *il Giornale*. Carlo De Benedetti, the owner of the giant Olivetti company, was famous for putting politicians in his thrall; Mr. Berlusconi was soon

> out-schmoozing him. Many Italians reveled in the outsider's success, others frowned, everyone noticed.[33]

An undeniable narcissism is also present in Berlusconi's personality profile, and there is a wealth of evidence to support this. After much back and forth with the media, Berlusconi confirmed reports of extensive plastic surgery he has undergone, including eye lifts, neck surgery, and other assorted nips and tucks.[34] Aside from all of the actions and comments associated with his affair with Veronica Lario, who eventually became his second wife,[35] there have been many direct statements that testify to how he sees himself. When asked about seeking office, he remarked, "I don't need to go into office for the power. I have houses all over the world, stupendous boats . . . beautiful airplanes, a beautiful wife, a beautiful family . . . I am making a sacrifice."[36] After having likened a German member of the European parliament to a Nazi death camp guard, he was quoted saying, "I'm not a traditional politician, and I have a sense of humor. I'll try to soften it and become boring, maybe even very boring, but I'm not sure if I'll be able to."[37] In 2011, he was quoted as saying "when asked if they would like to have sex with me, 30% of women said yes while the other 70% replied 'what again?' "[38] When asked what Italian citizens should do if they find themselves below the poverty line, he remarked, "Do it my way and earn more money."[39]

He has also been quoted as calling himself the "best political leader in Europe and in the world . . . because of my personal history, my professional skills and my business achievements, I am a man nobody can expect to compare himself with."[40] He has also stated, "I am absolutely sure to be the most democratic man who ever became Prime Minister in Italy."[41] He reportedly is greatly annoyed by "being heckled, questioned, or interrupted except by cheers."[42] Further, as mentioned earlier, he has revered his parents in a way that is wrapped up in a narcissistic notion of his origins.

Sometimes the line between narcissism and megalomania is blurred, as is evidenced in his other public comments. Some of these clearly point to a man obsessed with the notion of himself as someone who was chosen by God with delusions of great power and omnipotence. One solid example of this is the building of his tomb, which he reportedly constructed before he entered the world of Italian politics and has been relatively silent about since. David Willey, a BBC correspondent, was given a tour and described it as follows:

> Silvio Berlusconi's underground mausoleum has 100 tons of marble abstract sculpture on top . . . you enter it by a stairway reminiscent of pre-Roman burial sites, pass through a narrow corridor and enter an imposing square burial chamber with a pink marble and granite sarcophagus in the center. It looks for all the world like the tomb of a pharaoh.[43]

Continuing this messianic theme, he has been quoted as stating "I am the Jesus Christ of politics. I am a patient victim, I sacrifice myself for everyone."[44] He has also claimed to be a victim of a "communist plot" by the judicial system in Italy as the culprits of an organized conspiracy against him.[45] In fact he himself has estimated that he has made "2,500 court appearances in 106 trials, at a legal cost of 200m euros" over a 20-year period.[46] His view of himself as omnipotent and above the law is evidenced in his clever and successful attempts to avoid prosecution in the many lawsuits related to his financial dealings. His answer to the allegations is to gain power and create new laws, which ultimately prevent him from standing trial, and in the process water down an already tenuous Italian judiciary.[47] In January 2008, for example, he was acquitted of several acts of "false accounting" that had allegedly occurred in the 1980s due to a new law that his 2002 government passed, effectively decriminalizing the acts at the heart of the accusation.[48] These many lawsuits stem from allegations that Berlusconi used capital from "highly suspect sources," implying mafia involvement.[49] These issues remained unresolved, as questions still remain over how the 22 holding companies that he set up in the 1970s were originally funded.[50] Berlusconi has been tight-lipped and secretive about any information related to finances during this period in his professional life. Has Berlusconi manipulated the system or simply demonstrated self-confidence in his dealings, regardless of where the capital funds originated? His demonstrated behaviors seem to connect his personality with other leaders who "hold fast obstinately to their own way of doing things" and exhibit "negativeness, secretiveness and vindictiveness."[51] Further, the evidence suggests that he is motivated by the pursuit of power as a means to facilitate self-interest, rather than the good of the people.

His second wife Veronica Lario has described him as "the most charming liar I have ever met."[52] Facts indicate she may have a point, as Berlusconi's own accounts of his life differ from reality, making it again difficult to differentiate fact from fiction. He has falsely claimed to have been a "student at the Sorbonne" and that he toured with his band (and friend Fedele Confalonieri) in Lebanon. In reality, he attended the University of Milan and did not accompany the band to Lebanon.[53] Many of these accounts come from his "autobiography," *Una Storia Italiana.* In the book, Berlusconi hoped to portray himself as the Italian everyman or at least an "idealized archetype . . . from humble, working-class origins, ready to accept sacrifice, part of a strict but affectionate family, true to his word, devoutly loyal to parents, energetic, enterprising and even slightly mischievous but ultimately obedient to authority, both parents and Church" and to show himself as a larger-than-life leader with a legendary almost god-like quality.[54] In part, as aforementioned, by cleverly co-opting the battle cry of A.C. Milan—Forza Italia—for the name of his party, Berlusconi tapped into the Italian identity and nationalism. This type of populist appeal effectively fits into what Hermann et. al would call the "evangelistic" motivational relationship focus: a leader whose "focus is on persuading others to accept one's message and join one's cause."[55]

The evidence suggests that Berlusconi has a talent for truth-bending and exaggeration—in effect creating his own revisionist history. For example, after facing immediate heat from making a comment that Mussolini was "benign" and "killed nobody," he publicly apologized to the Jewish community. However,

> Mr. Berlusconi tried to blame his remarks on the two British journalists who interviewed him for deliberately getting him drunk. He claimed that Boris Johnson, editor of *The Spectator,* and Nicholas Farrell, formerly of *The Sunday Telegraph* and now a columnist with *Voce di Romagna,* " took advantage of me. They were with me for hours and hours. And that's how it was, at the end of a very long day, in front of a bottle of champagne, you understand." Mr. Johnson retorted: "Il Presidente's memory must be playing him tricks . . . Alas, no champagne at all. We were plied with about a gallon of iced tea . . . It was always clear that it was an interview." [56]

Evidence of manipulation and the bending of facts can also be found in prior years, and his attempts to manipulate those around him for material gain are also evident. One story recounts him filling a rental office of one of his properties with relatives posing as interested customers in order to convince investors that the property was valid and desirable.[57] During one of his early construction deals, he had built a large housing complex, that:

> by his own admission, had literally no appeal on the " free" market, because they were in a dreary, isolated area where no one wanted to live. [Berlusconi] [first] tells us he knew no one in Rome, but suddenly has friends there who can present him to the secretary of the vice president of the pension fund . . . he tells us that he seduced a secretary in order to get an opportunity to be alone with the man who could bail him out of trouble. A pension fund ended up spending millions, perhaps tens of millions, of dollars on apartments it didn't originally want, not because Berlusconi convinced the vice president that they were a good investment, but because he got him drunk and established a "common cultural" bond based on a discussion of the genitalia of women of the Caucasus.[58]

Thus Berlusconi bends the truth for personal and professional gain, creating what has been called *hyper-fiction.*

> Berlusconi's advantage is to subvert the rules of theatre, if you will. His environment is the institution he represents, while his agency perches on his awareness of the institutional framework and the performance of cynicism.

> In a way, he is an actor aware of being an actor who is aware of not being perceived as an actor. This is, in a nutshell, *hyper-fiction*, Berlusconi's agency.[59]

Yet could these same examples be used as evidence of extreme self-confidence as much as evidence of his manipulative and persuasive talents? Could these actions be connected to an ego-defense? Even his father has alluded to Berlusconi's fragile ego, referring to him as proud, stubborn, and independent. His father commented on his son, "If you touch his pride, then *look out*."[60] During the decade of his 20s he was known as a "player" or "ladies" man. "His lack of height being amply compensated, according to his friend Confalonieri, by his charm and expensive wardrobe."[61] In fact, it is generally agreed that Berlusconi is only 5'5", although he usually claims to be two inches taller than that. He is known to have been the butt of jokes about his lack of stature and his wearing of platform shoes. In his own words, "Satirists describe me as a dwarf, but I am actually 170 centimeters (5'7") tall. In my day that was considered quite tall." Pride about not only his height but his general appearance has made hair mysteriously appear on election posters and at least one of the magazines in his media holdings, *Panorama*, has been known to have made "a shiny bald patch on the back of his head" disappear.[62]

Later in life, he publicly aired the dirty laundry of his marital problems, and addressed head-on the rumors that his wife was having an affair with a former mayor of the city of Venice, Massimo Cacciari. While at a press conference with Denmark's Prime Minister Anders Fogh Rasmussen, Berlusconi commented "Rasmussen is the most handsome prime minister in Europe . . . I think I will introduce him to my wife, because he is even more handsome than Cacciari."[63] His celebrated sexual exploits continued, as he became caught up in scandals involving "bunga bunga" parties, an underage prostitute, and his 2013 conviction and multiyear sentence for abuse of power and paying a minor for sex.[64] Of course, those who see Berlusconi as a fine and upstanding leader, deliberately wronged by many, think otherwise. One such quote in his defense is as follows; "Italians are smart enough to know that running a country is not the same as running a monastery. And that, therefore, leadership is preferable to holiness."[65]

Even though he had a reputation for having a need for control, those in his party reject this notion. Pointing to his own writings on behalf of *Forza Italia* and before the 2001 election, Berlusconi wrote:

> We believe that . . . the state must be the servant of the citizen and not the citizen the servant of the state. The citizen must be sovereign. For this reason—actually—we believe in the individual and we believe that everyone should have the right to carry himself, to aspire to the welfare and happiness, to build their own future with their own hands, and to be able to educate their children

> freely. For this reason we believe in the family, the fundamental nucleus of our society. And we also believe in companies, to which are assigned the great social values of job creation, welfare and wealth.
>
> We believe in the values of our national culture that the whole world admires and envies. We believe in the values of our Christian tradition, the inalienable values of life, the common good, in the fundamental value of freedom of education and learning, of peace, solidarity, justice, of tolerance towards all, starting with one's opponents. And we believe above all in respect and love towards those who are weaker: the sick, children, the elderly, and the marginalized.[66]

Berlusconi's populist-oriented writing taps into all of the emotional points a skilled politician would want to emphasize in order to woo voters, including a nod to nationalism. What some may call smart politics, others would call emotional manipulation, and in fact his charisma and political cunning led to his manufacturing a culture of adulation, elevating his leadership to a quasi-personality cult. Again, we witness the creation of a reality for personal and political gain, or a *hyper-fiction*.[67] Defeating the left thereby preventing them from acquiring a majority in parliament was his first "significant miracle . . . [which] meant not only that collective anxiety was soothed but also that 'the leader' acquired the never-ending gratitude of those who had felt distinctly threatened by a Communist rise to power."[68] However, even MPs were clear about Berlusconi's power and the structure of his party, Forza Italia. In 2007, an MP remarked, "Forza Italia is an avowedly leader-dominated party even if it is now becoming a little more firmly structured. That is [to be a candidate] it may be important to have local support, but what counts always is the opinion of the charismatic leader." The same year, another MP commented on Forza Italia as "a party established by a charismatic leader who speaks to the people directly, bypassing all party structures including the departments."[69]

In terms of policies, Berlusconi's time in office was a mixed bag albeit one with a minimum of substance. While one could point to some successes both domestic and foreign, at the same time he and his allies expended considerable energy passing laws that would benefit him and his closest partners, shielding him from further convictions. On the other hand, despite a multitude of evidence that indicates Berlusconi as being a power-loving narcissist, there is some evidence of at least a minimum of willingness to enact policy for the public good. Whether one gleans an underlying self-serving nature in these policies is up for discussion. For example, in a moment that can perhaps be characterized as atypical, Berlusconi approved the payment of $5 billion in reparations to Libya for colonial atrocities the Italians had committed.[70] In 2001, he "increased child benefits; [and] raised the salaries of teachers, policemen and soldiers. He . . . put the minimum public pension, helping out two million people, up to at least 1m Lire ($475) a month."[71]

However, these actions and policies, among others, can also be seen as attempts at shoring up his legacy so as to appear as an omnipotent, yet benevolent, leader, a goal that would fit his personality traits. The reality is that his many promises of economic recovery during the 2001 election cycle never managed to materialize, and Italy's economy stagnated, experiencing no fewer than three recessions in the five years of Berlusconi's term. It was during this same period that he managed to circumvent the law by creating new laws that made his previous personal financial shenanigans appear within the law, a move that during those bad economic times created unfavorable perceptions of Berlusconi's moral standing. He subsequently lost the 2006 election for just that reason.[72]

While, as mentioned, the Berlusconi government passed many laws that benefited ordinary Italians such as those creating large public works projects, school reforms, anti-mafia laws, and pension and retirement reforms, there were just as many that were questionable in nature. According to Freedom House, "the 2004 Gasparri Law on broadcasting was heavily criticized for provisions that enabled Prime Minister Silvio Berlusconi to maintain his control of the private media market, largely through his ownership of the Mediaset Group."[73] Even though the law was vetoed by the then president Carlo Azeglio Ciampi, it was nonetheless adopted shortly thereafter. Other such laws such as those decreasing the statute of limitations on corruption charges, one imposing a moratorium on criminal trials for the five highest office holders in Italy while they were serving,[74] and a law providing for the decriminalization of false accounting practices[75] give the impression that their sole purpose was to benefit Berlusconi and his closest allies and business partners. Gianfranco Pasquino sums it up this way:

> Berlusconi also had the opportunity to enact major reforms of institutions and even of the Italian Constitution itself. Yet he proved entirely unable to fulfill the task of institution-builder. When his parliamentary coalition approved a constitutional reform in 2005, not only was the reform poorly drafted and full of contradictions but Berlusconi never tried to promote it or engage his supporters. It is little wonder that voters resoundingly rejected a referendum on the reform in June 2006. Rather than constructing a more efficient institutional circuit, Berlusconi preferred to challenge the existing ones—above all, the judiciary and, to a lesser extent, the presidency of the republic. He has regularly confronted the opposition, often resorting to Manichean statements: for example, his party is the "party of love," while the opposition is the "party of hate." Berlusconi's leadership has exhibited truly toxic qualities and certainly deserves to be labeled as such.[76]

Two areas in which the Berlusconi government did affect change in the economic arena are in the areas of labor and pensions, although the advantage gained by these laws depended on which side of the economic spectrum you were on. Laws such as the 2003 Biagi Law, which changed the rules of business so that many new jobs that were to be created did not need to be permanent or full time, resulted in more part-time and temp employment. This created increased flexibility in the labor market, albeit to the marked advantage of business. In 2004, the Berlusconi government "presented a law that combined cutbacks in pensions, increasing pension system revenue along with innovations to increase the employment rates of older age cohorts (65 years for men and 60 years for women)."[77] A few years later, Berlusconi scored a few more successes, albeit controversial, on the domestic front.

In 2008, in a rare fulfillment of a campaign promise made before his third election, Berlusconi abolished a tax on primary residences. He commented that "this tax caused Italian families worry, anxiety, and fear of the future," saying that it had an adverse effect on both the housing industry and consumer spending.[78] His "saving" of Alitalia from the abyss, and worse, the French, was perceived as a victory for Italy.[79] Even though Berlusconi has often commented that the cleaning up of the garbage in Naples in 2008 as "one of his biggest successes,"[80] three years later the problem still lingered and the mayor of Naples referred to him as "having washed his hands, like Pontius Pilate" while residents lit the garbage piles on fire.[81] He was praised for his quick response to the 2009 6.3-magnitude earthquake in L'Aquila, spending countless hours meeting with locals and looking for ways to rebuild, despite his Berlusconian gaffe comparing the experience of the now homeless who were forced to stay in tents to a "camping weekend."[82] In an attempt to slow down government spending and lower the country's debt, Berlusconi's controversial education reform program that would "cut the number of courses and faculties, reduce funding for grants and introduce non-academic university deans to the education system" passed the Italian Senate in 2010 but was met with massive protests.[83]

An often stubborn person, as his father described him, and not easy to deal with, he has demonstrated his penchant for intractability. His relentless pursuit of power in the midst of constant scandal indicates that there is a part of him that is simply driven by the power and prestige of high office. All of these attributes indicate an authoritarian leadership model, which, through Berlusconi's own commentary, he seems to embrace. However, his self-confidence in business, with women, and in an almost mythical ability to skirt the law coupled with his strong sense of personal efficacy indicates a chaotic or impulsive model along with a need for control. Despite some policy successes, flexibility is not one of his personality traits, and while he is loyal to his inner circle of friends and advisers, there are no other indications that he could be classified as a delegative type. Our typology illustrated in this book takes into account that personalities will include some traits of other types. Thus, Berlusconi fits primarily within the authoritarian type with some characteristics of an impulsive personality. These do not necessarily contradict each other, but reinforce his personal need for power, not necessarily as an avenue for improving the public agenda.

His managerial style indicates a "Berlusconi-style hierarchical" model, in which he relies heavily on himself and few closest partners or advisers, who are fiercely loyal to him. He also depends on his personality and ability to sway voters and colleagues to get his way. His relationships with close friends and partners such as Fedele Confalonieri began in school and followed throughout his career. He once boasted that "all of my old high school mates but one are still on my team."[84] His is a style that would rather rely on party machinery only inasmuch as it allows him to win elections. Writing about Berlusconism, Claudia Mariotti adds, "it is Berlusconi himself who impedes any aggregative tendencies inside the party, obstructing, for example, all opportunities for the creation of internal groups (which would compel him to engage with his party officials), seeking, as he does, to avoid anything that would limit his power, even partially."[85]

Even the U.S. government characterized him in this way: "he displays an overweening self-confidence born of stable and strong political popularity that has made him deaf to dissenting opinion. The strict control he exercises over his government and party inhibits his staff from giving him unpleasant messages."[86] What is important to note is as in other countries no politician in Italy can survive without the skills at coalition building, regardless of the methods employed to do so. The layers of control that a successful politician may exercise begin at the voting booth with the citizenry, but must continue within the political machinery.

The evidence suggests that Silvio Berlusconi indeed lives up to the stereotypes that come to mind. He could have used his charismatic personality to grow Italy's economy. However, given the economic and political woes facing the nation it is difficult, I would say almost impossible, to argue that Berlusconi's legacy has left Italy stronger. Nevertheless, he still maintains a public following and has personally amassed a huge fortune in part aided by his ability to pass laws that shielded him and his close allies from prosecution.

During his career Silvio Berlusconi has been accused of tax fraud, embezzlement, bribery, and false accounting, yet he has always maintained his innocence. These accusations have resulted in a circus of acquittals and overturned convictions. In late 2012 Berlusconi was sentenced to four years in prison, later reduced to one, for tax fraud and was barred from holding office. In August 2013 Berlusconi lost his final appeal, struck down by the Italian courts, meaning that he would be required to serve time in prison. However, because of his age, Italian law would only require him to remain under house arrest rather than prison. In the end, he opted to serve the time in community service in a nursing home outside Milan.[87] His many legal troubles have included being accused of paying for sex with an underage prostitute and leaking information related to a police investigation to a newspaper under the control of his brother.[88]

His promise of a government without corruption was no more than a fairytale. Defending himself and his ego, Berlusconi would tell you that he has experienced "judicial harassment unmatched in the civilized world," and he states that he is "without a doubt the person who has been the most persecuted in the entire history of the world and the history of man."[89] Even this statement illustrates his megalomaniacal penchant for exaggeration combined again with his sense of victimization. Yet he has time and again been able to cleverly elude prosecution and return to public life. It seems that his biggest accomplishment has been to perpetuate the political culture in Italy, a culture that has been described as having "an operatic flourish, with governments regularly falling"[90] based in "a selfish, corporatist, fragmented society that despises politics and considers politicians to be useless and obnoxious." The Italian political culture is commonly said to be rooted in *anti-politics*, this particularly Italian type of politics having existed since the country's unification. According to Gianfranco Pasquino:

> Italy has also been since its founding a country where anti-politics has dominated. From 1861 to 1919, democracy was quietly accepted and was even expanded, but the "politicians" never enjoyed prestige of any kind, and anti-parliamentarianism ran rampant . . . the many problems left unsolved by the development of the first long phase of the republic (1948–1992), as well as the many scandals exacerbated by the pentapartito, opened a wide window of opportunity for Berlusconi, a wealthy media tycoon, who felt threatened by the disappearance of all his political friends, utmost among them fugitive Bettino Craxi. Berlusconi felt further threatened by the distinct possibility of an electoral victory by the left . . . Berlusconi did not come from Mars. He is the logical product of the political/non-political/antipolitical culture of Italy.[91]

Berlusconi's success has been described within the political culture as based on "a complex mixture of misplaced individualism, selfishness, distrust of others, anti-parliamentarism, and a lack of civil religion," sometimes referred to as *berlusconismo*.[92] During his time in power Berlusconi has blocked any possibility of that culture changing or progressing in any substantive way. It has been said that "Berlusconi's legacy will be the further weakening of institutions that were not strong to begin with, and an even greater tolerance for damaging conflicts of interest. Fifteen years of verbal assaults on Italy's courts have left many people believing that the legal system is a conspiracy of diehard leftists trying to undermine the government."[93] Further, "Silvio Berlusconi's parties are organizations neither of which has represented a specific social category, a uniform political culture, or a distinct political identity. Berlusconi's parties have always represented nothing other than Berlusconi."[94]

Berlusconi's childhood provides clues to his future behavior, which was clearly "goal-driven" and centered on an ego-defensive need for power and control. Yet, he tapped into the desires of the Italian public. As Mascitelli and Zucchi comment, "Berlusconi built his political platform and election campaign on the need for Italians to be freed from the cudgels of the state, to take opportunities to progress and realize individual expectations. He talked about the need for liberal market values and rewarding individual initiative. It was a message which sought to imitate his own successful climb to the top as the self-made man free from oppressive state control."[95] Aside from the general goal of the acquisition of personal wealth, if one looks at his electoral promises in advance of his first election, his goals for Italy, centered on the economy, are clearly defined. These were "(1) a lowering of taxes; (2) a major reduction in the crime rate; (3) a minimum monthly pension allowance of 1,000,000 lira; (4) the creation of 1,500,000 new jobs; [and] (5) a massive program of public works." Unfortunately for Italy, not only was he unsuccessful, but he betrayed his promise of not running for office again if he did not accomplish at least four of these goals,[96] pointing to the theme that his time in government "seemed more to pass laws which favored his private empire rather than to put in place real economic reforms."[97]

When it comes down to a stark analysis of his personality type, Berlusconi has proven to be authoritarian, controlling, dogmatic, close-minded, highly ideological, and ego-defensive. In referring to himself as the "Jesus Christ of politics,"[98] his megalomania is obvious, as is his unwavering narcissism. His extremely aggressive business dealings and the passing of laws that benefited him and his closest friends and partners demonstrated his skill for manipulation and his ability to operate secretively. Also, many of his words and actions reveal a closed-minded tendency to put things in black-and-white terms: his political friends as good (the in-group) and his political foes as evil (the out-group).

A young boy separated from his father in war-torn Italy with the backdrop of totalitarianism created a desire to be in control within an environment that was out of control and unstable. Berlusconi brought that need for control with him into his adult life and used it to his personal economic and political advantage, but unfortunately to the economic and political disadvantage of the Italian people.

NOTES

1. Oliver Burkeman, "Silvio Berlusconi Is Not Jesus Christ," *Guardian*, February 14, 2006, http://www.theguardian.com/world/2006/feb/14/italy.religion.

2. Milton Rokeach, *The Open and Closed Mind: Investigations into the Nature of Belief Systems and Personality Systems* (New York: Basic Books, Inc., 1960), 7.

3. As of March 2013, his net worth was estimated at $6.2 billion. See *Forbes Magazine Online*, March 2013, http://www.forbes.com/profile/silvio-berlusconi/.

4. Paul Ginsborg, *Silvio Berlusconi: Television, Power and Patrimony* (London: Verso Press, 2005), 11.

5. Ibid., 12.

6. Benito Mussolini, with Giovanni Gentile, "The Doctrine of Fascism" (1932), from *Fascism Doctrine and Institutions* by Benito Mussolini (Ardita Publishers, Rome, 1935), 7–42. Translation online at: http://www.upf.edu/materials/fhuma/nacionalismes/nacio/docs/muss-doctrine.pdf.

7. Gianfranco Pasquino, "Silvio Berlusconi and Anti-Political Leadership in Italy," *Bologna Center Journal of International Affairs* 14 (Spring 2011), http://bcjournal.org/volume-14/silvio-berlusconi-and-anti-political-leadership-in-italy.html.

8. "In Quotes: Berlusconi in His Own Words," *BBC News Online*, May 2, 2006, http://news.bbc.co.uk/2/hi/europe/3041288.stm.

9. Alexander Stille, *The Sack of Rome: How a Beautiful European Country with a Fabled History and a Storied Culture Was Taken Over by a Man Named Silvio Berlusconi* (New York: Penguin Press, 2006), 21.

10. Ibid.

11. Francesca Caferri, "Silvio Berlusconi, Self-Styled Man of the People," *CNN Italia*, 2001, http://web.archive.org/web/20010707053152/http://edition.cnn.com/SPECIALS/2001/italy/stories/berlusconi/.

12. Ginsborg, *Silvio Berlusconi*, 13, 41.

13. Silvio Berlusconi, *Una Storia Italiana* (Mondadori Printing, 2001). http://www.madvero.it/pernondimenticarefile/unastoriaitaliana.pdf

14. David Lane, *Berlusconi's Shadow: Crime, Justice and the Pursuit of Power* (London: Penguin, 2005), 42.

15. Ibid.

16. Berlusconi, *Una Storia Italiana.*

17. Ibid.

18. Stille, *The Sack of Rome*, 21–22.

19. Fred I. Greenstein, *Personality and Politics: Problems of Evidence, Inference, and Conceptualization* (New York: W.W. Norton, 1975), 29.

20. Ginsborg, *Silvio Berlusconi*, 13–14.

21. Lane, *Berlusconi's Shadow*, 43.

22. Ginsborg, *Silvio Berlusconi*, 15.

23. Lane, *Berlusconi's Shadow*, 43–44.

24. Stille, *The Sack of Rome*, 24.

25. "The Cavaliere and the Cavallo: What Silvio Berlusconi Promised—And What He Has Delivered," *Economist Online*, June 9, 2011, http://www.economist.com/node/18780867.

26. Bruno Mascitelli and Emiliano Zucchi, "Expectations and Reality: The Italian Economy under Berlusconi," *Journal of Contemporary European Studies* 15, no. 2 (August 2007): 131–140.

27. "The Cavaliere and the Cavallo."

28. "Silvio Berlusconi's Rise, Bungles and Bunga-Bunga: A Timeline of the Italian Politician's Controversial Career," *Giampiero Sposito/Reuters*, April 29, 2013, http://www.cbc.ca/news/interactives/berlusconi-timeline/index.html.

29. Caroline Frost, "Silvio Berlusconi: The Italian Tycoon," *BBC Online*, June 9, 2005, http://www.bbc.co.uk/bbcfour/documentaries/profile/silvio_berlusconi.shtml.
30. Caferri, "Silvio Berlusconi."
31. "Basta, Berlusconi," *Economist*, April 6, 2006.
32. "Silvio Berlusconi, Italy's Would-Be Napoleon," *Economist*, March 22, 2001.
33. Ibid.
34. "Berlusconi Admits Plastic Surgery," *BBC News*, January 28, 2004,
35. Ginsborg, *Silvio Berlusconi*, 28–29.
36. "In Quotes: Berlusconi in His Own Words."
37. "10 Questions for Silvio Berlusconi," *Time World*, July 19, 2003, http://www.time.com/time/world/article/0,8599,465796,00.html.
38. "In Quotes: Berlusconi in His Own Words."
39. Interview, *Telelombardia*, March 6, 2006.
40. Caferri, "Silvio Berlusconi."
41. *Agenzia Stampa Quotidiana Nazionale*, January 25, 2002, www.asca.it.
42. "Silvio Berlusconi, Italy's Would-Be Napoleon."
43. "Portrait of a Marriage," *Independent Online*, July 23, 2003, http://www.independent.co.uk/news/world/europe/portrait-of-a-marriage-587690.html.
44. Burkeman, "Silvio Berlusconi Is Not Jesus Christ."
45. "Silvio Berlusconi: Unfit to Lead Europe," *Economist*, May 8, 2003.
46. "Profile: Silvio Berlusconi, Italian Ex-Prime Minister," *BBC News Europe*, August 1, 2013, www.bbc.co.uk/news/world-europe-11981754.
47. "Basta, Berlusconi."
48. "A Leopard, Spots Unchanged," *Economist*, April 3, 2008.
49. Ginsborg, *Silvio Berlusconi*, 23.
50. "He's Sitting Pretty: Italy, Its Prime Minister and the Law," *Economist*, July 18, 2002.
51. Alexander L. George and Juliette L. George, *Presidential Personality and Performance* (Boulder, Co.: Westview Press, 1998), 33.
52. Malcolm Moore, "Berlusconi Takes Mama to Polls as Vote Opens," *Telegraph Online*, April 10, 2006, http://www.telegraph.co.uk/news/worldnews/europe/italy/1515331/Berlusconi-takes-mama-to-polls-as-vote-opens.html.
53. Stille, *The Sack of Rome*, 23.
54. Ibid., 22–23.
55. Margaret G. Hermann, Thomas Preston, Baghat Korany, and Timothy M. Shaw, "Who Leads Matters," *International Studies Review* 3, no. 2 (Summer, 2001): 95.
56. Peter Popham, "It Was the Drink Talking, Claims a Rueful Berlusconi," *Independent*, September 19, 2003.
57. Stille, *The Sack of Rome*, 25.
58. Ibid., 26.
59. Filippo Spreafico, *Between Theatre and Politics: The Hyper-Fiction of Silvio Berlusconi* (University College London BSc Anthropology 2011 personal thesis), 44, 45, http://cinquecentmilliondewiskey.files.wordpress.com/2012/10/anth3048dissertationfilippospreafico.pdf.
60. Georgio Ferrari, *Il Padrone del diavolo: Storia di Silvio Berlusconi* (Milan: Camunia 1990), 7.
61. Ginsborg, *Silvio Berlusconi*, 25.

62. "Silvio Berlusconi Has Eye Job," *BBC News Europe*, January 15, 2004, http://news.bbc.co.uk/2/hi/europe/3400755.stm.

63. Moore, "Berlusconi Takes Mama to Polls."

64. "Profile: Silvio Berlusconi."

65. Giglio Reduzzi, *Berlusconi: The Truth about Italy's Much Maligned Premier* (Dallas: St. Paul Press., 2010), 56.

66. Silvio Berlusconi, *L'italia che ho in mente* (Milano: Arnoldo Mondadori Editore S.p.A., 2000), 22.

67. Spreafico, *Between Theater and Politics*, 4.

68. Pasquino, "Silvio Berlusconi."

69. Claudia Mariotti, "Berlusconism: Some Empirical Research," *Bulletin of Italian Politics*, 3, no. 1 (2011): 49.

70. Jeff Isrealy, "Italy Pays Reparations to Libya," *TIME*, September 2, 2008.

71. "Bad Luck and Clumsy Driving—On a Rocky Road," *Economist*, October 4, 2001.

72. Steve Scherer, "Berlusconi Seeks Place in History with Comeback Bid," *Bloomberg.com*, April 11, 2008, http://www.bloomberg.com/apps/news?pid=20601109&refer=home&sid=aymIkiJ2eyaM.

73. Freedom House, "Italy: Freedom of the Press 2011," *Freedom House Online*, http://www.freedomhouse.org/report/freedom-press/2011/italy.

74. "Italian Court Rejects Prime Minister's Immunity," *New York Times*, October 7, 2009.

75. Pierpaolo Schiattone, "Il nuovo "falso in bilancio": aspetti sostanziali e metodologie investigative," August 29, 2003, http://www.altalex.com/index.php?idnot=6413.

76. Pasquino, "Silvio Berlusconi."

77. Mascitelli and Zucchi, "Expectations and Reality."

78. Frances D'Emilio, "Berlusconi: If I Win, Italians Get Home Tax Back," *Associated Press*, February 3, 2013, http://bigstory.ap.org/article/berlusconi-if-i-win-italians-get-home-tax-back.

79. Jacopo Ieranò, "The Alitalia Saga Is Finally Over," *BlogEuropa.eu*, February 2, 2009, http://blogeuropa.eu/2009/02/02/the-alitalia-saga-is-finally-over%E2%80%A6/.

80. Silvia Aloisi, "Naples Trash Crisis Highlights Berlusconi Weakness," *Reuters*, November 23, 2010, http://www.thestar.com/news/world/2010/11/23/naples_trash_crisis_highlights_berlusconi_weakness.html.

81. "Naples: Exasperated Residents Set Fire to Rubbish," *BBC News Europe*, June 24, 2011, http://www.bbc.co.uk/news/world-europe-13904216.

82. Peter Wilkinson, "Berlusconi Praised despite Quake Gaffe," *CNN.com/Europe*, April 9, 2009, http://edition.cnn.com/2009/WORLD/europe/04/09/italy.quake.berlusconi/.

83. "Italy Senate Approves Education Reforms," *PressTV Online*, December 23, 2010, http://edition.presstv.ir/detail/156842.html.

84. "The Secret of Silvio Berlusconi's Success," *BBC News Online*, November 12, 2001, http://news.bbc.co.uk/news/magazine-15629283.

85. Mariotti, "Berlusconism," 54.

86. U.S. Embassy Cable, "Scenesetter for Italian PM Berlusconi's June 15 Visit to Washington," *To the President from the Charge D'affaires*, Classified by Elizabeth L. Dibble, June 9, 2009, http://www.theguardian.com/world/us-embassy-cables-documents/210920.

87. "Profile: Silvio Berlusconi, Italian ex-prime minister," *BBC News Europe*, May 9, 2014. http://www.bbc.com/news/world-europe-11981754

88. "Profile: Silvio Berlusconi."
89. In Quotes: Berlusconi in His Own Words."
90. Jim Yardley and Gaia Pianigiani, "Has Berlusconi Finally Run out of Political Lives?" *New York Times Online*, September 8, 2013, http://www.nytimes.com/2013/09/09/world/europe/has-berlusconi-finally-run-out-of-political-lives.html?pagewanted=all.
91. Pasquino, "Silvio Berlusconi."
92. Ibid.
93. "The Cavaliere and the Cavallo."
94. Mariotti, "Berlusconism," 55.
95. Mascitelli and Zucchi, "Expectations and Reality," 130.
96. Ibid., 131.
97. Ibid., 134.
98. Burkeman, "Silvio Berlusconi Is Not Jesus Christ."

12

Eva Peron: Spiritual Leader of the Nation

Evette Rivera and Jean Krasno

Affectionately known as Evita, Eva Peron was born Maria Eva Ibarguren Duarte on May 7, 1919, in the village of Los Toldos in rural Argentina. While never holding elective office, Eva's legendary image as Argentina's First Lady set the stage for other women to emerge into leadership positions in Argentina. The first female elected to the presidency in Argentina in 2007, Cristina Fernandez de Kirchner, has said that women owe a debt to Eva, due to "her example of passion and combativeness."[1] It is difficult to assign a type to Evita because she did not hold a formal office, but created her own position in the Argentine government by founding a set of social programs unique to her leadership. She used her relationship with her husband, Juan Peron, as president of the country to leverage her own goals, and in that sense was pragmatic as she was somewhat forced to be flexible in that relationship. But her gradual, even obsessive, dedication to her social programs led her to become more controlling and authoritarian. In addition, she strategically utilized her charismatic passion and glamor to garner the support she needed to achieve her goals, which were both personal and morally compassionate.

Maria Eva grew up in abject poverty and her childhood memories were filled with thoughts of her mother, Juana Ibarguren, struggling to raise five children who were the illegitimate offspring of a wealthy rancher, Juan Duarte, who had taken her on as his mistress. Before abandoning Juana and the children, he signed a document stating that he was the father of the five children, thus allowing them to take the name Duarte.[2] Both Juan Duarte and Juana Ibarguren were descendants of Basque immigrants from Spain.[3] After the father abandoned the family and disowned them, withdrawing all support, Juana moved to a very small apartment in the town of Junin where she and her daughters took jobs as household cooks to support themselves. Juan Duarte passed away when Eva was just six years old. Early on in her life, Eva witnessed the injustices of the social classes, where her wealthy father lived one type of life and his mistress and second family lived in miserable poverty. Eva would remember this as she matured.

> As far as I can remember the existence of injustice has hurt my soul as if a nail was being driven into it. From every period of my life I retain the memory of some injustice tormenting me and tearing me apart.[4]

Eva attended school in Junin and began to participate in school plays and developed a passion for acting. For Eva, escaping her real life into the world of make-believe was exhilarating. In 1933, Eva played a role in a play called Arriba Estudiantes (Students Arise), a patriotic melodrama, after which she was determined to become an actress.[5]

The next year, at the age of 15, Eva escaped her poor village and ran off to Buenos Aires to pursue her acting career.[6] Buenos Aires at the time was considered the Paris of Latin America with cafes, theaters, movie houses, and shops. Eva recalls:

> That there were other places in my country and in the world where things could happen is some other way . . . I imagined, for instance, that large cities were marvelous places where only wealth existed; and everything I heard about them from other people confirmed this belief. They talked about the great city as if it were a wonderful paradise from what they said, that people there were more real people than those I saw in my own town.[7]

The city of Buenos Aires became a magnet for migrants from the interior seeking jobs, but many ended up living in outlying shanties or tenements, a miserable existence. But Eva was able to launch her acting career and opened in a play called "La Señora de Perez." As a beautiful and talented young woman, Eva later toured Argentina with a theater company, worked as a model, and appeared in a few low-budget films. Around this time, Eva began coloring her hair from its natural brunette hue to the bright blonde tone she is known for. In 1942, she was hired to play in a radio soap opera drama that aired everyday on Radio El Mundo, the biggest radio station at the time.[8] Eva was very ambitious and with her modest successes in radio and film, she was able to build up some financial earnings enough to move into her own apartment in a good neighborhood in Buenos Aires. She also became one of the founders in 1943 of what was to become an important political radio station, Argentine Radio Syndicate.[9]

In January 1944, Argentina was hit by a major earthquake, killing some 10,000 people. Juan Peron was secretary of labor at the time and initiated a fund-raising campaign by launching an art festival to benefit the victims, inviting radio and film stars to perform and entice people into giving.

At the gala, Colonel Juan Peron, met the beautiful Eva Duarte and the new couple left the gala together at around two o'clock in the morning and were married the following year.[10] However, before they were married, Peron as secretary of labor, announced that broadcast performers would form a union and shortly after the union's formation, Eva was elected its president. Eva then began a daily radio soap opera drama called "Toward a Better Future," which highlighted Peron, his work, his goals, and his personality.[11]

Threatened by Juan Peron's growing power and popularity, particularly with the *descamisados*, a movement made up of the "shirtless" poor, on October 9, 1945, his opponents arrested him and he was thrown into jail. Within a few days on October 17, a rally of protesters organized by descamisado leaders gathered in front of the government house, demanding his release. A few hours later, a free man, Peron stepped onto the balcony of the Casa Rosada government house and dramatically addressed his followers in the traditional caudillo style, adopting even a quasi-religious tone.[12] Within a few months, a member of the ruling class and socially connected Peron married Eva Duarte, despite her illegitimate origins, thus giving her a societal status she had not known but only observed as a poor outsider.

In 1946, Juan Peron ran for president and won an overwhelming victory. Utilizing her acting skills and radio access, Eva delivered passionate speeches promoting Peron during his campaign. She was the first woman to appear in public on a campaign trail and was enormously popular with the general public, if not with the wealthy members of the Argentine oligarchic elite who resented her background. It was during this period that Eva introduced to her public the more endearing name "Evita" as "little Eva."

EVA PERON: EUROPEAN TOUR

After her husband won the presidency, in June 1947, Eva ventured on a two-month European tour, which started in Spain and included visits to Italy, France, Portugal, and Switzerland. Initially, Juan Peron had received an invitation to visit Spain by the country's dictator Francisco Franco, but instead asked Eva to respond to the invitation. Two years after the end of hostilities in World War II, many countries continued to suffer the appalling consequences. Spain had remained neutral, but was in the throes of the repression that followed the Spanish Civil War—an atrocious war that Franco instigated in order to establish his regime. As a result of Franco's fascist government, following the defeat of fascism in Germany and Italy, the international community began to isolate Spain. In 1946, the diplomat and economist Oscar R. Lange regarded Spain as a "threat to world peace."[13] This led to serious discussions on discontinuing diplomatic relations with Spain. The Soviets were particularly resentful of Spain and for that matter, Argentina's well-known co-operation with the Axis powers, so much so that Stalin tried to block Argentina's participation in the writing of the UN Charter in San Francisco in 1945. The founders of the nascent United Nations considered Franco's fascist regime out of alignment with the United Nations' objective of attaining peace and security. Therefore, the organization proceeded to demand that Franco "surrender the powers of government to a provisional government broadly representative of the Spanish people."[14] The United Nations then required Spain to remove Franco from power in order to become a member of the organization. Since Spain failed to follow the United Nations' request, the organization recommended all member states to cease all diplomatic relations with Spain and close down their embassies in Madrid.[15] Argentina, among a few other countries such as Portugal and Ireland, refused to comply.

During times of hardship, increasing poverty and hunger in Spain, Argentina came to its assistance. While the war had brought devastation throughout Europe, Argentina remained the wealthiest country in South America and one of the richest nations in the world. Part of Argentina's assistance to Spain came in a loan of 400 million pesos and a trade agreement that provided Spain credit to purchase food.[16] For two years during Peron's regime, imports of Argentine products amounted to 25 percent of all the goods that came into Spain.[17] In wheat alone, the agreement assured Spain at least 400,000 tons in 1947 and 300,000 tons in 1948.[18] The quantity of grain and beef sent to Spain from Argentina saved the nation from starvation.[19]

Due to Spain's gratitude to Argentina for this needed assistance, Franco had invited Juan Peron to a state visit, but as stated earlier, he demurred and Eva went in his place. There were no clear explanations as to why Peron declined Franco's invitation. It is likely that Peron was avoiding any compromising implications that a visit to Spain would have stirred, mainly receiving a cold shoulder from the United States and the Soviet Union. It was never a secret that Peron admired fascist leaders such as Mussolini and Hitler. While serving as a military envoy in fascist Italy, Peron grew more interested in fascism. He essentially admired fascists' ability to control the masses and believed it was an effective way to implement power. As Juan Peron explained:

> The value of the people ... does not reside in the number of men who are organized. Its value resides in the rulers who lead the people, because action is never generated by the mass or by the people, but by the rulers who lead them. The mass goes wherever its ruler takes it; otherwise, it overflows, and God forbid![20]

Despite his admiration for Mussolini, Peron acknowledged his mistakes and assured himself that he would follow Mussolini's footsteps but also avoid his errors.[21] Peron adopted some of the political ideologies of fascist Europe, but did not fully implement them nor did he establish a fascist regime in Argentina.[22] *Peronism* had characteristics of fascism but also affected policies that pure fascism would have never approved—particularly the support of women's participation in politics, which Eva successfully modeled.[23]

During a seemingly inopportune time for Peron to visit Spain, Eva decided to make the trip and Peron did not dissuade her. In order to give credible cover for her visit to Spain, more countries were added to her tour. The Argentine government justified this trip by stating that its sole purpose was to bring "a message of peace" to Europe,[24] or "stretch a rainbow of beauty between the New World and the Old World."[25] Consequently, they nicknamed it the "Rainbow Tour" and added Portugal, France, Britain, Italy, and Switzerland to Eva's itinerary.

The Spaniards gratefully received Evita, due to the long history of strong diplomatic ties between the two Spanish-speaking nations. Furthermore, Spain's isolation made her visit particularly significant for the whole country. Thousands of Spaniards waited to welcome Eva at the airport and others congregated at the Royal Palace of El Pardo. Once Eva landed in Spain, Generalisimo Franco welcomed her personally at the airport. As a display of welcome and gratitude, Franco awarded Eva with the Cross of Isabel the Catholic. Eva was invited to many receptions in Spain and had the opportunity to address the people. She apologized for Juan Peron's absence, but also reminded the people of her husband's good heart.

> People of Spain, I hand to you along with my own heart, the heart of my husband, the president of Argentina. I know my presence does not fulfill your wishes; you wished that General Peron had visited personally, General Peron, who during the bitter hours of your nation's history, while battling for the honor of Spain, announced to the world, with the courage of a well-born son, his full support for the mother [country]. I bring to you warm greetings from the workers of Argentina, from the cities and the countryside, hoarse from cheering for the dawning of a great people marching forward, our people, full of pride, as I feel proud of belonging to the Hispanic lineage.[26]

However, Eva's very exuberant, successful, and warm welcome in Spain was not repeated during the rest of her Rainbow Tour. Europe was emerging from the appalling aftermath of World War II and the bitterness against fascism was deep-seated. Argentina's trade agreement with Spain in 1946 provoked animosity with anti-fascist countries, which led to demonstrations and protests against the "Fascism of Peron and Franco" during the rest of her tour.[27] Peron's regime was already deemed as fascist regardless of Eva's visit to Spain. The visit just furthered this belief.

In Italy, Eva's reception was cool and she did not receive any special awards, as she had in Spain. She did have a meeting with Pope Pius XII and was given the "customary rosary bestowed as a token of an audience."[28] Eva then traveled to France and met with Charles De Gaulle, promising relief shipments. In addition, she met with President Vincent Auriol and the minister of foreign relations, George Bidault. During her visit in Paris, Eva signed a treaty that granted France a loan that allowed France to purchase wheat and meat in Argentina.[29] Eva retained her glamorous profile during her visit to France, which added to her reputation for extravagance:

> A reception was given at the Cercle d'Amerique Latine, in a large hall with a grand marble staircase. The entire diplomatic corps from Latin America filed before her, the women curtseying and walking back three paces when they greeted her. Evita was dressed extravagantly in a golden dress, skin tight and décolleté, with a long fish-tail train. She wore a gold veil over her blond hair, and an enormous jeweled necklace, long earrings to match, and three jeweled bracelets.[30]

The First Lady was then scheduled to visit Great Britain. Both the English and Argentine press had covered the anticipated visit and Eva was looking forward to seeing London for the first time. The Argentine press emphasized that their First Lady "was to be a guest of the royal family at home in London" while English reports clarified that "such a visit would be neither proper nor desirable."[31] While in France, Eva received news that the Royal Family was planning to be in Scotland during her visit to England and therefore could not receive her.[32] Feeling snubbed, Eva canceled her trip to England, claiming exhaustion.

Switzerland was the last country in Eva's itinerary before leaving Europe and was not the best end to her European tour. Many questioned Eva's visit to Switzerland. Some thought that the real purpose of her visit was to deposit money into Swiss bank accounts and that she organized the trip to conceal the deposit.[33] Nicholas Fraser explains that it is common for rich Argentines to deposit money in Swiss bank accounts, but he believed that there were better ways to conceal such transaction without going through the trouble of organizing a trip and meeting the Swiss foreign minister.[34] The true reasons for her trip to Switzerland remain unclear. The welcome Eva received in Switzerland was hostile and continued so throughout her time there. Protesters threw tomatoes at her during one of her visits and rocks were hurled at the vehicle that had been arranged to drive her around, smashing the windshield.[35]

Eva made little mention of her European tour in her autobiography, *In My Own Words*, but she did emphasize her eagerness to travel to Europe and learn about its social reform programs.[36] She was intent on exploring different social projects in the European countries she visited. To her disillusionment, Eva did not encounter strong social reform; instead, with few exceptions, Eva saw what Argentine social reform should *not* look like. "Social work in Europe is, in their vast majority, cold and poor."[37]

During her trip to Europe, Eva wrote a letter to Peron explaining her interpretation of European social work. She reminded Peron of how he wanted their social doctrine to be Christian, but in an innovative way.

> Our doctrine must be Christian and humanist but in a new way, in a way that the world has yet to know. The Christianity of our movement, just as you dream to attain it, was not what I saw in the European countries I visited . . . I will help you through my work. From now, I request your help.[38]

During her time in Europe, Eva noticed that everything on the European continent was about history, while she envisioned a new Argentina. As she visited cathedrals and ancient sites, she visualized the new homes and schools that she would start once she returned to Buenos Aires. Nevertheless, Eva was impressed with Paris fashion and when she returned to Latin America, she toned down her hairstyle for a more sophisticated brushed back French chignon, and began wearing more conservative but stylish Dior suits.[39]

As she wrote in her autobiography, Eva reflected on her experience in Europe and was proud of herself for accomplishing what once was a dream for Argentina. She asked her husband:

> "Did I fulfill the promise that I made to you when I returned from Europe, when I offered to help you attain the social work, the Christianity of your doctrine?" Peron replied, "I wouldn't have been able to do anything without your help. You have taught us to build with love."[40]

Charity and affection for the poor were key elements of Eva's work. She made it her goal to expand Peron's policies through her social work. Her commitment was first to her husband and then to the Argentine people. Eva added emotion; she gave Peron's policies a heart.

In this new democracy, Peron needed the support of the working class, the descamisados, and Evita had a natural and passionate connection to the poor to rally them in support of Peron.

HER WORK AS FIRST LADY

Eva occupied her days with work that promoted her husband and his policies. She understood that policies alone were meaningless without implementation. Consequently, she voluntarily made it her responsibility to guarantee that Peron's policies were put into action and she did so with generosity and love. Remembering her own childhood, her heart went out to children, women, and the elderly, while zealously advocating for the poor and working class.

> We cannot forget that I have always tried to think and feel as Peron thinks and feels. And his soul is too large to be understood by the mediocre. The wonderful greatness of his soul has definitely remained in my work and that can only be comprehended with generosity and not selfish mediocrity.[41]

Soon after Peron became president, Argentina's most deprived people began to congregate in front of the presidential residence in hopes of speaking with their advocate and now president. When Peron was secretary of labor, the workers had direct access to him and he invested time in listening to their appeals. But the newly elected president now had to attend to other responsibilities that came with his new position. Eva, in turn, saw the people's urgency to express their needs and gave them her attention. As a resolve to reach out to the people's needs, in an old garage in the presidential property, Eva prepared packages with food and clothing and distributed them to the people. Through this initiative, Eva received donations but most of the expenses were covered with her own funds. The poor thought of this garage as the store of delights (*Tienda de las Delicias*).[42]

By fall of 1946, Eva was given a suite of offices in the newly created Ministry of Labor. Eva occupied the office that Peron once had when he was secretary of labor and kept the "open door policy" that her husband had. The people knew where to find Eva and frequently visited her office. Eva was well aware of the problems that afflicted her people and she always had them in mind. She continued to meet individually with poor people, always giving them small amounts of money and helping them find housing and resolve other needs. The poor flocked to meet with her and she always made time for them, working well into the night.

It was not until she returned from her trip to Europe when Eva, overflowing with ideas, started the Maria Eva Duarte Social Help Foundation (later shortened to the Eva Peron Foundation). Through her foundation, she created homes for children and the elderly, schools, and hospitals.[43] Eva did not limit herself to providing basic needs; she went over and beyond to give the best and expected those who worked with her to emulate this same dedication.[44] In Eva's speeches and writing, she constantly stressed the importance of delivering assistance with excellence and mirrored this through her foundation. The foundation was supported by contributions in money and goods from unions, businesses, and the Confederacion General del Trabajo, as well as taxes on movie and lottery tickets and other sources.[45]

Eva established children's homes that were also schools. The focus was to provide the children with a safe place to live while assuring them a proper education. After witnessing how other charities assisted poor children, Eva knew what she would not allow her schools to practice. For instance, the Society of Beneficence was a charity run by 87 older wealthy women who exploited their employees and the children. The treatment children received by these women aggravated Eva. Their schools were focused on training instead of education. They had the children work long hours and the women employees were paid 45–90 pesos when the minimum wage was 120 pesos. The children from the orphanages roamed the streets of Buenos Aires with shaved heads, grubby uniforms, tin cans in hand, and signs that read, "Collection for Poor Children."[46] All of this took place while 95 percent of the charities' income went to the 87 wealthy ladies' salaries. These were the injustices that the rich inflicted on the poor that intensified Eva's animosity toward the wealthy. Even though she was rich herself, Eva did not shy away from the cry of the poor. Her long hours of work took on an Evangelistic demeanor and she became increasingly angry at the social injustices inflicted by the upper class:

> Sometimes I have wished my insults were slaps or lashes. I've wanted to hit people in the face to make them see, if only for a day, what I see each day I help the people.[47]

In contrast to other children's homes in the city of Buenos Aires, Eva assured that the children she helped were enjoying the best she could provide for them. The architecture, interior decoration, and furniture of the schools and homes were all of the highest quality. In her schools, students were not just a number, or rejected because they were poor. They were called by their names and cared for.[48] The home schools sheltered about 16,000 children at a time.[49] Once a child was admitted into the school, he or she received medical examinations twice a month. The homes had doctors, nurses, dentists, dietitians, and hygienists who attended to the health of the staff and children.[50] The home schools had both day children and resident children. The day children attended the school during the day and returned to their homes after school. The poorest children and those who lived too far to commute to school everyday were the resident children. All children received books, school supplies, clothing, shoes, and medical attention. In seven years, the Eva Foundation built 1,000 schools.[51]

One of the First Lady's projects intended for children was the Children's Football (soccer) Championship. This event mobilized all the children of each village in every province of the country.[52] Each village was asked to organize a team and select a name and color. After the teams were organized, the foundation supplied each team with the resources they needed to participate.[53] Through this project, hundreds of thousands of children had their first medical examination and put on their first pair of shoes.[54]

The Eva Foundation addressed the needs of people beginning from childhood to the elderly. She established the Amanda Allen Children's City and the President Peron Student City. The children's city was a safe home for children whose parents needed temporary child care. This complex operated similarly to the home schools, but was designed and constructed to simulate a city. It had the main features of a city: police stations, lodges, schools, city hall, gas stations, a shopping center, pharmacy, and so on. The children had the opportunity to take on the role of a public servant with the aim to "integrate marginalized children into society, prepare them for school and help them develop healthy relationships by means of play."[55] It had the capacity to house 450 children. The President Peron Student City was a complex for adolescent boys.[56] All the boys attended regular high schools with specialized programs in engineering, law, medicine, business, and so forth. After school, the boys would return to the complex and were tutored by professors. The goal was to "prepare future leaders from among the working classes by involving them in the decision making process of governing the student city."[57] The students also received scholarships to study abroad.

In addition to the homes Eva established for children and adolescents, she also founded various homes that attended the specific needs of women and senior citizens.[58] Some of these homes were:

- Temporary homes: These homes were for people who needed a place to live until they were able to solve personal problems such as housing, employment, or medical matters. Women with children were given priority. The foundation opened three temporary homes. In 1954, the homes sheltered 2,280 people; most were single mothers and people who needed medical care.
- Senior citizens' home: On March 11, 1949, Eva's Dialogue of the Rights of the Seniors was incorporated into the revised 1949 Constitution. This provided seniors rights that the foundation incorporated in its home. For instance, if a senior were abandoned or not cared for by family, then the state would be his or her caretaker. The seniors had the right to assistance, housing, food, clothing, health care, spiritual care, entertainment, work, tranquility, and respect.[59] The compounds had everything the seniors needed and provided different activities for them to participate in. Eva created a space for them to feel motivated to live instead of waiting for death to knock on their doors.[60] These homes offered assistance to 200 senior residents.
- General San Martin Home for Women Employees: This home was named after the prime leader of Argentina's independence. The home was created for young women who were from small towns and had traveled to the big city in search of work.

All of these programs clearly reflect the conditions that Eva herself had experienced and demonstrated her strong will to rectify the injustices that continued to agitate her sense of fairness in the world.

Eva's legacy went beyond her work and her ability to put good words together in a heartfelt speech. She modeled her beliefs through gestures of generosity and affection that often made people uncomfortable—even Peron. One day a man came up to Peron and kissed him and Peron told him not to be a pig. Peron said that this cry came from his heart "because being kissed by a man, I don't know . . . it disgusts me."[61] Eva went to the man and tried to make him feel better by apologizing for Peron's reaction, giving him a kiss. In another occasion, Eva's maid tried to wipe the First Lady's face with alcohol after she had kissed a man with syphilis. This really upset Eva so she took the bottle from her maid's hands and threw it against the wall.[62]

The First Lady genuinely treated those rejected by society as her equal and did not hesitate to confront those who tried to interrupt her. Fraser and Navarro recount the various times Eva hugged and kissed the homeless, touched open wounds, and kissed the leprous. After observing Eva at work, the Catholic poet José María Castiñeira de Dios said:

> There were human beings in that room with dirty clothes and they smelt very bad. Evita would place her fingers into their suppurating wounds for she was able to see the pain of all these people and feel it herself. She could touch the most terrible things with a Christian attitude that amazed me, kissing and letting herself be kissed. There was a girl whose lip was half eaten away with syphilis and when I saw that Evita was about to kiss her and tried to stop her, she said to me, "Do you know what it will mean when I kiss her?" . . . When I watched her for a few days, she said, "How are you, Oligarcha, are you beginning to understand how people suffer?" . . . It was hard for me not to love her when I had seen her at work, as though she thought I was not worthy of everything that went on in that room. Even when I had been there three months I felt I couldn't wash the feet of those people . . . I had had a sort of literacy perception of the people and the poor and she had given me a Christian one, thus allowing me to become a Christian in the profoundest sense.[63]

Eva described her social work as an attempt to attain social justice and acknowledged her inability to resolve all social inequalities. In the meantime, she was content with being a drop of love in a world that needed a shower of justice.[64]

> My work is in my heart, my poor humble heart, who does everything, yes everything, out of love. For my love to Peron. For the love of his shirtless ones . . . and why not say it? For all the shirtless ones in the world.[65]

In addition to her work with the poor and the creation of her foundation, Eva formed the Peronist Women's Party in July 1949. By 1952, the women's party had 500,000 members and thousands of branches around Argentina. While the party gave women a political role and Eva spoke about the injustices toward working women, the main focus was to garner support for Peron among women as voters.[66] In the running of the party and the foundation, Eva's authoritarian leadership style began to emerge:

> It soon became apparent that there was no room in the party for anyone who was not a staunch loyalist, and many of the more intelligent people around Evita, when they realized this to be the case, left. Those who stayed, but questioned her authority in any way, were often expelled.[67]

Through her foundation, Eva helped improve the lives of thousands of Argentines. Before her death in 1952 at the age of 33, the foundation managed 1,000 schools and hundreds of homes and hospitals. Remembering her own suffering as a child due to her poor circumstances, she poured her soul into finding retribution for those who are weak and victims of injustice. However, many of these initiatives began to deteriorate following her death. The conditions that led to the neglect of these facilities were primarily due to external events. Argentina's economy, considered one of the wealthiest during the early years of the twentieth century, started to sharply decline. The economy went from a per capita income of $700 in the early 1900s[68] to negative growth in the 1980s.[69] From 1929 to 1983, the Argentine economy grew at an annual rate of less than 1 percent per capita.[70] In spite of the economic circumstances that affected the accomplishments of her social programs and Eva's legacy, her unwavering principles remain a strong force in Argentine politics today. She enjoyed the powerful position she had attained in Argentina, but used her position and charismatic personality to address those who were not as fortunate, thus finding a personal remedy for her own sense of injustice that had been meted out to her, her mother, and her siblings by a wealthy father who had turned his back on them. She appeared determined not to turn her back on her people. Shortly before her death, the Argentine congress awarded Eva the title of Spiritual Leader of the Nation, to acknowledge her work. In addition to her work with the poor, she was acknowledged for her work as a strong advocate for women's rights and personified the achievements that a woman could accomplish.

It is difficult to assign her a management style or type in our typology structure. She was both dictatorial and controlling in her relentless implementation of social policy as she saw it. Nevertheless, she did not want this power that had been handed to her for itself, but to right the injustices she experienced in the daily life of the people. To some extent she was impulsive and narcissistic, but she managed even to use her glamor and the spotlight to serve her mission. When some members of congress suggested that she might dress more quietly, Evita responded:

> Look, they want to me beautiful. Poor people don't want someone to protect them who is old and dowdy. They all have their dreams about me and I don't want to let them down.[71]

To some extent, Evita was Argentina's Cinderella, rising from the ashes of poverty into the ruling class. But unlike the fairytale that simple ends with marriage to the prince, Eva demonstrated to the people what their Cinderella could do once she arrived in the palace. She was well aware that she had to preserve this dream.

She was also pragmatic in the sense that she had to always balance her relationship with her president husband in order to continue her social programs. Peron also needed her to build political support among workers and women, and in that sense they were a team. Nevertheless, toward the end of her life, she became so obsessively overtaken by her work, that she and her husband rarely saw each other. He would work all day, and Eva would work sometimes late into the night. She began to develop political ambitions through her successful women's party and before she became terminally ill, she began an effort to run for vice president, but had to abandon this due to her advancing cancer. She died so young at 33, so we will not know what she might have done had she been able to continue.

NOTES

1. *Time Magazine*, Interview, "Cristina Fernandez de Kirchner of Argentina," September 29, 2007, http://www.time.com/world/article/0,8599,1666879,00.html.
2. John Barnes, *Evita, First Lady: A Biography of Eva Peron* (New York: Grove Press, 1978), 15.
3. Nicholas Fraser and Marysa Navarro, *Evita: The Real Life of Eva Peron* (New York: Norton, 1996), 3.
4. Fraser and Navarro, *Evita*, 5.
5. Barnes, *Evita, First Lady*, 15.
6. Lesli J. Favor, *Eva Peron* (Singapore, SG: Marshall Cavandish Corporation, 2010), 27.
7. Fraser and Navarro, *Evita*, 11.
8. Ibid.
9. Ibid., 27.
10. Ibid., 33.
11. Ibid., 43.
12. Robert D. Crassweller, *Peron and the Enigmas of Argentina* (New York: W.W. Norton, 1987), 170–171.
13. Antonio Cazorla-Sanchez, *Franco: The Biography of the Myth* (Abingdon, Oxford: Routledge, 2013), 119.
14. Ibid., 120.
15. United Nations General Assembly Resolution 39, Relations of Members of the United Nations with Spain, December 8, 1946, http://daccess-ods.un.org/TMP/4676149.1894722.html.
16. Frazer and Navarro, 77.

17. Stanley G. Payne, *The Franco Regime, 1939–1975* (Madison, WI: University of Wisconsin Press, 1995), 361.
18. Enrique F. Widmann-Miguel, *Eva Peron en España*, 3rd ed. (Buenos Aires: Quisa, 2014), 3.
19. Omar G. Encarnación, *Spanish Politics: Democracy after Dictatorship* (Cambridge, UK: Polity Press, 2008), 27.
20. Michael Newton, *The Path to Tyranny: A History of Free Society's Descent into Tyranny* (Phoenix, AZ: Eleftheria Publishing, 2010), 181.
21. Ibid.
22. Stanley G. Payne, *A History of Fascism, 1914–1945* (Madison, WI: University of Wisconsin Press, 1995), 349.
23. Ibid.
24. Fraser and Navarro, *Evita*, 88.
25. Favor, *Eva Peron*, 65.
26. La Aventura de la Historia, "16 días con Evita Perón en España," May 30, 2013, http://www.laaventuradelahistoria.es/2013/05/30/16-dias-con-evita-peron-en-espana.html [translated from Spanish to English].
27. Julie Taylor, *Eva Perón: The Myths of a Woman* (Chicago: University of Chicago Press, 1979), 44.
28. Ibid.
29. Loris Zanatta, *Eva Peron: Una Biografía Política* (Buenos Aires: Sudamericana, 2011).
30. Fraser and Navarro, *Evita*, 98.
31. Ibid., 45.
32. Ibid.
33. Fraser and Navarro, *Evita*, 98–99.
34. Ibid., 99.
35. Taylor, *Eva* Perón, 45.
36. Eva Perón, *La Razon de mi Vida* (Buenos Aires: Peuser, 1951); reissued by Peuser in London and New York in 1953 and 1978, 164.
37. Ibid., 165.
38. Ibid.
39. Fraser and Navarro, *Evita*, 91.
40. Ibid.
41. Perón, *La Razon de mi Vida*, 170.
42. Ibid., 60–63.
43. Eva Peron Foundation, Legacy, http://www.evitaperon.org/evita_peron_legacy.htm.
44. Fraser and Navarro, *Evita*, 126.
45. Crassweller, *Peron and the Enigmas of Argentina*, 209–210.
46. Eva Peron Foundation. Legacy. Accessed November 1, 2013.
47. Fraser and Navarro, *Evita*, 126.
48. Ibid
49. Ibid
50. Ibid
51. Ibid
52. Ibid, 128.
53. Ibid
54. Taylor, *Eva* Perón, 49.

55. Eva Peron Foundation, Legacy.
56. The foundation did not have a student city for adolescent females; therefore, the girls stayed at the home schools.
57. Eva Peron Foundation, Legacy.
58. Ibid.
59. Monica Esti Rein, *Politics and Education in Argentina, 1946–1962* (Armonk, NY: M.E. Sharpe, 1998), 66.
60. Eva Peron Foundation, Legacy.
61. Fraser and Navarro, *Evita*, 127.
62. Ibid.
63. Ibid.
64. Perón, *La Razon de mi Vida*, 174–175.
65. Ibid., 175.
66. Fraser and Navarro, *Evita*, 107.
67. Ibid., 108.
68. William C. Smith, *Authoritarianism and the Crisis of the Argentine Political Economy* (Stanford, CA: Stanford University Press, 1989), 16.
69. Todd Landman, *Issues and Methods in Comparative Politics: An Introduction* (Abingdon: Oxford: Routledge, 2003), 88–89.
70. Smith, *Authoritarianism*, 16.
71. Fraser and Navarro, *Evita*, 82.

Part IV

FLEXIBLE AND PRAGMATIC TYPES

13

Angela Merkel: The Outsider Who Became Chancellor

Sean LaPides

How did a pastor's daughter and trained physicist from communist East Germany become the first female chancellor of a unified Federal Republic—from a conservative party? The rise from such unlikely origins to become the world's most powerful woman[1] makes Angela Merkel a rigorous case study for this theoretical model. Perhaps initial comparisons to Margaret Thatcher were inevitable; both became the first female head of state of a great power, both entered politics late, both took on the existing power base to lead conservative parties, and "both became party leader against the will of the establishment, largely because their parties were in crisis and longing for a new face."[2] Nonetheless, Mrs. Merkel quickly dispelled any notion of similarity to the *Iron Lady* through her entirely different personality archetype, leadership style, and decision making process.

RETURNING TO THE DDR

Angela Kasner was born in Hamburg on June 17, 1954. Her father, Horst Kasner, originally from Pankow, had just completed his seminary training within the Lutheran church. Herlind Kasner, Angela's mother, was a teacher from Hamburg. Despite the communist regime, Horst intended to return to the Deutsche Demokratische Republik (DDR; German Democratic Republic) to minister a congregation and raise his family. Reluctantly, Herlind agreed and the young family moved to her husband's home town outside of Berlin in the fall of 1954. The Soviet Union had already partitioned off its sector two years earlier, transforming it into a German state allied to Moscow. Despite the clear demarcation line, traffic between the two German states continued with few impediments until construction of the Berlin Wall closed off the entire DDR in August 1961. Angela could have been raised in the West—a fact that has generated speculation surrounding the impact of that decision on the future chancellor and the possible motivation for her father's choice. Merkel, however, always understood her father's desire to return:

> He came from Pankow, always with the intention of going back to the Soviet Zone as a pastor. Such decisions were not as rare as many seem to think, because that generation had the impression that the church, even in the Soviet-occupied territory needed to have a solid base. One could get a better education in the west and he did that, in Bielefeld and then in Hamburg as a vicar, where he met my mother and where, ultimately, I was born. But when I was six weeks old, we went back to the DDR.[3]

Only a year or so before the Kasner family arrived at their first post in the Soviet zone, the government had waged a brutal campaign against youth ministries of both the protestant and catholic churches. Horst Kasner's first assignment was to take over the youth ministry in Quitzow just as the state ramped up its harassment of religion. In some churches, clergy and flock alike found themselves condemned to penal servitude for longer sentences than nonreligious citizens.[4]

During this time, the Lutheran church in the DDR operated as a part of the Lutheran Church of Germany, centered in the West. However, no facilities existed in the East to train pastors and young seminarians could no longer travel to the West to study. Three years after arriving in Quitzow, the family moved to Templin, where they lived in a building that had once been a small college called Waldhof. The building offered sufficient room for the Kasner family, which now included Angela's younger brother. Their baby sister would arrive six years later. In the remaining space, Horst opened a seminary, complete with dormitory to train protestant pastors in liturgy and Lutheran theology. Adjacent to the school, an institution for the mentally and physically handicapped had existed for decades, known as the Stephanus-Stift mit Heim und Werkstatt für Behinderte. Until the end of World War II, they had been two separate institutions, but in the DDR, the state would only take care of the mentally handicapped it deemed trainable. The remainder, adults and children, were consigned to the church for care.[5] Growing up alongside the handicapped residents allowed young Angela to become comfortable with people who otherwise embarrassed visitors to Waldhof. Her mature perspective at such a young age shows the germination of the tolerance and open-mindedness Merkel has come to exhibit as chancellor:

> I first noticed that others had difficulties with disabled [people] when my classmates reacted [towards them] with fear whenever they came to visit me. It was

> always just normal for me. As a child, your abilities grow but only slowly beyond the abilities of disabled adults.[6]

By the mid-1950s, East Germany had already begun to reshape its society into the Soviet model. The economic aspects of Lenin-Stalinism—collectivization of agriculture, transferring the means of industrial production from private control to the state, and the redevelopment of military hardware—constituted the easiest transformation. The more cumbersome task was to rewrite a new historical meta-narrative in which the war had been a natural outgrowth of fascism and capitalism. Within this revised national identity, socialism became the savior of the German nation and the DDR the legitimate continuation of the German state. Like other totalitarian communist regimes, religion became an unwelcome nuisance that called for an allegiance above the party apparatus. The antagonism inherent between the East German state and the church calls into question why a clergyman would return to an environment hostile to his vocation, especially a pastor already physically in the West.

It seems clear that Kasner did not base his decision on ideological grounds or any particular sympathy to the DDR. The family often discussed politics at home and both parents did not hesitate to criticize the East German government. Yet, everyone knew that the State Secret Police (*Stasi*) could have been listening. Whenever controversial topics came up in the family living room, someone would take the telephone receiver off its cradle and lay it next to the phone, though Merkel concedes that she does not quite know why that would be an effective means of insuring privacy. The parents tended to focus on the failures of communist politics but in a purely theoretical way since there was no action they could take to change it. They remained much less concerned about the economic aspects of the DDR. Conversely, Merkel came to the conclusion quite young that, on economic grounds alone, the DDR could not sustain itself forever. Yet, despite the obvious proscriptions and the seeming omniscience of the *Stasi*, the family felt no particular sense of oppression at home. "Naturally, there were a few topics one would rather discuss in the woods, for instance, when a friend was in some kind of trouble or when it concerned escape plans . . . we had simply learned to live with it."[7]

Far from a communist ideologue, pastor Kasner represents, nonetheless, the dichotomous aspect of the chancellor's upbringing and a rudiment of her psychology. He declined a job offer from the *Stasi* yet became a member of the *Weißenseer Arbeitskreis*, a brotherhood of leftist Lutheran clergy in DDR, which proved to be heavily influenced by the security ministry. After the war, the Church in Germany was governed by Bishop Dibelius, whom the brotherhood considered to be tainted by a nationalistic, Western orientation and enjoyed a privileged relationship with the government of the

Federal Republic of Germany. The theology of the *Arbeitskreis* argued that since the love of God extended to all mankind, the work of the church should benefit all, believers and nonbelievers alike.[8] This belief system set the group in direct opposition to church leaders in the West but in congruence with the state leaders in the DDR and allowed them to coexist with the totalitarian regime. After reunification, the significant influence of the *Stasi* on the group became clear. Kasner's work with the brotherhood and its connection to the communist state seems inconsistent with a pacifist who never chose to vote. Kasner believed that the "greater good" concept in socialism was consistent with the work of the church. His "Church in Socialism" approach was intellectual and pragmatic; he felt it should be grounded in the reality of life in the DDR and not remain on the sidelines, mired in religious dogma.[9] On the question of her father's sympathetic view of socialism and the DDR, Merkel offered a measured response, which illustrates his pragmatism and foreshadows her own:

> There were various phases. He had long since come to terms with a divided Germany and did not believe reunification would occur within his lifetime. He said it didn't make any sense to [operate] as though we were one church with one structure. He worked with the *Weißenseer Arbeitskreis* ... but also lived through many disappointments. A turning point [in his belief in the communist regime] came in 1968 when the Russians marched into Czechoslovakia.[10]

GROWING UP AT WALDHOF

As a preschooler, Angela Kasner displayed a remarkable verbal aptitude but her physical coordination was underdeveloped for her age. At three, she could shift indifferently between the Hamburg and Berlin dialects (of her mother's and father's families, respectively), but could not manage to walk down a flight of stairs by herself.[11] Merkel claims she learned to appreciate clarity of logic in debate from her father, and from her mother, she learned to improvise in daily life and "to make eight portions of food out of four, when necessary."[12] Others recall Horst's logical mind as well. His former colleague at the pastoral college, and later mayor of Templin, found the pastor to be a "niche thinker"—one who could critically argue a point but who "knew where the boundaries are in order not to come into conflict with the state." Angela's teachers and classmates remember him as an intellectual power as well, who was himself "a great listener" but "when he talked, everyone would stop and listen to him." Angela's former math teacher recalled the family living room lined with books. He found that pastor Kasner "exuded authority, understood human nature, and knew a great deal."[13]

Those statements are more telling than they appear. As Merkel's psychological profile emerges, we begin to see the pattern of dichotomies I alluded to previously—born in the free West, raised in the communist East; high verbal, low physical prowess. Her father exemplifies that pattern both in his person and in the psychological imprint he left on his daughter. For example, he became the pastor who returned to an unfriendly political environment and compromised the structure of the church for a tidy accommodation with the antagonistic regime. The guardian of the flock who conferred sympathy on parishioners was also a distant intellectual who required perfection from his children and a critical thinker who hesitated to criticize the state. Merkel's style as head of state reflects the imprint of her father's dualities: "she demands fair and perfect policy solutions but usually in a very cold manner."[14]

In other aspects, Angela Merkel had a typical childhood for her generation. She and her siblings had a strict upbringing in which failure to obey rules would result in punishments ranging from loss of allowance to grounding, and only occasionally a spanking. She enjoyed getting together with friends to listen to records but while "most of her contemporaries liked the Rolling Stones, she preferred to dance to the Beatles," with Paul McCartney a personal favorite. One of her favorite childhood memories was going into the forest with her father to chop down a Christmas tree. As a kid, apple juice was rationed so whenever there was enough for her to drink her fill, it was like a dream come true.[15] However, versions of the young Merkel vary depending upon the source. The Kasners admonished their children not to be confrontational with teachers; to be neither provoking nor antagonizing. Teachers, therefore, invariably remember a diligent student, always prepared and who did not have the capacity for typical schoolgirl silliness. Her mathematics teacher found her to be hardworking but not overly ambitious, and displaying no real leadership talent. He has expressed surprise that she ultimately went into politics. His views seem to echo a common theme among the adults in Merkel's adolescence. Her classmates, on the other hand, consistently describe in Merkel a class leader, a social animal who was a real *Grupenmensch* (people person) within the FDJ—Freie Deutsche Jugend—the communist youth organization. Her fellow teens described her as the classmate willing to help someone with an assignment or organize a party. One friend insists she was helpful but headstrong and her motto was "show no incompetence!"[16]

Once again, the conflicting versions of the youthful Angela Merkel repeat the duality pattern in her psychological profile. We find a young woman of above-average intellect whose peers regarded her as a natural leader. Yet, she hid those traits from other adults in order to avoid political complications due to her father's job. More importantly, she had no *need* to display her ambitions, her leadership skills, or her desire to urge her friends to be their very best. She also did not exhibit the adolescent need for adult approval. The psychological imprint remaining in the adult is a person with healthy self-esteem and low ego-defensiveness.

A FATHER'S PSYCHOLOGICAL IMPRINT

The middle-aged Angela Merkel has a complex relationship with her father. Though not exactly estranged, they maintain a distance. Biographers and journalists have noted that in interviews, Merkel almost exclusively mentions her mother and only discusses her father when pressed by specific questions. Though Merkel claims that the end of the "Prague Spring" soured her father's view of socialism, Horst Kasner grew "much closer to the socialist state than was previously known . . . [and] by the beginning of the Seventies, he had opened an increasingly intensive cooperation with the organs of state."[17] Pastor Kasner had participated in other events during the mid-1960s, which have only recently come to light, actions on Kasner's part that affirm the conflicting psychological dichotomies I have discussed previously. In 1966, the Berlin-Brandenburg Synod voted a West German pastor as bishop and wanted to merge with the West Berlin Bishopric. According to an SED (the East German Communist Party) document, Kasner and two other theologians undermined the synod on instructions from the East German government, specifically, the Office of Clerical Affairs and the Ministry for State Security.[18] So, the conflicting images of Horst Kasner consist of a pastor who criticized the West and the DDR publicly and privately, admonished his children to remain unseen by teachers but encouraged them to take part in a church confirmation, and finessed the boundaries of state tolerance to rebuild a forbidden youth ministry but undermined a synod on behalf of the communist regime.

In 1992, the first year Angela Merkel served as a member of Helmut Kohl's cabinet, Kasner wrote a guest editorial in the newspaper of the Lutheran Church of Berlin-Brandenburg. The commentary presents a scathing rejection of his daughter's party, the Christian Democratic Union (CDU), and its policies. He warned that the reunited Germany would face a "dictatorship of party politics." Again in 1994, he railed against the limited intellect of politicians. True to form, however, he commented in 2000 "anyone could see Angela doesn't speak from the bowels like all the others—she's tip top." As head of the party, the CDU threw Merkel a 50th birthday celebration in 2004. Her mother and two siblings attended—her father did not.[19]

REUNIFICATION AND A RADICAL CAREER CHANGE

As a physicist, Merkel had shown no inclination toward politics. In the heady days following the fall of the Berlin Wall, Merkel still had no intention of changing professions. She soon realized that a new era had begun and new people would be needed; and she wanted to become a member of one of the new political parties, concluding that these groups would become politically very powerful.[20] She took a long look at the Social Democratic Party

(SPD) but since her political outlook favors the individual over the collective, she decided the SPD "had nothing for her." Merkel's belief in a social market economy led her to *Demokratische Aufbruch* (Democratic Awakening). Its chaotic, "uncoordinated" atmosphere appealed to her.[21] Internal dissent within *Demokratische Aufbruch* forced Merkel to reappraise her politics once more and in 1990, she became a member of the (East German) CDU. In March of that year, just months prior to reunification, the DDR held its first free election since the inception of the East German state and the last as an independent country. Thus was born the political career of Angela Merkel. She stood as the CDU candidate for Mecklenburg-Vorpommern and was elected to the *Volkskammer* (People's Chamber), the unicameral legislature of the former DDR. When Lothar de Maizière became prime minister, Merkel became the party's deputy spokeswoman for the new government. Following reunification, her seat was transferred to the Bundestag in Bonn, where she became an acolyte of Helmut Kohl. Under his tutelage, she experienced her meteoric rise through the party ranks, holding cabinet positions as federal minister for women and youth (1991–1994) and federal minister for the environment, conservation, and nuclear safety (1994–1998). As political roads go, hers was not especially rocky, largely due to Kohl's mentorship. Her first real test came in 1995, when she attempted to push through an initiative designed to reduce smog during the summer driving months. That year in particular saw a spike in Ozone levels. As environmental minister, Merkel found herself under extraordinary pressure from both the public and the political opposition to take substantive action. She cared passionately for the environment and saw this initiative as "innovative—something the bureaucrats should attempt more often."[22] Though working against a time limit, Merkel did her due diligence with party and coalition leaders, gaining consensus with the minister of transport, Matthias Wissmann (CDU), and the minister of economics, Günter Rexrodt (FDP [Free Democratic Party]). However, when the discussion came up in the cabinet meeting, Merkel found herself at odds with both department heads, who openly criticized her plan as controversial, unworkable, and damaging to the economy.[23] Kohl asked whether she had gained the concurrence of the CSU (Michael Glos) and the FDP (Hermann Otto Solms) and when she had not, decided to table the discussion for further debate. Merkel felt betrayed by her cabinet colleagues:

> [Glos and Solms] were essentially the only ones I hadn't talked with. I felt blind-sided. I had spoken at length with the Chancellery but not with the Chancellor himself because I didn't want to bother him. Now I was left with the sinking realization that it would no longer be possible to pass an initiative by summer. In such a situation, I think a man might have screamed; I burst into tears.[24]

Despite the setback, she went on to become the general secretary of the CDU in 1998—with a political career spanning a mere eight years. This role confronted Merkel with her first crisis of power.

A SHORT ROAD TO POWER

In addition to reunification, 1990 brought reform of the political donation system. The CDU pushed through legislation designed to bring greater accountability and transparency by requiring parties to disclose any donation greater than DM 20,000. In November 1999, the treasurer for the Christian Democratic Union, Walther Leisler Kiep, was arrested for tax evasion regarding a 1991 donation of DM 1 million by an arms lobbyist named Karlheinz Schreiber. The money never appeared in CDU account disclosures. As details emerged, "it became clear that the CDU had accepted illegal donations throughout the 1990s and had developed a money laundering system to deal with them."[25] At the time of Kiep's arrest, Helmut Kohl had already lost his reelection bid to Gerhard Schröder and as former chancellor, assumed the role of honorary chairman of the CDU. On November 30, Kohl admitted to the existence of secret accounts, which he had used for the party at his discretion, and stepped down as honorary chairman. He denied that he had ever personally benefited from the illegal slush fund. His hand-picked successor as party chairman, Wolfgang Schäuble, insisted that he knew little of these "accounting maneuvers," since "Helmut Kohl led the party in a patriarchal way, [which] meant that the rules were not adhered to exactly in the way we might want today."[26] The Bundestag questioned Schäuble and he denied ever having accepted a donation personally from the arms lobbyist. Toward the end of December, Merkel discovered that Schäuble had lied to the Bundestag. She concluded that salvation of the party—and presumably her own career—would require bold action. On December 22, Angela Merkel publicly turned on her former mentor and his anointed successor. In her official capacity as general secretary of the CDU, she wrote an editorial piece in the *Frankfurter Allgemeine Zeitung*, in which she admitted that despite his 25 years of extraordinary service to Germany and the CDU, Kohl had brought shame onto his party. Merkel declared that "this tragedy" had ended the Kohl era:

> The party has a soul. So for us, there can be no alternative "explanations for mistakes" and no "preserving our heritage." When it comes to the image of Helmut Kohl, his legacy and the CDU are inextricably linked. So only upon the fundamental truth can an accurate historical picture emerge. Only upon the fundamental truth can we rebuild [for] the future. Helmut Kohl must accept this realization and so must we. Only then can we cease to be vulnerable to attack at every new report of alleged donations by those who only wish

> to use [Kohl's] actions to cripple the CDU. . . . It falls to those of us who remain responsible for the party to chart a new course into the future. This year, we won [local] elections neither because of, nor despite Helmut Kohl. We won . . . due to our campaign against Gerhard Schröder's chaotic policies. In the future, the party will have to learn to run, to trust itself, and to confront its political enemies without its old work horse, as Kohl liked to call himself. . . . This process will not be painless . . . our party will have changed but at the crux we will remain the same—with our strong core values, our self-confidence, and our proud tradition . . . with a plan for the future in the post-Kohl era.[27]

Within weeks, Schäuble admitted to having received the unreported donation and resigned as party chairman. Kohl refused to believe that Merkel had written the piece without Schäuble's knowledge, which not only destroyed the relationship between the two men but also sparked a vicious public campaign by each against the other. Thus with a stroke of the pen, Merkel succeeded in distancing herself from her own party's scandal and framing herself as the only one who could offer the CDU a fresh start. Suddenly, no one stood between her and the party chairmanship. There can be no doubt that she knew what she hoped to accomplish, and for the autocratic Kohl, this must have been quite an unbearable humiliation.[28] In Merkel's own words, "the only thing, quite rightly, that Kohl—or any party chairman—could not abide was personal disloyalty. . . . I had to [lead the fight] to save the future of the CDU."[29]

At age 46, Angela Merkel became the first female chairman of the CDU and stood to become the first *Bundeskanzlerin* (female chancellor). To the German electorate, this "fresh face" was still a mystery with the public persona still very much in development. Pundits and voters alternatively described Merkel as honest and mousey; lame and sharp-as-a-tack; arrogant and self-confident. When asked about her various public monikers—most of which would seem to be mutually exclusive—Merkel responded that she liked being "an enigma [because] it heightened the suspense. . . . I am multifaceted . . . yesterday I was mousey, today I am brutal and heartless."[30] Decades after she left school, we see the dichotomous pattern within her personality that I noted from her adolescence. This duality had served her well in her youth by allowing friends and foe alike to project onto Merkel while allowing her to remain noncommittal. Therefore, in the wake of the CDU scandal, this amalgam of contradicting adjectives likely contributed more to her rise to power than her policy positions. In fact, no one knew quite what her policy positions were. As an outsider from the former East, she had no inherent power base within the party apparatus. Instead, a growing number of disillusioned (mostly younger) conservative MPs "rallied to her cause—not because of what she [stood] for, but because she is 'convincing' as a person."[31]

Merkel injected a type of "libertarian" conservatism into the party. For example, even as minister for women and youth, her talk of family values centered on people caring for one another rather than children per se, or the institution of marriage. Ulrich Merkel was actually her first husband. They married quickly at age 23 "for a chance to get jobs and an apartment in the same city, which was only possible if one were married."[32] Though the marriage only lasted seven years, she kept his name professionally. For many years, she had lived with long-term partner, Dr. Joachim Sauerher, only marrying him in December 1998. This type of "liberalism" caused some consternation among the right-wing members of the CDU but they were not able to block her accession.[33]

Her tenure prior to becoming chancellor offers a foreshadow of her leadership style, as well as a glimpse into her personality. At the CDU/CSU party conference in April 2000, she made her bid to become party chairman in the wake of Schäuble's departure. Her speech effectively blended the same criticism of the party scandal that she leveled at Kohl, with the optimistic message of a party confident in its vision. In the remarks lies the ever-present duality of her personality—at once chastising for the party's failure, yet uplifting for the party's resilience "following the now famous breach of our own party rules. ... We are the party for the rule of law, like no other ... who, if not we, can meet the challenges of our time?"[34] She won her bid to become party chairman with more than 95 percent of the delegate votes. Within her first 100 days as leader of the CDU, an interviewer noted her relatively short career in politics and asked if she were particularly ambitious. She responded, with a politician's flourish, that she was

> "not unambitious" ... [and] would otherwise have sought a different job. ... A politician must be comfortable with power. He must be ambitious. He must be able to place demands on himself. ... I believe I am capable of fighting but I don't engage in every struggle. Does the fight promise success? Are there sufficient resources? One can't engage in a fight on all fronts. Some battles you have to delegate and others you have to let go.[35]

These remarks show a personality that is cognizant of the trappings of power but not dictated by them. She had already displayed her ambition and willingness to fight when she publicly ousted Kohl. Here, she proves that her mettle is not purely pugnacious for the sake of ambition, but rather centered on the tactical value of any given battle. This stratagem is indicative of the pragmatism she would later imbue in her chancellery, preferring to give ground to opponents rather than squandering resources on ideological squabbles that have little chance of prevailing. The same interview revealed hints of Merkel's insecurity. She stated how she sometimes feels queasy when faced with all the people she encounters, who feel as though they know all about her, but whom she does not know at all. She finds the resulting sense of imbalance "unsettling."[36] There is definitely a vulnerability about Angela Merkel that the *Iron Lady* Thatcher never revealed, from her tears over frustration within the cabinet dynamic to these articulated fears surrounding the enormity of her position.

In 2004, the CDU party chief celebrated her 50th birthday—16 months before becoming chancellor. In an interview with the popular magazine *BUNTE,* reporter Patricia Riekel noted how much more attractive and charming Angela Merkel is in person than she appears on television, where she sometimes comes across as cold. In focus groups at the time, 71 percent of respondents had rated her assertiveness as "high," while only 40 percent found her "sympathetic." Merkel appeared untroubled:

> At the beginning of my political career, I was, for many people, a blank slate, onto which, they could project their hopes and wishes. Thus I was once the "Queen of Hearts." In the interim, my name has become synonymous with hard, if not unpopular decisions. . . . According to research analysts, in the last couple of years, what I have lost in "sympathy," I have gained in "assertiveness."[37]

The piece offers little in terms of policy but it presents a valuable insight into the future chancellor's personality traits. Merkel had indeed been a "blank slate" but as I have argued, she likely nurtured the perception through her chameleon-like ability to utilize the dichotomies that make up her past and her very personality, to effectively become whatever a situation necessitated and minimize those aspects of herself that would detract from it. This is a trait she clearly shares with her father. In these remarks, she comes across as a leader, unafraid to make tough choices, and suggests that voters had already accepted this persona. But her comments elsewhere in the piece belie the blasé tone of the response. Some claim that ousting party officials or firing staff was never particularly stressful for the cold CDU chairperson. Merkel, however, insists these are the most difficult decisions and that they bring her considerable sadness. Yet, neither could she afford to appear too emotional because it would "likely be seen as crocodile tears." She is "astounded" when the press describes her as cold and calculating; Merkel sees herself as a "happy person, quick with a joke, an eternal optimist." She claims to be more comfortable with herself at 50 than in her youth, when she would frequently berate herself for anything she could not do that others could do better. She once aspired to be a figure skater and wasted years under the delusion that it might be possible—despite her glaring deficiencies in sports.

Merkel also addresses the question of women and power—the choices women must make that men need not. For instance, male leaders routinely opt for an entourage, but Merkel had to learn to utilize such accoutrements of power. In her earliest political roles, she turned up for meetings alone but quickly discovered the usefulness of knowledgeable staff in presenting a professional demeanor. Men worry little about their physical appearance, but like Thatcher, Merkel ultimately concluded that "appearance is important—[both] hair and makeup. In practice, it can't really be any other way if you don't want to look like a feather duster."[38]

The emerging picture presents a leader who is ambitious but sometimes ill at ease with ambition. It shows an image of a woman, who publically displays self-confidence—sometimes to the point of seeming arrogant and cold—but who is also plagued by self-doubt. Unlike the authoritarian Kohl, Merkel is willing to question herself, to allow personal doubts to force introspection. It points to a flexible-pragmatic leadership style and a personality willing to learn on the job. The result is a decision making process that has withstood public scrutiny as well as criticism from the political opposition.

DIE KANZLERIN (THE CHANCELLOR)

Governing coalitions are a fact of political life in postwar Germany. Following decades as the opposition party, the CDU regained power in the 1980s by forming a coalition with the FDP and Helmut Kohl became the new chancellor in 1982. Merkel's ascension to the chancellery in 2005 began auspiciously with her CDU bruising Schröder's SDP in state elections. In the September 2005 federal elections, the CDU/CSU and governing SPD received the largest percentage of votes but neither garnered enough to form a government. The resulting political stalemate forced the SDP and CDU/CSU into "an awkward embrace. . . . The SDP insisted that Mr. Schröder remain at the head of the government, while the CDU/CSU did not even want to start real negotiations until he was pushed aside and Ms Merkel had been accepted as the new chancellor."[39] After weeks of negotiation, the parties reached an agreement that forced Schröder to step down and allowed Angela Merkel to ascend as chancellor in Germany's second "Grand Coalition" since World War II.

The fragile nature of the "right-left" coalition would require finesse and political acumen if Merkel were to enact any of her political agenda. Three weeks before the Bundestag officially elected her chancellor, two key players in her coalition resigned. Many critics and observers wondered whether the partnership would implode, forcing new elections. Others felt that she had been forced to concede too much for her coveted prize: though she would be chancellor, 8 of 16 cabinet posts went to the SDP, including the powerful foreign affairs, labor, and finance ministries.[40] Nonetheless, she managed to complete the coalition by the November deadline. In forging the partnership, Merkel exhibited those flexible-pragmatic leadership skills that surprised her critics, delighted voters, and won her reelection in 2009 with the more politically homogenous FDP as a coalition partner.

Angela Merkel epitomizes the flexible-pragmatic leader within this theoretical model. Her ascendance to power in the first place required a flexible style not present in her immediate predecessors. Schröder had been prone to emotional outbursts and Kohl ran his governing "system" with an authoritarian intolerance of disobedient subordinates. Merkel, conversely, displayed her tolerance for alternative views in her willingness to concede the most powerful cabinet positions to the junior partner. It clearly indicates her capacity to see a larger goal and a longer-term plan, without losing focus on her basic governing structure. She never saw this pragmatism as weakness. Yet, her compromises angered members of her own party since they negated the basis of the CDU platform: she scrapped her intent to extend the working lives of nuclear power plants, reversed a planned tax cut for the wealthiest earners and replaced it with a 3 percent tax surcharge, and acquiesced on giving greater autonomy in collective bargaining to local factories.[41] Through her pragmatic willingness to accept the partner's alternative agenda, she succeeded in putting a government together when most thought it impossible—between political parties from antipodal ends of the political spectrum. Voters did not see her pragmatic acquiescence as weakness either. Instead, it sowed the seeds for a more formidable reelection with a greater mandate and a more like-minded coalition partner.

Merkel's adult personality with its (often) mutually exclusive dualities derives in large part from the dichotomies she experienced as a child: a pastor's daughter in an atheist country; a father who spoke against certain state policies but worked with the secret police (*Stasi*); a father who offered solace to the flock but only harsh expectations to his children; a family that insisted on baptizing her, yet also compelled her to join the communist youth organization. She was the social animal to her friends, organizing get-togethers, yet her teachers saw in her no leadership capacity and no ambition. Thus, the middle-aged Merkel heads a center-right party but believes strongly in social democracy and tight regulation of financial markets. She is ambitious and comfortable with power but also feels vulnerable and she "must legitimize [herself] more strongly [than other politicians]."[42] From her father she gets her respect for rules; for example, she hates to be late, considering it to be the height of rudeness.[43] From her mother she gets her pragmatism (making food for eight out of portions for four). From her father she gets her intellectual curiosity and a pastor's capacity for empathy. From her mother she gets her humor. One parent is Eastern, the other Western. And Merkel feels like an outsider in both realms, which "feeds her unwavering insecurity, her dearth of situational intuition."[44]

This recurring theme of duality within her personality is likely the key ingredient in shaping the chancellor's leadership and management style.

Her ability to take on whatever the person across the table needs her to be is a direct result of her dichotomous persona. All her life, she has become a "blank slate" whenever necessary. The *Economist* described her as "neither charismatic, nor flashily intellectual, nor domineering . . . [and in] temperament, [t]he opposite of . . . Sarkozy."[45] Embedded in this apt description is a head of state who affectively subsumes her own ego for the sake of the negotiation—in domestic and foreign affairs.

This substantiates a correlation between her personality and her leadership style. In this theoretical model, we also hypothesize that particular leadership styles will correlate with particular management styles; for example, the flexible-pragmatic leader will opt for the collegial/consensus-building management style. Angela Merkel bears out the concept.

Once in office, the new chancellor implemented the collegial management style she had developed in the Bundestag while trying to enact environmental legislation. In fact, the nature of the Grand Coalition privileged her flexible-pragmatic leadership. On the seventh floor of the chancellery, there is no colloquy and "Merkel's closest circle of staff are as structured as she: logical, business-like, pragmatic, and extraordinarily discreet and loyal."[46]

Her natural curiosity and management style were highly conducive to her work as a scientist, which often necessitated collaboration with colleagues. But her propensity to understand alternative viewpoints has arguably engendered her success abroad. Immediately, she picked up the mantle of European unity begun by Helmut Kohl. At a summit in 2007, the fate of the constitution of the European Union hung in the balance. The Poles threatened to scupper the effort and all eyes were on Merkel as term president of the European Council. With only two years' tenure in office, she had become a leading figure in European diplomacy. Her success in forging a compromise on climate change with both the EU and the recalcitrant Bush administration made her a superstar, especially in Germany. Following the summit, even her detractors at home and abroad backhandedly conceded, "she doesn't do so badly."[47] As one foreign diplomat expounded, "she has basically been very lucky; she leads a powerful country, she has a very affective advisory apparatus, and she filled a power vacuum when her country needed it. Nothing more."[48] This flippant dismissal of her diplomatic success belies the strengths she brings in terms of her leadership. Merkel ultimately prevailed in ratifying the EU Constitution because she understood that "conflating strength with pomposity or undiplomatic behavior" was not always the path to victory. Those capable of "compromise without losing sight of the objective"[49] will find success. The German press described her tactics as "so unerringly does she influence events, that it seems afterwards as though things were just automatically moving in the right direction."[50] Merkel's capacity for such statesmanship without self-aggrandizement speaks to the "flexible-pragmatic" leader in Krasno's theory.

She would clearly need a level of self-esteem sufficient to allow her to accomplish the end goal without letting everyone know what part she played in it. Absent the empathy to appreciate an alternative worldview, she could not have allowed potential dissenters to the EU Constitution to vent their positions without becoming defensive of her own. As journalist Margaret Heckel noted, "Merkel would never stake out a negotiating position that was unacceptable to the other. Instead she prefers to pursue innumerable discussions beforehand to sound out how far the opponent is capable of moving and what would be doable."[51]

International relations brings her greater personal satisfaction than domestic politics, even though "successes are harder to come by."[52] The scope of the international system, with its multiple actors and layered complexity, "fascinates the scientist in Merkel."[53] She prefers direct conversation to written communication such that when she wishes to articulate or clarify her official position, interviews are her method of choice.[54] During her simultaneous presidencies of the G8 and the European Council, she developed a method of collecting the pieces of information that make up the international "puzzle." She visited every European and the most important non-European heads of state. Whenever she traveled to a country for the first time, her staff prepared a psychographic portrait of the state leader. She then gleaned from each conversation a portion of the larger, holistic view of the world and Germany's place in it. Though state leaders often visit Berlin, "Merkel finds it far better to observe them in their homeland, how they tick, and what they really mean when they talk."[55] When travel is not viable, Merkel must rely, like all state leaders, on conference calls. With some, they stick to prearranged talking points; with others, they start with an agenda and digress off script occasionally. But about a dozen state leaders fit into a third category. This elusive club comprises presidents and prime ministers who freely engage in a meaningful exchange of thoughts and opinions; who will occasionally make a joke or interrupt each other. Some of these leaders even exchange text messages with the chancellor. Nonetheless, Merkel enjoys the face-to-face contact with other heads of state at international summits. Ever since her school days, Angela Merkel has to be the best at whatever she does and international summits give her an ego boost. She reads the dossiers of other leaders that her staff prepares so that she can be better informed than her colleagues.[56] Jose Manuel Barroso, president of the European Commission, remarked that when Merkel attends a summit, she personally engages in bilateral discussions rather than delegating to subordinates. Moreover,

> she is a scientist. She accords herself neither like a man, nor like the typical head of a large country. Many heads of state like grandiose plans and principles but Merkel likes the details. I am always surprised at how informed she is on the details. She bargains hard but remains authoritative.[57]

Barroso's remarks summarize the link between Merkel's flexible-pragmatic archetype and her personality, both reflected in her penchant for diplomacy. She relies on the tolerance and sensitivity she learned as a child, living among the physically and mentally handicapped. The same curiosity that propelled her into theoretical physics imparts a genuine desire to learn the nuances of her colleagues' personas and belief systems—and objectify her own *disbelief* system by "observing colleagues in their natural habitats." Unlike the more rigid Helmut Kohl or Gerhard Schröder, she remains open to ideas from any quarter, no matter the point on the political spectrum from which they originate. The nature of foreign affairs allows a head of state in most political systems greater latitude than that exists in domestic politics. So, in order to examine her management style, we must interject an international issue with a tangible domestic component. The banking crisis in 2008 provides an excellent starting point.

The financial collapse of 2008 became Merkel's second crisis of power after ousting Kohl—and her first as chancellor. Both of her immediate predecessors, Kohl and Schröder, governed with an authoritarian style, in coalitions that were far less fragile than Merkel's. Consequently, their cabinets tended to rubberstamp government policies with little or no discussion. Both chancellors also led their cabinet meetings without a detailed knowledge of legislative content. Conversely, Merkel fosters actual debate on issues, encourages open discussion, and tries to find consensus. Her cabinet is "often surprised how intensively she studie[s] files, including advisory positions."[58] This is not the first reference to Merkel and her facility with detail. One of the traits in Krasno's authoritarian archetype is an obsession with detail. We could cite this as overlapping typologies, but in Merkel's case, this speaks more to personality than leadership style. It is the scientific personality, propelled by natural curiosity to assimilate vast amounts of data, including details. The fact that Merkel allows open debate and works toward consensus speaks directly to her collegial management style.

By the end of 2008, bank bailouts around the world became inevitable. Merkel knew that some infusion would be necessary but her primary focus was on the causes of the crisis. Within her cabinet, she floated the idea of a one-time bailout and "want[ed] to hear her advisors' positions. Nonetheless, she [knew] that she had already decided but . . . consider[ed] it very important to come to a consensus for a step of this magnitude."[59] During those long workdays as the crisis progressed, the chancellor stopped by her chief of staff's office and asked if she would like to join Merkel for a bowl of soup, which they shared over Merkel's worktable.[60] Though she demands a great deal of her staff, formal hierarchies are not part of her management style. As the G20 met for the summit in Washington in November 2008, it was important to Merkel that leaders come to a consensus on the cause of the crisis because she felt that, otherwise, they would be merely treating the symptoms.[61] Her concerns are telling since they are consistent with the collegial nature with which she interacts with both her subordinates and her counterparts around the world. Consensus for Merkel confers legitimacy on legislation as well as bilateral agreements. However, her reliance on consensus, especially in the international arena, is not merely a function of political pragmatism. The euro crisis has long since superseded the financial crisis of 2008. And Germany has become, arguably, the most powerful country in Europe. Yet the Germans have shown a discouraging lack of political will to become Europe's hegemon. Angela Merkel has never shied away from the demands of leadership, but in terms of the current crisis, she "pandered to Germans' small-country mentality and their belief that responsibility for fixing the euro lies elsewhere. The one country with the capacity to lay out a strategic vision for the single currency's future is unwilling to do so." Germany's discomfort with an international leadership role is entirely predicated on its twentieth-century history and its fear of instability.[62] Merkel, therefore, repeatedly insisted on austerity for southern European recipients of bailout funds, even in the face of empirical evidence that it may slow growth rather than spur recovery. This reluctance and the novelty of Germany's position in the twenty-first century partially explain her collegial style and adherence to consensus. Here, the cultural memory of the past collides with a geopolitical situation that has confronted no other chancellor since the founding of the Federal Republic.

Another explanation for her collegial style rests with her own empiricism. In 2009, healthcare reform was a prominent issue among all parties. Merkel's CDU/CSU wanted to inject market competition and user-paid premiums into Germany's healthcare system. The SPD, however, feared a lump-sum approach that Merkel had articulated years before as a party operative. She made this reform a top priority and declared that she would guide the efforts personally. Merkel pursued a top–down approach, which she hammered out with SPD minister for health, Ulla Schmidt. Her early stake in the legislation and her personal stamp on it placed her prestige as chancellor at stake. If the Bundestag or the federal states voted down her signature reform, maintaining the coalition might be impossible. This top–down approach constituted an enormous change from Kohl and Schröder. Each of her immediate predecessors "would have asked for recommendations from the appropriate ministers and opposition factions, then waited to see how the majority of voters reacted to each proposal and weighed in accordingly, insisting they had always held that particular position." Although Merkel prevailed in her healthcare reform, she realized that the top–down approach "bore no fruit" and in most subsequent policy debates, took on the role of moderator, allowing her ministers a greater hand in crafting policy.[63]

Margaret Heckel asked the chancellor if "trial and error" were a fair characterization of her political style. Merkel replied, "when I was studying mathematics earlier and had to prove something, I often thought 'many roads lead to Rome'; why should we take the shortest?"[64] In a similar vein, political biographer, Gerhard Langguth, adds that she also has a tremendous capacity for "rapid course corrections." He described her style as a departure from the conventional CDU policies, framed in terms of values and "expressed in frequently fussy language." Merkel represents "a new type of politician, concentrating less on fundamental and traditional considerations and more on efficiency and rationale as decision calculi. . . . her scientific training [makes her] non-ideological. That many consider her an outsider results from this ideological freedom."[65]

CONCLUSION

We all carry the imprint of our past on who we are in the present. Angela Merkel and her father may be diametrically opposed politically but psychologically they have much more in common than either would probably wish to admit. A complex set of dichotomies forms each of their personalities but they have channeled their often conflicting dualities in different ways. The pastor with a great capacity for tolerance in others demanded perfection from his eldest daughter. And she grew to demand it from herself. On the other hand, a driven young woman, who accepted no less perfection than her father demanded of her, remained content to let teachers find her uninspiring as a student. A teenager, who routinely marshaled her friends, became a middle-of-the-pack follower in the communist youth organization. A politician with "no charisma" heads the most powerful country in Europe. It is Angela Merkel's greatest gift as a politician to shift effortlessly between opposing personas, allowing people to project the Merkel they need. This is the "mousey" woman who convinced President Bush to back the G8 climate initiative. This is the lame "Kohl girl" who stared down Vladimir Putin on Chechnya. This is the "blank slate" that no one noticed but everyone voted for.

Merkel is clearly aware of this aspect of her personality; it is, after all, how she channels her dualities. Her father remains conflicted—at times tortured—in his belief systems that communism offers a better quality of life despite its antagonism to religion. Merkel is unencumbered by the conflicting dualities of her nature. She grows more comfortable with herself the older she gets. She no longer berates herself for her shortcomings, but by demanding perfection in everything, she achieves it in many things. What some see as cold is really the detached precision of a scientist. These aspects of her personality she got from her father. The self-esteem she gets from her successes and her ability to forgive herself for her failures she gets from her mother.

It is precisely her high self-esteem and sense of efficacy, combined with a capacity for honest introspection, that place Merkel within the flexible-pragmatic leadership archetype. Her natural curiosity leads her down nonideological decision pathways, which by definition, makes her open-minded. With no need for self-aggrandizement, she allows ideas to flourish and others to take credit. This fosters innovation among policy decisions from potentially all sides of the political spectrum. A case in point is the healthcare reform. Though it was not well received by the electorate, Merkel worked with a minister from the center-left coalition partner to reach a bipartisan accord that both parties could support. Her willingness to foster new ideas speaks directly to her collegial management style as well as her flexibility. Having been blindsided by Kohl in a cabinet debate, Merkel uses her role to moderate and insure that no member of the cabinet is marginalized in the process.

In foreign policy, Merkel is a staunch supporter of the United States. As a person who lived under the DDR regime, she has no real love of Moscow, particularly in light of some heavy-handed tactics. Her first foreign policy decision was to restore relations with the United States that Schröder had allowed to deteriorate. To Sarkozy's chagrin, she reaffirmed NATO's centrality to European security. Yet, she has not distanced herself from Russia, opting largely to maintain Schröder's relations with Moscow. With both Bush and Putin, she used a "mix of friendly directness and uncommitted positioning, [which] signaled a new style in diplomatic engagement."[66] When the United States decided to place antiballistic missiles in Poland, Russia was predictably outraged. At the EU–U.S. summit in May 2007, Merkel interceded between the two in her capacity as president of the EU. She stated that ordinarily, she could not represent Germany's interest through the EU presidency; but felt, conversely, that Germany had been its most successful when acting as intermediary and not adding to the polarization. Her good offices worked and Bush was able to ameliorate Putin's concerns.[67] We clearly see Merkel as the pragmatist in her foreign policy: maintaining closer ties with Russia than she might personally prefer, and bending the rules to act as intermediary. We also see Merkel as the blank slate in her "uncommitted positioning" that allows her to openly criticize the United States and Russia, without destroying either relationship.

One further thought on Merkel's willingness to bend rules is worth a mention. A respect for rules (a notable German value in itself) is one of the earliest traits she inherited from her father. However, as she has grown as a state leader, she has discovered that flexibility with rules can be pragmatic in its own right: "the one who always wins is the one who isn't a stickler for the rules of the game. For a long time, I didn't want to believe that but it is so."[68] For Merkel to be able to move beyond so fundamental a personality trait signals a very open belief system and a leader unafraid to learn on the job.

One final but very important piece places her squarely within Krasno's flexible-pragmatic archetype: Merkel's "not unambitious" view of power as a means of bringing about policy, rather than an end in itself. Her critics charge just the opposite—that Merkel's "flexibility" and willingness to share credit are based on the fragile Grand Coalition. They argue that in the interim, she has sought to consolidate power by removing rivals, even within her own party.[69] However, most of the criticism from the right comes from voices that are irritated by Merkel's incessant compromise with the middle. Höhler, in particular, comes across as shrill, insisting that Merkel's status as an outsider from the East renders her incapable of understanding capitalism. I argue that critics from within the CDU/CSU are likely to fall into the authoritarian leadership type—as Kohl did. Any open-minded approach from the chancellery would be met with derision. There may be some truth to Merkel's removing internal obstacles—she has done it before and would not be chancellor now had she not. But any kernel of truth in it makes her a politician, not an authoritarian.

NOTES

1. *Forbes* has ranked Angela Merkel number one on its list of "The World's Most Powerful Women," almost every year since 2006; only in 2010 was she displaced by Michelle Obama.

2. "Maggie of Mecklenburg," *Economist*, October 23, 2003, http://www.economist.com/node/2156683. See also Rob Broomby, "The Rise of Angela Merkel," *BBC News*, March 20, 2000, http://news.bbc.co.uk/2/hi/europe/683187.stm.

3. Frank Schirrmacher, "Interview with Angela Merkel: Ihr wißt gar nicht wie viele sozialistische Elemente ihr habt," *Frankfurter Allgemeine Zeitung*, May 28, 2005, 34.

4. Gerd Langguth, *Angela Merkel: Aufstieg zur Macht* (Munich: Deutsche Taschenbuch Verlag, 2005) 19.

5. Angela Merkel, *Mein Weg* (Hamburg: Hoffmann und Campe Verlag, 2004), 38.

6. Ibid.

7. Ibid., 41–44.

8. Jürgen Schöller, "Zur Geschichte der Weißenseer Arbeitskreises," *über Uns*, Website of the Weißenseer Arbeitskreis, http://www.weissenseerblaetter.de/uns.htm.

9. Merkel, *Mein Weg*, 44–45.

10. Schirrmacher, "Interview with Angela Merkel."

11. Langguth, *Angela Merkel*, 23.

12. Merkel, *Mein Weg*, 37–38.

13. Langguth, *Angela Merkel*, 40.

14. Ibid., 24.

15. Ibid., 42–47. See also Merkel, *Mein Weg*, 40.

16. Langguth, *Angela Merkel*, 48–61.

17. Ibid., 65.

18. Ibid., 68–69. The author concedes his inability to ascertain any of Kasner's reasons for his actions or whether he was under any specific pressure from the state.

19. Langguth, *Angela Merkel*, 71–72.

20. Schirrmacher, "Interview with Angela Merkel."

21. "Interview with Angela Merkel: Das Leben ist erbarmungslos; es deformiert," *Stern*, July 20, 2000, 40. LexisNexis Academic.

22. Merkel, *Mein Weg*, 96.

23. Langguth, *Angela Merkel, 188–189.*

24. Merkel, *Mein Weg*, 97.

25. Gerd Langguth, "Germany's Schreiber Affair: The Scandal That Helped Merkel Become Chancellor," *Spiegel Online International*, August 7, 2009, http://www.spiegel.de/international/germany/germany-s-schreiber-affair-the-scandal-that-helped-merkel-become-chancellor-a-640938.html.

26. "Kohl Scandal: Europe's Old Master Admits He Ran Secret Slush Fund," *Independent* (London), December 1, 1999, http://www.independent.co.uk/news/world/kohl-scandal-europes-old-master-admits-he-ran-secret-slush-funds-1124613.html.

27. Angela Merkel, "Die von Helmut Kohl eingeräumten Vorgänge haben der Partei Schaden zugefügt," *Frankfurter Allgemeine Zeitung*, December 22, 1999, 2.

28. Langguth, *Angela Merkel*, 209–210.

29. "Interview with Angela Merkel."

30. Ibid.

31. Broomby, "Rise of Angela." Karl Feldmeyer, parliamentary correspondent for the *Frankfurter Allgemeine Zeitung*, made this observation to Broomby.

32. Merkel, *Mein Weg*, 56.

33. Broomby, "Rise of Angela."

34. Angela Merkel, "Keine Alternative zu unserem Kurs der Aufklärung," in *Machtworte: Die Standpunkte der Kanzlerin*, ed. Robin Mishra (Breisgau: Verlag Herder, 2010), 122–126.

35. "Interview with Angela Merkel."

36. Ibid.

37. Patricia Riekel, "Mit 50 Jahren fängt das richtige Leben erst an," *BUNTE*, July 15, 2004, 40–45. LexisNexis Academic.

38. Ibid.

39. "A Difficult Pairing, an Uncertain Outcome," *Economist*, October 13, 2005, http://www.economist.com/node/5025748.

40. William Horsley, "Analysis: German Coalition Deal," *BBC News*, November 15, 2005, http://news.bbc.co.uk/2/hi/europe/4438212.stm. See also "Merkel Clinches It, but the Price Is High," *Economist*, October 12, 2005, www.economist.com/node/5013718/print.

41. Horsley, "German Coalition Deal."

42. "Interview with Angela Merkel." See also

43. Margaret Heckel, *So Regiert die Kanzlerin* (Munich: Piper, 2009), 225.

44. Langguth, *Angela Merkel*, 390.

45. "The Mystery of Mrs. Merkel," *Economist*, June 25, 2009, http://www.economist.com/node/13900135.

46. Heckel, *So Regiert die Kanzlerin*, 13–14.

47. Petra Pinzler, "Die Methode Merkel: Warum die Kanzerlin gerade in der Aussenpolitik so erfogreich ist," *Die Zeit*, June 21, 2007, http://www.zeit.de/2007/26/Angela-Merkel-Europa-Bilanz.

48. Ibid.

49. Ibid.

50. Pinzler, "Die Methode Merkel."

51. Heckel, *So regiert die Kanzlerin*, 219.

52. Ibid., 103.

53. Ibid.

54. Heckel, *So regiert die Kanzlerin,* 54.
55. Ibid., 152.
56. Langguth, *Angela Merkel,* 391.
57. Heckel, *So regiert die Kanzlerin,* 123–125.
58. Langguth, *Angela Merkel,* 344.
59. Heckel, *So regiert die Kanzlerin,* 16.
60. Ibid., 21–22.
61. Ibid., 154.
62. "Europe's Reluctant Hegemon," *Economist,* June 15, 2013, 4–6.
63. Langguth, *Angela Merkel,* 349–351.
64. Heckel, *So regiert die Kanzlerin,* 238.
65. Langguth, *Angela Merkel,* 393–394.
66. Ibid., 361.
67. Ibid., 368–369.
68. Langguth, *Angela Merkel,* 392.
69. See Getrud Höhler, *Die Patin* (Zürich: Orell Füssli Verlag, 2012); and Dirk Kurbjuweit, *Angela Merkel: Die Kanzlerin für alle?* (Munich: Hanser Verlag, 2009). Höhler is a strategic communications consultant and sits on the board of several Swiss and German companies. Kurbjuweit is a novelist and journalist.

14

Benazir Bhutto: Personality, Beliefs, and the Empowerment of Women

Nicole DiMarco

In the years prior to Benazir Bhutto's accession to prime minister, Pakistan was ravaged by civil war and controlled by a militant ideology, which was oppressive to women and destabilized the nation. Her belief in equal rights and particularly the rights of women were fundamental in formulating her policies to address the repressive actions that had developed against women in Pakistan.

PERSONAL DEVELOPMENT OF BENAZIR BHUTTO

Benazir Bhutto, born June 21, 1953, was the firstborn daughter of Zulfikar Ali Bhutto, the fourth president of Pakistan from 1971 to 1973 and the ninth prime minister of Pakistan from 1973 to 1977. He was also the founder of the Pakistan People's Party (PPP) and served as its chairman until he was executed in 1979. According to many family histories, her father was delighted and did not share the prevailing Pakistani attitude that a daughter was a disappointment.[1]

She was the eldest child, raised to speak both Urdu and English, although English was her primary language. She came from a wealthy, powerful family and it was her privileged background that gave her a strong sense of confidence and entitlement that enhanced her later attempt at leadership.[2] She was the eldest of four siblings, two brothers and one sister, and she stated many times in the past that there was no question she and her sister were allotted the same opportunities as her brothers. She writes in her autobiography that there was no gender discrimination whatsoever in her family, unlike many others and that if anything, she was favored and received the most attention as the oldest of four siblings.[3] She also notes that her father wanted "to make examples out of us, the next generation of educated, progressive Pakistanis."[4] Her mother was also a strong influence in her life and no stranger to politics; she acted as chairperson of the PPP during Zulfikar's imprisonment.[5] Benazir describes her mother as a "strong woman" who "battled military dictatorships and was a pioneer for women's rights" and whose "mere presence" gave her strength.[6] When Benazir reached puberty, Benazir's mother wanted her to start wearing a burka (a tent-like black covering) when she traveled but her father said it was not necessary, "let her be judged by her character and her mind, not by her clothing."[7] With regard to this matter she mentioned "I was the first Bhutto woman to be released from a life spent in perpetual twilight."[8]

After completing her early education in Pakistan, she pursued her higher education in the United States. Her father had been very hard on all his children with regard to education. Lucky for Benazir, she was an excellent student, which she says was important "for he had great plans for me to be the first woman in the Bhutto family to study abroad."[9] From 1969 to 1973, she attended Radcliffe College at Harvard University, where she earned a bachelor of arts degree with cum laude honors in comparative government. Bhutto later called her time at Harvard "four of the happiest years of my life" and said it formed "the very basis of her belief in democracy."[10] These experiences that shaped her belief system reflect the theories of those who claim that adult experiences can be very important, as important as childhood experiences, in formulating how a person views the world around him or her. The next phase of her education took place in the United Kingdom. Between 1973 and 1977, Bhutto studied philosophy, politics, and economics at Lady Margaret Hall, Oxford, during which time she took additional courses in international law and diplomacy. After Lady Margaret Hall she attended St Catherine's College, Oxford.[11]

It is clear from political histories that Benazir's father had leadership in mind for his daughter's future. In 1972, Benazir recollects her father wanting her to be present for his summit with Indira Gandhi, the prime minister of India. He told her the first week of her summer vacation junior year at Harvard, "Whatever the result, this meeting will be a turning point for Pakistan's history. I want you to witness it firsthand."[12] She did indeed witness history in the making and the political process at work. Negotiations between Zulfikar and Indira remained contentious. Zulfikar almost left without an agreement, due to his unwillingness to compromise anything that he felt would jeopardize the people of his country. The turning point of the summit was Zulfikar's final attempt, an appeal to Mrs. Gandhi, which proved successful. This diplomatic endeavor produced an agreement that would become known as the Simla Accord—which ushered in the longest lasting peace on the subcontinent—and Benazir was there, by her father's side, to witness it.[13]

Benazir learned constantly about the world of politics via her father. She recounts that, when they were young, he would take his children to meet foreign delegations visiting Pakistan.[14] These meetings served as a means for her father to teach his children about the Chinese Revolution when they met with important men from China. In other words, he used his job to teach his children in the most hands-on way about politics, history, diplomacy, and democracy. She also recalls a time she was traveling with her father in the autumn of 1963. He shook her awake from her slumber and said, "this is not time to sleep. There has been a great tragedy! The young President of the United States has been shot."[15] She said her father had met President John F. Kennedy several times at the White House and that he admired him a great deal for his liberal social views.[16]

Upon completion of her formal education in America and the United Kingdom, Benazir Bhutto returned to Pakistan in 1977, and was placed under house arrest after the military coup led by General Mohammad Zia ul-Haq overthrew her father's government. Benazir remained in varying degrees of detention for seven years. She took this opportunity to write condemnations of Zia and his administration and defenses of her father's domestic and foreign policies.[17] It was an obvious attempt made by Zia to break her spirit but it only increased her determination and "added another layer of anger."[18]

The formation of her strong personality was certainly encouraged by her family and much of the data supports this but another layer of this formation came from Benazir's belief that it was her destiny to better Pakistan through political participation and ultimately the implementation of democracy. Her autobiography opens with the line, "I didn't choose this life; it chose me" and then goes on to state that although it was not the life she would have chosen for herself, it had been a life "of opportunity, responsibility and fulfillment."[19] She continues, "few in this world are given the privilege to affect change in society, to bring the modern era to a country that had only the most basic infrastructure, to break down stereotypes about the role of women and give hope for change to millions who before had no hope."[20] These quotes illustrate the strong obligation Benazir felt to better her country, an obligation that was perhaps greater than herself and something she was called to do. Her father arguably instilled this sense of obligation when upon her departure for Radcliffe he said to her:

> You will see many things that will surprise you in America and some that may shock you, but I know that you have the ability to adapt. Above all, you must study hard. Very few in Pakistan have the opportunity you now have and you must take advantage of it. Never forget that the money it is costing to send

> you comes from the land, from people who sweat and toil on those lands. You will owe a great debt to them, a debt you can repay with God's blessing by using your education to better their lives.[21]

Her father's words illustrate quite clearly his vision for her future and leave no doubt that he instilled in her a sense of obligation to the people of Pakistan—an obligation that motivated her to pursue politics.

One year after Zia ul-Haq became president in 1978, the elder Bhutto, her father, was hanged after his conviction on charges of authorizing the murder of an opponent.[22] Benazir then inherited her father's leadership of the PPP. It is clear that based on her personal history, leadership and the desire to create democracy in Pakistan were in her blood and in her family tree, and she would go on to follow in the footsteps of her father.

On December 18, 1987, she married Asif Ali Zardari in Karachi, an arranged marriage that was a political decision on her part and a calculated move because being a single woman in Muslim society was considered dangerous and suspicious.[23] The match was selected by her mother and aunts and was agreed upon because he was the same age as Bhutto, had been educated in the West, and had no personal political ambitions. The marriage was, as she said "the price in personal choice I had to pay for the political path my life had taken."[24]

Benazir became the first ever female prime minister of a Muslim nation on December 1, 1988. She claimed her father had asked her to take up his "mission," and so she did.[25] She also was quoted as saying "the suffering in the country, the suffering of my family, of all of us, had risen above the barrier of gender."[26] This comment demonstrates that her familial link to the male martyr (her father) not only helped her overcome traditional barriers that blocked women from positions of political power, but also linked her to her father's martyrdom, almost as if to show that she was going into politics not by choice, but out of a necessity to pick up where her father left off at the time of his death.[27] Whether this was a calculated move on Bhutto's part remains to be seen, but it does provide an explanation as to how a woman was able to win such high office.

BACKGROUND: HISTORY OF PAKISTAN

The history of Pakistan is tumultuous and complex. Pakistan, along with parts of western India, contains the archeological remains of an urban civilization dating back 4,500 years but it was not until the eighth century that Islam was introduced to Pakistan by Muslim traders in Sindh.[28] The collapse of the Mughal Empire in the eighteenth century provided a chance for the English East India Company to spread its control over much of the subcontinent.[29] The Sikh adventurer, Ranjit Singh, stamped out a territory that went from Kabul to Srinagar and Lahore, encompassing much of the northern area of modern Pakistan but British rule replaced the Sikhs in the first half of the nineteenth century.[30] In a decision that had enormous consequences, the British allowed the Hindu maharaja of Kashmir, a Sikh, to continue in power.

Pakistan emerged from an extended period of agitation by Muslims in the subcontinent to express their national identity free from British colonial control as well as control by what they perceived to be a Hindu-controlled Indian National Congress.[31] Muslim anticolonial leaders formed the All-India Muslim League in 1906.[32] Initially, the league adopted the same objective as the Congress—self-government for India within the British Empire—but the Congress and the league were unable to agree on a formula that would ensure the protection of Muslims' religious, economic, and political rights.[33]

The idea of a separate Muslim state in British India first emerged in the 1930s and on March 23, 1940, Muhammad Ali Jinnah, leader of the Muslim League, formally endorsed the "Lahore Resolution," calling for the creation of an independent state in regions where Muslims constituted a majority.[34] However, the Congress Party and the Muslim League could not agree on the terms for a constitution or establishing an interim government. In June 1947, the British government declared that it would bestow full dominion status upon two successor states, India and Pakistan, formed from areas in the subcontinent in which Muslims were the majority population.[35] Under this arrangement, the various states were free to join either India or Pakistan. On August 14, 1947, Pakistan, comprising West Pakistan with the provinces of Punjab, Sindh, Balochistan, and the North-West Frontier Province (now Khyber-Pakhtunkhwa), and East Pakistan[36] with the province of Bengal, became independent.[37]

INDEPENDENCE AND INSTABILITY

With the death of Muhammad Ali Jinnah in 1948, the first head of state, and the assassination in 1951 of its first prime minister, Liaqat Ali Khan, political instability and economic difficulty became prominent features of postindependence Pakistan.[38] On October 7, 1958, President Iskander Mirza, with the support of the army, suspended the 1956 Constitution, imposed martial law, and canceled the elections scheduled for January 1959.[39] Shortly thereafter, the military sent Mirza into exile, and General Mohammad Ayub Khan assumed control.[40] After Pakistan's loss in the 1965 war against India, Ayub Khan's power diminished.[41] Simultaneously, political and economic grievances ensued, which ultimately inspired protests that led to his resignation in March 1969.[42] He handed over responsibility for governing to the commander in chief of the army, General Agha Mohammed Yahya Khan, who became president and chief martial law administrator.[43]

THE RISE OF THE PAKISTAN PEOPLE'S PARTY (PPP)

General elections held in December 1970 polarized relations between the eastern and western sections of Pakistan. The Awami League, which advocated autonomy for East Pakistan, swept the East Pakistan seats to gain a majority in Pakistan as a whole.[44] The PPP, founded and led by Ayub Khan's former foreign minister Zulfikar Ali Bhutto (Benazir Bhutto's father), won a majority of the seats in West Pakistan, but the country was completely divided.[45]

On March 26, 1971, following a bloody crackdown by the Pakistan army, Bengali nationalists declared an independent People's Republic of Bangladesh.[46] On April 17, 1971, Bengali nationalists formed a provisional government in an area bordering India, and in November 1971, India sent its military into East Pakistan to intervene on the side of the Bangladeshis.[47] On December 16, Pakistani forces surrendered in Dhaka, and East Pakistan became the new nation of Bangladesh. Yahya Khan then resigned the presidency and handed over leadership of the western part of Pakistan to Zulfikar Ali Bhutto, who became president and the first civilian chief martial law administrator.[48]

Bhutto moved decisively to restore national confidence and pursued an active foreign policy, taking a leading role in Islamic and Third World forums.[49] Domestically, Bhutto pursued a populist agenda and nationalized major industries and the banking system, and in 1973, he promulgated a new constitution accepted by most political elements and relinquished the presidency to become prime minister.[50] Although Bhutto continued his populist and socialist rhetoric, over time the economy stagnated, largely as a result of the dislocation and uncertainty produced by Bhutto's frequently changing economic policies.[51] When Bhutto proclaimed his own victory in the March 1977 national elections, the opposition Pakistan National Alliance (PNA) denounced the results as fraudulent and demanded new elections. Bhutto resisted and later arrested the PNA leadership.[52]

With the increasing antigovernment unrest, the army grew restless. On July 5, 1977, the military removed Bhutto from power and arrested him, declared martial law again, and suspended portions of the 1973 Constitution.[53] Chief of Army Staff General Muhammad Zia ul-Haq became chief martial law administrator and promised to hold new elections within three months.

Zia released Bhutto from prison but after it became clear that Bhutto's popularity had survived his government, Zia postponed the elections and began criminal investigations of the senior PPP leadership.[54] Subsequently, Bhutto was convicted and sentenced to death for an alleged conspiracy to murder a political opponent. Despite international appeals on his behalf, Bhutto was hanged on April 6, 1979.[55]

The loss of a father is traumatic for any child, but to a daughter as close to her father as Benazir was, the loss was devastating. She recounts the pain by describing that she felt "as if my body was literally being torn apart. How could I go on?"[56] She describes the days that followed her father's execution and the impact it had on her:

> For days after my father's death, I couldn't eat or drink. I would take sips of water, but then I'd have to spit it out. I couldn't swallow at all, nor could I sleep. Every time I closed my eyes I had the same dream. I was standing in front of the district jail. The gates were open. I saw a figure walking towards me. Papa! I rushed to him . . . Just before I reached him, I would wake up and have to realize once again that he was gone.[57]

Perhaps the most striking details about her father's execution are the ones that illustrate the immense closeness between Benazir and her father. She was the only child to see her father before his execution. None of the other children were called for, just she and her mother. Zulfikar said to them both the day before his execution, "Give my love to the other children. Tell Mir and Sunny and Shah that I have tried to be a good father and wish I could have said good-bye to them."[58] Perhaps the most heart-wrenching detail is when Benazir recalls her father's last words to her: "You don't know how much I love you, how much I've always loved you. You are my jewel. You always have been."[59] Perhaps it was this fatherly love and adoration that gave Benazir the confidence and strength to rise to political power. In her book she writes:

> Now, in the nightmare that had engulfed Pakistan, his cause had become my own. I had felt it as I stood by my father's grave, felt the strength and conviction of his soul replenishing me. At that moment I pledged to myself that I would not rest until democracy returned to Pakistan. It was up to us to continue.[60]

This is arguably the single most telling insight into her motivation; she felt an obligation to continue the fight for democracy, a fight that began with her father that would hopefully be successful throughout her leadership.

Zia assumed the presidency and called for elections in November. However, fearful of a PPP victory, Zia banned political activity in October 1979, and postponed national elections. In Zia's search for legitimacy, he implemented a religiously based legal code (Shari'a law) unparalleled in the modern history of Islam in South Asia.[61] For the first time, the resultant laws regarded men and women as having different legal rights and paradoxically compromised the rights of women.[62] He also passed into law the Hudood Ordinances, which implemented harsh Quranic punishments for violations of these new laws, which directly affected women in a negative way. For example, of the 4,500 women who were imprisoned in 1989, 80 percent of them were sentenced under the new, harsh, discriminatory laws implemented by Zia.[63] It is important to understand this harsh treatment of women under Zia to fully appreciate the environment facing Benazir Bhutto when she took office.

SHARI'A LAW

Also meaning "path" in Arabic, shari'a guides all aspects of Muslim life including daily routines, familial and religious obligations, and financial dealings. It is derived primarily from the Quran and the Sunna, the sayings, practices, and teachings of the Prophet Mohammed. These laws are oppressive to both men and women, but affect women's daily life more directly.

Marriage and divorce are the most common themes in Shari'a law. This is a result of the commonly held view that women are property with no rights of their own, a view that is deeply rooted in Islamic culture according to Tahira Shahid Khan, who is a professor specializing in women's issues at the Aga Khan University in Pakistan. He wrote in *Chained to Custom*, a review of honor killings published in 1999 that "women are considered the property of the males in their family irrespective of their class, ethnic, or religious group. The owner of the property has the right to decide its fate. The concept of ownership has turned women into a commodity which can be exchanged, bought and sold."[64] Other practices that are woven into the shari'a debate, such as female genital mutilation, adolescent marriages, polygamy, and gender-biased inheritance rules, elicit a massive amount of controversy in other parts of the world, but exact statistics concerning women victimized by these laws are not easy to find because many of the indicators used to assess gender equality and human development did not exist at that time.

THE RISE OF BENAZIR BHUTTO

In 1980, most center and left parties, led by the PPP, formed the Movement for the Restoration of Democracy (MRD). The MRD demanded Zia's resignation, an end to martial law, new elections, and restoration of the Constitution, as it existed before Zia's takeover. His opponents, led by the MRD, boycotted the new elections. When the government claimed a 63 percent turnout, with more than 90 percent approving the referendum, many people questioned the figures.[65]

On August 17, 1988, a plane carrying President Zia and 28 Pakistani military officers crashed on a return flight from a military equipment trial near Bahawalpur, killing all on board.[66] In accordance with the Constitution, chairman of the Senate Ghulam Ishaq Khan became acting president and announced that elections in November 1988 would take place and that they would take place on a party basis.[67] On one side was an eight-party alliance and on the other, the PPP. In the 1988 elections, the PPP won 94 seats out of 207 and the Islamic Democratic Alliance won 54 so the president was bound to invite the PPP to form the government.[68] Ultimately, President Khan asked PPP Co-chairperson Benazir Bhutto to form a government.[69] From the very start of Bhutto's tenure as prime minister, a debate broke out on whether a woman could hold such a high position in government under Shari'a law. After much analysis, they decided that since she was not president, which was a position reserved for men, but the leader of a political party, it was fine.

PRIME MINISTER BENAZIR BHUTTO (1988–1990)

Benazir Bhutto's performance as prime minister has been criticized from every angle: friends, opponents, feminists, mullahs, and pacifists. It must be stated before examining her tenure that the problems she confronted were so formidable that it is difficult to imagine how any leader could have governed successfully.[70]

Immediately after the November 1988 election, the PPP released a manifesto outlining a number of reforms for the empowerment of the Pakistani people, including provisions for securing basic human rights, employment, and political participation. The manifesto was consistent with the goals pledged in the "Awami budget" of 1986 in which Benazir stated that:

> The Pakistan People's Party believes the role of the government is in creating a society free from social and economic inequalities—a society where there is respect for the individual dignity and opportunity for development and mobility. . . . We want to see that our people are free from hunger and disease, free from oppression and exploitation, free from unemployment and injustice.[71]

The 1988 manifesto included a pledge to eliminate all forms of discrimination against women and promised that a new PPP government would:

1. Sign the [United Nations] Convention on the Elimination of all forms of Discrimination against Women (CEDAW);
2. Actively support women's right to work, to free choice of employment, to just and favorable conditions of work, to protection against unemployment, to equal pay for work of equal value, and for payment of maternity leave;
3. Repeal all discriminatory laws against women;
4. Take special measures to promote the literacy of women;
5. Ensure that Jahez [dowry] would be "eradicated by enlarging social consciousness and strictly enforcing the relevant laws and Dowry Act."[72]

These are just a few of the many measures outlined in the PPP manifesto but one thing remained clear: the empowerment of women became one of the major themes of the PPP's manifesto and platform. However, the economic conditions in Pakistan during this time were dire, with inflation running at about 15 percent and foreign exchange reserves at an all-time low. Some critics claimed that she had no right to make promises that she knew she would be unable to fund, especially since the government was borrowing money to pay its own employees.[73]

In support of women's rights as prime minister, Benazir Bhutto freed many female prisoners from Pakistan's jails.[74] Some argued it was merely a symbolic gesture, but on the contrary, the very act of releasing women from unfair imprisonment and oppression demonstrated courageous support for the treatment of women. Most of these women were very poor and their freedom sent a clear message to the previous administration, stating a blatant objection to the "social prisons" they had built. The new government also allowed for the revival of trade unions, which included a sizeable number of women in their ranks and, perhaps more importantly, the government lifted press censorship, which resulted in a marked difference in the media's portrayal of women.[75]

Author Anne Weiss visited Lahore in 1988 and many poor craftsmen and traders spoke with her about the dream of the PPP that Zulfikar Ali Bhutto, Benazir's father, had espoused: women, the poor, and other disenfranchised would get land and political rights. She claims that the people believed that Benazir has built on that dream, as when she stated in 1987: "I like to think I'm carrying on my father's vision of a federal democratic Pakistan. He set the way for a society in which there should be no discrimination on the basis of sex, race, or religion, and I too am fighting for this."[76] Benazir clearly expresses here the strong influence her father had on her belief system.

A good measure of women's welfare is to look at the health of their newborn babies. Infant mortality rates (IMR) in Pakistan in 1988 (at the time of her election) were 108 out of 1,000 live births.[77] By 1990, this number dropped to 96 according to one source[78] and 91 according to another.[79] Either way, there is a notable drop in IMR while Benazir Bhutto was prime minister.

Importantly, under Bhutto's administration, Pakistan made huge leaps in repairing its relationship with the United States. Her team was able to get the White House and Congress to increase aid to Pakistan, making it the third-largest recipient of foreign aid from the United States, after Israel and Egypt. After her defeat in the 1990 elections, the United States formally cut off all foreign aid to Pakistan. However, during her tenure she was able to not only sustain incoming aid but also increase the flow, including military assistance.[80]

In her book *Reconciliation*, she lists the numerous advances she and her team made during her first term as prime minister. These advancements included: freeing political prisoners; restoring free, open, uncensored print and media; removing constraints and conditions to the free operation of nongovernmental organizations (including women's and human rights groups); lifting the ban on student and labor unions imposed by the Zia administration; granting amnesty to political exiles, introducing computer identity cards; introducing microcredit and protecting minorities; and beginning the separation of the judiciary from the executive (which was completed in her second term).[81]

In the field of women's rights, she and the PPP government made advancements by appointing several women to her cabinet; creating women's studies programs in the universities; establishing a women's development bank to give credit to enterprising women; creating institutions to help women with family planning, nutrition, child care, and even birth control; and legalizing and encouraging women's participation in sports (previously banned under the Zia administration).[82] All of these initiatives were a solid start to changing a society where Islam had been used to exploit and repress the position of women.

Nevertheless, there is sharp criticism of Bhutto and her lack of politically empowering women during her first term as prime minister. According to Weiss, aside from herself and her mother, only one other woman was given a PPP ticket to run for a national assembly seat and few women were given provincial assembly tickets.[83] Initially, no women were given ministry positions, but in March 1989, Bhutto increased the federal cabinet size to 43 members, ultimately including 5 women.[84] Of the 19 ministers of state, 4 were women: Begum Shahnaz Wazir Ali (minister of state for education), Begum Rehana Sarwar (initially appointed as minister of state for the women's division, and later headed the ministry for women's development), Dr. Mahmooda Shah (minister of state for special education and social welfare), and Begum Khakwani (minister of state for population welfare).[85]

While these may not seem like huge feats on the part of gender development, the symbolism of these appointments cannot go unnoticed; during Bhutto's first term as prime minister, women were encouraged to participate actively in public life. It is important to gender development that participation was permitted, encouraged, and even possible. I should also note that coming to power in a country after previous male leaders had been executed and assassinated, including her own father, must have affected her and made her cautious when deciding which issues to push to the foreground.

When examining military expenditures in Pakistan during Bhutto's first term, it is interesting to see how it decreased during the course of her tenure. In 1988, military expenditures consumed 6.2 percent of GDP, 6 percent in 1989, which then were reduced to 5.8 percent in 1990.[86] She signed an agreement before entering office, stating that she would not decrease the military budget while she was in office, but it is apparent that based on these statistics, she did decrease the budget. Whether or not she was directly responsible for this decline remains unclear.

Bhutto launched several policy agenda items that were extremely controversial. She vehemently opposed Zia's *Islamization* programs and urged the repeal of the Hudood Ordinances and the Law of Evidence and all "cruel and inhuman laws that degrade women and make us second class citizens."[87] When her father was in power and fighting for gender equality it was not as controversial as when Benazir took a similar stand years later because in between the two Bhuttos' tenure there was an enormous rise in Islamic fundamentalism, perpetrated by Zia. Also, supporters of Benazir say that because she was a woman, it raised more suspicion and resistance for women's rights because of the generally held fear of female power.[88] Although it was not successful in overturning the laws, her administration was able to prevent the implementation of both the proposed Ninth Amendment, which would have made Islam the law of the land, and the Shari'a Bill, which would have put religious courts above civil courts.

But some women's groups thought she did not go far enough in promoting women's rights and believed she had a lack of commitment. They accused her of having more interest in politics than in women's rights while others believed she went too far and, therefore, remained opposed to her leadership.[89] In 1990, criminal charges were brought against her for corruption, abuses of power, and ineptitude.[90] This signaled the end of her first term as prime minister of Pakistan.

Immediately following the election of Nawaz Sharif, the administration reversed many of the social programs Benazir implemented: press censorship was reinstated; student unions were once again banned; access to the media by opposing political parties was blocked; and funds were immediately shifted from the social sector back to the military. Women's health and population control centers were also closed and Pakistan was once again thrown back into political turmoil and civil unrest.[91]

SECOND TERM (1993–1996)

In 1993, the PPP won the elections for the National Assembly and Benazir was reelected for a second term. She did not waste any time getting back to work.

She worked quickly to implement a social action program that addressed the needs of the Pakistani people, concentrating on education, health, housing, sanitation, infrastructure, and women's rights. While in office, Pakistan was able to attract four times more private sector international investment than during the previous year.[92] This money was strategically used to jump-start the Pakistani economy but also used toward women's empowerment. Some 100,000 women were trained to work in the villages of Pakistan in health and family planning.[93] Her administration is also credited with building 48,000 new schools and also instituted a remedial education program targeting women because she believed the most effective way to expand child literacy was to have literate mothers.[94] However despite these advancements, the 1995 statistics concerning primary and secondary enrollment rates of males versus females still show a staggering discrepancy: 50 percent of men enrolled in secondary schools and only 22 percent of women.[95]

In 1990, the first year the United Nations Human Development reports began, Pakistan was listed with a Human Development Index (HDI) score as the 36th lowest in development out of 130 countries in the report.[96] This index, which always represents information collected two years prior to its publication date, was compiled shortly after Benazir took office, so it gives an idea of where Pakistan stood in comparison to the rest of the world during her tenure. It also gives us a comparative base to see where Pakistan was ranked during her second term and if anything actually changed while she was in office. In 1993, Pakistan was ranked at 132 out of 172 countries,[97] which again was extremely low. Please note that in this report the best score is one and the lowest score is 172, so the higher the number, the lower the HDI is considered. But by 1995, two years into Benazir's second term, Pakistan moved up to 128 out of 172,[98] a marked increase in the HDI of Pakistan. Looking further ahead, by 1996, the year she left office again, the HDI was back down to 134,[99] even lower than when she came into office and by 1997 it had sunk even further to 139.[100]

Other growth indicators include the gross domestic product which in Pakistan doubled while Benazir was prime minister, growing from 2.1 in 1993 to 4.37 in 1995.[101] This is a marked growth in GDP that can fairly be attributed to Benazir and her administration.

PERSONALITY ASSESSMENT

Benazir Bhutto's personality type would best be described as flexible/pragmatic due to her high level of self-esteem and her ability to manage disagreement and disapproval in office. She recounts that, "Even though I was the newest elected Prime Minister in the South Asian Association of Regional Countries (SAARC), the youngest and the only woman, I wasn't shy and asserted my views."[102] She also writes that when she invited Rajiv Gandhi and his wife Sonia to Islamabad to take steps toward a legacy of peace, there were many who accused her of being "soft" on India. To this she replied, "I couldn't play their games—I had work to do."[103] This also illustrates that she had an innovative, open-minded approach to issues that had been plaguing the country for years. She was also able to work with others and prides herself in the bilateral talks she held with India during her time in office and recalls how together the two countries set up several committees to develop "confidence-building programs" aimed at nuclear installation security.[104] And finally, she was willing to listen to both peers and subordinates. She recalls that when she insisted that Pakistan explore a peaceful transfer of power in Kabul with Shevardnadze in 1989, her intelligence chief made an emotional appeal to her. He said, "Prime Minister, will you deny your men and the Afghan Mujahideen the right to march victoriously into Kabul after all the sacrifices they have made?"[105] She agreed to send forces into Afghanistan on the premise that the city would fall quickly. When this turned out to be false, she rejected a later proposal for Pakistani soldiers to join the fighting. This illustrates her flexible personality and open mind—she listened to staff but also had the courage to realize a mistake had been made and she quickly corrected it.

Her management style fits best under the collegial model; she met quite regularly with staff and was diplomatic in handling issues at hand. The example in the previous paragraph regarding Pakistani troops in Afghanistan is also an example of her collegial management style; there was an open dialogue about options, but in the end, when things did not go as planned, she ultimately made the final decision. She was very hands on, meeting with staff and diplomats regularly. She had many sources of intelligence, but in the end, she called the shots.

It was not long into her term before ghosts of the past came back to haunt Benazir. Her brother was brutally gunned down in September 1996, a brother with whom she had just recently reconciled, and a few months later in November, Benazir was overthrown again. After several years in exile, Benazir returned to Pakistan to lead the PPP and run once again for office. Tragically, in December 2007, during her campaign she was brutally shot in the head and instantly killed. It is clear Pakistan lost a true leader and possibly one of the few people in government who strongly supported women's rights and stood for real democracy.

It remains to be seen what she could have accomplished were she alive today. Perhaps she would be in office, or perhaps Pakistan would have made real progress toward democracy and gender equality; but these are all speculation. Some critics argue that she would not have been able to follow through on her promises to make women full members of society and that eventually she would prove to be only the daughter of a wealthy rural landlord and not a democratic symbol for Pakistan, and that this would have major implications for the realization of a just, equitable, and democratic order ever emerging.[106] Others believe the exact opposite; that if anyone was capable of making real changes for women in Pakistan, it was Benazir. Unfortunately, we will never know and the debate will continue without any resolution.

One thing that is unquestionable is the determination of her personality and her unwillingness to give up. She felt that the "forces of destiny and of history" had thrust her forward.[107] Her strong belief in women's rights was the influence of a strong woman, her mother, whom she considered a women's activist. But more importantly her father directly influenced this belief. He broke all the traditional gender rules prevalent in Pakistan during that time by educating his daughters alongside his sons and sending his daughter to America to learn and witness democracy firsthand. More importantly, this man who brought his daughter to political meetings so that she could see how diplomacy worked was also a man who loved her with all his heart and saw her as the one who could continue his legacy of democracy.

The Pakistan of today is still plagued by instability, poverty, violence, inequality, and utter chaos. The Taliban retains its grip, women are still second-class citizens, and the country is still poor and underdeveloped. And even though much of the legislation she implemented has been changed, forgotten, or erased, she still left a legacy for women and accomplishments can still be found, however small they may be. Perhaps what she did accomplish is a testament to possibility—that it is possible for women to be educated; it is possible for them to enter government; it is possible for them to speak out against injustice and inequality; it is possible for a woman to dress as she chooses; and more importantly, it is possible for a woman to have a vision and be a leader. She herself understood the impact her leadership had on her country: "My election empowered all women, promoted the image of a moderate interpretation of Islam and gave hope of a better life to the people of Pakistan."[108]

NOTES

1. Michael Genovese, *Women as National Leaders* (Newbury Park, CA: Sage Publications, 1993), 44.
2. Ibid.
3. Benazir Bhutto, *Daughter of Destiny* (New York: Harper Perennial, 2007), 33.
4. Ibid.
5. Ibid., 5.
6. Ibid., xix.
7. Ibid., 36.
8. Benazir Bhutto, *Reconciliation: Islam, Democracy and the West* (New York: HarperCollins, 2008), 47.
9. Bhutto, *Daughter of Destiny*, 35.
10. Biography.com, "Benazir Bhutto," http://www.biography.com/people/benazir-bhutto-9211744.
11. Ibid.
12. Bhutto, *Daughter of Destiny*, 60.
13. Ibid., 65.

14. Ibid., 37.
15. Ibid.
16. Ibid.
17. Genovese, *Women as National Leaders*, 48.
18. Ibid.
19. Bhutto, *Daughter of Destiny*, xi.
20. Ibid.
21. Ibid., 44.
22. Ibid.
23. Ibid.
24. Bhutto, *Reconciliation*, 350.
25. Genovese, *Women as National Leaders*, 42.
26. Mark R. Thompson, *Democratic Revolutions: Asia and Eastern Europe* (Oxford: Routledge, 2003), 546.
27. Ibid.
28. U.S. Department of State, "US Relations with Pakistan," http://www.state.gov/r/pa/ei/bgn/3453.htm.
29. Ibid.
30. Ibid.
31. Ibid.
32. Ibid.
33. Ibid.
34. Ibid.
35. Ibid.
36. East Pakistan later became the nation of Bangladesh in 1971.
37. U.S. Department of State, "US Relations with Pakistan."
38. Ibid.
39. Ibid.
40. Ibid.
41. Ibid.
42. Ibid.
43. Ibid.
44. Ibid.
45. Ibid.
46. Ibid.
47. Ibid.
48. Ibid.
49. Ibid.
50. Ibid.
51. Ibid.
52. Ibid.
53. Ibid.
54. Ibid.
55. Ibid.
56. Ibid.
57. Bhutto, *Daughter of Destiny*, 15.
58. Ibid., 9.
59. Ibid.

60. Ibid., 10.
61. Anita Weiss, "Benazir Bhutto and the Future of Women in Pakistan," *Asian Survey* 30, no. 5 (May 1990): 8.
62. Ibid.
63. Genovese, *Women as National Leaders*, 42.
64. "Thousands of Women Killed for Family 'Honor,'" *National Geographic*, October 28, 2010.
65. Ibid.
66. Ibid.
67. Ibid.
68. Ibid.
69. Ibid.
70. Genovese, *Women as National Leaders*, 60.
71. Weiss, "Benazir Bhutto," 3.
72. Ibid.
73. Genovese, *Women as National Leaders*, 60.
74. Weiss, "Benazir Bhutto," 3.
75. Ibid.
76. Ibid.
77. Zeba Sathar, "Changes in Mortality Rates in Pakistan 1960–88," *Pakistan Development Review*, Winter 1991.
78. World Health Organization, "Health Status and Demographics," Health Systems Profile-Pakistan, http://gis.emro.who.int/HealthSystemObservatory/PDF/Pakistan/Health%20status%20and%20demographics.pdf.
79. Population Reference Bureau, "Pakistan Still Falls Short of Millennium Development Goals for Infants and Maternal Health," http://www.prb.org/Articles/2007/pakistan.aspx.
80. Bhutto, *Reconciliation*, 203.
81. Ibid., 198.
82. Ibid.
83. Weiss, "Benazir Bhutto," 6.
84. Ibid.
85. Ibid.
86. Stockholm International Peace Research Institute, http://portal.sipri.org/publications/pages/expenditures/country-search.
87. Genovese, *Women as National Leaders*, 54.
88. Ibid.
89. Ibid.
90. Ibid.
91. Ibid.
92. Ibid.
93. Ibid.
94. Ibid.
95. 1997–99 United Nations ESCAP Fact Sheets.
96. United Nations Development Program, http://hdr.undp.org/en/media/hdr_1990_en_indicators1.pdf.
97. United Nations Development Program, http://hdr.undp.org/en/media/hdr_1993_en_indicators1.pdf.

98. United Nations Development Program, http://hdr.undp.org/en/media/hdr_1995_en_indicators1.pdf.

99. United Nations Development Program, http://hdr.undp.org/en/media/hdr_1996_en_indicators1.pdf.

100. United Nations Development Program, http://hdr.undp.org/en/media/hdr_1997_en_indicators1.pdf.

101. Trading Economics, "Pakistan GDP Growth Rates," http://www.tradingeconomics.com/pakistan/gdp-growth.

102. Bhutto, *Daughter of Destiny*, 395.

103. Ibid.

104. Ibid.

105. Ibid.

106. Weiss, "Benazir Bhutto," 14.

107. Bhutto, *Daughter of Destiny*, 392.

108. Ibid.

15

Ellen Johnson Sirleaf: Personal Experience and the Promotion of Women

Nicole DiMarco

ELLEN JOHNSON SIRLEAF: BIOGRAPHICAL HISTORY

Ellen Johnson Sirleaf was born on October 29, 1938, in Monrovia, Liberia. Her father was the son of a Gola chief, who was taken in as a ward by the McGrity family. In the name of assimilation, he was renamed Carney Johnson. He benefited from his time as a ward because the McGrity family sent him to school and he was given a solid primary education, which opened up the world for him. Eventually, he apprenticed with a practicing attorney in Liberia and became a lawyer himself. He began looking toward a life in politics as a way to serve his country and build on his career, as Sirleaf describes in her memoir.[1] Her mother Martha was born to a woman from Sinoe County and a father who was a trader from Germany. This made Martha stand out in the village where she grew up because she had fair skin and wavy hair. Nonetheless, the two were married and, according to Sirleaf, determined and eager to create a better life for themselves and their family.[2]

Her father was eventually elected to the House of Representatives and was the first indigenous man to achieve such a major accomplishment. President Tubman was in office at this time and not only appointed Sirleaf's father to many foreign delegations but often visited their home, she recounts fondly in her memoir. Her father traveled frequently for work, and her care was left to her mother. She describes her father as a womanizer, who had extramarital affairs, but Sirleaf also seems forgiving of this, writing that "this was not particularly frowned upon at that time. Polygamy was the dominant form of marriage in Liberia and most of West Africa before the arrival of settlers and colonists."[3] She also describes him as a worldly man, who spent much of his free time away from his family.[4] Sadly, her father suffered a massive stroke in his 40s, the prime of his life, while he was vigorously pursuing his goal to become Speaker of the House. She does not speak about their relationship or the impact his sudden illness had on her specifically; she only says that "to my father President Tubman was a man who opened the door. Then illness slammed that door shut again, with a suddenness and ferocity that shook us all to our core."[5] She talks about the drastic effect the stroke had on her family—one day they were a wealthy, prominent family, and the next day the family income plummeted, her father's colleagues vanished, and the family was forced to adjust to a new life.[6]

Her mother, a devout Catholic, kept any strain in the marriage away from the children.[7] She found solace in religion and focused her energy on education, eventually opening a school close by, which was attended by dozens of children as well as Sirleaf and her siblings. During this time it was not unusual for children of wealthy families to be educated, including girls. Her mother also became an itinerant minister in the Presbyterian Church and traveled the countryside to preach. Sirleaf acknowledges that it was rare for a woman to serve as a traveling pastor in those days, perhaps alluding to her mother's strength of conviction. Her mother was a role model for her and Sirleaf says "growing up, all I had ever wanted was to be an English teacher, like my mother."[8] Her mother also cared for Sirleaf's children while she was in school and even moved to Virginia for a few years to help her care for her youngest son, so it is clear the two were close and that Sirleaf depended on her help. Sirleaf does mention the influence her grandmothers had on her. Neither of her grandmothers could read or write in any language but she describes them as hard-working women, who loved their country, loved their families, and believed in education.[9] Sirleaf says of the two women: "They inspired me then, and their memory motivates me now to serve my people, to sacrifice for the world and honestly to serve humanity. I cannot and will not betray their trust."[10] Clearly, the women in her family had more of an influence on her personality development than the men.

Ellen Johnson Sirleaf has led a distinguished career spanning nearly four decades in the private and public domain in Liberia and internationally. While growing up in Liberia she attended high school at the College of West Africa in Monrovia, studying at Madison Business College, the University of Colorado, and Harvard University's Kennedy School of Government, where she obtained a master's degree in public administration in 1971.[11] In 1965, she joined the Treasury Department in Liberia, where she was eventually selected to be minister of finance in 1979, during which time she implemented measures to limit the mismanagement of government finances. After the military coup d'état in 1980, Sirleaf served as president of the Liberian Bank for Development and Investment (LBDI) but fled Liberia that same year to avoid the suppressive government that was gaining momentum.[12] She went to Kenya and served as vice president of Citicorp's Africa Regional Office in Nairobi, and later moved to Washington, DC to assume the position of senior loan officer at the World Bank, and eventually, vice president for Equator Bank. In 1992, she joined the United Nations Development Programme as assistant administrator and director of its Regional Bureau of Africa with the rank of assistant secretary-general of the United Nations.[13]

In 1956, her senior year in high school, she married a man named Doc, seven years her senior, with whom she had four sons. Her sister Jeannie, who at the time was in nursing school in England, was not happy about the marriage, fearing that Ellen was too young and that her ambition would be "squashed beneath the requirements of being a good Liberian wife."[14] Her sister was not far off, because by December of 1957, Ellen was already the mother of two children.

Though not widely known, Sirleaf's husband verbally and physically abused her throughout the entirety of their marriage.[15] Sirleaf noticed his jealousy from the moment they started dating, but admits she paid little attention to it. She writes, "I was young and in love and believed a man had the right to protect the virtue and reputation of the woman he loved."[16] When the couple left their children with their parents in Liberia and moved to Wisconsin, so that Doc could complete his master's degree, the situation deteriorated. In the onslaught of abuse, Sirleaf realized he was also an alcoholic. One day she came home from work and Doc was furious that dinner had not been made. He pulled a gun on her and struck her in the head with the butt of the pistol. She seems to rationalize this behavior by writing that in the late 1950s and early 1960s:

> Women simply took the occasional slap, or even worse, as part of life. There was no recourse . . . no police to seek or court administrator to whom you might appeal . . . the only thing you could do—and I did this more than once—was to run from home and straight to your mother's house. Your mother though, was equally helpless. Perhaps she would soothe you, tend your bruises . . . but in the end she would leave and the husband would either change or more likely, beat you harder next time. This was simply part of life. In my case, the increasing verbal and physical abuse led me to ask myself a simple question: How can I get out of this life?[17]

It finally got to the point where they agreed they could not continue to be together. Both had engaged in extramarital affairs and the violence had escalated. Doc took the children, and she was once again separated from them. About this separation she writes:

> Like nearly everywhere else in the world at this time, Liberia was very much a male-dominated society. Though Liberian women had long worked outside

> the home and held positions of prominence in government they were not regarded as equals . . . This was traditional in our society—children belong to the father first and foremost.[18]

Perhaps the most surprising detail of all is how she credits this tumultuous past with giving her the strength she needed to overcome the obstacles in her life. She writes, "living with a person like that also strengthened me. I have to thank him for that, because it was the strength I would need in the days and years to come."[19] These experiences as an adult impacted her personality and ultimately her policy decision making and point to one of many reasons why she has made women's empowerment a priority during her administration. She poignantly writes in her memoir:

> Domestic violence knows no geographical boundaries. It exists in every nation, every society, every corner of the world and neither Africa in general nor Liberia in particular is immune to this particular disease. Right from the start of my administration, even in my inaugural address, I pledged to bring the full weight of the government against those who would continue this terrible abuse. Those who violate our women and girls know that they will bear the force of the law.[20]

In the 14 years prior to Ellen Johnson Sirleaf's election, the country was ravaged by civil war during which many Liberian women were systematically raped and abused. Over the course of those years, murderous warlords supported by rebel groups in Sierra Leone fought government forces and each other. Both sides conscripted child soldiers and inflicted wanton violence against women and the civilian population, killing an estimated 200,000 people and driving 850,000 more into refugee camps in neighboring countries.[21] The chaos and violent history of Liberia provide an important backdrop to the efforts of Sirleaf to restore stability and create space for the rule of law.

HISTORICAL BACKGROUND OF LIBERIA

Liberia, "land of the free," was founded by free African-Americans, freed slaves from the United States beginning in 1820.[22] Thousands of former American slaves and free African-Americans arrived during the following years, leading to the formation of more settlements and culminating in a declaration of independence of the Republic of Liberia on July 26, 1847.[23] In Liberia's early years, the American settlers periodically encountered stiff and oftentimes violent opposition from indigenous Africans, who were excluded from citizenship in the new republic until 1904. At the same time, British and French colonial expansionists invaded Liberia, taking over much of its territory.[24] Politically, the country was ruled by the True Whig Party (TWP) after independence in 1847. Joseph Jenkins Roberts, who was born and raised in America, was Liberia's first president. The style of government and the country's constitution were fashioned on those of the United States; however, the Americo-Liberian elite controlled political power and restricted the voting rights of the indigenous population.[25] The TWP dominated all sectors of Liberia from independence in 1847 until April 12, 1980, when indigenous Liberian Master Sergeant Samuel K. Doe (from the Krahn ethnic group) seized power in a coup d'etat.[26] Doe's forces executed President William R. Tolbert and several heads of his government, mostly of American descent. One hundred thirty-three years of American-Liberian political domination ended with the formation of the People's Redemption Council (PRC).[27]

Over time, the Doe administration began endorsing members of Doe's Krahn ethnic group, and they soon dominated political and military life in Liberia. This raised ethnic tension again and caused frequent hostilities between the dominant Krahns and other ethnic groups in the country.[28]

After the October 1985 elections, Doe solidified his control. The period after the elections saw increased human rights abuses, corruption, and ethnic tensions, and the standard of living further worsened.[29] Life under the Doe military regime for women was especially fearful. A statement given by a man who had grown up in Monrovia described it this way:

> Doe proceeded to take the law into his own hands, effecting murders and rapes with impunity. Everyone was frightened; if a man were walking with his wife or daughter on the street, Doe's men or others would simply take the woman and rape her. I personally witnessed such an event one day in the vicinity of the radio station. When I saw three soldiers take a woman into a building, I ran to find their commander; but by the time the commander arrived the woman, presumably raped by all three, simply sat weeping on the ground. Only one of the perpetrators was detained, and the next day he was released.[30]

According to countless reports, this was a commonplace practice. Women's empowerment did not exist under the Doe administration and human rights violations were not limited to women.

1989–1996 CIVIL WAR

The Liberian civil conflict began in December 1989 when the National Patriotic Front of Liberia (NPFL), led by Charles Taylor, crossed into Liberia from the Ivory Coast to overthrow the government of Samuel Doe. The NPFL initially encountered support from the people but the Armed Forces of Liberia (AFL) eventually launched counterattacks against Taylor's forces.[31] Ethnic tensions that had increased under Doe's rule fueled the fighting. Ten months after the war began, the Economic Community of West African States (ECOWAS) peacekeeping force, ECOMOG, entered the conflict under a cease-fire and peace arrangement, albeit without the support or agreement of the NPFL.[32] The NPFL continued to make military gains in the capital of Monrovia, and widespread atrocities were reported in Krahn and Mandingo areas.[33] The Mandingoes were still largely victims of the NPFL onslaughts until 1991, when they, along with the exiled Krahns, organized the United Liberation Movement for Democracy in Liberia (ULIMO).[34]

In September 1990, President Samuel Doe visited the ECOMOG headquarters in Monrovia, where officials urged him to accept exile outside of Liberia. At the port, Doe was captured and taken to the Caldwell Base of the Independent National Patriotic Front of Liberia (INPFL) led by Prince Johnson. The circumstances that led to Doe's visit to Free Port are still unclear; however, after Doe arrived, Prince Johnson's INPFL attacked the headquarters and captured, tortured, and killed him.[35] Johnson's INPFL and Taylor's NPFL continued to struggle for control of Monrovia in the months that followed.

In September 1995, in accordance with the Abuja Peace Accords, the seven factions involved in the continual fighting joined to form the Liberian Council of State, mediated by ECOWAS. Despite this agreement, fighting continued until 1996 and it was during this time that some of the war's deadliest battles took place. However, in accordance with the timetable laid out in a supplement to the accords (the "Abuja Supplement"), elections were conducted in July 1997 and Charles Taylor was declared winner, with nearly 75 percent of the vote.[36] Some have speculated that Taylor won because many citizens believed that electing him was the only way to end the war.

Nearly half of Liberia's 2.5 million people were forced to flee their homes at least once during the civil conflict, giving Liberia the largest percentage of refugees and internally displaced people of any country in the world at the time.[37] Liberians who fled to Monrovia lived in and traveled through parts of the country that were under the control of one or more factions before they reached Monrovia and the relative protection of a West African peacekeeping force.

A survey conducted in 1994, which consisted of 205 women between the ages of 15 and 70 years of age, reported that 49 percent of these women had experienced at least one form of physical or sexual assault by a soldier during the first civil war.[38] An additional 17 percent had been beaten or held captive and 15 percent had been brutally raped.[39] Another 32 percent of women were subjected to strip searches and fondled.[40]

1997–2003: CIVIL WAR

Peace in Liberia, if it ever really existed, was short-lived. By the late 1990s, it was clear from reports that Taylor was supporting the Revolutionary United Front (RUF) in the civil war in neighboring Sierra Leone. As a result, the

United Nations imposed sanctions on the Liberian government, including the following:

- An arms-importation ban
- A ban on foreign travel by high-ranking members of the government and their immediate families
- A ban on trading "blood diamonds."[41]

At the same time there was a growing opposition movement to Taylor's government within Liberia, based largely in northern Lofa County. This opposition group, Liberians United for Reconciliation and Democracy (LURD), headed by Sekou Conneh (a businessman married to the daughter of Guinean president Lansana Conté), began to engage in sporadic fighting with the AFL in 1999.[42] By 2000, many believed that LURD controlled nearly 80 percent of the countryside.[43] Fighting continued through 2002, but Taylor maintained control of Monrovia.

Throughout the fighting, both the AFL, commanded by Taylor, and LURD were accused of widespread human rights violations against innocent civilians as well as child soldier recruitment.[44] With fighting intensifying, Charles Taylor agreed to participate in an ECOWAS-sponsored peace summit in Ghana. In the hope that Taylor would be arrested by his Ghanaian hosts, the Office of the Prosecutor of the Special Court for Sierra Leone unsealed an indictment against him. Reportedly caught by surprise and unwilling to arrest Taylor, Ghana refused to detain him. Within hours Taylor returned to Monrovia. In the following months, fighting intensified in and around Monrovia.[45]

Finally, in August 2003, Taylor accepted an ECOWAS-brokered peace agreement that offered him asylum in Nigeria and proposed an ECOWAS vanguard intervention force. Taylor's vice president, Moses Blah, finished the remaining term and was followed by a transition interim government headed by Liberian businessman Gyude Bryant.[46] In October 2003, the United Nations took over peacekeeping operations from ECOWAS and established the UN Mission in Liberia (UNMIL). In the years that followed, active disarmament, demobilization, and reintegration and rebuilding efforts unfolded.

WOMEN'S ORGANIZATIONS IN LIBERIA

The role women's organizations have played in Liberia throughout the course of the civil wars is important to discuss here, especially because they are credited with helping Sirleaf become elected.

Although many women suffered a great deal of violence during the civil wars, many other women, uniting for peace, created organizations aimed at ending the conflict. Women were tired of seeing their husbands and sons killed, and their daughters raped and kidnapped, so they organized together to peacefully protest and call for an end to war. A group of four women eventually turned into 500, and so the Women of Liberia Mass Action for Peace Campaign was created[47] to lead a peaceful initiative for international intervention in Liberia's civil conflict. They sat on the streets together dressed in white shirts holding signs that begged the soldiers to lay down their guns; they held prayer vigils and petitioned the heads of the ECOWAS to arrange peace talks in Accra, Ghana, in July of 2003—the talks that gave rise to the Comprehensive Peace Agreement (CPA), which brought an end to the civil conflict.[48]

Another organization, Women in Peacebuilding Network (WIPNET), is actually credited with helping President Sirleaf become elected. WIPNET made it a point to ensure women's representation during the 2005 election. Initially, many women expressed an indifferent attitude to voting, believing that the previous government structures had never done anything to advance them as a group. Five days before the last day in the registration period, WIPNET realized that market women were not registering to vote. In response, a coalition of 200 women, led by WIPNET, provided transportation, childcare, and supervision of market stalls to allow women the means to leave their work and register to vote. At the end of five days, an additional 7,400 women had registered to vote.[49]

THE PRESIDENCY OF ELLEN JOHNSON SIRLEAF

When President Ellen Johnson Sirleaf won the election in 2006, she inherited a country that had been ravaged by civil conflict; there were displaced citizens, traumatized combatants, a broken economy, and shattered society. It was clear from the start, when she was inaugurated, that gender issues would be a part of her agenda, in addition to her promises to rebuild the nation's economy, government, and society. In an excerpt from her first inaugural speech she said:

> My Administration shall thus endeavor to give Liberian women prominence in all affairs of our country. My Administration shall empower Liberian women in all areas of our national life. We will support and increase the writ of laws that restore their dignities and deal drastically with crimes that dehumanize them. We will enforce without fear or favor the law against rape recently passed by the National Transitional Legislature. We shall encourage families to educate all children, particularly the girl child. We shall also try to provide economic programs that enable Liberian women to assume their proper place in our economic revitalization process.[50]

Thus President Ellen Johnson Sirleaf made it a priority to include women in Liberia's reconstruction: women were named to head the ministries of commerce, justice, finance, youth and sports, and gender and development. They also comprised 5 of the 15 county superintendents.[51]

Sirleaf followed through with her stated goals from the beginning and, one could argue, in the footsteps of her mother by focusing on education for young girls. In August of 2006, President Sirleaf created the Liberian Education Fund (LEF)—Monrovia. Some of the accomplishments attributable to this organization include the building of 50 schools, reaching 500 teachers through short-term programs, and providing scholarships to 5,000 girls/women in formal schools and women in literacy programs.[52] LEF has reportedly reached every county in Liberia through construction, literacy, or scholarships.[53] Additionally, LEF has implemented a scholarship program for 100 girls in the Southeast and has also undertaken a scholarship program for 200 impoverished but high-achieving girls at the F-SHAM School of Girls with support from PLAN Liberia.[54]

Another noteworthy program is the National Gender Policy (NGP) that emerged in 2009 from a participatory process involving Liberian government ministries and agencies, public and private institutions, women's nongovernmental organizations, religious leaders, cultural leaders, the national legislature, media practitioners, other civil society organizations, and youth and community-based organizations nationwide. The NGP is a powerful tool, calling for the integration of gender perspectives in all policies and programs on behalf of Ms. Vabah Gayflor, the Liberian minister of gender development. Gayflor outlines why this policy is so important to Liberian stability and development:

> The Government of Liberia is strongly committed to gender equality as a means of maintaining peace, reducing poverty, enhancing justice and promoting development in the country. It is in furtherance of this commitment, that a National Gender Policy was developed in 2009 through a wide consultative process with input from various stakeholders. The Policy recommends that gender mainstreaming and gender budgeting should be adopted as a development approach and shall inform the economic reform agenda, medium and long term development planning, value re-orientation, social transformation and other development initiatives of government.[55]

The goal of the NGP is to mainstream gender in the national development processes, enhance the empowerment of women and girls for sustainable and equitable development, and create and strengthen gender responsive structures and mechanisms in which both women and men can participate and benefit from development programs on an equal basis.[56] A policy such as this sends a very clear message: women's empowerment is one of the main priorities of the Sirleaf administration.

The findings of a report created by the ministry of gender development reveal that women and girls in Liberia play an essential role in Liberia's economy but face countless obstacles that prevent them from full participation in economic activities. The report explains that these obstacles have grown out of gender segregation in the labor market and women's multiple roles in the family that limit their opportunities for economic empowerment. Women are major players in the agricultural sector, providing all marketing and trading services and linking rural and urban markets through their personal networks.[57] However, despite their important contribution, they neither own land nor have secure tenure to the land they work, compared to men.[58] For these reasons, and countless more outlined in the policy itself, the ministry for gender development was created and is currently implementing the NGP.

The education of women and girls has grown significantly during Sirleaf's time in office. In terms of literacy rates, in 2005, 47 percent of women over the age of 15 could read and write, but by 2009, that number rose to 55 percent.[59] In her first year in office she created the Free and Compulsory Education Program, which abolished all fees and tuition for public primary schools and drastically reduced the tuition and fees for high school. This program was so successful that after the first year of implementation there was a 40 percent increase in school enrollment. In Liberia and many countries around the world, men are traditionally educated first due to the economic strain it can put on a family to educate both girls and boys, but this policy directly benefited women because it allowed them free access to education.[60]

Before Sirleaf came to office, 8 women held seats in parliament; by 2009, the number had risen to 13. This still represents a small portion of the electorate but also an increase of over 50 percent.[61] According to the World Bank, in 2005, the female labor force participation rate in Liberia (percentage of women between the ages of 15–64) was 69 percent. By 2009, this number had not changed. Nevertheless, this proportion of women workers is about average when compared to statistics for other sub-Saharan countries.[62] Fertility rates among women were 5.6 children per family in 2005, and this number decreased only slightly in 2009 to 5.3.[63] While these statistics seem to be heading in the right direction, it is still an indication that there is much work to be done.

Another important measure is the United Nations' Human Development Index (HDI). The HDI is measured by three dimensions, namely health, education, and living standards. It also has four indicators, which are life expectancy at birth, mean years of schooling, expected years of schooling, and gross national income per capita. The HDI sets a minimum and a maximum for each dimension, called goalposts, and then shows where each country stands in relation to these goalposts, expressed as a value between 0 and 1.[64]

The HDI initially improved under Sirleaf and her administration, which was at .265 in 2004, compared to the 2010 data of .300, so it is clear that incremental progress is being made, regardless of how slow it may seem.[65] But in 2009, Liberia was still ranked under "very-low human development" at 169 out of 186 countries surveyed,[66] and sadly, as of 2013, that number decreased even further to 174 out of 186.[67] Whether this is a testament to a lack of leadership or the insurmountable damages of civil war is unknown.

Another important measure of the condition of women is infant mortality rates (IMR). In 2006, when Sirleaf took office, the IMR in Liberia was the highest it had ever been, with 152 children out of 1,000 under the age of one year dying.[68] In addition, the maternal mortality ratio, estimated at 1,200 deaths per 100,000 live births, was one of the highest in the world in 2006.[69] Comparing these numbers to the more recent data for Liberia, progress in this area is much clearer. In 2010, the IMR in Liberia was calculated at 74 out of every 1,000 live births. Still a staggering number when compared with the rest of the world, but a decrease of more than 50 percent, which is significant.

Military expenditure as a percentage of the Liberian gross domestic product (GDP) was 0.6 percent in 2006 and remained the same until it increased slightly in 2009 to 0.8 percent.[70] This is a rather low when compared to other postconflict countries like Nicaragua that had defense spending at 4 percent of the GDP, post conflict. In contrast, the total government expenditure on education was 12 percent of the government budget in 2008 according to the World Bank.[71] Since Sirleaf has been in office, the percentage of government spending on health has increased from 11.9 percent in 2004 before she became president to almost 17 percent in 2008.[72] It is also worth noting that Liberia received an estimated $229 million from the United States in 2010 for the purpose of development.[73]

According to a UN report, Liberia has created a task force to implement recommendations in the 2009 report of the Committee on the Elimination of Discrimination against Women (CEDAW).[74] Also under Johnson Sirleaf, the ministry of gender and development in Liberia has launched a program that is gaining positive feedback from the international community. The Economic Empowerment of Adolescent Girls & Young Women project is a joint initiative between Liberia, Denmark, the World Bank, and Nike. An excerpt from the program proposal claims that the goal is to:

> Smooth the path of adolescent girls to productive employment through job skills training and business development services. The training offered to participants will focus on technical skills, as well as the integration of life-skills training to address some of the crucial barriers to the development of adolescent girls in Liberia. These include, for example, early pregnancy, social restrictions from family and community members, and forms of GBV, including sexual exploitation and abuse.[75]

This program is important because many public work programs in Liberia have previously been geared toward assimilating male ex-combatants into the job market and the few skills training programs that did exist for girls taught primarily "female" job skills, such as cooking or sewing. The program is targeting nine counties in Liberia and an outreach to 2,500 young girls.[76] Although it is obvious that the needs of Liberia's women and girls reach far beyond what the project will be able to deliver, the program is nonetheless an indication that gender issues are on the list of priorities for the Johnson Sirleaf administration.

However, despite all these positive achievements and huge advances, violence against women is still a primary concern for the administration. Since 2007, rape has been the highest reported crime in Liberia and there are innumerable unreported cases.[77] Doctors without Borders (DWB) reported in 2011 that 92 percent of females treated for rape in its Liberia facilities were under 18. A DWB study published in November said that of about 1,500 females treated for rape in Monrovia clinics in 2008 and 2009, 4 out of 10 were younger than 12.[78] Worse still is the staggeringly small number of prosecutions and punishment for these crimes, because prosecutors in Liberia have no access to DNA testing or other forensic techniques.

Sirleaf vowed to continue the fight for women's empowerment during her second inauguration in 2011. She was quoted in the UK *Guardian* as saying: "in studies conducted in many of the counties of Liberia in 2004, a large percentage of women and girls reported that they were victims of various forms of violence and abuse. International organization reports show that a large percentage of these women were raped."[79] Additionally, Liberia has the highest teenage pregnancy rate in the world with a staggering 38 percent of teenage women getting pregnant before the age of 18, according to a recent study conducted by the United Nations Population Fund,[80] so it is clear this effort must continue.

Based on the typology created for this volume, Ellen Johnson Sirleaf can be classified as the flexible/pragmatic personality type and her management style is best described as collegial. While it is difficult to find actual proof of this in the research, there is evidence that supports this claim, specifically because of her open-minded approach to issues and her ability to work with others. Since in office, with the help of her administration, many new government oversight ministries have been created to oversee the problems Liberia faces. She states that "governments must respond to changing times and come up with new measures to increase economic prosperity without creating new tensions,"[81]which illustrates her flexibility. She is also clearly open to working with others to solve problems and writes about many conferences in which she represented Liberia, including a 2007 conference of 30 countries in Africa that met to discuss small arms control and ways to solve the issue collectively.[82] Etweda "Sugars" Cooper, founder of the Liberian

Women's Initiative, describes Sirleaf as "the kind of person who works with everyone for the interests of Liberia. She puts Liberians first. It's for them she works."[83] She is also working with President Obama on a new initiative entitled Power Africa, which aims to double electricity access in sub-Saharan Africa by responsibly building on the continent's potential in gas and oil as well as its huge potential to develop clean energy.[84] The 23 years of civil war that ravaged the country before her presidency has left a country of 4.1 million people literally in the dark, with only 1 percent of people residing in urban areas with power. Almost no one living in rural areas has electricity.

She is lovingly called "Ma Ellen"[85] by all Liberians, young, old, friends, and enemies alike, which says a lot about the maternal instincts that influence her leadership. A recent documentary film entitled "Iron Ladies of Liberia" reveals the combination of caring and toughness that is the key to Sirleaf's leadership. In one gripping scene, her maternal nature as a leader becomes quite apparent when she is able to peacefully resolve a potentially volatile protest. Soldiers threatened to stage a coup if their demands were not met. The president invited them in to hear their grievances but only if they promise to continue peaceful demonstrations and stop threatening a coup. She listens to the grievances with a patient and caring ear and promised to look into the issues they were complaining about. The men refer to her as "Our Ma" and, despite their anger, still have a level of respect and love for her.[86] It shows her ability to listen to others, be tolerant of other viewpoints, and effectively handle disagreements.

I will also argue that she seeks power in order to implement policy and better her country, not simply for the sake of power. We see this in one of the most recent developments in Liberia. She has cracked down on her country's widespread corruption. Sirleaf issued an executive order last March requiring all presidential appointees to declare their assets to Liberia's Anti-Corruption Commission. When 46 appointees failed to comply, she suspended them all until further notice, including her own son, Charles Sirleaf. According to a statement released to the media recently, Sirleaf said the 46 officials could be reinstated only after she had confirmation from the commission that they have complied.[87]

President Sirleaf stated from the beginning that development and women's empowerment would be the focus of her administration and it is clear she tried to do everything she said she would. Due to years of civil war, she inherited a country that was economically and socially ravaged, so progress was sure to be slow. Perhaps her goals were greater than one president could manage. It seems clear she made progress, albeit through small steps. Internationally, Johnson Sirleaf has generated a great deal of goodwill and single-handedly raised the country's profile in the rest of the world. Her efforts have somewhat paid off through debt-forgiveness and increased foreign investment. According to critics, however, not enough of these benefits have translated into tangible improvements for the country's people.[88]

In 2011, she won the Nobel Peace Prize along with two other women "for their non-violent struggle for the safety of women and for women's rights to full participation in peace-building work," so her work has clearly caught the attention of the international community.[89] She told the *New York Times* in 2010 that she would appoint women to every ministry position, if she could find enough who were qualified, saying, "Women are more committed. Women work harder. And women are more honest; they have less reason to be corrupt. They don't have so many diversions. Men have more than one wife; they have their concubines."[90] And she followed through with these words upon her reelection in 2011, when there were 14 possible government appointments and Sirleaf appointed half of the positions to women.[91] In May of 2013 she was ranked 87 out of 100 in *Forbes Magazine*'s "Power Women," but the question still remains: Is all this publicity and international acclaim enough to see tangible improvements for women and the people of Liberia? The jury is still out and only time will tell what her legacy will be. President Johnson Sirleaf has stated repeatedly that women are her priority. The women of Liberia and the rest of the world will watch and wait to see if she is able to follow these words with tangible results.

NOTES

1. Ellen Johnson Sirleaf, *This Child Will Be Great* (New York: Harper Collins, 2009), 11.
2. Ibid.
3. Ibid.
4. Ibid., 17.
5. Ibid., 25.
6. Ibid.
7. Ibid.
8. Ibid.
9. Ibid.
10. Ibid.
11. http://www.emansion.gov.lr/content.php?sub=President's%20Biography&related=The%20President.
12. Ibid.
13. Ibid.
14. Ibid.
15. Sirleaf, *This Child*, 38.
16. Ibid.
17. Ibid., 39.
18. Ibid., 41.
19. Ibid., 36.
20. Ibid.

21. Ruthie Ackerman, "Rebuilding Liberia, One Brick at a Time," World Policy Institute, 2009.
22. http://www.state.gov/r/pa/ei/bgn/6618.htm#history.
23. Ibid.
24. Ibid.
25. Ibid.
26. Ibid.
27. Ibid.
28. Ibid.
29. Ibid.
30. Advocates for Human Rights, "Human Rights Violations during the Rice Riots and Doe Era," http://www.theadvocatesforhumanrights.org/uploads/chapter+5human+rights+abuses+during+the+rice+riots+and+doe+era.pdf.
31. Peter Dennis, "A Brief History of Liberia," International Center for Transitional Justice (May 2006).
32. Ibid., 4.
33. Ibid.
34. Ibid.
35. Ibid.
36. Ibid.
37. S. Swiss, P. Jennings, and G. Aryee, "Violence against Women during the Liberian Conflict," *JAMA* 279 (1998): 625–629.
38. Ibid.
39. Ibid.
40. Ibid.
41. Dennis, "A Brief History of Liberia," 5.
42. Ibid.
43. Ibid.
44. Ibid.
45. Ibid.
46. Ibid.
47. http://www.thescavenger.net/.
48. http://www.theperspective.org/2005/feb/struggleofwomen.html.
49. http://www.usip.org/publications/women-s-role-liberia-s-reconstruction.
50. Inaugural Address of H. E. Ellen Johnson Sirleaf, January 16, 2006, http://www.emansion.gov.lr/doc/inaugural_add_1.pdf.
51. "Women's Role in Liberia," http://www.usip.org/publications/women-s-role-liberia-s-reconstruction.
52. http://www.peopletopeople.info/id490.html.
53. Ibid.
54. Ibid.
55. Ministry of Gender and Development, *Liberia National Gender Policy* (Monrovia: Liberia, 2009).
56. Ibid.
57. Ibid.
58. Ibid.
59. Gender Statistics of Liberia, http://web.worldbank.org.
60. Sirleaf, *This Child,* 292.

61. Ibid
62. Ibid.
63. Ibid.
64. http://hdr.undp.org/en/statistics/indices/gdi_gem/.
65. United Nations (2010). World Population Prospects: 2008 Revision. New York.
66. http://hdr.undp.org/en/media/HDR_2009_EN_Complete.pdf.
67. http://hdr.undp.org/en/media/HDR2013_EN_Summary.pdf.
68. http://www.unicef.org/har08/files/har08_Liberia_countrychapter.pdf.
69. Ibid.
70. http://milexdata.sipri.org/result.php4.
71. http://www.tradingeconomics.com/liberia/public-spending-on-education-total-percent-of-government-expenditure-wb-data.html.
72. http://www.tradingeconomics.com/liberia/health-expenditure-public-percent-of-government-expenditure-wb-data.html.
73. http://www.usaid.gov/locations/sub-saharan_africa/countries/liberia/liberia_fs.pdf.
74. United Nations Security Council, 21st Progress Report of the Secretary-General on the United Nations Mission in Liberia, August 11, 2010.
75. http://www.supportliberia.com/assets/108/EPAG_one-pager_1_.pdf.
76. Ibid.
77. Jordan Ryan, "Prevention and Response to Sexual Exploitation and Abuse in Liberia (PSEA)," Country Report, Monrovia, Liberia, August 2008.
78. http://www.frontpageafricaonline.com/politics/42-politics/5221-rapists-nation-rape-stalking-liberias-kids-1-in-10-victims-age-5-and-under.html .
79. http://www.guardian.co.uk/global-development/2010/oct/06/guardian-development-network
80. http://www.theinquirer.com.lr/content1.php?news_id=739&main=news.
81. Sirleaf, *This Child,* 300.
82. Ibid., 302.
83. http://www.pbs.org/wnet/women-war-and-peace/features/what-has-ellen-johnson-sirleaf-done-for-liberian-women/.
84. http://www.foreignpolicy.com/articles/2013/08/29/let_s_power_africa_ellen_johnson_sirleaf_liberia_energy.
85. Sirleaf, *This Child,* 272.
86. http://www.imow.org/wpp/stories/viewstory?storyid=924.
87. http://abcnews.go.com/blogs/headlines/2012/08/liberias-president-suspends-son-in-anti-corruption-push/.
88. Women's Campaign International Assessment Report: Transforming Protracted Conflicts through Women's Empowerment: Liberia, February, 2008.
89. http://www.nobelprize.org/nobel_prizes/peace/laureates/2011/johnson_sirleaf.html.
90. http://www.nytimes.com/2010/10/24/magazine/24sirleaf-t.html?pagewanted=all.
91. http://allafrica.com/stories/201203050458.html.

16

Mikhail Gorbachev: The End of the Cold War

Natasha Zemtsova Miller

This chapter examines Mikhail Gorbachev's personal characteristics and their influence on his decision making process against the background of the historical events that took place in the USSR (Union of Soviet Socialist Republics) in 1985–1991.

Gorbachev as a political leader is a unique and very controversial figure. His name is associated with the most crucial changes during the final years of the Soviet Union. During his six-year term as Communist Party secretary-general, he initiated more reforms than his communist predecessors ever did and much more than anybody expected from him. Some 30 years later, Gorbachev's personality and his achievements in international and domestic affairs are still often misunderstood. Most of his countrymen blame him, and cannot forgive him, for the collapse of the Soviet Union and the subsequent economic decline. But in many other countries people are thankful to him for the unification of Germany and Europe and the peaceful end to the Cold War.

Mikhail Gorbachev was a product of the Lenin-Stalinist system and a staunch supporter of it. Paradoxically, he emerged as a more vociferous internal enemy of the communist system than all its external opponents. Following the deaths of so many of its aging leaders, the regime wanted a young, vigorous man who could take the USSR forward into the coming decades. But they gained a young, vigorous reformer who tried "to improve" the

---

This chapter relies on information from "Mikhail Gorbachev and His Role in the Peaceful Solution of the Cold War," a master's thesis written by Natasha Zemtsova at the City College of New York in 2011.

system in order to save it. After thwarting innovation and entrepreneurship for decades under secretive, centralized political and economic controls, the Soviet system was imploding from within, something that many Russians have forgotten. Taking over the helm, Gorbachev tried to turn the system around by introducing transparency and political and economic reforms. However, the system was too ossified and corrupt to be able to adapt to the new world environment and even Gorbachev's optimism could not bring about the needed changes fast enough. The paradox is that he tried to bring about peaceful change and that very peaceful process led to the collapse of the Soviet Union and its communist system. Gorbachev's unique personal characteristics such as his high sense of morality and unwillingness to use force, endless energy and optimism, and idealism in combination with his ability for political pluralism were all positive leadership qualities but could not prevent the inevitable.

This analysis of Gorbachev's personality and his performance in the political arena is based in part on the theoretical framework developed by Alexander L. George and Juliette L. George, who believe that a closer look at a person's childhood and early years will provide us with a better understanding of the person's policy decisions and character.

EARLY YEARS

Mikhail Gorbachev was born on March 2, 1931, in the small southern village Privol'noye, in the Stavropol region, Republic of Russia. His ancestors were Cossacks who had been pushed from the Ukraine and the Don River area in search of virgin soil and religious freedom, settling in the southernmost wilds of the territory of Stavropol, known as the Northern Caucasus.

Mikhail was born into a family of hard-working Russian and Ukrainian migrants. In his early years, Mikhail experienced the influence of two different political temperaments: those of his two very different grandfathers.

His maternal grandfather, Panteley Gopkalo, was an active communist, a party member and a collectivization[1] participant. He also was chairman of the local collective farm, or *kolkhoz*, which made him the most important person in the village.

His paternal grandfather, Andrew Gorbachev, was a total antipode to Mr. Gopkalo. Being a staunch opponent of collectivization and of Stalin's ideology, Andrew Gorbachev refused to share his harvest even with his son Sergey because his son had become a collective farmer. In his memoirs, Mikhail Gorbachev described this family episode as evidence of a broader struggle, almost a fight, because his grandfather had hidden the grain in the space under his roof. Later on, during World War II, when German soldiers occupied the village for a few months and were going to annihilate the communist families, it was his nonparty grandfather Andrew who hid, not the grain, but the 12-year-old Mikhail on his farm.

Nevertheless, despite their very different political views, both grandfathers suffered under Stalin's repressive policies during the 1930s. Mr. Gopkalo, though a committed communist, was charged as "an active member of provocative organization" and escaped execution by a miracle, spending some time in prison. Meanwhile, Andrew Gorbachev was arrested and deported to Siberia for a few years, purportedly for having hidden 40 pounds of grain for his family from the collective harvest.

Despite the fact that Stalin-era repressive measures affected both the families of Gorbachev's parents, neither of the grandfathers blamed Stalin for it. They considered zealous, local executives responsible for their troubles. During this era of repression, reporting on other people, including neighbors and friends, was highly encouraged by the KGB, the Soviet secret service. Even political anecdotes among coworkers could result in arrest, imprisonment, or even execution if the secret police were informed. Later, Mikhail Gorbachev would say: "Stalinism demoralized not only hangmen but their victims as well. Betrayal became a very popular illness of the society."[2] Mikhail Gorbachev's first lessons in political pluralism and tolerance were learned not only from his politically polarized grandfathers but also from his family lifestyle. There were portraits of Lenin and Stalin in one corner and Orthodox icons brought by his grandmother from Keiv-Pecherskaya Laura in another corner of their house.

The two conflicting political viewpoints of his grandfathers contributed to the dual nature of Gorbachev's character, which allowed him to rise to the top of the ruling establishment as an active communist and then, from a party loyalist point of view, turn around and destroy the Soviet communist system.

World War II left young Gorbachev with memories of a troublesome period told to him through his father's letters, the starvation, and extreme poverty. The village way of life, very close to serfdom, combined with his curiosity and unrestrained energy, paved the way for Mikhail to change his life completely and enter a very different world: the world of studies. He read books avidly, taking an interest in everything including math, physics, and literature. School theater was another passion of his during high school. He played many roles in amateur plays, and even considered embarking on an acting career.

Young Gorbachev also felt very comfortable playing the role of a *komsomol*[3] leader during his school years. He was very strict with those who were late or undisciplined but also showed respect for adults and goodwill for classmates.

Gorbachev began helping his father on the collective farm when he was 14 years old. At the age of 17, Mikhail was awarded a State Labor Order for his work as a combine operator. This honorable acknowledgment made him special among his schoolmates and helped in his future career.

Hard labor and working together in the field strengthened Mikhail's relationship with his father Sergey. Until the very end of his father's life, they were close friends, spending time together. Mikhail inherited his father's chivalrous respect for women and his passion for discovering all kind of information. Sergey Gorbachev had only four years of secondary school education but always enjoyed reading newspapers, watching the news on TV, and discussing issues with his son.

His relationship with the mother, Maria Gorbacheva, was not so easy. She was a very strong and outspoken woman in contrast to her intelligent and mild husband. In one of his interviews, Gorbachev, talking about his "constant hesitations" during a decision making process, mentioned that his "mother has never had any doubts. She never went to any kind of school and everything has always been clear to her."[4] Maria Gorbacheva was very conservative and refused to change her way of life and habits under any circumstances. Only in 1992, after Gorbachev resigned, was she convinced and finally agreed to leave the village where she had spent all her life and move to Moscow.

The image of a strong woman around Gorbachev in his childhood explains why he conceded so much power to his wife, Raisa, whom he consulted at times and whom he regarded as a full partner, referring to her as "my General."

In 1950, Mikhail asked his father's permission to apply to a university. Because of the war, he had lost two years and was already 19 when he finished high school. His dad was very brief and said: "If you're enrolled, we will help you as much as we can. Otherwise you can always come back and continue working together in the farm."[5] The determination to escape peasant life and his endless thirst for knowledge were so strong that Mikhail applied to five schools at the same time, including engineering, diplomacy, and finally the law department of Moscow State University (MSU), one of the most prestigious and highly competitive programs in the country. In high school, young Gorbachev had been given a silver medal: a special award given to excellent students after completing their program of studies. The medal and the State Labor Order given to him earlier contributed to his admission to MSU without taking any exams. Hedrick Smith, a famous American journalist who worked in Moscow for a long time and wrote a book about Gorbachev, said that for someone from a small southern village to be admitted to the famous Moscow university is like a black kid from Louisiana becoming a Harvard student.[6] Gorbachev commented modestly about this crucial step in his life, mentioning that after the war, the whole country was starving for qualified people, and just an application was enough to get enrolled.

In September 1950, after covering more than 1,500 kilometers (about 930 miles) by train and arriving in the capital, a completely new period in his personal development began for the future leader.

STUDENT YEARS AND MARRIAGE

Speaking of his origins in his memoirs, Gorbachev says: "In order to make the reforms you have to live the life I've lived and see the things I've seen; to be from the family that went through the drama of collectivization and repressions of 1937. To graduate from Moscow University is the most important thing in this to-do list."[7]

The law program in MSU was very hard and intense. Some of the professors had been working there since before the revolution. In addition to the theories of Marx and Lenin, students from all over the Soviet Union had to study Roman law, history of political science, oratory, constitutions of the greatest bourgeois states including America, and so on. This intellectual atmosphere contributed to Mikhail's political pluralism and tolerance of noncommunist ideologies. Many years later Gorbachev would be criticized for his sympathy for the Western way of life. The Soviet people would blame him for "giving up" to American culture and would informally call him Michael Gorby, in an Americanized manner. However, according to behavioralist Milton Rokeach, Gorbachev was simply demonstrating the classic characteristics of open-mindedness, curiosity, and openness to different systems and points of view.

The future president lived in a dormitory where, due to general poverty, there were 15 to 20 people per room. As one of his former roommates recalls, there were constant discussions about philosophy, political ideologies, Lenin, Stalin, and other leaders. Some of those men were arrested and sent into exile later for not being careful enough in their jokes and comments about Stalin.

Gorbachev, in his memoirs, says that the university transformed his passion and curiosity into a stable interest in philosophy, politics, and theories. The first year in Moscow was the most difficult for him since his classmates from the big cities had better academic backgrounds. He quickly compensated for the lack of knowledge by his purposefulness and persistence. Having a strong thirst for knowledge, he spent most of his time in the library, reading books. Such qualities were not rare for students of that time. After the war, many young people considered education the only way to succeed in life.

The individual traits of everybody in the dormitory were especially visible due to the severe economic conditions of students at that time. Young men were sharing food and gifts from home with each other; it was not abnormal to borrow a warm coat from a friend: "[a]student's wardrobe never was personal, we all were sharing with each other," recalls Gorbachev about his student life.[8]

During his university years, Mikhail was known as a friendly and open person. His former classmates point out his provincial openness and leadership qualities. He was elected as a *komsorg* (komsomol) leader—and then, in 1952, a Communist Party member.

In 1953, Mikhail Gorbachev married Raisa Titarenko, a girl from a small city in the Altai region of Siberia, the eldest of three children of a Ukrainian-born railway engineer. Since the family was very poor, Raisa could not always afford even warm clothes and shoes while living in Moscow. She looked very modest, had never been a coquette, and, as her husband certifies, did not start to use lipstick until after she turned 30.

Mikhail and Raisa had a lot in common. Both spouses were half-Russian and half-Ukrainian. Both had come to Moscow from poor, diligent families, considering studies as a logical continuation of their hard-working way of life. Both were provincial and foreign to the big city. Raisa spent all her early years in the Ural Mountains region and came to Moscow to study philosophy at the same university as Mikhail. They had common habits and interests. For example, both loved evening walks, and it became their sacramental ritual for many years.

Despite all those similarities, Raisa was much stronger, much more organized, and a more meticulous person than her husband. All the books in their home library were placed in alphabetical order. She could leave a theater in the middle of a show and go home if she had to finish reading a book or to prepare for an upcoming exam. When Mikhail was promoted and the couple began traveling abroad, Raisa prepared for their first trips as for an exam, reading historical literature, visiting museums, and taking notes. When the couple came back to Moscow in 1978, after 23 years in Stavropol, Raisa organized for her and her husband a more thorough exploration of the capital. Every Sunday, they visited historical places in chronological order, starting from the earliest.

Raisa's discipline and extreme fastidiousness crystallized during her years of study in Moscow and then in her teaching career in Stavropol. Those qualities were her means to compensate for the lack of knowledge and "universal culture" that she had not been able receive from her family and which had made her feel inferior in Moscow.

However, Raisa Gorbacheva created a furor in the international political arena when she appeared in the mass media as an elegant, independent, and up-to-date First Lady, which was not expected from the Soviet Union at that time. Despite spending 23 years in provincial Stavropol, where her husband brought her after graduation, Raisa followed all the current political and fashion trends on an international level. She also became her husband's personal image-maker, though the concept was unknown to Soviet people at that time. Raisa played the role of his unofficial political adviser, being his so-called personal minister of international affairs. Gorbachev was broadly criticized for his inability to make more or less important political decisions without conferring with his wife. One could assume that the roles of a strong principled mother and more malleable and intelligent father contributed to the fact that Gorbachev felt comfortable with the super-organized and active Raisa,[9] jokingly referring to her as the "secretary-general in their family."

Everyday walks together became their unbreakable family tradition. Partially, it was caused by the fact that, outdoors, they could discuss all the political issues and be sure nobody else was eavesdropping. Lukyanov, who worked closely with Gorbachev during his time as the secretary-general, recalls that Mikhail, if reminded by the end of the day about an urgent decision to be made, would often say "Let me call you later." As Lukyanov assumes, it meant the issue was going to be discussed in the "family *politbureau*" with Raisa during their walk. And closer to midnight, Gorbachev would always call him back with the decision.[10]

Like millions of Soviet people, Gorbachev and his wife felt devastated after Stalin's death in 1953 and asked themselves "What will happen to us?" Even though both Mikhail's grandfathers suffered under Soviet-style repression and Raisa's grandfather was executed in Siberia during the 1930s, none of them blamed Stalin. As some of Gorbachev's former classmates certify, Mikhail never was a big fan of Stalin nor demonstrated any signs of criticism or disagreement with the leader. His anti-Stalinism and determination to reform the political environment emerged much later while working in Stavropol after graduation.

Since education in the Soviet Union was totally sponsored by the government, recent graduates were unable to freely choose their place of work right after the completion of their studies. Most of the students after graduation were distributed to various locations and positions based on their major, grade-point average, state needs for specialists, and other factors. There was an option to continue in graduate school, but since Mikhail's background had been in farming, he was offered the study of peasant law instead of law and political science, which he preferred. The strong-minded Gorbachev refused to sacrifice his professional interests for life in Moscow. And even though Raisa was offered the chance to stay in graduate school, they decided to move to provincial Stavropol, the capital of the region where he was from.

EARLY CAREER AS A YOUNG POLITICIAN

Stavropol in the 1950s was "more than provincial," as Raisa characterized it later.[11] The whole city had neither a sewer system nor an urban water supply. There was one major street and almost no public or personal transportation. People commuted mostly on foot. After five years spent in Moscow, Stavropol seemed extremely undeveloped to the young couple.

After several unsuccessful attempts to seek employment as a lawyer, Mikhail went to the local office of the komsomol. There he presented all his achievements, including his Communist Party membership, State Labor Order for work as a combine operator, a university diploma, and his activity in student life. Gorbachev's personality and persistence were favored by the komsomol secretary, and the recent MSU graduate was hired in a position where energy, responsibility, and communication skills were much more important than his specialized knowledge.

Not only his diligence and endless activity but also his organizational and speaking talents and his ability for off-the-cuff public speaking made Mikhail distinct among local komsomol workers and brought him to the attention of the local leadership. Gorbachev's career developed dramatically. In March 1961, at the age of 30, he was already elected as the first secretary of the komsomol in the Stavropol region and was given his first separate apartment instead of room in a dormitory.

Meanwhile, Raisa was not as successful during their first four years in Stavropol. Having her diploma with distinction from Moscow University, she was considered overqualified for regular positions in the province. In 1957, she gave birth to their only daughter, Irina. Raisa later defended her master's thesis and then became a lecturer in a local university. Raisa's example inspired Mikhail to continue his education and write a master's thesis as well. Gorbachev passed the initial exams but never accomplished his scientific dreams. His political career went on, and in 1969, his former chiefs, who had moved to Moscow by that time, decided to promote the young promising secretary. In April 1970, Gorbachev visited the Moscow office of the secretary-general, having no idea he was going to run it in 15 years. The same year, at the age of 39, he was appointed First Party Secretary of the Stavropol *Kraikom* (regional committee), becoming one of the youngest provincial party chiefs in the nation. The Stavropol region was considered one of the most economically important in the country, and its territory was as large as Belgium, Switzerland, and three times the size of Luxemburg, all together. In this position, he helped reorganize the collective farms, improve workers' living conditions, expand the size of their private plots, and give them a greater voice in planning. These policy decisions and positions were most likely a result of his experiences growing up as a peasant farmer.

He soon became a member of the Communist Party Central Committee in 1971. Three years later, in 1974, he was made a representative to the Supreme Council of the Soviet Union and chairman of the Standing Commission on Youth Affairs. He was subsequently appointed to the Central Committee's Secretariat for Agriculture in 1978, replacing Fyodor

Kulakov, who had supported Gorbachev's appointment, after Kulakov died of a heart attack.

Although he was one of the more privileged people in the Stavropol region, Gorbachev saw how primitive the living conditions were of simple, hard-working people in small towns. Observing this inequality seems to have stimulated reformist "rebel thoughts" in his head, but due to everyday duties he did not really think about significant changes. Gorbachev modestly refused many benefits given him due to his position. Even though he had a personal service car, he always walked to his office. The city dwellers used this habit in order to approach him right on the street and ask him for something in person. His daughter Irina attended regular school instead of the only special English school for children of important people. The question whether the service car and a personal driver should be used for her was not even open for discussion—the idea itself was considered inappropriate. His biographers describe it as an attempt to keep family traditions and stay independent despite his position, not forgetting where he came from.[12] This is clear evidence that as a personality, Gorbachev did seek power for its own sake, but was more of an achievement-oriented person. A power-seeking personality would have enjoyed flaunting his position.

Gorbachev first heard in 1968 the ideas for the future *perestroika*, the policy of economic and political reformation of the country, from docent F. Sadykov, who strove to present his prescriptions for renovating the communist system soon after Czechoslovakia's attempt at political liberalization.[13] As Gorbachev recalls in his memoirs, political elites, including himself, tore down all Sadykov's ideas, but later on Mikhail had second thoughts, recognizing the docent was right. All these regrets or "bad feelings" combined with childhood memories of collectivization, the repression of his family members, and extreme poverty multiplied by his university training in political science became a springboard for changes in his internal ideology and spurred his open-minded approach to political reform.

His participation in international delegations and his trips abroad provided him with elementary lessons in political pluralism and a better view of what was going on in other countries. In 1957, Mikhail organized the participation of an Italian delegation in one of the youth festivals in Moscow. The Italian perception of time, protocol, and discipline appeared to be very different from what the punctual and responsible Gorbachev was used to. His first trips to the Western bloc countries—France, Italy, Belgium, and West Germany—were surprisingly different from the socialist bloc countries such as Bulgaria or East Germany. The future secretary-general came to at least two very important conclusions after visiting Westernized countries. First, he realized that the Soviet people were not living in the best of worlds, as the party had tried to convince them. In the West, not only the leadership class but also simple people lived and worked in conditions that even party leaders in the USSR had never seen before. Second, Gorbachev and his wife were amazed by the relaxed atmosphere of the imperialistic environment. The Soviets had invested most of their budget in the military to protect themselves from the capitalist threat, but the people representing this threat were surprisingly friendly and benevolent with them. After one of those trips, Raisa, who was also impressed by the beauty and culture of Western Europe, asked her husband an anti-Soviet question, "Why do we live worse, Mikhail?" While residing in Stavropol, Gorbachev could not find an answer to this question. Things started to change when the family moved back to Moscow in December 1978.

BACK TO MOSCOW

During the 1970s, the USSR was living through a period of so-called Brezhnev stagnation, the time of socioeconomic slowdown under Leonid Brezhnev that started in the 1970s and continued during the short administrations of his successors Andropov and Chernenko.

From the moment Gorbachev's family was transferred back to Moscow in 1978, Mikhail already had made a successful Komsomol party career, becoming the first secretary of one of the most important regional committees. He already felt comfortable entering offices of high-ranking leaders. Though in his 40s, he was the youngest secretary of the Central Committee of the Communist Party in the USSR at that time. His wife Raisa was ambitiously thinking about a scientific career in a university, but recognized that as her husband's personal adviser and consultant, she had a much greater opportunity to put her intellect to use.

Mikhail's career rose dramatically due to a lucky concurrence of conditions: the decades that the country spent under overaged leadership, three secretaries-general in less than three years, Andropov's[14] protection of Gorbachev, and the favor of other authoritative people. The Soviet people were pleasantly surprised to see a young, educated, and lively leader on the political stage. In March 1985, Mikhail Gorbachev became secretary-general of the USSR.

The year 1985 also became the year of big changes in the Soviet Union. The Brezhnev epoch of stagnation was over. Energetic Gorbachev started his famous innovative project of perestroika. The word literally means "reconstruction" or "rebuilding," and meant the improvement of socialism and the economic system that was on the brink of bankruptcy. The moment he became secretary-general, Gorbachev had realized the urgent need for changes in the political and economic situation. The plan was to carry out reform within the system by means of democratization. The idea of perestroika was complex and included many politically and economically crucial decisions, for which Gorbachev is still heavily criticized within the former USSR and highly praised in the West.

Gorbachev began with the famously failed large-scale antialcohol campaign. Alcoholism had grown sharply and cut heavily into productivity. The prices of liquor were increased, retail sale was very limited, and many nationally famous vineyards were cut down. This brought a whole new level of complexity to the problem. The consumption of home-made low-quality vodka increased dramatically, the state budget incurred losses, and people who were forced to stand in long lines outdoors to buy licensed alcohol criticized the government for the inconvenience.

The campaign against alcohol was imposed on a country still shocked by the disaster in Chernobyl, in the Republic of Ukraine. In April 1986, one of its nuclear reactors exploded in the middle of the night, causing an expulsion of highly radioactive fallout into the atmosphere, killing and mutilating thousands of people. The Chernobyl accident became the worst nuclear disaster in world history, but the Soviet leader waited days before acknowledging the disaster and was criticized for hiding the truth. He responded by creating *glasnost,* Gorbachev's policy of openness and the democratization of all the aspects of social life. The word *glasnost* is derived from the Russian *golos*—voice—and can be translated as "policy of openness." The communists had originally conceived the idea of glasnost as freedom for constructive (loyal) criticism or self-criticism but not the absence of censorship in mass media. However, during the perestroika years, due to efforts by progressive journalists and activists, glasnost was interpreted to be freedom of speech. The law regarding the press that was passed in March 1990 allowed the Soviet mass media to reach some certain level of independence from the party's control.

The Chernobyl disaster vividly exposed all the ugliness and ineffectiveness of the Soviet system. Leaders realized the actual scale of the tragedy only a few days after the explosion. During those days, the local Ukrainian leaders understated the real number of victims in order "not to distress Moscow," and the central government was not sharing any clear information about the case with its citizens and the world press. Gorbachev kept silent for 14 days. It took him a while to overcome the psychological barrier developed by the communist system and honestly tell the country the truth, exposing the internal reasons for the disaster. "It's all because most of our 'closed' ministries and scientific centers stayed out of control. That's where monopoly in politics, science, [and] industry led us. Closeness entails the spirit of servility, fawning and corruption." Gorbachev's words said after the tragedy indicate both his attitude toward the communist system as a whole and his romantic faith in openness and glasnost as a means of real socialism.[15]

Gorbachev's innovations became the subject of mass criticism. Some opponents considered his reforms too slow and inconsequential while others blamed him for hastiness. All the critics mentioned the contradictions in his actions. For example, right after the law of cooperation development, which gave birth to the spread of a shadow economy, the act against "speculation," was also passed, meaning additional restrictions on any kind of private retail business. Another law increasing central planning followed a law supporting democratization in corporate management. A law reforming the political system and allowing free elections preceded the law of "consolidating the role of the Party," and so on.

It is worth mentioning that the power of the secretary-general was not unlimited and these decisions depended also on the Central Committee's opinion. The whole system of Stalin-Leninist socialism resisted the reformation. Constrained in domestic affairs, Gorbachev had more freedom in the international arena. Relying on the support of Edward Shevarnadze, the minister of international affairs (later the president of Georgia), Gorbachev acted vigorously and effectively. From 1985, after a six-and-a-half-year break, the leader of the USSR was annually meeting presidents and prime ministers of other countries, including the U.S. leaders Ronald Reagan and then George H. W. Bush. Mikhail also had a good relationship with the UK prime minister Margaret Thatcher who told Western leaders that they (the West and Gorbachev) could "do business together."[16] In 1989, Gorbachev initiated the withdrawal of Soviet troops from Afghanistan and, by not sending in Soviet troops as had been done in the past, contributed to the fall of the Berlin Wall and the unification of Germany. In 1990, the signing of the "Charter of Paris for a New Europe" with other heads of European states and American and Canadian leaders ended the period of the Cold War, which had lasted for more than 50 years.

With the best intentions for reform, Gorbachev was destroying the communist system and his own career by not realizing that the ideology of the Cold War was the main support to the party's domestic policy. With the image of an "enemy," the Soviet people were willing to sacrifice their comfort and wealth in order to support the military complex and national interests. Nobody asked the party government to report expenses. Realizing that the threat of war was over, and that the potential aggressor was becoming a partner and then, possibly, a friend, people started asking themselves questions that were inconvenient for the government.

Meanwhile, the Soviet Union was on the edge of a serious political and, especially, economic crisis. When he started economic reforms, Gorbachev had neither a strong program for transition to a market economy nor enough investments to stimulate such a transition. A significant part of the budget had been spent on military armaments and for the antialcohol campaign. The shortage of day-to-day goods was dangerously increasing. The political system started to fall apart in 1989 and the Soviet republics were beginning to declare their independence. Attempts to prevent secession using military force led to counterproductive results and increased dissident tendencies, especially in the Caucasus and Baltic republics. In the first half of 1990, many of the Soviet republics had declared their independence. The Russian Republic did so on the 12th of June, 1990, yet the Soviet Union had still not dissolved. Overwhelmed with all the domestic events, Gorbachev sent his deputy instead of himself to receive his Nobel Peace Prize in 1990.

In the summer of 1991, a new treaty among the Soviet republics was prepared for ratification, but the attempted military coup against Gorbachev in August of the same year made it clear that the treaty would never be signed, giving a strong impetus for the country's disintegration. Ironically, it was Boris Yeltsin, president of the Russian Republic, who saved Gorbachev from the military takeover, only to oust the leader just a few months later to take his place as the head of the newly created Russia, which replaced the Soviet Union. As the events were spinning out of Gorbachev's control, on December 8, 1991, the leaders of Ukraine, Belorussia, and Russia (represented by Boris Yeltsin) secretly met in a place called Belovezhskaya Pushcha, Belorussia, and signed the treaty of liquidation of the USSR and the establishment of the Commonwealth of Independent States. After that, Gorbachev had nothing to do but to announce his resignation on December 25, 1991.

GORBACHEV AFTER 1991

According to George and George, Gorbachev's leadership style can be characterized as collegial. It was typical for the Soviet leader to open major questions for discussion with his team, sharing responsibility for decisions with his group of advisers. He used democratic means, giving his people the right to freely express their opinions and involved them in finding solutions as a group. His wife Raisa played the role of his special political and personal adviser until the day she passed away in September 1999.

When talking about his personality, people who used to work with Gorbachev describe his high sense of morality. His ethical positions and aversion to the traditions of Soviet leadership, which originated in his childhood and during his student years, combined with his romanticism and idealism caused him to play a unique historical role. He truly believed in the ideal of communist equality and that the system could be reformed and thrive. On an international level, those traits helped him not only to build trust with other leaders and end the Cold War, but also to contribute to the future peaceful image of the country. At the same time, this idealism and perhaps an overly optimistic point of view doomed his domestic reforms to failure. Historians consider Gorbachev's unrealistic belief in his ability to reform socialism and the Communist Party, without first changing the whole system to be his major mistake.

As his former adviser Cherniaev reminisces, "Gorbachev was not a great person, but he performed a great mission liberating Russians from a totalitarian communist regime which is more important for history."[17] For his endless energy and optimism, Gorbachev is often compared to one of his predecessors Nikita Khruchshev, who also was opposed to tyranny and believed in the reformation of socialism.

Another of Mikhail Gorbachev's important characteristics, recognized by both his friends and opponents, is his inability to make risky but necessary decisions and affect them sequentially. As Egor Gaydar, the famous political journalist and activist, notes, Gorbachev was very good at the proposal of innovative ideas and always tried to reach a consensus, but ended up with quasi-decisions while the situation in the country demanded more firm and unambiguous actions.[18] Chronic inconsistency and a lack of any kind of strategy affected the process of *perestroika* most of all and were the major causes of the fiasco. Gorbachev's favorite expressions were "the processes have started," "life will show," "history will judge," and so on. A gifted orator and professional lawyer, he was excellent at public speaking, using colorful words to express his many ideas. But if a situation required fast and crucial decisions, he usually preferred to wait until the "processes" would finish their job and "life would show." As an example, Gorbachev postponed the inevitable decision for troop withdrawal from Afghanistan for three years.

Gorbachev had another key trait that did not allow him to exert maximum control. By nature, he was averse to any use of force. It was especially difficult for him to authorize the use of force against civilians for political purposes. He always tried to avoid bloodshed, remembering the brutal political repression exercised by the regime against his and Raisa's grandfathers and the time of the Nazi invasion in his home village. Because of his refusal to use military force, the key principle of realist theory, other party members considered Gorbachev and his supporters "Martians."

Writer Olas Adamovich summarized Gorbachev's personality and ideas, using the image of a cabbage: "Gorbachev believes that if he takes off the decayed leaves there will be a healthy cabbage inside. The *apparatchiks*—people working for the Party apparat—know it's dangerous to strip off the leaves, because it's rotten inside; it will all have to be thrown away. Gorbachev is the last romantic socialist."[19]

As of mid-2013, Mikhail Gorbachev was still active in political and social life. In 1992, he became the president of the Gorbachev Foundation, known as the International Foundation for Socio-Economic and Political Studies, a nonprofit educational foundation. Since 1993, Gorbachev has been the president of the environmental organization, Green Cross International, with branches in more than 20 countries. He is a prolific writer, the winner of many various awards from all over the world, and the holder of academic ranks of honor from a number of international universities. Through his life, Gorbachev has kept his sense of high morality, energy, idealism, and optimism.

Despite his faults as a leader, Mikhail Gorbachev is a good example of a person who retained his idealism and personal and moral dignity during a time of political crisis. In April 2013, at 82 years old and increasingly frail, Gorbachev delivered a poignant address in Moscow. In his remarks he aggressively attacked Putin's policies of clamping down on nongovernmental organizations, saying, "For goodness sake, you shouldn't be afraid of your own people."[20] Gorbachev also stated, "I'm often accused of giving away Central and Eastern Europe. But who did I give it to? I gave Poland, for example, back to the Poles. Who else does it belong to?"[21]

NOTES

1. Collectivization—A policy pursued under Stalin between 1928 and 1940. The goal of this policy was to consolidate individual land and labor into collective farms (*kolkhoz;* plural: *kolkhozy*).
2. Andrew Grachev, *Gorbachev* (Moscow: Vagrius, 2001), 35.
3. Komsomol—Young Communist League, the youth wing of the Communist Party in the Soviet Union. The organization was officially established on October 29, 1918.
4. Mikhail Gorbachev, *Memoirs* (London: Bantam books, 1996), 67.
5. Grachev, *Gorbachev*, 41.
6. http://www.hedricksmith.com/books/bookTheRussians.shtml.
7. Grachev, *Gorbachev*, 133.
8. Ibid., 175.
9. 9 See Alexander George and Juliette L. George, *Presidential Personality and Performance* (Boulder, CO: Westview Press, 1998).
10. Grachev, *Gorbachev*, 193.
11. Ibid., 64.
12. Ibid., 168.
13. The events were called the Prague Spring, a period from January to August 1968, when reformist Alexander Dubcek came to power and tried to grant additional rights to the citizens and partially decentralize the economy. The Soviets, after failed negotiations, sent troops to occupy the country. Although there was no military resistance, Czechoslovakia remained occupied till 1990.
14. Yuri Andropov (1914–1982), the Secretary General of the Soviet Union, Nov. 1982–Feb. 1984.
15. Mikhail Gorbachev, Размышления о прошлом и будущем [Thinking about the Past and the Future] (Moscow: Terra, 1998), 136.
16. Margaret Thatcher, interviewed by John Cole for BBC, http://www.margaretthatcher.org/speeches/displaydocument.asp?docid=105592
17. Grachev, *Gorbachev*, 178.
18. Ibid., 182.
19. Ibid., 197.
20. David M. Herszenhorn, "An Ailing Gorbachev Makes a Fierce Attack on Putin and His Restrictions," *New York Times*, April 2, 2013, A7.
21. Ibid.

17

William Jefferson Clinton: Promise, Persistence, and the Will to Be Adored

Jean Krasno

Born in Hope, Arkansas, on August 19, 1946, William Jefferson Clinton first took the oath of office on January 20, 1993, as the 42nd president of the United States. He served 2 four-year terms, completing his eight years in office on January 20, 2001. Ironically, Bill Clinton snatched a second term away from George Herbert Walker Bush in a three-way race in 1992, only to be replaced in 2001 by Bush's son, George W. Bush, in a very tightly contested electoral outcome pitted against Al Gore, Clinton's vice president.

PERSONALITY TRAITS

Bill Clinton is the ultimate charismatic person, charming, and an artful speaker with a quick and retentive mind who takes thorough pleasure in working a crowd and winning their adoration. On the other hand, he is narcissistic, a political manipulator, always taking the pulse of the body politic to set his achievement agenda.

Margaret Hermann analyzes Bill Clinton's leadership style through an examination of "seven different characteristics that have implications for how political leaders will behave, the kinds of actions they are likely to urge on their parties and governments, and the way they structure and interact with their advisory groups."[1] She analyzes interviews with Clinton by the press rather than speeches because these informal venues are to a greater extent unscripted. As stated in the introductory chapter of this book, I agree with Hermann that embedded within personality lie the characteristic behaviors that inform management style, worldview, motive, and decision making skills in a leader. Therefore, her analysis of Clinton's personality characteristics is very informative for our study. She finds that Clinton—in comparison to others in her study—is moderate in his need for power and in his belief that he can control events. However, he scores high in his self-confidence and his capacity for conceptual complexity, is open-minded to differing perspectives, and will even seek different points of view from a variety of constituents. His high self-confidence indicates, according to Hermann, that he is strategic in his behavior and focuses on what is feasible at the time. Leaders of this type see information as power and prefer to place themselves "as the hub of such networks," which allows them to be at the center of the decision making process.[2] And for Clinton, who thrives on interpersonal interaction, this places him at the center of attention.

Hermann also finds that Clinton is generally trusting of others and, along with his self-confidence, is therefore optimistic about his ability to achieve his policy goals. Clinton shows a rather low score on in-group bias, which indicates that he is independent of what his advisers might prefer. Hermann suggests that he sees politics as a "game board" in which players must compromise, and for Clinton, winning is the "art of the possible."[3] Because he does not take a zero-sum position, with a clear winner or loser, his actions can be perceived as having no principles. I will illustrate this decision making process when I discuss his specific policies on both national and international issues later in the chapter.

David Winter analyzes Clinton's motivations as a political leader, examining three characteristics: his desire for power, achievement, and affiliation. We can describe power as the ability to control events, people, and policy decision making. Clinton sees achievement as both personal achievement in terms of career ambitions and policy achievements that address his goals. The latter includes not only advancing the Democratic Party agenda of attending to the needs of the less advantaged, but also moving the Party to the center of American politics to make its candidates more electable. Winter defines "affiliation" as the ability to communicate with the public, engage in personal relationships, identify and empathize with others, and thrive on feedback and even adulation. He found that Clinton's motivations changed somewhat over time. During his 1992 campaign and his initial months in office, Clinton scored higher in achievement and affiliation as motivators. But as his term progressed, his motivation for power, while rather low initially, grew to comparable levels to his need for achievement and affiliation. This became particularly true after the 1994 elections, when the Democratic Party lost the majority in the House of Representatives and the face-off with Republican Speaker Newt Gingrich went into full gear.[4]

Based on Hermann and Winter's analyses, Clinton's personality traits fit perfectly into our flexible/pragmatic type: open-minded; strong sense of efficacy and high level of self-esteem; innovative; listens to others; ability to handle disagreement and synthesize perspectives into a larger picture; tolerant of different points of view; nonideological; capacity to see the big picture and still retain a structural focus; and finally, power is sought to be able to implement policy, not simply for the sake of power. As Hermann points out, however, Clinton appears at times to take on some traits of our chaotic/impulsive type with the inability to focus, often changing his mind. But that could also be attributed to his perception of the "art of the possible" if he sees that the timing or the political climate is not ripe for a particular policy position.

William Leuchtenburg, in his book *In the Shadow of FDR*, offers insight into Clinton's identification with the personality of Franklin D. Roosevelt, the icon of the Democratic Party and founder of the New Deal. He points out that one of the first trips that Clinton took outside Washington, DC, only four weeks after his inauguration, was to FDR's home in Hyde Park, New York. The political implication was that Clinton would continue the Democratic support for the poor and disadvantaged along the New Deal policy ideals. However, Clinton saw his identification with FDR not as continuing the socialist ideology but in emulating FDR's sense of strong leadership, overcoming adversity, and the ability to persuade and capture the American public's attention to embrace his policies through his skills as a communicator, along the lines of FDR's fireside chats.[5] In addition, Clinton's management style reflects a similar personality characteristic. Both FDR and Clinton chose advisers and cabinet members from a wide spectrum of viewpoints so diverse that it demonstrated not only their ability to absorb and synthesize differing perspectives but also their capacity to actually enjoy sorting out conflicting ideas and stepping in at the right time to capture the policy decision.[6]

THE GENESIS OF PERSONALITY

The origins of psychological personality are *dynamic* as a product of early childhood and family experiences. They are also *developmental* as a person experiences critical belief-shaping events throughout life. I will discuss both here. Bill Clinton's early childhood was riddled with stress and instability. He never knew his real father, William Blythe, who died in a car accident a few months before Bill was born. His mother, Virginia Kelley, widowed and a single parent, lived with her parents at the time of the baby's birth in August 1946. When Bill was a few months old in the spring of 1947, his mother decided to leave home for two years and study to become a nurse-anesthetist in New Orleans, leaving the baby with his grandparents in Hope, Arkansas. "Thus young Bill Clinton not only lost his father before he was born but was psychologically abandoned by his mother during the crucial developmental period between the ages of one and three."[7] Bill's endless need for attention and affection may stem from this early emotional deprivation. When his mother returned from her training, her busy social life revolved around her new boyfriend, Roger Clinton. Young Bill was just under four years old when they married and Roger gave Bill his surname. His mother, Virginia, was affable, sociable, and enjoyed a good time, much like her son. She was a woman who "worked hard and played hard, with an affinity for the night-clubs and the thoroughbred horse-racing tracks."[8] She also had a narcissistic streak, enjoyed her reflection in any mirror she passed, and would do whatever was necessary to be the center of attention.[9] Clinton remembers his stepfather trying to take an interest in him as a boy, but his alcoholism always threatened to throw the family into violence and crisis. Like any child growing up in an alcoholic family, young Bill had to walk a careful line not to set things off. He had to appease both his mother and his stepfather and find his own middle ground to save his own sense of worth. Bill tells the story of one of these episodes:

> One night his drunken self-destructiveness came to a head in a fight with my mother I can't ever forget. Mother wanted us to go to the hospital to see my great-grandmother, who didn't have long to live. Daddy said she couldn't go. They were screaming at each other in their bedroom in the back of the house. For some reason, I walked out into the hall to the doorway of the bedroom. Just as I did, Daddy pulled a gun from behind his back and fired in Mother's direction. The bullet went into the wall between where she and I were standing. I was stunned and so scared. I had never heard a shot fired before, much less seen one. Mother grabbed me and ran across the street to the neighbors. The police were called. I can still see them leading Daddy away in handcuffs to jail, where he spent the night.[10]

Children who grow up in a volatile family often try to find common ground between the two warring sides, a skill that Bill Clinton honed in his later political life. Nevertheless, Bill Clinton adored and respected his mother. In an interview with Charles Allen, he stated:

> She was, I thought, a good role model in three ways. She always worked, did a good job as a parent; we had plenty of adversity in our lives when I was growing up and I think she handled it real well, and I think she . . . gave me a high pain threshold, which, I think, is a very important thing to have in public life. You have to be able to . . . take a lot of criticism—suffer defeats and get up and fight again.[11]

Thus we can see several influences shaping young Bill's personality in his early years: a need for attention and love in a situation where he had felt abandoned early in his childhood, the adoring affection of his mother who had also put him in a very hostile and dangerous living situation, and yet an admiration for her as a role model of perseverance and a tough skin.

To add to the drama in the Clinton household, the fighting and drinking grew more out of control with not only verbal but also physical abuse by the stepfather. His mother filed for divorce and asked Bill to testify against his stepfather. After putting Bill through this tremendously stressful position, the two parents reconciled three months later and were remarried on August 6, 1962.[12] Having betrayed the stepfather, Bill now had to tolerate living with him again. Young Bill hid his violent and chaotic home life from his schoolmates, teachers, and all outsiders, as many children in this situation will do. John Harris in his biography of Clinton explains: "Childhood friends like David Leopoulos and Carolyn Yeldell Staley, who were in the Clinton home nearly every day, never learned until decades later—by reading articles about candidate Clinton's youth—that there was any problem in his home life."[13] As a child, he also felt the responsibility to be the conciliator between these two parents embroiled in heated arguments, a kind of family unifier. He brought that sense to his political ambitions. In his acceptance speech in 1992 on the night of the election, he said of his goals, "perhaps most important of all, to bring our people together as never before, so that our diversity can be a source of strength in a world that is ever smaller, where everyone counts and everyone is part of America's family."[14] Clinton lived two distinct lives, one deeply hidden away and another one where his wit and intelligence could thrive unburdened by his inner suffering and disgrace. This ability to separate a secret life from his public demeanor was one he carried with him into adulthood. For him, it was perfectly justified to hide parts of one's life. However, this suffering enabled Bill to empathize with others. During his 1992 campaign for the presidency, the public discovered this quality in Clinton.

> "Empathy" was a word Clinton brought into political vogue that year. "I feel your pain," he told audiences, a phrase that quickly became a parody. But Clinton's gift was not simply a put-on: He did have an authentic superior sense of human dynamics.[15]

Like many children whose home life is chaotic, Bill took refuge in school where he began to shine and thrive with his quick wit and intelligence. He enjoyed school and raised his hand so many times in class that the teacher, in desperation to keep him under control, gave him a poor grade in deportment, just to get his attention. When in fourth grade he started at a new school, one of the students said later that he, "within days seemed to be running the place. . . . He just took over the school. He didn't mean to, but he just took the place over."[16] Seeking the attention he had not received at home, Clinton found school the perfect arena for showing off in as many areas as possible. In an interview with Carolyn Staley, his childhood friend, she recalled, "He had to be the class leader, he had to be the best in the band.

He had to be the best in his class."[17] But his competitiveness at times became obsessive:

> As governor, Clinton had a pinball machine installed in the basement of the governor's mansion. When the son of one of his staff ran up a score of 800,000 points, breaking Clinton's record, Clinton stayed up until two in the morning trying to reclaim his record from the seven-year-old.[18]

Clinton's competitive nature certainly was an important factor in his ability to ride out two rigorous campaigns, never giving up, and drawing on every inch of his self-confidence and sense of efficacy. All these personality traits have enabled him to persevere, often against the nasty mud slinging and attacks on his personal character. In balance against what might be considered an obsession, Renshon places Clinton's competitiveness in perspective, "[i]n Clinton's case his competitiveness is buttressed by his idealized sense of doing good for the right reasons and being very confident that his views are right."[19]

CLINTON'S VIEW OF HIS PRESIDENCY AND THE DEMOCRATIC PARTY

Every political leader operates within a belief system that has formed in early childhood experiences, interaction with the outside world, and testing out role models as guides along the way. Clinton's childhood was challenging but through his mother's unconditional love and his achievements in school, he developed a belief that a person could overcome adversity and not only survive, but thrive. His absent father and abusive stepfather certainly did not provide workable role models. And even his mother, who adored her son, was not an appropriate role model. His discovery of FDR, not so much for his more socialist policies of the times but for his strength as a leader, gave Clinton the role model he was searching for. Yet Bill believed in his ability to walk his own path. His obsession with achievement and his highly motivated drive and dogged perseverance kept him going, facing down challenges as they popped in front of him. He had become the first Democrat to be elected president in sixteen years. The charismatic Republican Ronald Reagan had moved the country's leadership significantly to the right. And while George Herbert Walker Bush had stepped more toward the center, it appeared that Republican conservatism had grasped a strong hold on U.S. policy. Clinton believed that for Democrats to be elected president and see at least some of their policies enacted, the party had to move to the center. He would have to struggle to draw Republicans into his left of center policy tent, but he also had to convince Democrats to enter and move to the center with him. Both the House and Senate already had Democratic majorities before the Clinton election in 1992. Far from being Clinton followers, congressional Democrats were not beholden to him and could go their own way if they saw fit. He believed he had to establish a third way by creating a new Democratic Party with a centrist policy agenda, but he was challenged from both sides of the aisle.[20]

Presidential author Stephen Skowronex describes Clinton's leadership style as "preemptive," meaning that he would suck the wind out of the Republican's agenda by preempting their policies with his own centrist positions like: balancing the budget, cutting federal spending, reducing taxes, and reforming welfare. Far from welcoming Clinton's more centrist stand, Republicans hated him for snatching what they considered their proprietary agenda.

> The distinctive thing about preemptive leaders is that they are not out to establish, uphold, or salvage any political orthodoxy. Theirs is an unabashedly mongrel politics; it is an aggressive critique of the prevailing political categories. These leaders bid openly for a hybrid alternative.[21]

For the preceding three terms, no Democrat had been in the White House and Clinton had won less than a majority of the popular vote in a three-way race with Bush and Ross Pirot. Therefore, like other presidents who had only won about 40 percent of the popular vote, he believed he had to adopt strategies that would reach out to the majority who had not voted for him. Thus when he tried to slip in his more liberal agenda, for example, on gays in the military and his expanded healthcare proposals, he lost. Without the loyalty of Democrats in Congress, without a majority public mandate, and with the pushback from conservative Republicans, he was unable to deliver. Skowronex describes how this ad hoc approach can create a sense of unprincipled leadership:

> The characteristic risk in leadership of this sort is that in trying to chart a third way the president will appear to be wholly lacking in political principles; that in exploiting the indeterminacy of his opposition stance, he will be branded unscrupulous and cynically manipulative.[22]

Furthermore, by his preempting the Republican agenda, conservatives found themselves in the awkward position of not being able to oppose Clinton's most successful policy achievements. That left them with one alternative, to go after him personally, and they did. They searched every scandal angle they could and finally zeroed in on his weakness—his sensual appetite for women. And, stupidly for an intelligent person, Clinton fell into the trap. Clinton had always been able to keep his secret life separate from his public persona, and he truly believed he had a right to do that, having led a double life since childhood. But his exaggerated sense of self-confidence led him to believe that as president, he could do the same, even in the face of a very hostile Republican Party. As we know, in 1998, the House impeached him for "lying" about his relationship with a White

House intern, but the Senate denied the conviction that the Republicans had hoped for.

Clinton suffered from a lack of impulse control whether it was donuts and fast food on the campaign trail or pretty women, placing him at times in our chaotic/impulsive type. He may have felt that he did not have to comply with these perhaps middle-class moral standards of fidelity. And on the other hand, he had managed in the past to wriggle his way out of these transgressions by mincing words and using semantic double talk. For example, when Clinton announced that he had cut the White House staff by 25 percent, keeping a promise to reduce the number of federal employees, the actual number was more like 16 percent, because many of the people had simply been moved to other departments.[23] He tried to use this semantic strategy again, thinking he could wriggle around the accusations regarding his sexual encounters with the intern, by saying he had not had "sex" with that woman. What he was referring to, so that it would not be a lie, was that he had not physically penetrated her. However, stories about cigars and the semen stains on the infamous blue dress made his pronouncement of innocence appear completely fake.

> The point here is not that there are differences between President Clinton's words and behaviors. Few people are totally consistent. Nor is it that there are not some possible, even plausible, explanations for some of these matters. It is quite simply the *sheer volume* of such discrepancies that draws attention.[24]

In summary, Clinton believed that he had to move the Democratic Party to the center and his strong sense of self-confidence and belief in his ability to achieve whatever goal he set his mind to undertake, assured him that this was achievable. However, he had not anticipated the strength of the opposition. He was in some ways ahead of his time as an open-minded social liberal but he had also misread the intransigence of many who were not ready to openly take gays into the military or to provide universal healthcare. Years later, the public would catch up to him. Capturing the middle ground and coaching his American "family" to join hands proved much harder than he had anticipated.

BILL CLINTON'S FOREIGN POLICY AND DECISION MAKING

Clinton ran his campaign in 1992 on domestic policy issues and the economy, as most American presidential candidates do. In fact, Clinton at the onset had little interest in foreign affairs, calculating that the American public was not engaged in such issues and he did not want to waste valuable political capital on something the public did not care about. His National Security Adviser Anthony Lake and Secretary of State Warren Christopher were both told to keep foreign policy from distracting the president from his domestic agenda. Meetings on foreign policy were rare and even canceled. Eventually, Warren Christopher had to tell the president "point blank that he had to become more engaged in foreign policy by spending at least *an hour a week* with his national security adviser."[25] As a result, President Clinton was unaware and uninformed on events as they were coming to a head in Somalia.

The unfolding crisis in Somalia unleashed a cascade of foreign policy missteps that led to dire tragic proportions. As the George H. W. Bush administration was drawing to a close at the end of 1992, President Bush had decided to send American troops into Somalia to provide robust security to ensure the delivery of United Nations–led humanitarian aid efforts to starving people who were dying by the hundreds every day. The combination of clan warfare that had forced people from their homes and a devastating drought had plunged Somalia into a humanitarian crisis that the United States viewed continuously on CNN to the horror of the American people. The U.S. effort had been successful in securing the delivery of badly needed food and other humanitarian supplies but had cost the lives of some 100 American soldiers in the process. The famine had subsided, and many of the U.S. troops had been withdrawn, but a crisis that occurred in October 1993 under Clinton's watch would repaint all the successes with a wash of darkness. A U.S. Delta Force team had remained and had decided to attempt the capture of a group of clan leaders suspected of obstructing the peace process. The Delta strategy failed miserably, with two Blackhawk helicopters downed and 18 U.S. soldiers killed before UN troops could rescue them. The most dramatic event was the rope-dragging of a dead U.S. soldier through the dusty streets of Mogadishu to cheering Somalis. The photo of the soldier made all the news headlines and was seen on CNN over and over, to the horror of Americans who were asking, "Why are we in Somalia?"

As a consequence of the debacle in Somalia, U.S. troops were eventually withdrawn and Clinton began a "careful scrubbing" of a policy being developed by his administration on U.S. involvement in multilateral peace operations, something Clinton had previously supported. Republicans, looking for ways to criticize Clinton even though it was President Bush who had sent the troops to begin with, were in an uproar. Democrats were also concerned about the reaction of their constituents at home. "Ambassador Albright was sent to the Hill to reassure an increasingly jittery Congress that the administration was aware of their concerns."[26] In January 1994, Senator Robert Dole introduced legislation that would bar "placing US forces under UN or foreign operational control and proposed other restrictions on US participation in and support of UN peacekeeping operations."[27] In reaction, Clinton overhauled his policy directive.

When completed, the administration had fundamentally altered the tone of Clinton's Presidential Decision Directive 25 (PDD-25). While the directive still expressed support for UN peacekeeping, especially when U.S. interests were involved, the report emphasized the limited role peacekeeping played in U.S. national security policy and that American forces were to protect U.S. national interests. This marked a move away from proactive multilateralism to a more wary support of UN peacekeeping. Clinton viewed his electoral mandate as placing domestic concerns ahead of foreign policy, especially where U.S. interests were not at stake. Ironically, during his campaign Clinton had viewed UN action as a means of burden sharing.

> Multilateral peace operations, it was thought, offered a way for the United States to remain engaged internationally without having to bear alone all the burdens in international leadership. . . . in the wake of the Somali debacle, the administration chose to join its critics rather than defend its policy, believing that in so doing it could better protect its domestic political agenda.[28]

However, by stepping back from multilateral engagement, Clinton stepped into probably the worst foreign policy decision of his administration, the refusal to act in the face of genocide in Rwanda, which erupted a mere six months following the Delta Force disaster in October 1993. In April 1994, news of genocidal killings in Rwanda spread around the world. In just the first few weeks the *New York Times* was reporting tens of thousands killed and massive numbers of people displaced from their homes, fleeing across borders into neighboring countries.[29] The United States with its permanent seat on the UN Security Council and the power of the veto characterized the fighting as a civil war, invoking recent memories of Somalia. While the media was already calling it genocide, the Clinton administration still clung to its view that it was a civil war and the United States should not intervene where it did not have interests involved. In the opening days of the killing, the Hutu-led Interahamwe had strategically shot dead 10 Belgian UN troops, resulting, as they had predicted, in Belgium withdrawing all its soldiers, leaving only a little more than 300 UN troops in Rwanda. It was not until six weeks into the massacre that the UN Security Council, at the urging of New Zealand, took any action. The Security Council resolution called for 5,500 troops to secure humanitarian safe areas, but did not authorize the use of force under Chapter VII. New Zealand was unable to insert any reference to genocide due to concerns that using the word "genocide" would induce a legal requirement to take action under the Genocide Convention, something the United States, and others following along behind, did not want to do. In addition:

> Some Council members felt that the United States was unnecessarily delaying action by demanding that the proposed new mandate satisfy the "factors of consideration" included in US Presidential Decision Directive 25, a new statement of US policy on peace operations. For its part, the United States was

> uncertain if adequate troops and equipment, complete consent of the belligerents, and coherent operational plans were available for the proposed mission.[30]

While all these delaying tactics were going on, thousands more people were dying each day. Meanwhile, Romeo Dallaire, the UN Force Commander in Rwanda under the United Nations Assistance Mission for Rwanda (UNAMIR), was begging for armed troops. Tragically, most of the deaths were carried out with machetes and clubs, and Dallaire, who had been left with only some 325 troops, claimed he could have stopped most of the killings if the United Nations would just send him a well-trained contingent. "The only maneuverable forces under UNAMIR's control from late April to mid-August 1994 were two partially equipped companies of the Ghanaian infantry battalion, consolidated in Kigali."[31] When the genocide finally ended in July 1994, with no intervention by the outside world, some 800,000 to 1,000,000 people were dead and many more were displaced. It was a global disgrace. Clinton deftly shifted the blame onto the United Nations. And to this day, people blame the United Nations for this tragedy.

Four years later in March 1998, Bill and Hillary visited Rwanda. They were there for just three hours and never left the airport. But inside the airport lounge he sat quietly and listened to one story after another told by people who had lost their families. Josephine Murebwayire told her story: "The Hutu soldiers dragged them outside and began swinging their machetes. She was badly cut. Her husband, two brothers, and six children were all killed."[32] Clinton listened and whispered a thank you to her when she had finished. Few presidents ever have the courage to face directly the consequences of their decisions, "or, in this case, his non-decisions."[33] Afterward, in addressing a larger group of Rwandans, Clinton stated that "he accepted his share of the responsibility for not intervening," and also that the international community should not have "dithered in rhetorical debate about whether the killing amounted to 'genocide.'" It was not exactly an apology and he inserted "the international community" in an effort to share the blame with the rest of the world, but at least he was willing to face the horrendous disaster that he had failed to stop. "The visit, Clinton later told friends, was the most emotionally searing moment of his presidency."[34]

Haiti and Haitian refugees, however, were something Clinton clearly saw as an American interest. During his campaign, he had expressed sympathy for Haitians trying to reach U.S. shores and escape a brutal military regime that had recently overthrown a freely elected government under President Jean-Bertrand Aristide. But just before Clinton's inauguration in January 1993, reports of some 100,000 Haitian refugees preparing to forge the waters on makeshift boats seeking asylum under Clinton's anticipated new policy caused him to abruptly backtrack, again mincing words about differences between purported economic and political refugees. Yet a year later in the spring 1994, the refugee problem was increasing and diplomatic efforts to end military rule and return the elected government to Haiti had failed. Clinton felt he had to bring an end to the refugee crisis and he went on national television to make the case for an invasion of Haiti to the American people and to Congress, who overwhelmingly opposed an American military attack. Two days before his speech, Clinton had grumbled to his aides, "I guess we'll have something to show those people who say I never do anything unpopular."[35] Fortunately for Clinton another avenue opened up. Former president and fellow Democrat Jimmy Carter made Clinton a proposal, and after pondering the options, Clinton allowed Carter to go to Haiti to meet with Haitian General Cédras to inform him that he could leave peacefully or face a U.S. attack. "[T]alks were still going on, even as planes were taking off from Pope Air Force Base in North Carolina, only a couple hours from their destination."[36] The clearly imminent attack had the effect of focusing the minds of the military junta and they agreed to leave peacefully. "The planes did a U-turn in the sky back to North Carolina. At 10 p.m., Clinton announced to the nation that a crisis had been resolved."[37]

Staying out of foreign affairs became an impossible task for Bill Clinton. While the termination of the Cold War brought an end to East–West tensions and the proxy wars over spheres of influence between the two major rivals, other conflicts like Somalia and Rwanda in Africa, and the breakup of the former Yugoslavia in Europe followed their own agendas. The United States attempted to delegate the problems in the former Yugoslavia to the Europeans and to the United Nations. Former president Bush had been preoccupied with the 1991 Gulf War to expel Iraq from Kuwait and hoped Europe would sort out its own issues. When Clinton took office in early 1993, the conflict had spread to Bosnia-Herzegovina and stories of ethnic cleansing were increasing. The United Nations had passed a resolution imposing an arms embargo, which on the ground meant that all the military power of the former Yugoslavia fell into Serb and Bosnian Serb hands while the Bosniaks were left to their own devices. UN efforts to deliver humanitarian aid were often thwarted by Serb intervention and blockades. Ethnic cleansing by all sides continued, however, and by most accounts the Serbs were the major perpetrators. Attempts at mediating a peace agreement failed as the fighting continued, each side trying to gain more territory to their advantage before agreeing to a cease-fire that would lock in boundaries. Bosniaks meanwhile were smuggling heavy weapons across their borders to try to match Serb fire power. Safe areas created by the United Nations were never given enough manpower or resources, and in mid-summer 1995, Serb forces overran the UN Dutch troops and took the Srebrenica safe enclave. Mass graves found later showed that some 8,000 Bosnian men and boys had been slaughtered. Safe areas Zepa and Gorazde fell to Serb forces within weeks.

The Clinton administration was increasingly interested in being more proactive and National Security Adviser Anthony Lake began cabinet-level meetings to address the issue. At the end of August 1995, Clinton had given the go ahead for NATO to begin a two-week air campaign against Bosnian Serb holdings.[38] A combination of the NATO air campaign, a strengthened UN presence, and territorial gains by the Bosniaks, now aligned with Croatian support, finally brought the parties to accept a mediated peace agreement. In October, Clinton envoy Richard Holbrooke had achieved a cease-fire, and on November 1, 1995, Clinton had managed to bring the three presidents—Izetbegovic (Bosnia), Milosevic (Serbia), and Tudjman (Croatia)—for talks at Wright-Patterson Air Force Base in Dayton, Ohio. Under Holbrooke's able management, the three heads of state initialed the Dayton Agreement on November 21.[39] Hurt by inaction in Rwanda, Clinton demonstrated his ability to learn from adversity and take action to achieve what others had been unable to do. He was now irrevocably embroiled in foreign policy.

Winning a clear majority in his reelection in 1996 handed Clinton the political mandate he had lacked in his first term. His success at Dayton in 1995 and gaining a majority in the popular vote a year later secured Clinton a much stronger footing in the coming years. He no longer backed away from foreign affairs. He moved Madeleine Albright from ambassador to the United Nations into the position of secretary of state. She had been instrumental in replacing Boutros Boutros-Ghali as UN secretary-general with the more proactive Kofi Annan who took office in January 1997 a few weeks before Clinton's second inaugural address. These moves were important for what was about to unfold in Kosovo, as the turmoil in the former Yugoslavia now turned to this small province in greater Serbia. In 1998, around the time of Clinton's visit to Rwanda the conflict in Kosovo was turning ugly and rumors of ethnic cleansing and genocide were once again making headlines. Having been unwilling to intervene in Rwanda and unable to stop genocide in Bosnia, Clinton morally could no longer stand by and "dither" over terminology. He had survived the personal and political crisis of his impeachment during the fall of 1998, and, by January 1999, had sent Albright to Rambouillet, France, to mediate an end to the violence. Unlike Dayton, this time Milosevic remained defiant, and on March 20, Serb forces launched a full attack into Kosovo. Under Clinton's persuasion on March 24, NATO began a 78-day siege of Serb military targets.

> That night Clinton spoke from the Oval Office, with a large map of Serbia on his desk as a visual aid to explain to a largely baffled public what Kosovo was

and why it mattered. . . . Noting that genocide had plagued this region before, he implored, "Ending this tragedy is a moral imperative."[40]

He had said "never again" would he allow genocide to take place on his watch and his own sense of moral worth depended on following through on this commitment. He was no longer afraid of public opinion; he was determined to lead it. When Milosevic finally capitulated, the United Nations asked Kofi Annan to establish a UN-led operation in Kosovo, UNMIK, to administer and stabilize the territory. NATO's KFOR mission provided the needed security while the United Nations and European Union began the process of nation building. Clinton had now realized his original commitment to multilateralism and PDD-25 was forgotten. The United States had no national interests in Kosovo, other than becoming a moral leader.

Only a few months later in August 1999, Clinton was challenged again. Violence broke out on the other side of the world, in yet another continent, in East Timor, a half-island seeking independence from the archipelago Indonesia. At the end of August, the East Timorese people voted overwhelmingly in a popular referendum for independence; Indonesian military-supported militias then began a rampage of killing, setting the capital of Dili up in flames. Kofi Annan had carefully mediated a solution to the enduring tensions in the territory by convincing the interim president Habibie to allow the referendum,[41] but Habibie did not have control of Indonesia's entrenched military led by General Wiranto. Now Kofi Annan needed Clinton to keep this initiative from becoming a disaster. On September 9, Clinton arrived in New Zealand for the APEC (Asia-Pacific Economic Cooperation) summit. The crisis in Indonesia was the central issue at APEC. The solution involved a three-pronged strategy, including a proactive role by the U.S. administration: (1) a delegation of the UN Security Council forced General Wiranto to join them on a visit to Dili to press him to admit what was going on[42]; (2) Clinton's direct role in pressing Habibie to accept UN intervention; and (3) pressure on General Wiranto from U.S. Admiral Dennis Blair, Commander-in-Chief of the U.S. Force in the Pacific. Admiral Blair met with Wiranto on September 8 to convey the serious consequences of Indonesia's complicity in the violence in terms of the country's relationship with the United States and the rest of the world, for example, cutting off economic and military aid. In addition, both Albright and Secretary of Defense Cohen spoke directly with General Wiranto with the same message.[43] President Clinton described the discussions at the APEC meeting in New Zealand:

Most of the APEC leaders favored an international peacekeeping mission for East Timor and Australian Prime Minister John Howard was willing to take

> the lead. At first the Indonesians were opposed to it, but soon they would be forced to relent. An international coalition was formed to send troops to East Timor under the leadership of Australia, and I pledged to Prime Minister Howard that I would send a couple of hundred American troops to provide the logistical support our allies needed.[44]

Clinton acted swiftly in response to the unfolding crisis, using both the economic and military power of the United States as leverage. Without Clinton's proactive and rapid intervention, East Timor would have fallen into chaos—something Kofi Annan dreaded. Like in Kosovo, the United Nations immediately played the role of nation building in East Timor, and by 2002, the new country became a member of the United Nations.

While these events forced him to engage beyond domestic issues, Clinton also grappled with another set of decisions regarding international involvement: global trade. Free trade was considered a Republican issue and President Bush had negotiated the North American Free Trade Agreement (NAFTA) but was unable to get it through the Democratically led Congress during his term. Yet, Clinton believed in the economic benefits of easing trade restrictions and anguished over what direction to take.[45] He finally decided to go with his own beliefs despite his own party's concerns over job losses, and he began pushing for NAFTA. His advisers believed that the Senate would come along, so the focus was on the House.

> [T]he House of Representatives was the focus of a furious round of lobbying. A steady stream of lawmakers went to the Oval Office with hands out. They got what they wanted—special deals for everyone from broom makers to citrus growers. But Clinton got what he wanted: NAFTA passed the House by 234 to 200.[46]

NAFTA passed the Senate 61 to 38 and Clinton signed it into law on December 8, 1993; the agreement went into effect on January 1, 1994. In the first years, unemployment decreased and trade with Mexico grew, giving Clinton the success he had hoped for. A year later in December 1994, both houses of Congress passed the GATT (General Agreement on Tariffs and Trade) resolution that created the new World Trade Organization (WTO) that would open previously closed markets to U.S. goods and services and would create uniform trade rules for all countries who were members and launch a means for adjudication of disputes. Clinton was a big supporter of the WTO and labor was less opposed to GATT than it had been to NAFTA.[47] The two trade agreements taken together catapulted the United States into a system of multilateral trade, symbolizing the integration of world economies following the collapse of the Cold War. Clinton saw these as essential to U.S. future growth.

However, he was not successful in bringing along the Senate on two other global agreements: the ICC and the CTBT. Clinton had strongly supported the creation of the International Criminal Court (ICC), a permanent court that would hold accountable those who bore the greatest responsibility for heinous crimes like genocide and crimes against humanity that had been perpetrated in Rwanda and Bosnia. But once the Republicans held the Senate majority and Senator Jesse Helms took over the chairmanship of the Senate Foreign Relations Committee, Clinton lost his chance to secure the needed Senate ratification for the United States to join the court. The Rome Statute establishing the ICC was completed in June 1998 and ultimately went into force without Clinton's signature. Near the end of Clinton's second term in 2000, Kofi Annan asked him to sign the agreement as a symbolic gesture to the rest of the world that the United States was a supporter of the court and human rights. Clinton obliged. "Finally, on the last day of the year, I signed the treaty by which America joined the International Criminal Court. . . . I had been among the first world leaders to call for an International War Crimes Tribunal, and I thought the United States should support it."[48] Signing an international agreement, even though it does not become ratified, is significant because it means legally a state cannot undermine the agreement. Later George W. Bush unsigned the ICC agreement because his administration planned on undermining the court.

Another issue that became moribund in the Senate was the Comprehensive Test Ban Treaty (CTBT) that would ban all testing of nuclear weapons. In 1998, both India and Pakistan detonated a series of nuclear bombs in a stand-off of military might. Even though the Republican-led Senate was not likely to give up U.S. discretion on testing, the India/Pakistani explosions reignited fears of more nuclear rogue states looming in the shadows. Clinton condemned the tests but reaffirmed U.S. support for nuclear nonproliferation and the CTBT, which he signed.[49] Nevertheless, the mood in the Senate was very negative toward anything that smelled of international engagement, which even included the Senate withholding payments for UN dues and the refusal to pay U.S. contributions to the International Monetary Fund. Neither the ICC nor the CTBT have seen the light of day in the senate chamber.

In summary, Clinton's initial disengagement in foreign affairs led to catastrophic results. However, he regained his footing by learning from his mistakes, overcoming adversity as he had learned to do in his early years growing up in a constantly volatile home life. His motivation for achievement and his sense of perseverance enabled him to take a leadership role, something that came naturally to him once he became engaged in international relations. Also, his failure and the catastrophic results of his inaction effectively altered his belief system on his role in world affairs. Many people perceived his inaction in Rwanda as immoral. Nevertheless, this event resulted in an adult learning experience, which then shaped his personality and pushed him into the realization that he and the United States had to assume the role of international moral leadership. His timely and effective efforts on Kosovo and East Timor are examples of this change. In addition, his achievements on creating NAFTA and support for WTO were important and forward looking. On some issues, though important to him, he was unable to overcome Republican Congressional opposition. He had to choose his battles and work within the art of the possible, as Margaret Hermann so aptly describes Clinton's style.

DOMESTIC POLICY AND DECISION MAKING

Clinton had wanted to create a new Democratic Party by moving party policies more toward the center. However, he felt he had to bring along the party leaders and the base by enacting some policies that addressed Democratic values, such as expanded healthcare and the elimination of discrimination, particularly regarding gays in the military.

In the 1992 presidential campaign, Bill Clinton made gay rights a prominent plank. He advocated allowing gay military personnel to serve openly, a policy consistent with most NATO allies. Clinton had maintained that the president had the unilateral authority to allow gay soldiers to serve. His interest in the rights of gay soldiers stood in marked contrast to Pat Buchanan's vilification of gays during his speech at the Republican convention, as proof of America's moral decay. However, when he tried to honor his campaign promise, the backlash from both sides of the aisle caught Clinton by surprise. His efforts resulted in the faulty *don't ask, don't tell* policy. Clinton, wanting to maintain his larger, popular public support, characteristically retreated from his advocacy of gay rights. For the remainder of his presidency, he sided with Republicans on morality grounds. In 1996, he signed the Defense of Marriage Act, which prohibited the federal government from recognizing same-sex marriages performed legally in any state. The same year, he also signed the Telecommunications Act of 1996, including Title V, known as the Communications Decency Act. This provision outlawed the use of obscene language and broadly defined indecency on the Internet. One potentially chilling effect could have made it a crime —among other things—to promote abortion or homosexuality as a legitimate lifestyle on the Internet. A federal appeals court immediately struck down this portion of the law as contravening the First Amendment right to free speech. In June 1996, The U.S. Supreme Court upheld that ruling, adding that the law's concept of indecency was too vague.

Clinton retreated at that time from what we now consider a human rights issue and a truly moral stand, the elimination of discrimination against people on gender choice issues and sexual orientation. The Supreme Court struck down the Defense of Marriage Act in June 2013, declaring it unconstitutional and a violation of due process and equal protection under the law. Was Clinton ahead of his time on the issue of gay rights? Perhaps, but he lost a great deal of credibility by abandoning the gay community who had been his big supporters.

Both Bill and Hillary Clinton were shocked by the immediate challenges that faced them once they arrived in the White House. Bill had tasked Hillary with developing a more inclusive national healthcare plan, something strongly lacking across America, where some 37 million people were without health insurance. Bill Clinton tried to find compromises to achieve acceptance of their ideas consistent with the "effort of his lifelong penchant for finding a third way between traditional liberalism and the conservative alternative."[50] This penchant for trying to find the middle ground follows from his need as a child to mediate some kind of conciliation between his warring parents. But there were some parts of the health plan that apparently Hillary was not willing to concede to those who wanted a less ambitious and perhaps less universal policy. Also Bill, at the same time, was confronted with one scandal after another, including another sexual exposé. Clinton adviser David Gergen describes how Bill gave into Hillary's demands not to capitulate on the healthcare proposal,

> [I]t was very much like watching a golden retriever that has pooped on the rug and just curls up and keeps his head down. . . . I think it put him in a situation where on health care he never challenged it in a way he ordinarily would have, had he been under a different psychological situation.[51]

Once again Clinton had backtracked on one of his major campaign promises, and once again, he may have been ahead of his time on healthcare. But, the reality of governing and the inherent difficulties of finding a middle way combined with his personal weaknesses constantly nagged at his heels as he tried to find his footing as a New Democrat.

Welfare reform, on the other hand, emerged as a centrist issue where Clinton believed he could forge an agreement with the Republicans who had by January 1995 taken over both houses of Congress. After all, another one of Clinton's campaign platforms was to "end welfare as we know it." Democrats however thought that reforming welfare could instill devastating hardships on the poor. Clinton wanted a welfare reform bill but was not willing to go at it as drastically as the Republicans, and he had vetoed some initial attempts at cutting welfare put forward by the new Congress. Many believe that had Clinton promoted welfare reform initially with the Democratically held Congress, the policy would have been more humane, but he missed that opportunity. In 1996, with a new reform bill awaiting Clinton's signature, Bill called a meeting of his cabinet and advisers on August 22:

> Often in the Clinton White House, debates like this were roiling affairs, profanities flew, and people exaggerated their arguments for maximum effect. Not this time. It was as if all of them, recognizing the momentous nature of a choice that belonged to the president alone, chose to tone down their appeals. . . . Then quietly he posed the question again: What should we do?[52]

The bill that substantially curtailed six decades of aid to the poor included many of the things that Bill had campaigned on, such as placing a limit on the time someone could stay on welfare and also providing incentives to move off welfare into work. He had believed that the current welfare system undermined American values of work and responsibility and encouraged dependency. This time, the bill had passed both houses of Congress with a 70 percent majority. Ultimately, Clinton signed the bill that day, August 22, 1996, breaking with the old Democratic ideal of liberalism. "Unlike the two bills I had vetoed, the new legislation retained the federal guarantee of medical care and food aid, increased federal child-care assistance."[53] The bill also included the capability of states to convert welfare subsidies into wages to encourage employers to hire people formerly on welfare. What was missing, however, was an increase in the minimum wage that would have provided those going off welfare with a livable income.

In Clinton's first two years in office with a Democratically led Congress, he was able to achieve legislation that most Democrats wanted and that helped many Americans, especially working Americans. Shortly after his inauguration, he signed into law the Family and Medical Leave Act. "I believed that family leave would be good for the economy. . . . In the next eight years, and even after I left office, more people would mention it to me than any other bill I signed."[54] He also signed into law that year the Earned Income Tax Credit (EITC) that gave working people earning less than $30,000 a year a meaningful tax cut. "After we doubled the EITC, more than four million of them moved out of poverty into the middle class during my presidency."[55] Clinton had also run his campaign on improving the economy and reducing the deficit that had deepened during the Reagan and Bush administrations. The slogan, "It's the economy, stupid," hit a nerve with the American public and Clinton wanted to deliver once he was in office. Part of the purpose of the EITC bill and the family leave policy was to balance off against tax increases and spending cuts that were going to tighten the budget and bring spending and revenues into greater balance, which were inevitably going to impact the public. During his time in office, the economy grew, deficits dropped, and by 1999, unemployment was just over 4 percent.

> The gamble Clinton took four years earlier that deficit reduction would spur the economy was paying off extravagantly. Annual growth in 1997 was 8.2 percent. The tax revenue this growth produced was erasing the deficit far faster

> than anyone had projected—it was $22 billion in 1997, compared to $290 billion when Clinton took office. The deficit would be gone entirely by the first week of 1998—a milestone the *New York Times* called "the fiscal equivalent of the fall of the Berlin Wall."[56]

Another piece of legislation that Clinton signed into law that many feel allowed the economy to grow was the Gramm-Leach-Bliley Act signed on November 12, 1999. The purpose of the act was to modernize financial services, primarily, that is, to end regulations that prevented the merger of banks, insurance, and stock brokerage companies. However, the removal of these regulations raised significant risks. Financial institutions, under the new act, would have access to large amounts of personal information, with no restrictions. Prior to Gramm-Leach-Bliley Act, insurance companies that maintained health records were distinct from banks that held mortgages on people's homes and the stockbroker that traded that person's stocks. Once these companies merged, however, they had the capability to analyze, consolidate, and sell the personal details of their customers' lives. The new act freed these large mergers to take hold and thrive, driving the stock market up, increasing incomes, and therefore raising federal income tax revenues. This boom had a downside, however, and a decade later, in 2008/2009, the bubble burst.

Nevertheless, Clinton's legacy on the economy is positive and much of his continued popularity today derives from this memory. Clinton admired FDR for his strong leadership skills but also realized that America was now living in a different era. Roosevelt's emphasis on the state as a mechanism for growth was no longer needed and Clinton showed that placing greater trust in a market economy, both at home and in international trade through NAFTA and WTO, would eventually bring about the kind of growth where everyone could benefit. Reducing the deficit and lowering interest rates created millions of new jobs and drove down unemployment to the lowest point in a generation.[57] With no disrespect for Roosevelt, Clinton believed he had to move the Democratic Party away from the FDR legacy and create a political space for the party that reflected the current time, the last eight years of the twentieth century.

Presidents also leave their mark on the future by whom they nominate to the Supreme Court. As a liberal, Clinton made two very successful choices: Ruth Bader Ginsburg and Stephen Breyer who have both proved to be the kind of progressive-minded jurists Clinton sensed and hoped they would be. He appointed Ginsburg in 1993 and the Senate easily confirmed her by a 96–3 vote. A year later, Clinton nominated Stephen Breyer to the Supreme Court and he took his seat in August of that year. Clinton had interviewed Breyer in 1993 but had preferred Ginsburg at the time. However, Clinton had thoroughly studied Breyer's record in his 1993 decision and came back to him a year later when a new vacancy opened up. Clinton needed to balance the larger conservative membership on the bench and these two appointments have fulfilled the liberal Democratic agenda.

CONCLUDING REMARKS

Embedded in personality lie the characteristic behaviors that inform management style, worldview, motivation, and decision making. We acknowledge that personality is in some ways inherited, but is also shaped by early life experiences and adult events that form beliefs about the world environment and a person's role within that context. As stated previously in this chapter, the need for achievement and personal affiliation rank high in Clinton's sense of motivation. He is highly competitive, which complements his motivation for achievement. At the beginning of his first term, his motivation for power was relatively weak, but as he faced constant challenges from both the right and left, his desire for power increased, but solely for the purpose of achieving his policy goals. His need for personal acknowledgement appears to have emerged from his sense of abandonment in his very early years. He constantly needed personal affirmation whether it was being the center of attention or seeking the affection of women. He wanted to move the Democratic Party to the center of American politics so that it would be more relevant to the majority of Americans who had perceived the party as too far to the left and to make Democrats more electable. Achieving some social Democratic goals, he believed, was better than being out of office and not able to accomplish any of them. Preempting Republican policy positions like balancing the budget and reforming welfare while trying to carve out a middle agenda made Clinton appear unprincipled, constantly taking a zig-zag, sometimes incomprehensible, path. But as Hermann suggests, he was simply playing on a game board where the goal entailed the art of the possible.

His management style is illustrated in the example of his discussion with his advisers on welfare reform. He, like FDR, surrounded himself with strong-minded people who spoke their minds freely in meetings that were often, as Harris describes, "roiling affairs." Clinton's sense of self-confidence and efficacy enabled him to listen to competing viewpoints and then ultimately make his own decision. He enjoyed people, being in the center, and that is where he placed himself. He cultivated his quick mind and charismatic manner, but these qualities also came naturally to him.

Renshon warns that for anecdotal case material to become reliable, we must take into account the quality and source of the information, plus anecdotes should represent a pattern of behavior.[58] With that in mind, I would like to recount a few anecdotal events where I was a witness to the stories. Back in June 2004, Bill Clinton was invited to give the commencement address to some 2,700 graduating seniors at the City College of New York in Harlem not far from the location of his newly established office in the Adam Clayton Powell building on 125th Street.[59] In contrast to previous commencement speakers who would leave right after their speech, Clinton stayed throughout the ceremony that lasted about 90 minutes. Then afterward, to the astonishment of the faculty, he walked out among the beaming parents to congratulate them on their achievements in raising their children to graduate from college. Most of them were minority students who were the first in their family to ever go to college, let alone graduate. He shook hands, expressed his admiration for them, and asked questions, all the while smiling and taking pleasure in the whole affair. He honestly appeared to enjoy the interaction. At another event while he was still president, Clinton had hosted a large dinner party in the White House with about 600 guests, some at tables in the East Room and others in the Roosevelt room. After the dinner and during dessert, Clinton went to every table and engaged in conversation, welcoming everyone and making sure they were enjoying themselves.

Finally, in 2006, I attended a Global Leadership Award dinner in New York hosted by the United Nations Association of the United States of America (UNA-USA), honoring Bill Clinton for the creation of his Clinton Global Initiative just the year before. I was sitting at a round table of guests about 50 feet from the podium. Honestly, I was still angry at Clinton for his affair with the intern, bringing about his impeachment, and wasting valuable public time and American funds on the endless proceedings. Nevertheless, about five minutes after he began his remarks, all the women at the table simply sighed and looked at each other, "Ok, we forgive him." The lyrical tone of his voice, his gestures touching his heart, his easy body language all conveyed that magical charisma that is really beyond explanation or analysis.

Like many bright young students, Bill Clinton emanated promise as a boy growing up in Arkansas. Yet promise alone does not lead someone to become president of the United States and emerge as a world leader; that takes persistence and a driving motivation to achieve even the most challenging goals. All leaders enjoy some level of attention, but for Bill Clinton being at the center not only is enjoyable, but also fulfills a deep need for validation born from that sense of abandonment he had endured from an early age. He not only bears a need for adulation; he carries within him an insatiable will to be adored. And the cameras are still rolling.

NOTES

1. Margaret Hermann, "William Jefferson Clinton's Leadership Style," in *The Psychological Assessment of Political Leaders*, ed. Jerrold M. Post (Ann Arbor, MI: University of Michigan Press, 2003), 313.
2. Ibid., 315–318.
3. Ibid., 319.

4. David Winter, "Motivations and Mediation of Self-Other Relationships," in *The Psychological Assessment of Political Leaders*, ed. Jerrold M. Post (Ann Arbor, MI: University of Michigan Press, 2003), 306–312.
5. William E. Leuchtenburg, *In the Shadow of FDR: From Truman to Barack Obama*, 4th ed. (Ithaca, NY: Cornell University Press, 2009), 277–278.
6. Ibid., 271.
7. Stanley Renshon, "William Jefferson Clinton's Psychology," in *The Psychological Assessment of Political Leaders*, ed. Jerrold M. Post (Ann Arbor, MI: University of Michigan Press, 2003), 278.
8. M. L. Oakley, *On the Make: The Rise of Bill Clinton* (Washington, DC: Regnery, 1994), 23.
9. Renshon, "Clinton's Psychology," 281.
10. Bill Clinton, *My Life* (New York: Alfred A. Knopf, 2004), 20.
11. Charles F. Allen, "Governor William Jefferson Clinton: A Biography with a Special Focus on His Education Contributions" (PhD dissertation, University of Missouri, 1991), 20.
12. Renshon, "Clinton's Psychology," 279.
13. John F. Harris, *The Survivor: Bill Clinton in the White House* (New York: Random House, 2005), xx.
14. Ibid., xxvi.
15. Ibid., xxiii.
16. Renshon, Stanley, *High Hopes: The Clinton Presidency and the Politics of Ambition* (New York and London: Routledge, 1998), 148.
17. Allen, "Governor Clinton," 12.
18. David Maraniss, *First in His Class: A Biography of Bill Clinton* (New York: Simon and Schuster, 1995), 383.
19. Renshon, *High Hopes*, 127.
20. Stephen Skowronek, *The Politics Presidents Make: Leadership from John Adams to Bill Clinton* (Cambridge, MA: Harvard University Press, 1997), 447–448.
21. Ibid., 449.
22. Ibid.
23. Renshon, *High Hopes*, 132–133.
24. Ibid., 133.
25. Ibid., 137.
26. Ivo H. Daalder, "Knowing When to Say No: The Development of US Policy for Peacekeeping," in *UN Peacekeeping, American Policy, and the Uncivil Wars of the 1990s*, ed. William J. Durch (New York: St. Martin's Press, 1996), 57.
27. Ibid., 58.
28. Ibid., 59–60.
29. J. Matthew Vaccaro, "The Politics of Genocide: Peacekeeping and Disaster Relief in Rwanda," in *UN Peacekeeping, American Policy, and the Uncivil Wars of the 1990s*, ed. William J. Durch (New York: St. Martin's Press, 1996), 377.
30. Ibid., 378.
31. Ibid.. 383.
32. Harris, *The Survivor*, 319.
33. Ibid., 320.
34. Ibid.
35. Ibid., 138.

36. Ibid., 141.
37. Ibid.
38. William J. Durch and James A. Schear, "Faultlines: UN Operations in the Former Yugoslavia," in *UN Peacekeeping, American Policy, and the Uncivil Wars of the 1990s*, ed. William J. Durch (New York: St. Martin's Press, 1996), 246.
39. Ibid., 247–249.
40. Harris, *The Survivor*, 367.
41. Mark Quarterman, "UN Leverage in East Timor," in *Leveraging for Success in United Nations Peace Operations*, ed. Jean Krasno, Bradd C. Hayes, Donald C. F. Daniel (Westport, CT: Praeger, 2003) 160–161.
42. Ibid., 161.
43. Clinton Fernandes, *The Independence of East Timor: Multilateral Perspectives* (Eastbourne, UK: Sussex Academic Press, 2011), 197.
44. Clinton, *My Life*, 869.
45. Harris, *The Survivor*, 95.
46. Ibid., 101.
47. Clinton, *My Life*, 636.
48. Ibid., 942–943.
49. Ibid., 787.
50. Harris, *The Survivor*, 114.
51. Ibid., 115.
52. Ibid., 236–237.
53. Clinton, *My Life*, 720.
54. Ibid., 490.
55. Ibid., 494.
56. Harris, *The Survivor*, 263.
57. Leuchtenburg, *In the Shadow of FDR*, 289.
58. Renshon, *High Hopes*, 314.
59. Carl Camonile, "Uptown Bill Will Thrill CUNY Grads," *New York Post*, May 20, 2004.

Part V

COMBINING FLEXIBILITY WITH DELEGATION

18

Václav Havel: The Most Deserving Political Leader to Have Never Won a Nobel Peace Prize

Jakub Robert Walko

Guided by an open mind, unwavering morals, and an uncompromising belief in human freedom, Václav Havel was one of the most prominent opposition leaders and human rights champions of our time. Born into a prominent and wealthy family, he endured decades of communist oppression, becoming an enemy of the state almost overnight due to his family's socioeconomic status. His perseverance and a passion for fairness and freedom ultimately led him to become a leader of a movement that overthrew communism and created a modern and democratic state in Czechoslovakia. Havel's actions have earned him many accolades and labels. Often compared to the likes of Nelson Mandela and the Dalai Lama, many regard him as the most deserving political leader never to have won a Nobel Peace Prize. In fact, in September 2013, the former opposition leader Daw Aung San Suu Kyi of Myanmar disclosed that Havel rejected the Nobel Institute's efforts to nominate him in 1991, and instead suggested that Daw Aung San Suu Kyi herself be nominated.[1] The Nobel Institute keeps its information confidential for 50 years, but if true, this anecdote is reflective of the praise that Havel received in obituaries around the world upon his death in December 2011. The *Economist* called him a "humble man, [who] detested the pomposity, superficiality and phony intimacy of politics."[2] The *New York Times* described him as a "shy yet resilient, unfailingly polite but dogged man,"[3] while *Time* referred to him as "an irreplaceable moral leader," who "remained iconic and relevant" even after leaving office.[4] Which of these labels really fit, and to what extent, are questions we can answer only through an in-depth study of his life. An analysis of his youth, work as a dissident, and life as president shows that Havel was a pragmatic and flexible leader, using his office for the benefit of his constituents rather than personal power.

Havel's early childhood provided him with some of the experiences that would shape his later actions. Born in Prague in 1936, in what was then Czechoslovakia, he grew up in a prominent and wealthy family that appears to have influenced him profoundly. Bearing the name of several generations of his paternal line, he should have been born with a mind for engineering, capitalist enterprise, or real estate development—occupations that made his father's family well known among Prague elite. It is possible that it was his father's preoccupation with business enterprises that allowed Havel's affectionate and industrious mother, Božena, to have a greater role in his upbringing, passionately instilling in him an awareness of culture that she developed through her art and language studies during college. Havel began to notice differences between him and the people who surrounded him early on. Some of his earliest memories were the feelings he experienced toward the people employed by his family: cooks, maids, and laborers involved with the estate or his family's entrepreneurial pursuits:

> I was ashamed of my advantages, my perks; I pleaded to be relieved of them and I longed for equality with others, not because I was some kind of a childhood revolutionary, but simply because I felt separate and excluded, because I felt around me a certain mistrust, a certain distance, because I knew that between me and those around me there was an invisible wall, and because behind that wall – and this may seem paradoxical – I felt alone, inferior, lost, ridiculed.[5]

The feeling of separation, of forced exclusion beyond his understanding, gave him an early appreciation of social inequality and led to his lifelong inquiry into the human condition. It also led to what is considered to be one of his chief personality problems: his overwhelming sense of humility, the feeling of not deserving the praise and recognition he obtained for his achievements.

Young Václav satiated his yearning for answers and knowledge—at least partially—by what he described as a particularly intellectual upbringing. His maternal grandfather, Hugo Vavrecka, was a prominent Czechoslovak ambassador and a self-taught philosopher whose ideas would come to shape Václav in profound ways. Because of his grandfather's interests and profession, Václav had full access to what was one of the most exhaustive personal collections of literature in the country. He spent long periods of time digging up ever more esoteric works, an activity unavailable to most of his peers, or even adults, at the time. His environment also made it possible for Václav to interact with family friends occupied with writing and philosophy, such as the prominent Czech journalist Ferdinand Peroutka. Václav maintained correspondence with Peroutka and others despite his young age. As friends and patrons, the Havel family became a means of refuge for many intellectuals during both the Nazi occupation and the postwar communist regime.

Being surrounded by literature led Václav to develop a taste for writing. Having been occupied with it "since he learned the alphabet," he composed poems, essays, and articles, and at the age of 13, wrote a book on philosophy.[6] As a promising new literary talent, the teenage Václav began to experience the reality of life under the new communist regime. Because of their considerable socioeconomic status, his family was selected by the government for "Action B," a property seizure and relocation plan for wealthy Praguers, which relegated them to a border town. The government liquidated the Havel's wealth and assets, seized their properties, and nationalized everything from their art collection to their summer home. The family also came under scrutiny by the secret police.

The Havels, as a family, survived World War II, but the new system of government eventually led to their total undoing. As the communist regime declared war on everything considered bourgeois, jobs became restricted and the state offered no sympathy for those with a background incompatible with its designs. Over the following decades, Václav would see his father barred from any meaningful employment, and his mother become the breadwinner of the family, taking jobs as a tour guide, a caretaker in the Bethlehem Chapel in Prague, and at one point, as a box office and souvenir shop clerk at the town hall.[7]

For someone as acutely sensitive as Václav, these injustices might have been too much to bear, but he weathered them privately and chose to be proactive. Expelled from the private school he was attending due to his class status, he quickly organized an alternative means of education and grew close with fellow ex-student Milos Forman. Since he was no longer following a particular curriculum, he read whatever interested him and met others like him for lively debates and collaborative writing on intellectual subjects. In his spare time, he wrote poetry and devoured what was left of the family's collection of precommunist magazines. He worked as a carpenter and eventually managed to get an apprenticeship as a chemical lab assistant. This position allowed him to complete a secondary school education by taking night classes.

These experiences, combined with his childhood observations, demonstrated to him a particular absurdity of humankind in relation to his surroundings, in which intuitive rules of merit and morality seemed to have little consequence on where individuals found themselves. It appeared to young Havel as if one's place in this world not only resulted from chance but also seemed highly resistant to change. It would be difficult to designate a single origin point for Václav Havel's beliefs, since one can see so many influences. While the events of World War II and the communist regime that followed certainly shaped his development, the environment provided by his family and their acquaintances seems to have inculcated a passion for intellectualism in Havel. While his brother, Ivan, ended up using his natural talents in mathematics and engineering, Václav instead showed striking similarities to his grandfather, Hugo Vavrecka. Before becoming the director of the Ministry of Foreign Affairs, Hugo spent much of his time abroad, trying to realize his vision of a strong and fraternal Central Europe. While posted in Budapest, he was called "the Czech Optimist" for his belief that the nations of the region had more commonalities than differences and needed to come together to guard themselves against the ever-present danger of Germany and Russia.[8] He wrote prolifically on diverse subjects and served as a co-editor of a daily newspaper. From the memoirs he composed for his grandsons, one gets a distinct sense of an inexplicable and perhaps menacing undercurrent, a quality that Václav's writings would one day contain as well. He viewed Czechoslovakia as simultaneously the center of Europe and a fragile place held together by the strained collective hands of good and moral people.

His writings betray a sense of "our land," less in the sense of nationalism and far more in the sense of "our freedom," always on the cusp of oblivion by those waiting across its borders. On a more spiritual level, Václav found in his grandfather the building blocks of his inner faith and awareness of the immense frustration in trying to make sense of the world. The following passage from his grandfather's memoir offers a hint of Havel's worldview, having spent his life expounding on its premise in his essays and plays:

> It is impossible to refute the supreme natural law governing the whole world, the rule of cause and effect which rules all objects and phenomena. However, we also may not forget that no one can know all the causal conditions and links in the world – there are considerably more of them than there are cells and atomic combinations in a human brain. Even in pure mathematics, it is impossible to solve certain equations with total precision. As soon as there are three bodies in space, the simplicity and clarity of mechanics ends. . . . How can science manage the world when we do not know what is hidden in people?[9]

As Hugo Vavrecka's fears for the fate of Czechoslovakia materialized, Václav had to look inside these ideas for the strength to persevere through the mounting injustices against everything dear in his life. He found many answers to his questions about the cruelty of others coming from his tutor, the Czech philosopher J. L. Fischer, whose ideas on human character, as shaped by societal circumstances, held great explanatory power. Fischer's pragmatic approach to philosophy and the need for dynamism in any societal order account for Václav's view of society that is free to maximize efficiency but remains aware of the pitfalls of quantifying aspects of human life.[10] Havel's other teacher, Josef Safarik, complemented these perspectives with his own teachings on the "living constitution," or the value of personal experience in the formation of one's beliefs.

Safarik's assertion of the "despicable nature of the tendency to clothe oneself in moral obligation, in the service of external authority and power" provided an important philosophical comfort to the young Václav. The starkness of postwar Czechoslovakia heavily exacerbated his loneliness. His biographer, Eva Kriseova, makes an interesting observation about the influence of his favorite author, Franz Kafka, whose works were banned and their legacy nearly erased during these years. Kriseova finds great similarities between the two in

> [t]heir recognition of the absurd dimension of the world, their experience of exile, of shyness, of persistent doubt in themselves and their abilities, and a sense of guilt and of their own particular obscurity. Both are interested in the loss of an individual's identity, in a person's position as the victim and target of manipulation by an impersonal power.[11]

The impact of this background is evident when one analyzes the patterns of behavior in Havel's later life. Milton Rokeach asserted that a person's set of beliefs is less important than the way the person believes them, and Havel's upbringing made him believe strongly in his principles. Interestingly, he said something similar himself:

> The period you grow up in and mature in always influences your thinking. This in itself requires no self-criticism. What is more important is how you have allowed yourself to be influenced, whether by good or by evil.[12]

It is necessary to note that much of where he found himself was the result of external factors and not personal choices. Due to his class status, he was denied work in virtually all fields, and was denied admission to universities for many years. During this time, art was the only form of expression sufficiently ambiguous to avoid attention from secret police and yet attract more dissidents and other artists.

Havel desired to attend the Academy of Performing Arts in Prague, but was rejected for socioeconomic reasons. Still hoping for admission, he meanwhile spent his time as a student of economics at the Czechoslovak University of Technology, but soon gave up and enlisted in the military. This turned out to be fortuitous for Havel, since he was becoming increasingly notable due to his reckless public behavior. He published his first work, an essay of literary criticism in a dissident journal, in which he showed knowledge of banned works and made references to disapproved historical events. To make matters worse, he had delivered an incendiary criticism of censorship, condemned the oppression of literature, and made an appeal for freedom of speech at a conference for young writers. Had it not been for his departure from public life, Havel might have found himself in prison much sooner than he actually did. During this time, he also began dating Olga Splichalova, an outspoken aspiring actress, whose personality contrasted and complemented his own; Olga soon became his wife.

Going into the military proved to be a very different experience from life in the artistic circles in Prague. A friend said about Havel's military experience:

> [T]he service in the course of the two years makes a teenager into a man. In the service, a guy has to keep company with people he wouldn't hang out with on the outside, where he would have avoided them. After these two years he learns to bear his fate in this world. Vasek [*Editor's note: diminutive form of Václav*] can handle so many things today because he had a background in coercion. As a civilian he was coerced many times, but it started in the service . . . he could have come up with flat feet or something else, but he never shirked anything. . . . Nothing human was alien to Vasek.[13]

While in the military, Havel started a theater group, more in order to avoid drills and training exercises than to pursue that particular interest. He wrote a few short plays that appealed to his unit's political officer, but once acted out, the plays presented the characters, ostensibly seeming to represent communist ideals, in ways that revealed the plays to be more satire than the uplifting patriotic works that they appeared to be. The experience of "author's theatre" would dispatch Havel on a journey that blurred the distinction between reality and scripted fiction. His life began to resemble a play more than any rational or plausible story of a person caught in a hostile environment. After his military service, his familiarity with theater allowed him to obtain one of the only jobs he could—as a stagehand with the ABC Theatre in Prague. This exposure permitted the blossoming of a wider range of talents. He wrote, befriended others who found refuge in theater, and thus moved onto more serious and dramatic works at an emerging cultural institution of some significance, the Theatre on the Balustrade. Havel found great relief in this environment and decided on theater as his chosen profession.[14]

At this point, one can begin noticing the more apparent patterns of behavior stemming from Havel's childhood influences. Havel's first major play, *The Garden Party*, was presented as part of the *Theatre of the Absurd*, an artistic perspective of which he had an intimate knowledge and understanding. The play told a story of a man who, in pursuit of a job, betrays himself and changes beyond recognition, echoing the Czechoslovaks' growing complacency and metamorphosis within the communist system.

This approach forms a major part of his belief system, with each play showing the impact of his life experiences. Havel's highly didactic plays shine in their ability to demonstrate the intimately personal details within a scheme of an all-encompassing and perpetually controlling societal order, making him a prominent representative of this style of art. Havel reveals much about his identity and the underlying meaning of his work when he writes about this type of theater:

> [I]t demonstrates modern humanity in a state of crisis, as it were. That is, it shows man having lost his fundamental metaphysical certainty. The experience of the absolute, his relationship to eternity, the sensation of meaning – in other words, having lost the ground under his feet. This is a man for whom everything is coming apart, whose world is collapsing, who senses that he has irrevocably lost something but is unable to admit this to himself and therefore hides from it. He waits, unable to understand that he is waiting in vain. He is plagued by the need to communicate the main thing, but he has nothing to communicate. . . . The plays are not – and this is important – nihilistic. They are merely a warning. In a very shocking way, they throw us into the question of meaning by manifesting its absence. Absurd theatre does not offer us consolation or hope. It merely reminds us of how we are living: without hope. . . . The absurd playwright does not have the key to anything. He does not consider himself any better informed or any more aware than his audience. He sees his role in giving a form to something we all suffer from, and in reminding us, in suggestive ways, of the mystery before which we all stand equally helpless.[15]

Concurrent with the beginning of his theatrical success, Havel began his work with the Writer's Union. Because of his earlier writing, Havel was asked to join the rebellious, but state-approved *Tvar* (The Face) magazine, on the condition that he would attend the Writer's Union meetings. Because Havel saw the magazine as a rare opportunity to address some civic interests, he accepted and began attending the meetings. There he found the union extremely elitist and, despite their desire for moderate national change, highly ignorant of civic problems. Over time, as his plays gained popularity, his written opinions about the union became increasingly incendiary. In particular, he pointed out the rampant discrimination in the approval process for newly written works, and he began branching out into criticism of the national system.[16]

It is crucial to understand that Havel never had a particular inclination toward politics, and held back most of his political opinions, a pattern consistent in his early work, political endeavors, and post-presidential writing. His theatrical works faced censorship but, as was the case elsewhere in communist Europe, carried political messages as part of a subtext hidden within creative fiction. Under the guise of fiction or fantasy, these works allowed people to recognize their strife without putting the creators in danger. When writing about his reactions to the applause and thrill of a large portion of the Czechoslovak population, Havel remained reserved and self-deprecating, often questioning a work's creative strength and characterizing its message as only simple and human. Though speculative, it is quite likely that his lifelong feeling of being an outcast and the staunch belief in the right of human dignity made him think that he really was stating the obvious in his works, regardless of how revolutionary the issues tackled in them were. When asked whether he faced the "danger" of self-worship as a result of his success, Havel said:

> I don't feel threatened by that particular danger. It has to do with my nature, my disposition, my general type, both as an author and as a man. I'm the kind of person who is always doubting himself. I'm far more sensitive to critical voices than I am to voices that praise me. I hear many different expressions of sympathy, solidarity, respect, and admiration; some have even invested hope in me. . . . At the same time, however, I always find them somewhat embarrassing, and I continually ask myself whether I really deserve such attention, whether I'll manage not to disappoint all those expectations and live up to all those demands. After all, what have I really accomplished? I've written some plays, a few articles, I've done some time in prison. I ask myself these questions, and I harbor these feelings so perhaps the danger of self-worship is not my problem.[17]

Havel's statement about his works and his time in prison can be attributed as typical to both his self-image and the mediation of self-other relations.[18] The nature to which he refers, along with the moral principles he has exhibited throughout his life, seems to make up the primitive belief system that goes unquestioned, and as a result gives a person a feeling of some actions being natural.[19]

Following the suppression of the Prague Spring by the Soviet invasion of Czechoslovakia in 1968, Havel's works were banned, and with considerable pressure from other dissidents, he became convinced that he needed to take a greater part in the effort to bring human rights to the forefront of the then nonexistent public debate. His next plays and essays, and particularly the publication of the collaborative dissident manifesto, *Charter 77*, resulted in his detention and several stays in prison (with the longest lasting four years, from 1979 to 1983). Philosopher Jan Patocka, whose death at the hands of police interrogators gave solid validation to the authors of the Charter, often inspired Havel's work as a dissident. Havel's lack of status as a radical made the sham trials he faced very unpopular, even among people reluctant to express views against the establishment. Eventually his struggle would lead to Havel's becoming a symbol of struggle and increased social unrest. During his first and rather traumatic stay in prison, Havel wrote a customary petition for release, though he did not expect the state to take any action. Instead, the government told him that the opposition movement had given up, and he would be released if he signed a statement relinquishing his claim of being a Charter representative. Havel signed the statement, but upon his release discovered the state's lie, and felt that he had let the movement down by not standing his ground during his prison stay.

The stay in prison was followed by Havel becoming consumed by guilt. It shows off his fault as a moral perfectionist who failed to forget the experience, despite forgiveness and understanding shown by fellow dissidents. Havel was then happily arrested for a second time and viewed the next stay in prison as penance, which he used as a motivator for his actions, vowing to not show such weak principles again.[20] During his second prison experience, Havel focused and cemented his views on the lonely nature of *self* and the grounding of his principles. Writing to his wife on the destructive effects of idle imprisonment on his fellow inmates, he observed that those primarily attached to a group or circumstances, or to particular allies, felt greatest fear and anxiety. In other words, those who depended on external things for their beliefs in their causes were those who most readily fell victim to selfish behaviors. On the other hand, those whose beliefs were of a more self-created nature, focusing on values disconnected from organizations and movements or being a part of something, suffered less due to the comfort of certainty they had found in themselves.

His writings from this period became more hopeful and increasingly aligned with a broad, future-oriented perspective.[21] Two of his most famous essays, *The Power of the Powerless* and *Thriller*, exemplify this optimism:

> For the real question is whether the "brighter future" is really always so distant. What if, on the contrary, it has been here for a long time already, and only our own blindness and weakness has prevented us from seeing it around us and within us, and kept us from developing it?[22]
>
> I am unwilling to believe that this whole civilization is no more than a blind alley of history and a fatal error of the human spirit. More probably it represents a necessary phase that man and humanity must go through, one that man – if he survives – will ultimately, and on some higher level (unthinkable, of course, without the present phase), transcend.[23]

Havel found himself in need of such hope of better times, as he spent much of the 1980s in and out of prison and ill with repeated cases of pneumonia. However, the more he wrote on the subject, the closer he came to a statement he had made in his youth that "suggesting something better was a politician's job, and I've never been a politician and never wanted to be."[24] It was then only fitting that in 1989, he was approached, while still in prison, to be the leader of the entire opposition movement in Czechoslovakia. With mounting pressure from his fellow Czechoslovaks, he accepted. That same year, Václav Havel, the reluctant playwright who disliked the spotlight and thought the idea of himself as a politician laughable, was elected to become the first president of free Czechoslovakia by a unanimous vote of the Federal Assembly, composed entirely of Communist Party politicians. It was an outcome worthy of the *Theatre of the Absurd.*

Being elected president did not alter Havel's moral principles much: despite widespread and multidirectional pressure in his decision making, he adhered to his set of morals. We see this pattern of behavior in one of the most unpopular decisions of his political career: a broad amnesty for all those imprisoned by the Communist regime, not only opposition figures but criminals as well. Havel felt that, given the general level of injustice in the Communist regime, the court decisions could not be upheld on ethical grounds. In addition to demonstrating Havel's refusal to compromise beliefs for popularity's sake, such actions also brought a feeling of reconciliation to a country that desperately needed it in order to move forward.

Havel understood the impossibility of appeasing all political players while coming to power in a state with virtually no functioning government bodies. He attempted to establish a just and pragmatic rule, without altering the structure of the government overnight. For example, he insisted on a two-year transitional government and refused to meet others' demands to ban or jail Communist Party members. He felt he had no moral rights to do so, especially in an environment as unfriendly to proper justice. Such an action holds great explanatory power. Havel's refusal to cave into political demands ultimately protected Communist Party members whom he could easily view as indirectly or even directly responsible for destroying his life during his youth. As a younger dissident, Havel took plenty of jabs at the establishment, but in his new position he found greater wisdom than to simply exact revenge. He placed the practical need to maintain peace above popular demands for revenge and treated those who have previously harmed him with justice.

Rather than attempting to maintain his popularity, Havel's presidency focused on the politics and logistics of pulling society out of the Communist and Warsaw Pact systems, an admittedly complicated feat. He paid particular attention to the European Union, an organization with a strong focus on human rights promotion, believing that people needed to look to others with whom to stand in defense of the rights of people, an attitude reminiscent of his grandfather's view of international affairs. He worked to form the Visegrad Group of Central European States, which jointly negotiated a NATO entry, a position that brought him criticism both from those desiring greater Czech individualism in the matter and from those who saw it as too reactionary to the breakup of the USSR. As president, Havel did not have unlimited power to reshape his country, and he experienced both adulation and criticism.

Ignoring calls from his supporters for greater political party leadership, Havel remained an independent president. Despite occasional controversies, he was notoriously absent from political partisanship, often expressing critical opinion of infighting, deceitfulness, and attempts at personal gain. He identified his own definition of politics as little more than selfless public service rooted in moral codes of general conscience and responsibility. Havel saw his conviction of both personal responsibility toward others and adherence to higher ideals as being a "check" on political decisions long before the actual electoral "check" of the people. Resisting advice to strengthen his position by engaging in political battles, Havel said this about remaining faithful to his beliefs regardless of the political cost:

> [W]hat most concerns me: the simple fact that directness can never be established by indirection, or truth through lies, or the democratic spirit through authoritarian directives. Of course I don't know whether directness, truth, and the democratic spirit will succeed. But I do know how *not* to succeed, which is by choosing means that contradict the ends. As we know from history that is the best way to eliminate the very ends we set out to achieve. In other words, if there is to be any chance of success, there is only one way to strive for decency, reason, responsibility, sincerity, civility, and tolerance, and that is decently, reasonably, responsibly, sincerely, civilly, and tolerantly. I'm aware that in everyday politics, this is not seen as the most practical way of going about it. But I have one advantage: among my many bad qualities there is one that happens to be missing – a longing or a love for power. Not being bound by that, I am essentially freer than those who cling to their power or position, and this allows me to indulge in the luxury of behaving un-tactically. I see the only way forward in that old, familiar injunction: "live in truth."[25]

Havel's ability to consider multiple perspectives was an important component of his actions surrounding the break-up of Czechoslovakia. As president, he opposed the separation of Czechs and Slovaks, and hoped that the federation would continue. He had been a strong advocate of constitutional reforms that gave greater voting rights to the people. He often proposed that matters be decided by referenda. Havel allowed the Slovaks a referendum on moral grounds, stating, "[I]t would have been against all my principles had I tried to determine for the Slovak people a way in which they might or might not express themselves as a nation."[26] He resigned as president of Czechoslovakia (but was quickly elected president of the Czech Republic), feeling it would be wrong for him to sign an act of dissolution of a state whose integrity he swore to protect. This provides an interesting case of a pragmatic approach to matters of honor and faithful execution of one's duties as a leader, which, for the moral perfectionist Havel was, he could have seen as a personal failure. While he admits seeing it that way at the time, he reflected that he was not fully aware or understanding of Slovak sensitivities on the subject and his views on self-determination aided his decision as a matter of principle.[27]

Havel freely admitted to many mistakes, but held himself most accountable for the state of Czech society following the revolution and the dissolution. Havel saw his country as having as much potential as any other to develop a culture of morality after its experiences, but felt that this did not happen. He was frustrated when legislative work often took on strong shades of reactionary politics rather than true pragmatism. Capitalist politicians, particularly his rival and Prime Minister Václav Klaus, often considered many issues close to his heart, such as the environment, civil society, and the nonprofit sector, irrelevant. Havel wished he had been more forceful in his exercise of limited presidential powers in favor of such causes, though how much of this is due to his awkwardness and politeness, as he claims, is too difficult to see. Ultimately, he made the best of his position, advancing proposals for reform, decentralization, and diversity of representation of political opinions. These served as satisfying consolation prizes for the frustration of making grand moral speeches that were met with applause from civil society, only to be subsequently ignored by the parliamentarians.[28]

Havel took greatest pride in his part in the dissolution of the Warsaw Pact and re-unification of Western and Central Europe. Coming into power, he recalls being overwhelmed by the difficulties of negotiating on subjects considered taboo before the revolution. Throughout the Cold War, the Soviet Union stationed large numbers of troops in the territories of the Warsaw Pact countries, making it an uncomfortable proposition to negotiate separation and independence during what was a de facto occupation. Havel was symbolically rewarded for his efforts in 1991 when he was chosen to announce the end of the Warsaw Pact from the capital invaded by its forces just two decades prior.[29] Havel left office in 2003, and the Czech Republic joined the European Union the following year.

Rokeach theorized that knowing the way a person believes can be a predictor of how he will solve problems; Havel's life presents a fascinating example. His belief in nonviolent resistance, despite challenging circumstances, led to Havel's becoming a nonconfrontational problem solver, with consensus seeking, reconciliation, and inclusion apparent in the actions he took throughout his life. Accordingly, I can describe Havel only as a pragmatic and flexible leader.[30] His creative criticism through theatrical performances and hidden storylines shows mental flexibility, coupled with his empathy for the socially neglected, and victims of discrimination show him to be an open-minded individual.[31] This pattern of behavioral dynamics demonstrates that Havel acquired most of his beliefs from experiences during his youth, and he never shed the principles they instilled in him. About his childhood lessons, Havel said:

> [S]omething of that early self-awareness probably stayed with me: my bourgeois background – and this may seem odd, and you don't have to believe it if you don't want to – awakened (or, more exactly, strengthened) within me something like a social emotion, an antagonism towards undeserved privileges, towards unjust social barriers, towards any kind of so-called higher standing predetermined by birth or by anything else, towards any humiliation of human dignity. I think that everyone, as far as possible, should have the same chances.[32]

The peculiar nature of Communism provided a unique impetus for social, but more importantly personal-philosophical unrest. The Romanian scholar and expert on Communism Vladimir Tismaneanu condensed that nature to a simple essence:

> Communism was not simply a variety of political regime, one of the many forms of dictatorship mankind has experienced since ancient times. It was unique in its attempt to mold the human psyche, in its mythological hubris, in its endeavor to regiment people and to force them to behave in accordance with Pavlovian recipes of happiness.[33]

In order to understand Havel's development, it is crucially important to grasp the peculiar feeling produced by Communism in Central Europe. It was an environment where unjust jailing and entrapment were common, and that punished morality itself. Under the surface, it was an existential condition that made every individual keenly aware of their absolutely constant vulnerability to the state. Hypocrisy and apathy were the most desirable traits, and contrary to common thought, it was individuality and not the fraternal ideal that was most rewarded. After all, a true individual cared about himself first and at all costs. Thus, an individual could not ask questions or stand up for the rights of a group. The perfect communist was not a person whose understanding of good led to collective work for that purpose, but rather it was someone fully concerned with his or her own well-being, an unprincipled working consumer. The artificially constructed system provided peace and glorified selfishness at the expense of morality, spirituality, and the organic collective ideal—culture—that it sought to entirely wipe out.

With Havel's childhood love of philosophy, he would only emerge as more passionate and more creative, regardless of the traps devised for him. It is somewhat poetic that Havel ended up in theater and then rose to the top of opposition leadership. It may illustrate something about the faults of closed-minded regime planners, or perhaps more about the durability and inventiveness of the struggling human spirit. One of the last things Havel did before the Soviet invasion, and the subsequently imposed travel restrictions, was to participate in a memorial march for Martin Luther King Jr. in New York in 1968. Even before his significant dissident work began, Havel possessed a firm understanding of injustice and felt a motivational empathy for those mistreated by their governments.

Havel regretted staying in politics for as long as he did due to the intrusive nature of popularity into his private life. A shy man, disliking the star label so many have imposed on him, Havel held no self-criticism back, equating his friction with others, an extramarital affair, and other personal transgressions as sins major enough to mar his legacy. Havel often hid behind his writing, and it is only the volume of his work that permits us to snatch a glimpse of this complicated individual, who grew up with a harsh awareness of things that, he once commented, gave him "the opportunity, right from the start, of seeing the world 'from below', that is, as it really is. This helped me escape certain eventual illusions and mystifications."[34] When asked about his feelings on the Nobel Peace Prize, he responded, in a fashion typical of him, that while he could not deny wanting the prize early on, he would have felt awkward accepting it as president, being conscious of the fact that he was compensated for the job the prize is meant to encourage. He felt instead that, given the attention it brings, the prize should be awarded to someone presently struggling for its ideals, who, in prison or fighting impossible obstacles, might find the recognition necessary to keep going.[35]

Through his statements, we can see the impact of Havel's childhood experiences on his personality, and thus political behavior throughout his life. His early experiences cemented his perceptions of inequality, and provided him with seeds of thought that he would later nurture, such as his growing sense of hope and faith in the future. On becoming more hopeful throughout his life, he said:

> [A] state of mind, not a state of the world . . . it is an orientation of the spirit, an orientation of the heart; it transcends the world that is immediately experienced, and is anchored somewhere beyond its horizons. Hope, in this deep and powerful sense, is not the same as joy that things are going well, or willingness to invest in enterprises that are obviously headed for early success, but, rather, an ability to work for something because it is good, not just because it stands a chance to succeed. The more unpropitious the situation in which we demonstrate hope, the deeper that hope is. Hope is definitely not the same thing as optimism. It is not the conviction that something will turn out well, but the certainty that something makes sense, regardless of how it turns out. In short, I think that the deepest and most important form of hope, the only one that can keep us above water and urge us to good works, and the only true

source of the breathtaking dimension of the human spirit and its efforts, is something we get, as it were, from "elsewhere." It is also this hope, above all, which gives us strength to live and continually to try new things, even in conditions that seem as hopeless as ours do, here and now.[36]

Havel was rare in the world of political leaders—a disinterested artist, whose work in politics was based on his unwillingness to turn his back on people who asked for his help. He was steadfast in maintaining his opinions, befitting a man who gave great thought and moral consideration to his decisions. Much like the playwright of the Theatre of the Absurd, Havel showed the world the truth of what they were missing. He performed his role in a period of history that desperately required someone to gather the truth and put it together for everyone to see. His belief system is most evident in his statement that "the moral order stands above legal, political, and economic orders, and that these latter orders should derive from the former, not be techniques for getting around its imperatives ... this moral order has a metaphysical anchoring in the infinite and the eternal."[37]

Given the level of adversity Havel faced, one can ask whether he could have endured it had it not been for the early experiences that prepared him philosophically for his later struggles. Havel's personal motto, "truth and love will prevail over lies and hate," carried him through his difficult life. Clearly, the convictions of an individual with deep-seated beliefs about open-mindedness, fairness, and equality reflected in his dissident work and his political decisions. Havel's case illustrates what we all desire to be true—that if one only remains true to one's beliefs and maintains an intimate bond with his or her environment, one will find plenty of ways to keep hope and achieve what he or she sets out to do.

NOTES

1. Dan Bilefsky, "Vaclav Havel Refused 1991 Nobel Peace Prize Nomination, Says Daw Aung San Suu Kyi," *New York Times*, September 16, 2003.

2. "Living in Truth: Vaclav Havel, 1936-2011," *Economist*, December 31, 2011. http://www.economist.com/node/21542169.

3. Dan Bilefsky and Jane Perlez, "Vaclav Havel, Former Czech President, Dies at 75," *New York Times*, December 18, 2011. http://www.nytimes.com/2011/12/19/world/europe/vaclav-havel-dissident-playwright-who-led-czechoslovakia-dead-at-75.html?pagewanted=1&_r=0&adxnnl=1&adxnnlx=1381946046-BdUEHIqVaiAtGupPm67YNA.

4. James O. Jackson, "The Death of the Playwright-President: Vaclav Havel," *Time*, December 18, 2011. http://content.time.com/time/world/article/0,8599,2102748,00.html.

5. Václav Havel, *Disturbing the Peace: A Conversation with Karel Hvizdala* (New York: Alfred A. Knopf, 1990), 6.

6. Ibid., 23.

7. Eda Kriseova, *Vaclav Havel: The Authorized Biography* (New York: St. Martin's Press, 1993), 24.

8. Ibid., 29.
9. Ibid., 26.
10. Jiri Gabriel, Lubomir Novy, and Jaroslav Hroch, eds., *Czech Philosophy in the XXth Century: Czech Political Studies, II* (Washington, D.C.: Council for Research in Values and Philosophy, 1994), 101–104.
11. Kriseova, *Vaclav Havel,* 117.
12. Havel, *Disturbing the Peace,* 8.
13. Kriseova, *Vaclav Havel,* 20.
14. Václav Havel, interview with Jan Culik, University of Glasgow, Slavonic Studies Department. http://www.arts.gla.ac.uk/Slavonic/havel.html.
15. Havel, *Disturbing the Peace,* 53–54.
16. Ibid., 81.
17. Ibid., 70.
18. Fred I. Greenstein, *Personality and Politics: Problems of Evidence, Inference, and Conceptualization* (Princeton, NJ: Princeton University Press, 1987), 64.
19. Milton Rokeach, *The Open and Closed Mind: Investigations into the Nature of Belief Systems* (New York: Basic Books Inc., 1960), 40.
20. Kriseova, *Vaclav Havel,* 135–136.
21. Rokeach, *The Open and Closed Mind,* 51.
22. Václav Havel, *The Power of the Powerless* (New York: M. E. Sharpe, 1985), 96.
23. Václav Havel, *Open Letters: Selected Writings 1965–1990* (New York: Alfred A. Knopf, 1991), VII.
24. Havel, *Disturbing the Peace,* 8.
25. Václav Havel, *Summer Meditations,* translated by P. Wilson (New York: Vintage Books, 1992), 6–9.
26. Václav Havel, *To the Castle and Back,* translated by P. Wilson (New York: Alfred A. Knopf, 2007), 98.
27. Ibid., 100.
28. Ibid., 176–183.
29. Ibid., 293–294.
30. Rokeach, *The Open and Closed Mind,* 7.
31. Ibid., 62.
32. Havel, *Disturbing the Peace,* 7.
33. V. Tismaneanu, *Reinventing Politics: Eastern Europe from Stalin to Havel* (New York: The Free Press, 1992), IX.
34. Havel, *Open Letters,* 4.
35. Havel, *To the Castle and Back,* 24-25.
36. Havel, *Disturbing the Peace,* 182.
37. Havel, *To the Castle and Back,* 326.

19

Kofi Annan: From Ghana to the World Stage

Jean Krasno

In studying Kofi Annan's personality and its influence on his decision making, I will begin with an examination of the genesis of factors that shaped the formation of his personality, beginning with the social and cultural context of his family growing up in Ghana around the time of Ghana's independence from colonial rule, and continuing through his adult personality formation.

BRIEF BIOGRAPHICAL OVERVIEW

Kofi Annan was the seventh secretary-general of the United Nations, serving two five-year terms from January 1, 1997, to December 31, 2006. Born in Kumasi, Ghana, in 1938, he was the first secretary-general to be appointed from the ranks of the UN staff, where he had served for over 30 years. He began his work with the United Nations in 1962 when he joined the World Health Organization in Geneva as a young administrator. Kofi's first recognition for his abilities came when someone from the Ford Foundation, who was recruiting for a leadership program for students to study at a university in the United States, approached Kofi at a student meeting and asked him to apply. Kofi was then a student at the University of Science and Technology in Kumasi, Ghana. He won the fellowship and attended Macalester College in St. Paul, Minnesota, completing his undergraduate work in economics in 1961. After completing his BA, he was offered a grant from the Carnegie Corporation to study for one year at the Institut Universitaire des Hautes Études International in Geneva. To complete his education, Kofi later returned to the United States as a Sloan Fellow and received a Master of Science degree in management in 1972 from the Massachusetts Institute of Technology (MIT). For most of his early UN career, Kofi Annan served in administrative positions in accounting, personnel, and other posts.

UN secretaries-general have traditionally served two five-year terms, but the United States objected to a second term for Annan's predecessor, Boutros-Ghali. The African Group at the United Nations had insisted on an African as secretary-general when Boutros-Ghali, from northern Africa's Egypt, was elected. However, when he was not accorded the traditional second term, the Africans insisted that another African, preferably now from sub-Saharan Africa, should be chosen. Kofi Annan, by that time, had become known to the major powers as talented and trustworthy, and his candidacy emerged with the most positive votes and no vetoes in the Security Council, which must approve the nomination before it goes to a full-member vote in the General Assembly. Annan had enough support from the major powers during his first term to be elected early, some five to six months earlier than usual, to a second term. After completing his second term as UN secretary-general, Annan has continued to be involved in international issues, highlighted by his role in mediating a successful resolution to the conflict that arose in Kenya after its presidential election in 2007/2008 and in 2012 his selection by the United Nations and the Arab League as special envoy for Syria.

KOFI'S EARLY YEARS IN GHANA

Kofi, which means Friday, the day he was born, is part of an elite Ghanaian family. Born with a twin sister, Efua Atta, his full name is Kofi (Friday) Atta (twin) Annan. Both his mother and father are descendants of tribal chiefs from the dominant tribal groups in Ghana, his mother (Ruth) full Fante and his father (Henry) part Fante and part Ashanti. In Ghanaian tradition, a man may take several wives, and Kofi's mother, not being the first wife, did not live with them and Kofi did not see her very often until he was older. Both Kofi's parents were Christian, yet they gave their children African names. In describing his father, Kofi Annan states, "To him, there was no contradiction in being African in identity and European in outlook."[1]

Henry Annan, despite his noble heritage, was not elected in the traditional manner as a chief, yet he was certainly a leader. He became a top executive in the United African Company, a subsidiary of Lever Brothers, later known as Unilever, an Anglo-Dutch multinational. After independence in 1957, Henry was appointed as commissioner of the Ashanti region, an administrative position given to tribal leaders by the new government of Ghana.[2] In this way his tribal leadership was acknowledged, though in a more modern manner by the central government, instead of by tribal elders.

With the United African Company, Kofi's father moved the family from region to region around Ghana as he became district manager in different parts of the country. In an interview, Kofi explains: "It was very interesting for me to grow up dealing with and getting to know so many different groups in Ghana. It gave you a sense of being able to relate to everybody and different groups at a young age."[3] When Henry became director of the company, the family moved to the capital, Accra, and the household became a hub for political debate. Henry Annan became a leader in one of the parties that supported independence, the United Gold Coast Convention (UGCC), but took a more moderate stance, advocating a gradual move toward independence.

> Our house in these days became a gathering point for senior members of the UGCC – to the point where Nkrumah activists would hold rallies in the park across the street. As a young man, I was deeply influenced by discussions going on at home with my father and his friends. At the same time, I was emotionally drawn to the passion and urgency of Nkrumah's calls for "independence now."[4]

While Kofi's father was not a tribal chief, per se, it appears as though he operated as such and was given the respect accorded to a chief. In Ghanaian tribal tradition, and Ashanti law, the chief must peacefully resolve local disputes, listen to complaints, and not speak in a loud voice. Kofi Annan explains, "[A]mong Ashantis themselves there was an important priority placed on compromise and negotiation. Indeed, the Ashanti king did not have his own army, but had to convince tribes and subtribes to provide troops in times of war and crisis."[5] This sounds very familiar when thinking about Annan as secretary-general of the United Nations, not having any troops of his own at his disposal. In his autobiography, Kofi describes his observations of his father in a way that profoundly reveals how Kofi Annan sees himself:

> In this respect, my father was representative of a deeper cultural tradition of patience, negotiation, and reconciliation. For Ghanaians, the concept of the African palaver tree has always been a tangible part of our heritage, and a source of the relative peace and harmony among myriad tribes and religions. A place to meet and talk, to seek compromise and settle disputes, to bridge differences and foster unity – this was the meaning of the palaver tree.[6]

At all times, but particularly when resolving disputes, a traditional Ghanaian chief maintains a dignified, almost judgelike, repose. The chief then relies on a chief minister or spokesman, referred to as the linguist, to pronounce the judgment or give out any rebuke.[7] Kofi's very dignified reserve appears to be shaped by the observations of this tradition passed down through his father.[8] He also, by many accounts as secretary-general, listened very attentively as others spoke, not only other leaders, but his own advisers. A close colleague of Annan's, Ibrahim Gambari, who served as his under-secretary-general for political affairs, stated in an interview that Annan "listens to everybody, synthesizes, and makes his decisions. And we all respected him for that because we felt he listened to us."

Gambari, from Nigeria, goes on to explain further the role that African chiefs traditionally have had to develop as a manner of listening to their people or, as Gambari uses the term, the chief's subjects:

> In traditional African society, the subject insists on being heard, so people don't realize it's not just that the kings or the chief had the luxury of not listening to his people. He had to listen to his people, absolutely, no hierarchies, no protocol; they insist on being heard. The wise chief, the wise, traditional ruler was one that listens to his people, gives guidance; he has to lead by example. African traditions are very democratic in nature. They talk all issues out, almost to exhaustion before consensus, reaching consensus, because that is the goal. Talk everything through, and the chief has to listen, has to be patient, and that's how you judge a successful, good leader.[9]

But Gambari warns not to take that as essentially an African or tribal trait:

> Obviously, we are all in many ways the product of our culture, but it was him too and his family. Because there are also other African leaders who are not like that. I think it's something about his personality, about his values, about his upbringing. . . . So, I think one has to give credit to him.[10]

Kofi Annan grew up in a well-to-do, stable family unit where he was absorbed into a transitional balancing of traditional tribal culture into the more modern industrialized culture that was growing in Ghana. His father was a symbol of that transition, which combined both systems. A council of elders in the old system, as explained earlier, along with elite civic leaders in the modern system, would gather at his house discussing issues of the day. "Kofi once said he was brought up 'atribal in a tribal world.' "[11] An old photograph of Annan's extended family shows most of the men wearing suits, while about half the women wore European dresses and the other half had African head ties and traditional African dress.[12] While Kofi observed the dignified manner of his father and the Ashanti king who frequented their house, his father also diligently trained his children to "explain their behavior with honesty and confidence, without stuttering and shuffling."[13] This training by his father would explain Kofi's composure and his ability to speak very clearly and to the point.

Another trait that seems to emerge from Kofi's Ghanaian background, and particularly the mood of his years as a teenager, is his continual optimism.

Throughout his speeches, off-the-cuff comments, and press conferences, he often refers to being optimistic about an eventual positive outcome. In an interview with this author, Annan explains:

> I've always been hopeful. I feel one can make a difference. I think it's also my own experience as a youth. I came of age in the years of African independence. Ghana was the first [sub-Saharan] African colony to become independent, and I was a teenager. I was in my teens. When we got independence, with the struggle, watching it, I was eighteen, nineteen then. And so you live in a colony where the governor is an Englishman, the police commissioner is an Englishman, the headmasters of some of the schools are English, and the bank manager. The struggle for independence starts, and you follow it. My father was active even though he was not in politics. He knew most of the politicians. They would come home and they would be talking about changes, and the need for independence, and the pace at which one should push for it. So, as a boy, you listen to all this and it seems so far away when they are discussing it, how difficult and impossible. And then one day, this big exciting thing that everybody is fighting for, independence, is achieved. And in a way, you grow up thinking that change is possible, even a huge transformational change is possible because you've lived it and you've seen it. So I think in a way, I've always gone through life feeling that change is possible, and one should not give up; one should try.[14]

Kofi attended private schools in Ghana, and those days left an impression on him. At 15 he entered Mfantsipim, a prestigious, elite high school. Annan recalls a personal tale of his school years when asked if he ever had a nickname:

> They used to call me Demo – short for democracy. I grew up in Ghana [in West Africa] at the time the country was getting its independence [from Britain], and there were lots of discussions at school about political systems. I was always talking about democracy. There were two Annans at school, so they called me Annan Demo.[15]

Annan clearly absorbed the political environment at school and at home and demonstrated very early on his interest in political affairs and the world. Kofi was sociable at school and is remembered for his sense of humor, but was not always compliant. Whether it was the developing resistance movement and growing demands for democratic participation that inspired the young Kofi, he organized and led a boycott at the school, demanding better food in the cafeteria. He even made sure that the boys had eaten before the boycott. The strategy worked and the menu was changed.[16] What now appears odd, Annan was not considered a strong scholar by the head master and did not make a high enough score on his examinations for him to enter an academic college and instead he enrolled in the Kumasi Institute of Science and Technology. His leadership qualities were beginning to become apparent, nevertheless, and he was elected vice president of the Ghana national students union. This enabled him to attend a confer ence in Sierra Leone of African student leaders, where he made an impression on a representative of the Ford Foundation, as mentioned, who offered him a scholarship to attend Macalester College in the United States. Growing up in the Annan family and attending private schools in Ghana, Kofi was already becoming Westernized, but studying in the United States would profoundly shape his development.

THE UNITED NATIONS AND A TURNING POINT IN ANNAN'S CAREER

In 1962, Annan began his first job within the UN system at the World Health Organization. Once in the UN system, he found a natural affinity to the type of humanitarian work it stands for. During most of his years within the United Nations, Annan held bureaucratic management positions. This enabled him later to understand the United Nations inside and out, but he was not identified as a political officer until much later. A profound event that would shape Annan's career as well as his sense of efficacy came when Secretary-General Pérez de Cuéllar sent Annan, at that time within the UN department of personnel, to Iraq in late September 1990 to try to free the 900 UN hostages who had been taken by Saddam Hussein before the outbreak of the first Gulf War in 1991.

It was his first political assignment, and his skills at diplomatic negotiations successfully brought about the release of all the UN hostages. Annan had remained optimistic about achieving their release and did not leave Iraq until every last person had made it to Jordan for the airlift out, even though he had to struggle at the last minute to get a few out who had left behind their proper papers.[17] To further understand the way his conscience drove his behavior, in working to release the UN hostages, Annan discovered that some 500,000 Asians from India, Sri Lanka, Bangladesh, and many other countries could not leave Iraq or Kuwait and risked being slaughtered in the impending war. They had all suddenly lost their jobs, and because most banks had closed down, they could not retrieve any money they might have had to pay their way home. Annan explained, "These people were beggared overnight."[18]

> Annan attended several meetings of the Western Ambassadors in Baghdad who discussed ways of pressuring the Iraqis to release the Western hostages. Unfortunately, the Asian and African ambassadors had not organized in the same way. So he made the rounds of the Indian, Pakistani, Bangladeshi, and

> other ambassadors to collect estimates of the numbers of their nationals stranded in Iraq and Kuwait. "I got the figures from them," he said. "I think I was the first to give it to the Iraqi Foreign Ministry." [Tariq] Aziz soon agreed to allow the UN to organize airlifts to take the workers from Jordan to their homes.[19]

This achievement laid the groundwork for UN Secretary-General Pérez de Cuéllar to recommend Kofi Annan as assistant secretary-general for Special Political Affairs under Marrack Goulding. This achievement was not only a turning event in Annan's career but also a profound learning experience. He was beginning to act upon the leadership role his father had nurtured. Thus, we see that Kofi's personality, his response to a humanitarian crisis, and his sense of efficacy were not only shaped by early childhood and cultural experiences but would also be shaped by major events in his adult life. Others would follow.

THE PROFOUND EFFECTS OF ADULT TRAUMA: SOMALIA, RWANDA, BOSNIA, AND OIL-FOR-FOOD

Kofi Annan's sense of efficacy and diplomatic skills were emerging through this newly found political role. But along with high-level positions comes responsibility, not only for achievements but for missteps, debacles, and failures. The four traumas—Somalia, Rwanda, Bosnia, and the Oil-for-Food crisis—not only weighed heavily on the United Nations, but involved Annan and his decision making. Not that he was to blame; the parties to the conflict were the ones killing each other and Saddam was responsible for the extortion schemes under Oil-for-Food. Nevertheless, Annan was involved and the human tragedy and accusations bore deeply into his conscience. A detailed explanation of each of these crises is beyond the scope of this chapter, but a brief summary is important in order to explain Annan's role.

Annan began his position as assistant secretary-general of Special Political Affairs as the new Secretary-General Boutros Boutros-Ghali took office in early 1992. The Cold War had just ended and there was a general euphoria that the United Nations could now take on the role of world peace that the founders had anticipated. When Boutros-Ghali created the new Department of Peacekeeping Operations that year, Goulding became the under-secretary-general and Annan his assistant secretary-general. A number of old conflicts were in the process of being resolved under UN auspices, and perhaps leaders at the United Nations became overconfident. When massive starvation overtook Somalia in the early 1990s, Boutros-Ghali was interested in taking a proactive role. This met some resistance from Goulding, who took more of a traditional approach to UN peacekeeping, not sending troops until a firm peace agreement had been reached and with consent of the parties. Boutros-Ghali found a more willing partner in Annan. Both had stronger ties to Africa and most likely felt the United Nations ought to take a more active role in addressing the suffering.

When the Security Council voted to reinforce the UN mission in Somalia in early 1993, Goulding was hesitant and Boutros-Ghali moved Goulding back to the Department of Political Affairs (as it was now called) and Annan was promoted to under-secretary-general for peacekeeping. We now know, looking back, that clan warfare in Somalia made it impossible for the United Nations to achieve its goals of peace and stability in the country. When in October 1993, the U.S. Delta Force failed in its efforts to disarm clan leader Aideed and 18 U.S. soldiers were killed, with one soldier dragged through the streets of Mogadishu before CNN cameras, the United Nations was blamed. President Clinton then oversaw a new policy toward UN peacekeeping in which there would be a close examination of vital interests and an exit strategy before the United Nations would be committed to humanitarian operations. The Somali tragedy was a blow not only to the United Nations but also to Kofi Annan, now the head of peacekeeping.

The Somali tragedy was confounded and magnified geometrically by events in Rwanda. This was probably the crisis that has left the deepest wound in Kofi Annan's psyche. A peace agreement had been reached in 1993 in Rwanda between the Tutsi-led Rwandese Patriotic Front and the Hutu-led government. The UN Security Council had approved a peacekeeping operation (UNAMIR) of some 2,500 troops to be sent to Rwanda under Chapter 6 (use of force only in self-defense) to oversee the agreement. But by January 1994, barely three months after the Somali debacle, Force Commander Romeo Dallaire had received information that a Hutu militia, the Interahamwe, was preparing to carry out a directed genocide of Tutsi civilians.

Dallaire sent a cable to UN headquarters in New York addressed to the military adviser to Boutros-Ghali, General Baril, asking that the informant be given asylum outside Rwanda and informing Baril that UNAMIR was planning to raid the cache of suspected weapons. Annan and his assistant, Iqbal Riza, read the cable as well, and told Dallaire not to raid the cache of weapons but instead to inform the Rwandan Hutu government of the breach of the agreement and also, in Rwanda's capital, Kigali, to inform the ambassadors of the United States and France and, importantly, Belgium, who had the bulk of UN troops on the ground.[20] Annan was still conscious of the repercussions following the raid on Aideed in Somalia and thought that a more diplomatic approach might work better. We know now that those attempts were fruitless. In hindsight, Kofi's judgment seems in error, and the results were horrific, but he was reacting to the debacle in Somalia and had no way of knowing the tragedy that lay ahead.

Additionally, Annan has been criticized for not immediately informing the Security Council of Dallaire's cable. To understand that decision, one has to look at the way Boutros-Ghali had structured the Executive Office of the Secretary-General and who was allowed to report to the Security Council. Boutros-Ghali had very narrow restrictions on who could address the council. Only the secretary-general himself or his adviser, Chinmaya Gharekhan, were allowed to go to the council, and Gharekhan was always very reluctant to do so. Realizing this would be a stumbling block must have played a role in trying to resolve the problem without alarming the Security Council. Annan also must have anticipated that the U.S. mood, as a permanent member of the council, would not be receptive to any proactive raid. We have to remember that this was a time of uncertainty, and the whole role of peacekeeping was being watched. Still, Annan had insisted that those in Kigali be kept informed. When the genocide broke out in April 1994, even the most dramatic news coming out of Rwanda did not budge the Security Council nor the U.S. leadership until nearly 1 million Tutsis and moderate Hutus had been murdered. Nevertheless, one question remains, Why was the informant not given asylum? He was never heard from again.

In Europe, the war in Bosnia and Herzegovina was reaching its peak in early 1995. UN peacekeepers (UNPROFOR) were there as a humanitarian mission under Chapter 6 and did not have the mandate or the capacity to stop what became mostly Serb attacks on Muslim Bosnian civilians. Ethnic cleansing was rampant and climaxed during the Srebenica massacre of some 7,000–8,000 Muslim men and boys. This was followed by Serb-fired mortars on Sarajevo's Markale marketplace. The international community was crying for action. The United Nations had set up a system called duo-key whereby NATO and the UN secretary-general had to both agree before any NATO bombing of Serb areas could be undertaken. Boutros-Ghali in the past had been reluctant to authorize bombing even though the United States had been calling for a NATO response for some time. The French and British, who had peacekeepers on the ground and in the way, had also been cautious. But with these bold Serb attacks, they were ready.

> They regrouped their peacekeepers, circling the wagons in anticipation of the Serb response. The NATO hand was ready to turn the key. Madeleine Albright [U.S. ambassador to the United Nations] tried to get Boutros on the telephone to get him to turn it too. But he was in a commercial airliner en route to an official visit to the Caribbean. He was unreachable. Boutros had "passed the key" to Kofi during the brief time that he was unavailable. When Madeleine asked Kofi, he didn't hesitate. He said yes.
>
> Richard Holbrooke told Phillip Gourevitch of The New Yorker, "When Kofi turned that key, he became Secretary-General-in-waiting."[21]

The Dayton Accords in the fall of 1995 brought an end to the war in Bosnia, but the black mantle of shame once again fell over the United Nations as it was blamed for not protecting the safe areas and allowing ethnic cleansing to go unchecked for so long. While these three events happened before Kofi Annan became secretary-general, another and more deeply personal blow landed in Kofi's second term as secretary-general. Accusations erupted that Annan had some culpability in the extortion scandals that had emerged out of the Oil-for-Food program that involved the sale of Iraqi oil to purchase food for the Iraqi people, suffering from the sanctions imposed by the UN Security Council. These accusations, in the end, proved completely false. However, the tragedy of the Oil-for-Food controversy is that Annan deeply cared about getting food and medicine to the Iraqi people through the program. Resolution 986, which created the program, was passed in 1995, and by December 1996 the United Nations had everything in place to begin the sale of oil in order to buy the needed food and medicine. When Kofi Annan took office, the Secretariat was asked to make a full report on the program, up to that point, and in March 1997, the Report of the Secretary-General Pursuant to Resolution 986 was ready. Annan took the report very seriously, and while acknowledging the complexity of the undertaking, was very concerned about the slow pace of the distribution, stating:

> Nevertheless, I have strong concerns about the pace at which the provisions of resolution 986 (1995) are being implemented. I have directed that a number of steps be taken both within the Secretariat and in the Security Council Committee to look for innovative and flexible approaches to overcome the constraints that the Programme has encountered.[22]

The accusations against Annan hurt very deeply, not only because they were false but also because he had worked so hard to make the program a success in getting the needed provisions to the people of Iraq. The effects of these traumas will be further discussed in the next section.

ANNAN AS UN SECRETARY-GENERAL

Annan took office as secretary-general on January 1, 1997. Immediately drawing on his UN experience, Kofi Annan set out with a broad agenda. First, he wanted to overhaul the very tightly controlled manner in which his predecessor had operated the Executive Office of the Secretary-General. Kofi Annan wanted greater transparency, greater openness and communication among the departments, and the ability of those who knew the most about an issue to be able to report to the Security Council or to the press Spokesman, when needed. He was determined to open up the United Nations, both in its decision making processes and in its relations with the people. He created a "cabinet" of the top under-secretaries that met every Wednesday. He also held a lunch with the entire Security Council each month as the presidency of the council rotates on a monthly basis. He also reached out to the heads of all the UN agencies, funds, and programs, and worked to encourage them to coordinate their activities in a more productive manner. These ideas and actions are demonstrated in his papers even in the first several months of his first term. As we can clearly see, Annan's leadership management type falls into the collegial model.

By observing several secretaries-general, he knew the complex role he would have to play as administrator to the member states. He saw his role as a moral leader to the peoples of the world, upholder of international law, head of a large bureaucracy, and peace mediator in times of crisis. He also understood the United Nations needed to reform, and he began a reform effort in his first days that lasted throughout his tenure. Annan states that "the biggest impediment to change and reform in the bureaucracy is the restraint bureaucrats put on themselves."[23] This was most profoundly ingrained in him in the days just before the outbreak of the genocide in Rwanda when members of the staff decided not to take critical information to the Security Council, believing (and rightly so) that the members would do nothing. He tried through his more open policy process to empower the staff to speak freely.

When Annan took office in January 1997, he immediately began to restructure the Secretariat under a new paradigm of transparency and communication. One of his first acts, on January 6, was to dramatically change the policy of his predecessor, which had been to only allow the Secretary-General Boutros-Ghali or his adviser, Chinmaya Gharekhan, to brief the Security Council. In this short note to the under-secretary-general for political affairs, Marrack Goulding, signed by the secretary-general's chief of staff, Iqbal Riza, Annan completely changed this policy:

> Note to Mr. Goulding
>
> *Briefing to the Security Council on the situation in the Great Lakes region*
>
> The Security Council will hold informal consultations on the situation in the Great Lakes region on Wednesday, 8 January.
>
> The Secretary-General would wish you to brief on his behalf the members of the Security Council on this topic.
>
> Thank you.
>
> S. Iqbal Riza
>
> 6 January 1997[24]

On January 13, he broadened that policy, and made it very clear in this interoffice memo that he directed to several under-secretaries, including Chinmaya Gharekhan:

Subject: Briefings and reports to the Security Council

1. As substantive Departments assume enhanced responsibilities and authority for their functional areas, the reporting by your Departments should follow the guidelines below.
2. Where the Security Council is concerned, the Department of Political Affairs retains the primary responsibility for monitoring the deliberations of the Security Council and for providing it with the political information required. In parallel, the Department of Peace-keeping Operations and the Department of Humanitarian Affairs will attend Security Council meetings (both consultations and formal) as required and provide the Council with information relating to their peace-keeping and humanitarian responsibilities. Heads of Departments will determine when it is appropriate for them to brief the Council personally, or through their staff, ensuring consistency in this practice. Of course, it is vital that all three Departments coordinate closely, each acting as the lead Department where it has principal responsibility.[25]

While other secretaries-general, and particularly Boutros-Ghali, had been more reclusive and less transparent, Annan set out not only to change the atmosphere to one that was more open but also began to enhance policy coordination and build teamwork. As an insider, he had the advantage of experiencing the weaknesses of the organization when there was a lack of policy coordination. He immediately created the Senior Management Group (SMG), which included all the heads of departments, as a kind of cabinet to provide a structure for dialogue, exchange, and policy advice. In addition, he established a Policy Coordination Group: the Executive Committee on Peace and Security (ESPS), which would meet every month, with the three lead departments (political affairs, peacekeeping, and humanitarian affairs) meeting every week. The members of ESPS also included heads of legal affairs; human rights; development; refugees; the executive office of the secretary-general; and special representatives of the secretary-general as needed.[26]

Annan continued to emphasize teamwork, as he stated in this speech to a gathering of his special and personal representatives held in 2001, when he gave them this advice:

> Keep in constant dialogue with everyone in the United Nations team. Try to hold meetings with your immediate staff every day, and set aside time to thrash out deeper issues.[27]

Annan's emphasis on teamwork and open dialogue represents his early exposure to the kind of dialogue he experienced in his home with his father and the local leaders, elders, and the tribal tradition of listening and building consensus. As Gambari stated, this was not just his African experience, but how he absorbed that experience into his own personality.

Kofi always approached a problem with the need to see the larger picture and to be optimistic. He saw himself as being the giver of hope. As a world leader, he had some responsibility as a guide to hope and to ward off despair. Annan has said several times that he would often make declarations on people's human rights, so that those who had been victims and were still vulnerable to retribution could quote him on human rights, and not suffer the consequences, because they were just quoting what he had said. Another lesson that Annan incorporated into his lexicon of personal traits is his experience while at Macalester College in Minnesota when he first encountered the northern winter cold. After nearly freezing his ears, he finally gave in and started wearing earmuffs.

> I would put on layers and layers of clothing to get warm. But I was determined not to use earmuffs because I thought they were not elegant. Until one day I almost lost my ears to the cold, so I went and bought the biggest pair of earmuffs I could find. From that day on, I learned that you never walk into a situation and believe that you know better than the natives. You have to listen and look around.[28]

In a speech to the Foreign Policy Association, he reveals how that lesson has shaped the way he looks at policy formation:

> We start from the observation that our prevention efforts can only be effective if they are undertaken with the cooperation of Member States. In each case, we need to start by looking at the society we are trying to help. We cannot impose models or behaviours on the people we are working to support, but instead should look to them to guide what we do, and how we should do it. Conflict prevention must be a home-grown process.[29]

Annan was strategic in his approach to decision making. He would carefully lay the groundwork, build consensus, and cultivate a grassroots understanding of the issues, but he also played very close attention to timing. In an interview, Annan explains his strategy:

> Timing is very important in this Organization. You can kill a brilliant idea by moving too soon. And once they've shot it down, it can become very difficult to revive it. And I know it is difficult because we have a tendency to want to act, and it's much more difficult sometimes to sit back. But I believe that there is a time to sit and let things happen because whatever you do will not make a difference. And there comes a time when you need to move to make things happen because the timing is right.[30]

At an off-the-cuff encounter with the press after having met with the Security Council, Annan explains his decision making process as he was applying it to the Middle East question:

> I wouldn't call the discussions or the process I went through to decide "indecision." I think it was assessing the situation, analysing the situation, working with our partners for peace, and determining the right timing to go to the region, and when I thought it would be most opportune and helpful to go. So it was a question of analysis, a question of coordinating with others, and a question of timing. And so I am going at the precise moment that I think I should go. The other things, the previous discussions and all were part of the process.[31]

ANNAN AND AFRICA

While Kofi Annan had grown up in Africa, he had lived most of his adult life either in Geneva or in the United States. Therefore, he was not well known among Africans and at first the Africans did not have much empathy for him. But as Ibrahim Gambari explains, "[T]hey felt he understood them instinctively and that he cared really about Africa. . . . So I think in that sense his sympathy with Africa grew . . . looking over the years you also saw that the man grew in the job; there's no doubt about it." Gambari explains that in that regard only the African Kofi Annan could get away with criticizing African leaders and holding them accountable, as he did in his speech to the OAU summit when he challenged them to uphold human rights in their respective countries and to embrace democracy, not as a Western imposition, but out of responsibility to their own peoples. In an interview, Kofi explains what prompted him to make the now famous speech in Harare at the OAU summit in 1997:

> I think I felt that Africa had reached a stage where it should be able to keep its soldiers and generals in the barracks, and those who were in office, to send them back to the barracks. I was also looking at an evolution in Latin America, where they had been able and in a way were sending their soldiers back to the barracks. The economic and political development in Africa had been distorted because of the number of coup d'etats and the number of people who took part through the barrel of the gun. So, I was trying to encourage them to have a new beginning and really try and make sure that the people who were going to lead were elected by the people and are accountable to the people. When I made that speech, Salim, [secretary-general of the OAU at the time] . . . said to me, "Let me tell you, you are the only one who can make such a speech in this room at this time and walk away unlynched."[32]

What Salim was referring to was that there were a number of military dictators in the room, notably Robert Mugabe, because the meeting took place in Harare, Zimbabwe. As we know from Kofi's nickname in school "Annan Demo," he had grown up listening to discussions of politics at home and at school of African independence and democracy. These early impressions stayed with Annan, and he felt because he had grown up with these ideas, he would be able, by rights, to encourage African leaders to take a look at Africa through this lens. Annan talks about his role as an African at an off-the-cuff question-and-answer encounter:

> I think being a Ghanaian and an African, as Secretary-General it has had an impact and raised the profile of the continent, and from the reactions I get from black peoples everywhere and I think, I hope it has inspired some of them to work harder, and to reach out and live their dreams. I am often reminded of something that Eleanor Roosevelt said, advising a group of young women, but I think it also applies to other minority situations, she said, "No one can make you feel inferior, unless you give your consent." And I hope what I have achieved and done is an inspiration for others.[33]

Annan traveled frequently to Africa, attending conferences and working with leaders at side meetings as well as directly in their countries. Because most peacekeeping operations take place in Africa, Annan spent much of his time working to enhance the conflict resolutions that would inevitably arise on a day-to-day basis. In an effort to prevent the return to conflict, he met with the leaders of Nigeria and Cameroon to establish a boundary commission to peacefully oversee the demarcation of the border between the two countries once a decision was announced by the International Court of Justice (ICJ). In another case between Namibia and Botswana, Annan encouraged the two countries to resolve their dispute over some islands in the Caprivi River dividing the two neighbors by taking the issue to the ICJ. He then made available to them funds so they could have enough resources to support their arguments before the court and ultimately end the fighting through peaceful means. When allegations arose about UN humanitarian workers and peacekeepers in African missions abusing refugees or other vulnerable persons, Annan called for an investigation to uncover the truth about what was going on. The report was very blunt and honest about the problem and the United Nations set in motion new policies to address the problem. Much of Annan's focus on combating poverty and forming the Millennium Development Goals, while they applied to enhancing development worldwide, arose out of his sense of concern for the African continent. So, while many Africans did not really know him when he took office, he did more than any other secretary-general to bring the needs of Africans to the world stage.

HUMANITARIAN INTERVENTION AND THE RESPONSIBILITY TO PROTECT

We discussed earlier the personal role and impact that the humanitarian crises in Somalia, Rwanda, and Bosnia had on Annan before he became secretary-general. These horrific events weighed heavily on him, and soon after he took office in the spring of 1997, he hosted a dinner party at which he asked Elie Wiesel, a Holocaust survivor, to talk about the concept of humanitarian intervention. He then asked all the guests to discuss the issue and over dessert report to the whole gathering what they had discussed. Kofi listened carefully and absorbed what they said.[34] Several months later, he was asked to give a speech at Ditchley in the United Kingdom in June 1998, at a gathering of high-level dignitaries, and he asked Edward Mortimer, who would later become his speechwriter, to write the speech for him on the issue of humanitarian intervention. These early forays into examining the concept led the way to Annan's speech in the General Assembly in September 1999, after the events in Kosovo and East Timor had revealed once again the urgency of intervening on behalf of victims of genocide and crimes against humanity. Annan explains why he gave this controversial speech:

> I think I gave that speech in the General Assembly because despite the experience of the earlier years, and by that I'm talking about the Former Yugoslavia, Somalia, and Rwanda, we had quite a bit of debate about Kosovo and whether there should have been an intervention in Kosovo. So, it led me to believe that we haven't really resolved the issue, and here we were in 99 with Kosovo going through it again. I remember the Russian position and others. So, I thought I should put the issue on the table.[35]

The speech in the General Assembly represents a number of traits in Kofi Annan's personality. The trauma of adult experience shaped his concern for the suffering of innocent people at the hands of those who were seen as protected by the sovereignty of the state. His own personal need to address this issue on moral, ethical grounds would not let him be passive, even though his actions would become controversial. He also was building a strategy for timing, and first needed to build over several months his thoughts on the issue and then carefully chose the right time and place. The events of Kosovo, followed so rapidly by the rampage in Dili in East Timor, offered the media attention, and the General Assembly's opening session in September offered the right audience: all the member states. Some governments embraced the right to intervene, but many, particularly in the developing world, were vociferously against it. Kofi was heavily attacked by the president of the General Assembly for 1999, Theo Ben-Gurirab of Namibia. The Canadians came to Annan's rescue and formed a commission to study the concept that resulted in the well-known report, the Responsibility to Protect. In the report they turned the concept around by claiming that it is not just a passive right to intervene but a responsibility if the host nation is unable or unwilling to protect its citizens. Kofi has said, "I give them credit for being better diplomats than I am in the sense that I refer to humanitarian intervention, but they came up with the responsibility to protect, which is much more elegant."[36]

BULLY PULPIT

As Brian Urquhart has said, the secretary-general has no resources of his own to carry out policy; therefore, the public profile and figure of the office is the only base from which a secretary-general can build norms and challenge the international community. According to Annan, who has been perhaps the only secretary-general to use his office as a bully pulpit, "quite frankly, there's very little the Secretary-General can do himself or can do alone. . . . You have to come up with inspirational things, and then empower people and then encourage people to go out and do it. . . . So, if you don't use that bully pulpit and your voice, you restrain yourself severely, in my judgment." He acknowledges that had he served during the Cold War, it would have been quite different. "The end of the Cold War gave me some freedom in the sense that the world was changing. . . . So, on the issues of promotion of democracy, individual rights, human rights, since everyone claimed either they were democratic or imagined democracy, or aspiring to be democratic, they couldn't really take you on forcefully in public."[37]

Annan took great advantage of his office as a bully pulpit, promoting human rights, pressing the norm creation on the responsibility to protect, and developing a conscience in major corporations around the world by creating the Global Compact whereby companies would sign on to a code of conduct on human and worker's rights. He took on the fight against HIV/AIDS as a personal priority by forming the Global Fund for HIV/AIDS, malaria, and tuberculosis, and pressing countries to contribute funding. People who worked with him have said that he would create a "peg" of an idea he wanted to promote and then he would work over time hanging things on that peg. He also continued the practice of every secretary-general of trying to find peaceful solutions to conflicts around the world by using his "good offices" as a means of mediation.

Annan felt strongly that the United Nations must stand for the common good and be an organization for the peoples. Annan believed very deeply in the goals of the United Nations and upholding the rule of law as embodied in the Charter. When the war broke out in Iraq in the spring of 2003, he found himself in an untenable position. On the one hand, he believed in the peaceful resolution of conflict and the authority of the Security Council to approve any use of force, except in self-defense after having been attacked. Yet he also had to remain impartial in the face of all the member states, particularly the permanent members, including especially the United States. It was an impossible balancing act. Some of the members implored him to declare openly that the War in Iraq was illegal, but he resisted that pressure. What he continued to say when pressed by the media was that the war was "not in conformity with the UN Charter."

However, in a fateful interview with the BBC, after stating his mantra about not being in conformity with the Charter, the interviewer continued to push asking whether that meant the war was illegal? Most likely out of fatigue, Kofi finally agreed with the interviewer's perspective, although he never said the word "illegal." Nevertheless, that is how it came out in the press and Annan paid dearly for this. Members of the conservative right in the United States, who never support the United Nations, began an aggressive attack on Annan. The disclosures on discrepancies in the Oil-for-Food program became the ammunition that they were looking for and the onslaught was severe and persistent. Calls for Annan to resign bore down on him and he almost did resign. Only after a lengthy report by the Volcker Commission, which took over a year to complete, found Annan innocent of the allegations and criticized him only for not overseeing the program more aggressively did Annan emerge from a deep depression. Once this personal crisis was over, he began to recover. In his final years as secretary-general, he took up once again the fight against poverty and the Millennium Development Goals. At the 60th Anniversary of the United Nations, in 2005, Annan pushed for the heads of state attending the summit to sign on to a list of eight goals and criteria for their achievement by 2015. The Outcome Document, which also contained language on the support for the Responsibility to Protect, was accepted unanimously by a vote of consensus in the final day of the summit. With this achievement, Annan had recovered.

ANNAN: PERSONALITY TRAITS AND TYPE

Annan's personality traits of tolerance for different points of view, listening to others, being a team builder, and capacity to see the big picture place him into the type we call flexible/pragmatic. Annan fits well into the Rokeach model of open-mindedness, or what Winter and Hermann would refer to as cognitive complexity, the ability to seek differentiated information about others. He never really sought power for its own sake. And once he took office, he understood the limitations on his power. His motivations, according to Winter's classifications of power, achievement, and affiliation, would then not include power, but would definitely lean toward achievement and affiliation. He used his position to promote the values of the United Nations, and not his own ego. He has a strong sense of efficacy demonstrated by his constant efforts at strategically advancing norms and holding state leaders accountable. He was innovative while in office, constantly creating new structures, like the Global Compact; the UN Funds to fight

HIV/AIDS, malaria, and tuberculosis; and the Millennium Development Goals. His efforts at reforming management within the Secretariat were to create greater transparency, improve communication, remove the secrecy and the authoritarian framework of the past, and delegate responsibilities and trust. While some of these characteristics might be seen as falling into the delegative type, Annan was very interested in governance and was not easily manipulated. He listened to his advisers and took their advice, but he ultimately made the decisions. He was always curious to learn about other points of view and other cultures, saying that you cannot impose a solution on people; it must evolve out of their own understandings. He was pragmatic in his strategy to build consensus and waiting for the right timing to press an issue. If there is a fault, it might be his willingness to trust those around him and let them do their work. In the Oil-for-Food crisis, the Volcker report accused him of not directly overseeing the process. But that was not his style. He trusted the leaders of the Office of the Iraq Programme (OIP) to do their jobs and he trusted the Security Council's 661 Committee to do theirs. We now know that did not happen.

In our framework of analyzing traits, forming types from those traits, and then determining a management style based on George and George, the flexible/pragmatic type should assume the collegial management model. Annan's creation of his Senior Management Group and the Executive Committee on Peace and Security demonstrate that model. Advisers like Ibrahim Gambari confirm that these bodies were really team efforts and not just window dressing. George and George base their assumptions of this model on John F. Kennedy's style of working with his advisers. Annan's self-confidence and desire to work as a team follows this tradition.

As David Winter warns, while understanding the formation of personality, how it is shaped, and the linkage between personality and decision making, it is a much bigger leap of uncertainty to, with this understanding, be able to predict decisions in future unknown environments. Nevertheless, increasing our understanding can perhaps benefit how we select our leaders, deal with them in diplomatic situations, or even offer opportunities for self-examination.

While Kofi Annan's dignity, charisma, and support for UN values brought him great respect among some in the international community, others resented his overreach and even defiance in the face of some member states. On the extreme, some even hated him. Yet, his identification with the Secretariat staff always made him conscious of keeping up morale and he was appreciated for the respect he gave in that regard. On the day that he left office right before the holidays at the end of December 2006, he announced that he would say goodbye to the staff in the large UN cafeteria on the main floor of the UN headquarters in New York. I had an office in the Dag Hammarskjöld Library at the time and intended to go to the reception in the cafeteria, but when I approached the hallway to the cafeteria, I was met with an overwhelming crowd of staff members coming from all directions, even from across the street where many of the offices were located. Lines were out the doors to the United Nations and filled the hallways. It was impossible, even going early, to get into the cafeteria. Security guards were letting people in only when someone came out. Finally, Kofi Annan came out into the hallway and went down the line of everyone there, shaking hands with all who came to say goodbye. Even he was overwhelmed.

Kofi Annan and the United Nations were given the Nobel Peace Prize in the fall of 2001. However, a shadow fell over the announcement and the award ceremony. The horrific events of September 11, 2001, had taken place only a few weeks before the announcement of the Nobel Prize, and the award was lost in the media frenzy of the time. Nevertheless, at this writing, Kofi Annan still plays a leadership role in international affairs. Known for his skills at mediation and the respect he retains internationally, Secretary-General Ban Ki-moon named Annan in spring 2012 as the Special Envoy of the United Nations and the League of Arab States to find a peaceful solution to the conflict in Syria. He served as envoy for six months before he stepped down, saying that he had "lost his team on the road to Damascus," referring to the divisiveness within the UN Security Council.

In summary, Kofi Annan is known for his support of the "peoples" of the world, returning the focus of the United Nations to the words stated in the opening to the UN Charter: "We, the Peoples of the United Nations." His optimism and his achievement motivation enable him to believe that peaceful solutions are possible, but his sense of reality of the situational context also grounds him in the possible. As a proponent of human rights, he used his position as a world leader to give a voice to the voiceless and to set an agenda for the United Nations in the Millennium Development Goals to offer hope to the most vulnerable. As a norm entrepreneur, he has left his imprint through such initiatives as humanitarian intervention, the Global Compact to bring the business community into great harmony with the human rights goals of the United Nations, and his continued support for the rule of law. Through various key moments in his life, people have recognized Kofi Annan's capacity for leadership, but how he has applied these skills has depended on his internal compass and the totality of his personality.

NOTES

1. Kofi Annan with Nader Mousavizadeh, *Interventions: A Life in War and Peace* (New York: Penguin Press, 2012), 15.
2. James Traub, *The Best Intensions: Kofi Annan and the UN in an Era of American World Power* (New York: Farrar, Straus, and Giroux, 2006), 27.

3. Stanley Meisler, *Kofi Annan: A Man of Peace in a World of War (*New York: John Wiley and Sons, 2007), 12.

4. Annan, *Interventions*, 19.

5. Ibid., 20.

6. Ibid., 21.

7. Captain R. S. Rattray, *Ashanti Law and Constitution* (Oxford: Clarendon Press, 1929).

8. Of note is that according to Ashanti tradition, a chief and anyone in the presence of a chief must not cross his or her legs; in many of my meetings with Kofi Annan and observing him in other situations, he never crosses his legs, even while others in the room are doing so.

9. Interview with Ibrahim Gambari, by Jean Krasno, on June 3, 2009, at the United Nations in New York.

10. Ibid.

11. Meisler, *Kofi Annan*, 11.

12. Ibid.

13. Ibid.

14. Interview with former UN secretary-general Kofi Annan, by Jean Krasno, on Friday, March 21, 2008, in New York City.

15. This interview with young people was published in the May 2001 issue of *Nickelodeon Magazine,* in Jean Krasno, ed., *The Collected Papers of Secretary-General Kofi Annan: UN Secretary-General, 1997–2006* (Boulder, CO: Lynne Rienner Publishers, 2012), 1467.

16. Traub, *The Best Intensions*, 28.

17. Ibid., 49–50.

18. Ibid.

19. Ibid.

20. Annan, *Interventions*, 46–59.

21. Fred Eckhard, Draft Manuscript, October 31, 2008, 12.

22. Report of the Secretary-General Pursuant to Paragraph 11 of the Resolution 986 (1995), Security Council document: S/1997/206, March 10, 1997, paragraphs 24 and 25; in Krasno, ed., *Collected Papers of Kofi Annan*, 48.

23. Interview with Kofi Annan, by Thomas Weiss, on April 29, 2002, in Krasno, ed., *The Collected Papers of Kofi Annan*, xiii–xxv.

24. Note to Mr. Goulding of January 6, 1997, released from UN Archives, in Krasno, ed., *The Collected Papers of Kofi Annan*, 4.

25. Interoffice Memo from Kofi Annan to several heads of Departments on January 13, 1997, from UN Archives, in Krasno, ed., *The Collected Papers of Kofi Annan*, 8–9.

26. Note to the secretary-general from Marrack Goulding on February 5, 1997, from UN Archives, in Krasno, ed., *The Collected Papers of Kofi Annan*, 32–33.

27. Speech by the secretary-general on March 30, 2001, at the Seminar for Special and Personal Representatives and Envoys of the Secretary-General at Mont Pèlerin, Switzerland, document number SG/SM/7760, in Krasno, ed., *The Collected Papers of Kofi Annan*, 1437–1439.

28. This interview with young people was published in the May 2001 issue of *Nickelodeon Magazine,* in Krasno, ed., *The Collected Papers of Kofi Annan*, 1467.

29. Speech delivered to the Foreign Policy Association in New York on March 21, 2001, in Krasno, ed., *The Collected Papers of Kofi Annan,* 1422–1424.

30. Interview with former UN secretary-general Kofi Annan, by Jean Krasno, on Friday, March 21, 2008, in New York City.

31. Off-the-cuff comments by Kofi Annan outside the Security Council on June 8, 2001, in Krasno, ed., *The Collected Papers of Kofi Annan,* 1515–1516.

32. Interview with former UN secretary-general Kofi Annan, by Jean Krasno, on Friday, March 21, 2008, in New York City.

33. Question-and-answer session with the secretary-general following the Cyril Foster Lecture at Oxford University on June 19, 2001, in Krasno, ed., *The Collected Papers of Kofi Annan,* 1528–1532.

34. Traub, *The Best Intensions,* 92.

35. Interview with former UN secretary-general Kofi Annan, by Jean Krasno, on Friday, March 21, 2008, in New York City.

36. Ibid.

37. Ibid.

20

Nelson Mandela: A Leader with No Followers Is Just Someone Taking a Walk

Christopher Hammond

It matters who leads us. From bitterly contested elections, to vicious civil wars, to massive protest movements, human beings under a variety of political systems struggle, spend, fight, and, in some cases, die over the question of leadership. Decisions are made by leaders that can determine the course of human events: it matters who is making these decisions because politics are a matter of life and death, wealth and poverty, on a massive scale.[1] A leader's personality contains the embedded characteristic behaviors that inform management style, worldview, motive, and decision making skills.

This chapter will explore the decision making processes of Nelson Mandela, former president of South Africa following the fall of apartheid. Continuing from the premise established by Jean Krasno, this chapter is an analysis of Nelson Mandela's personality type and how that affected or determined his policy decisions. It is a study of how Nelson Mandela's personality influenced his decision making as a world leader. Mandela fits best into the flexible/pragmatic type, as this analysis of his experiences, deeds, and words will show. He has consistently demonstrated an open-minded approach, a focus on effective and pragmatic solutions, and a collegial management style.

BRIEF BIOGRAPHICAL OVERVIEW

Nelson Mandela became the first multiracial, democratically elected president of South Africa in 1994, bringing an end to apartheid, a racially based political and legal system that prevented South Africa's majority black and colored populations from attaining basic civil and political rights. He had participated in the struggle against apartheid throughout his life, rising quickly through the ranks of the African National Congress (ANC) to eventually become its leader. In 1964, he was found guilty of sabotage at the Rivonia Trial and sentenced to life in prison. He served 26 years and was released in 1990, emerging at the head of a movement that had come into its own against a government beginning to bow to the combined domestic and international pressure against it.[2] He served as president for one term, from 1994 to 1999, and in that time, South Africa's foreign policy was characterized by reconciliation with the international system, reintegration with the rest of the world, and re-identification with the African continent and the Global South more broadly.

Mandela entered into a leadership role early on in life. As a young man, he was being groomed to advise the future leader of his people, but in his early schooling he found himself leading his peers when they came into conflict with the administration. He was expelled from his first college in 1940, but eventually graduated in 1943 before moving on to the University of Witwatersrand for his LLB. Mandela worked as a clerk for one of the very few law firms that would hire blacks while he went to school, and became politically active. He cofounded (1944) and was elected national secretary (1948) of the ANC Youth League (ANCYL), and became its president in 1951.[3]

In 1952 the ANC began the Defiance Campaign, directed at the repeal of six racially biased "unjust laws." These were laws imposing limitations on travel for blacks and coloreds, the Group Areas Act, the Voters' Representation Act, the Suppression of Communism Act, and the Bantu Authorities Act.[4] In the same year he opened, with Oliver Tambo, the first black law firm in South Africa.[5]

In 1956 Mandela was arrested for treason along with 155 others. The protracted trial became a display for the defendants to articulate their argument against the government. All were acquitted by 1961.[6] Facing increasingly harsh repression by the apartheid regime, the ANC was forced to go underground in 1961. At that point the decision to incorporate limited violence into the struggle was made and an armed wing, Umkhonto we Sizwe (MK), was formed to carry out those attacks. In 1962, Mandela left the country to receive military training and to act as a diplomat, gathering support and funding for the ANC.[7] This diplomatic appeal, so useful in the 1960s to preserve the life of the fledgling movement, would lead to a learning experience for the more mature ANC in the 1980s. As Mandela's biographer Anthony Sampson writes:

> The ANC's hopes of support from independent black states were being dashed by the failures of their governments, and by successive coups and counter-coups. Over two decades twenty-eight African countries had experienced coups d'état and fifty governments had been overthrown; some were taken over by dictators who ignored all human rights, like Idi Amin in Uganda.

> By the early eighties only Nigeria, with huge oil revenues and a new civilian government, appeared economically hopeful. Western businessmen were writing off most of black Africa, while white South Africa depicted itself as the only viable part of the continent. The more mature Robben Islanders [that is, Mandela and his fellow prisoners] were learning lessons about the problems of democracy from the coups, wars and dictators to the north, and were determined not to take the same routes.[8]

The change from the euphoria of the immediate postindependence to the crash of democratic expectations in the 1980s demonstrates a key insight into Mandela's experiences. Due to the quirks of history, he was able to observe the failures of others before assuming the mantle of responsibility himself. Mandela learned mainly through observation, and having the pitfalls of a cult of personality or an economy ravaged by postcolonial revenge laid out before him allowed him to assimilate the lessons of history. In 1963, the Rivonia Trial began and in 1964, he was sentenced to life in prison along with Walter Sisulu, Ahmed Kathrada, Govan Mbeki, Raymond Mhlaba, Elias Motsoaledi, and Andrew Mlangeni. From 1964 to 1982, Mandela was imprisoned on Robben Island, and then until 1988 he was held in the Pollsmoor Prison. The last two years of his prison time were spent in the Victor Verster Prison in Paarl.[9]

Shortly after the ANC was legalized in 1990, Mandela was released from prison and then elected deputy president of the ANC. In 1993, he was awarded the Nobel Peace Prize with F. W. de Klerk, and in 1994 he was elected the first president of a democratic South Africa. Mandela chose to step down from the presidency after one term in 1999, in order to avoid the creation of a cult of personality and to focus on charity work.[10]

MANDELA'S EARLY LIFE

Nelson Mandela was born Rolihlahla Mandela on July 18, 1918. He was brought up in rural South Africa, in the village of Qunu. In his memoirs, he recalled those early days fondly, as he described the games he would play with the other children and the simple pleasures of living close to the land. At a young age, Mandela learned the sting of embarrassment. Two events early on in his development led him to avoid the kind of face-losing shame that he would later come to believe was built into race relations in apartheid-era South Africa. In the first incident, while playing with his friends, he was thrown from the back of a donkey. Though not hurt physically, Mandela felt shame due to his age and the public nature of his unfortunate accident. Later on, while courting a young girl, he was invited by her sister to eat lunch with the family. His experience in rural Qunu had not acquainted him with the regular use of a fork and knife, and he quickly realized he had been invited not for lunch, but to be laughed at by the older sister while he ineptly pushed tough chicken around his plate. These incidents caused him to develop strong emotions toward the notion of shame, and in his memoirs, he commented: "I learned that to humiliate another person is to make him suffer an unnecessarily cruel fate."[11]

Following his father's death in 1930, when Mandela was about 12 years old, he was sent to live with paramount chief, Jongintaba, the Regent of the Thembu people and head of the Madiba clan. The Regent became Mandela's caretaker, and Justice, Jongintaba's son, became Mandela's close confidant and near-brother. Justice was heir to lead the clan, and Mandela was to be an adviser.[12] The clan name Madiba is often used as a familiar name for Nelson Mandela.

The central part of Mandela's education at this age consisted of observing the Regent exercise his kingship at tribal meetings. Mandela often remarked that he learned best through quiet observation, not through asking questions. In fact, later in life he would express irritation when he saw how many questions children, particularly in white households, were permitted to ask their parents, and how the parents would patiently respond. In his experience it was better to watch, to observe from the outside, rather than to miss things while asking questions.[13] Thus, Mandela would sit and observe the Regent at work. He often credited the Regent with being the primary influence on his own leadership style; the Regent would listen for hours to his tribesmen, taking in their opinions silently. Finally, at sunset, he would attempt to synthesize their opinions and form a consensus, integrating all opposing views. Reflecting on the Regent's leadership style, Mandela remarked:

> One of the marks of a great chief is the ability to keep together all sections of his people, the traditionalists and reformers, conservatives and liberals, and on major questions there are sometimes sharp differences of opinion. The Mqhekezweni court was particularly strong, and the Regent was able to carry the whole community because the court was representative of all shades of opinion.[14]

Consensus-building would become an integral part of Mandela's leadership style, on both public and cabinet level, despite his intense disagreement with some interests. A leader should be like a shepherd, he would say, directing the flock from behind with skillful persuasion.[15] Not every opinion could be part of the final decision of the leader, but everyone's thoughts should be heard and taken into account, and all who spoke should be listened to by the leader. Meetings would take place until consensus was reached, and the Regent always strove for unanimity, an ideal Mandela would work toward in his own leadership.[16]

At this early age Mandela was greatly influenced by the idealized picture of tribal traditions of democracy that he learned from visiting old chiefs and headmen who would tell him stories of times past. He would often refer to the form of the tribal council as the pinnacle of democracy, wherein "all members of the tribe could participate in its deliberations. Chief and subject, warrior and medicine man, all took part and endeavored to influence its decisions."[17]

When Mandela was in his early twenties, he came home on holiday with a more politically inclined friend, Paul Mahabane, from the University College of Fort Hare, where he was enrolled as a student. Mahabane's father had been president-general of the ANC twice before, and Mahabane had the reputation of rebellious behavior. During the holiday a local magistrate, an older white man, stopped the two on the street and requested that Mahabane go inside and buy him some postage stamps.

It was common in 1939 rural South Africa for a white person to ask any black person to perform menial tasks. When the magistrate attempted to hand Mahabane the money for the chore, Mahabane refused. The magistrate grew angry and asked the two, "Do you know who I am?" Mahabane replied, "It is not necessary to know who you are. I know what you are."[18]

Throughout the exchange, Mandela watched nervously. While he was frightened by what his friend did, he also respected his courage. Mandela credits this exchange as foundational in his development as a political actor, saying, "I was beginning to realize that a black man did not have to accept the dozens of petty indignities directed at him each day."[19]

For Mandela, the racism inherent in the colonial, postcolonial, and apartheid systems of government in South Africa was not just a feature of a system, but also a mechanism of shame. It was a way by which black men and women were made to feel less worthy than their white counterparts, and this constituted a major motive for Mandela's future work. Not only did he want to end the system that shamed him and his people, he also wanted to help his people stand up for themselves and reclaim their pride. The power of a leader, according to Mandela, came from his people. In many ways his management style was to flow from his motives. If his motive was to empower black South Africa, then his management style was to follow public opinion and not try to control it with a patronizing hand:

> As a leader, I have always followed the principles I first saw demonstrated by the regent at the Great Place. I have always endeavored to listen to what each and every person in a discussion had to say before venturing my own opinion. Oftentimes, my own opinion will simply represent a consensus of what I heard in the discussion. I always remember the regent's axiom: a leader, he said, is like a shepherd. He stays behind the flock, letting the most nimbler go out

ahead, whereupon the others follow, not realizing that all along they are being directed from behind.[20]

LEAVING HOME

An early example of Mandela's leadership style took place during his schooling at Fort Hare. As a freshman, Mandela noticed that only upperclassmen, students who no longer lived in the dormitory, represented their House Committee. Mandela, along with a few classmates, decided to run for the committee in the elections. After winning the election, Mandela and his classmates assigned the upperclassmen the chores ordinarily assigned to freshmen. The upperclassmen appealed to the warden of the school to constrain their power, and the warden initially took their side. In his memoirs, Mandela described how the freshmen held firm and threatened to resign from the committee, "depriving it of any integrity or authority"[21] should the warden intervene. Their solidarity caused the warden to reconsider, and he decided to respect the decisions of the freshmen.

Shortly thereafter, Mandela ran for a seat in the Student Representative Council (SRC). He and the other representatives were elected even though some had boycotted the elections. Students were boycotting the elections to pressure the administration for better living conditions. Mandela and his cohort used the threat of resignation to express solidarity with the boycott and add to the pressure on the administration.[22] In response, the administration re-held the elections at mealtime, so that no student could say that they were not given the opportunity to vote. Mandela and his fellow representatives were then pressured to accept the legitimacy of the elections overriding the boycott. The representatives were elected again in the new voting. Mandela resigned again, but his peers stayed on, leaving him to stand alone against the administration. On account of his excellent record, the school administrator, Principal Kerr, met individually with Mandela and delivered an ultimatum. He could either respect the elections and serve on the SRC or continue to support the boycott and be expelled from Fort Hare. Mandela took a leave from school to consider his decision. As he says in his memoir, "I had never had to make such a consequential decision before."[23]

Several aspects of Mandela's personality come into focus in this story. He did not bow to the pressure applied to him directly by the administration. He did not accept the relative anonymity that would have come from siding with the rest of the elected representatives. He did what he thought was right, and he refused to add legitimacy to a system he found unfair by participation. Mandela was not one to accept slow change from the inside—rather he refused to participate in organizations he did not believe were legitimate.

Here, Mandela learned an important lesson in leadership: a leader with no followers is just someone taking a walk.

When Mandela arrived back at home with the Regent, he had not yet decided on whether or not to accept his elected position and lend his legitimacy to the boycotted elections, or accept expulsion. The Regent at that time was concerned about the future and decided to arrange marriages for his son Justice and Mandela. The young men were upset by this decision, and after depleting what they saw to be their limited options by complaining to the Regent's wife, No-England, they resolved to run away from home.[24] This decision resolved Mandela's problems at Fort Hare—running away would mean he would accept expulsion.

THE LAW

Mandela came of age at a time when the British were losing power in South Africa, and the Afrikaners—an ethnic group defined by their tongue, Afrikaans—originally descended from Dutch colonists, were gaining power. Apartheid, literally "apartness," was the new law of the land. Although the system was defined by the separate, and unequal, legal standards enforced for blacks and whites, Mandela nonetheless decided to pursue a career in law.

He began to work with Lazar Sidelsky in the early 1940s at the law firm of Witkin, Sidelsky, and Eidelman. Sidelsky was the first white man to treat Mandela with respect, and he argued that education was the best way to liberate the African people. Law, Sidelsky argued, could be a tool to change society.[25]

Sidelsky cautioned Mandela to stay away from politics, advice that Mandela thoughtfully ignored, and when Mandela and Oliver Tambo set up their law practice (the first black law practice in the country), Sidelsky lent them money for the venture.[26] Mandela's respect for the power of the law, and faith in the law's ability to be a positive force for change, were reinforced by his experience at Sidelsky's firm. It was at this time that Mandela was introduced to the ANC through Walter Sisulu, who had also connected him with Sidelsky's law firm.

DEFIANCE

In 1948, the Nationalists won the whites-only general election in South Africa. Dr. Daniel Malan led the nationalist party and quickly installed the broad range of policy measures that became the apartheid system, institutionalizing the de facto differences in South African society.[27] Laws were passed making sexual relations between whites and nonwhites illegal, labeling South Africans by race, and segregating living areas according to race.[28]

Mandela and the ANCYL believed the best response was to transform the ANC into a true mass movement. However, Mandela had reservations against working with Indians, another racially defined subgroup discriminated against in apartheid South Africa, and Communists, who were active in South Africa during the Cold War as well. "The spirit of mass action surged, but I remained skeptical of any action undertaken with the Communists and Indians."[29] Keeping an open mind, Mandela reversed course when confronted by his colleagues, namely Ahmed Kathrada, who he would later be imprisoned with on Robben Island, and by the Nationalist backlash against those groups. Under the broadly worded Suppression of Communism Act, all but the most lukewarm protests against the state were outlawed. "Here, I believed, was a sufficient threat that compelled us to join hands with our Indian and Communist colleagues."[30]

Still, Mandela had doubts about cooperation. At the outset of planning for what would become the Defiance Campaign, he argued, in his role as president of the ANCYL, that the campaign should be exclusively African. Walter Sisulu disagreed with him personally, and when the issue was voted on in the ANC National Executive Committee and the national conference, Mandela's viewpoint was voted down. "Now that my view had been rejected by the highest levels of the ANC, I fully accepted the agreed-upon position."[31]

In his biography of Mandela, Anthony Sampson indicates that it was during the Defiance Campaign that Mandela began to look like the leader he would eventually become:

> Mandela was soon looking more like a future leader of his people. On May 31, 1952, the ANC executive met in Port Elizabeth and announced that the campaign would begin on June 26. A banquet was held to say goodbye to Professor Matthews, who was leaving to spend a year in America, and Mathews' son Joe recalls Mandela saying that he (Mandela) would be the first black President of South Africa.[32]

Whether this anecdote is true or not, Mandela was clearly putting himself in the vanguard of the ANC. He offered to take the key position of volunteer-in-chief for the Defiance Campaign, a position responsible for national recruitment. It would give him an expansive, visible, and pivotal role in the organization as he traveled around the country to speak at large events and galvanize the people for the coming campaign.[33]

In the midst of the Defiance Campaign, Mandela was sent to the Eastern Cape to resolve a dispute between the ANC executive leadership and Alcott Gwentshe, a local leader of the campaign. Gwentshe was found to have ignored the advice of the executive, but he had the people on his side. The way Mandela handled this issue displays his strong sense of efficacy.

> Although I thought Gwentshe was wrong for disregarding the executive, he was doing a good job and was so firmly entrenched that he could not easily be dislodged. When I saw the members of the executive, I explained that it was impractical to do anything about the situation now, but if they wanted to remedy it, they must defeat him at the next election. It was one of the first times that I saw that it was foolhardy to go against the masses of people. It is no use to take an action to which the masses are opposed, for it will then be impossible to enforce.[34]

All leaders exhibit traits of attention-seeking and are at least somewhat charismatic. Here, we see that Mandela was beginning to exhibit traits characteristic of a strong leader, but he was nonetheless refining his particular management style, mainly focusing on including opposing opinions and consensus-building.

THE RIVONIA TRIAL AND PRISON

The Rivonia Trial, in which Nelson Mandela and his compatriots were sentenced to life in prison for inciting violence and committing sabotage, began on October 9, 1964. The defendants were facing the death penalty, and despite this they used the forum of the court to continue their political struggle against the apartheid system.

Mandela stated his plea to the judge, "My lord, it is not I, but the government that should be in the dock. I plead not guilty."[35] The strategy of the accused became clear from this first statement. This Rivonia Trial would be a forum for the political message of the ANC, which had been silenced since it was banned in 1960. Mandela, along with other defendants, chose to make a moral and political statement by clarifying their position rather than fighting the legal battle of the evidence against them. Although flexible/pragmatic leaders tend to be non-ideological, here we see a possible exception in Mandela's flirtation with the death penalty.

Their strategy brought them close to the death sentence, as the majority of them would be admitting to guilt on various charges. In response to this, the defendants were of one mind that they would not appeal the sentence, even if it were the death penalty. This strategy had the effect of breaking the state-imposed veil between the ANC and the general public, as well as making the political and moral case for the African majority to the international arena, which was by now focused on the trial.

Lionel Bernstein, one of the accused who was not sentenced to life in prison, wrote an article 25 years after the Rivonia Trial regarding the strategy of the accused:

> Here at last was the opportunity to break out of state censorship and press self-censorship, and replace unreliable rumor with an authentic policy guide for

> the whole people. The Rivonia trial must become the platform from which to tell the whole story, as it really was.[36]

The most important piece of the ideological defense was Mandela's statement from the dock. His speech stated that the ANC was fighting for a multiracial state where no race would be dominated by any other. Getting this message to the public was important to the accused, as it intended to draw support from all races to the anti-apartheid struggle, and disarm the state-sponsored propaganda that argued that the accused advocated black domination of whites.[37]

This particular strategy's shortcoming was that according to the law, the accused would be found guilty, and in this case the sentence would most likely be death, depriving the movement of its leaders. Mandela and other movement leaders decided that regardless of the sentence, they would not appeal. The main issue was that many of the defendants were the faces and leaders of the struggle, and without them, discipline within the movement would decrease, leading to an uncontrollable civil war.

The accused of the Rivonia Trial, through the use of an ideological defense, ensured they would be found guilty. When Harold Hanson was asked to read over Mandela's statement from the dock by Bram Fischer, he told Fischer, "If Mandela reads this in court they will take him straight out back and string him up."[38] The decision not to appeal, however difficult to make, was politically unassailable. They made this choice for political reasons, as the accused were afraid that an appeal would stifle international support, impede the campaign that would surely spring up, and end the trial on an anti-climax that would disappoint the people. The resolve of the defendants is shown in the short statements Mandela and Sisulu drafted in the event they were sentenced to death. Here the issue of the efficacy of their choice is debatable. Were they making an ideological choice or a political gamble? Given Mandela's general predisposition to err on the side of pragmatism, it is more likely that his insistence that they be found guilty and that they not appeal the decision was a calculated decision.

In 1985, the choice not to appeal was tried against a public offer for freedom by then president P. W. Botha. The offer was contingent upon Mandela's rejection of violence as a political instrument, and thus was an attempt to destroy both Mandela's international and domestic image along with his relationship to the ANC. Mandela responded through his daughter Zindzi to a crowd of cheering people, affirming his relationship with the ANC and the struggle that cost him a chance for freedom after 21 years of imprisonment.[39]

This trial had an enormous effect on the struggle against apartheid, on both international and domestic fronts. Internationally, Mandela was elected president of the Students' Union of London University as the

British government was being pressured to intervene on his behalf.[40] The UN Security Council, with a few abstentions, pressed the South African government to grant amnesty to the accused.[41] Lionel Bernstein, in the aforementioned article, claimed the impact of the Rivonia Trial was to tear down the veil of secrecy, misunderstanding, and propaganda to show the people of South Africa the policy of the ANC and to make the political case for the struggle. It reversed the trend toward defeatism that had characterized the early 1960s following the ban on the ANC. The leadership of the ANC in the public spotlight bravely standing up for what they believed in, even at the risk of their lives, reignited public sympathy for the ANC. For Bernstein, the Rivonia Trial was a key trigger of the resistance struggle of the 1970s and 1980s.[42]

In prison, Mandela continued to lead the movement. "In his letters Mandela was sounding not at all like a prisoner serving a life sentence, and much more like the leader of a government in exile who was waiting to create a new unified nation."[43]

Many of Mandela's fellow inmates automatically regarded him as their leader. He had been the leader of the ANC underground, and the position carried over into his incarceration. Visitors were referred to Mandela's cell, and he would represent the group.[44] The ANC prisoners created a High Organ structure to decide on the group's policy toward the prison authority. Mandela, Sisulu, Mbeki, and Mhlaba served on the Organ.[45]

When Mandela's lawyer, George Bizos, visited him at Robben Island in 1964, Mandela was taken by truck to meet Bizos outside the prison building. Eight guards surrounded Mandela, who was dressed poorly in shorts and shoes with no socks. "George," Mandela said when Bizos approached, "let me introduce you to my guard of honor."[46] He then named each of the guards in turn and introduced them to Bizos. This was Mandela's approach to incarceration. He would treat his captors as human beings, but he would never be subservient to them. Because he was open-minded about the guards, Mandela found that there was considerable variation among them. Some wanted to punish the prisoners and believed firmly that they should have received the death penalty. Some were just doing a job. Mandela began to talk with the wardens about the struggle against apartheid and the policies of the ANC. In many ways, these early discussions helped to prepare him for the eventual transition talks.[47]

FREEDOM AND THE PRESIDENCY

In 1990, following his pardon and release from prison, Nelson Mandela was invited to speak before the U.S. Congress. His speech there explained the terms of the struggle against apartheid from the perspective of the ANC. His narrative distanced the ANC from communist ideologies, though it made it clear that nationalization was a distinct possibility for the regime in order to pair growth with nonracial equity. He thanked the United States for imposing strict sanctions on the apartheid regime in South Africa and urged it to continue doing so. The tone of Mandela's speech was that of a world leader addressing equals.[48]

> Sanctions should remain in place because the purpose for which they were imposed has not yet been achieved. We have yet to arrive at the point when we can say that South Africa is set on an irreversible course leading to its transformation into a united, democratic, and nonracial country. We plead that you cede the prerogative to the people of South Africa to determine the moment when it will be said that profound changes have occurred and an irreversible process achieved, enabling you and the rest of the international community to lift sanctions.[49]

This passage from his speech is pivotal, as it shows Mandela as a leader coming into his own. He outlines his vision of the end of the struggle, and what he requires from the United States to get there. He asks the sole remaining global hegemon to put its foreign policy decision making power into the hands of the South African resistance rather than the regime. He proposes a vision of the future in which South Africa is a democratic and unified country, but stresses that the struggle is not yet complete.

During the lead up to the first democratic elections in South Africa, following his ascension to the presidency of the ANC, Mandela outlined the ANC's proposal for a new South African foreign policy in *Foreign Affairs*. The Cold War had recently ended, the Soviet Union had crumbled, and the South African regime was "one of the most isolated states on earth," due to the apartheid system.[50] Mandela's article discussed the strategy of reintegration with the world system that the ANC government would adopt should they win. The ANC's new pillars of foreign policy reflect Mandela's leadership style in their inclusiveness, pragmatism, and belief in the power of law.

> The pillars upon which our foreign policy will rest are the following beliefs:
>
> - that issues of human rights are central to international relations and an understanding that they extend beyond the political, embracing the economic, social and environmental;
> - that just and lasting solutions to the problems of humankind can only come through the promotion of democracy worldwide;
> - that considerations of justice and respect for international law should guide the relations between nations;
> - that peace is the goal for which all nations should strive, and where this breaks down internationally agreed and nonviolent mechanisms, including effective arms-control regimes, must be employed;

- that the concerns and interests of the continent of Africa should be reflected in our foreign-policy choices;
- that economic development depends on growing regional and international economic cooperation in an interdependent world.[51]

These six pillars accurately reflect some of the basic motivations upon which Mandela's decision making is based: the fight for dignity against the shame of apartheid, liberal democracy, belief in the rule of law, and execution of justice as a method of social change.

Up to this point we have not addressed Mandela's worldview. Worldview is the framework within which policy questions are interpreted. Motives help to form a worldview, but we must not conflate the two. The basis for Mandela's worldview is the Regent's court. All opinions should be heard, all participants' viewpoints acknowledged, and a decision should be made that is informed by the entire group. Mandela himself states that the court formed the basis of his ideal of leadership.[52]

Mandela lays out his worldview for foreign policy decision making in *Foreign Affairs.* He begins by asserting that governments do not always have the best interests of their citizens at heart; therefore, respect for human rights must be paramount. Whereas politicians closer to the realist perspective on foreign policy find the world dangerous and therefore stress the buildup of national security, Mandela saw the world as a community and the human rights crusade as an extension of the anti-apartheid crusade. The basic premise of the Regent's court was that every participant, at least in Mandela's interpretation, stood at the same level. All humans begin with the same premise of basic rights.

From a worldview where the most basic assumption is that human beings deserve to be heard, Mandela's insistence on human rights and democracy follow naturally, as does his commitment to a cooperative approach to international conflict and economic relations. The most important aspect of Mandela's leadership was the way he was able to reconcile South Africa following years of apartheid and civil strife, and reintegrate South Africa with the rest of the world.

FOREIGN POLICY DECISIONS

Reconciliation was a theme of Mandela's campaign, and it became the primary policy goal of his presidency. In his inaugural address, President Mandela argued that only the seeds of a better society had been planted and that in order for that society to blossom there was much work left to be done:

> We have triumphed in the effort to implant hope in the breasts of the millions of our people. We enter into a covenant that we shall build the society in which

all South Africans, both black and white, will be able to walk tall, without any fear in their hearts, assured of their inalienable right to human dignity - a rainbow nation at peace with itself and the world.[53]

In order to realize the promise of reconciliation, Mandela retained many people from the apartheid regime. One in particular was an Afrikaner major, who was kept on Mandela's staff despite being warned by security services that the man had helped to bomb an ANC building. "So what?" Mandela responded, "I work in government with people who have done worse things than that."[54]

As president, Mandela began to change his management style. He became more detached from political decision making and governance. While he had directly led the ANC during the negotiations with the apartheid regime over the transition and elections, he now saw himself as a figurehead. He referred most policy problems, and even visitors, to his deputy president, Thabo Mbeki.[55] Mandela feared the creation of a cult of personality of the sort that had been common and fatal in many of the short-lived postcolonial African democracies. He became more delegative in his management style, using the prestige of his office when necessary, but leaving decision making to others. Mbeki became the gatekeeper and heir-apparent, acting as a filter for the president and leading many of the cabinet meetings himself.[56]

Mandela still believed fervently in the power of personal diplomacy. In 1995 Ken Saro-Wiwa, a vocal opponent of the Abacha dictatorship and of the Royal Dutch Shell company in Nigeria, was executed while President Mandela was attending the Commonwealth Summit in New Zealand. Mandela had been pushing Abacha to release Saro-Wiwa in behind-the-scenes talks.[57] Mandela was outraged by the execution. "If Africa refrains from taking firm action against Nigeria," he argued, "then talk about the renaissance in Africa is hollow, is shallow."[58] He urged the international community to sanction the Abacha regime, both in Africa and at the UN Security Council. Mandela was disappointed by the tepid response of the international community to both the tragedy and his call for action. Nigeria was eventually expelled from the Commonwealth, but overt oppression in Nigeria did not end until Abacha's death.

By the time Mandela was elected president, the world was beginning to recover from the fall of the Soviet Union and the end of the Cold War. The Non-Aligned Movement adapted to the post-Cold War world by becoming a more Global South-oriented organization. In 1998–1999 Mandela was elected the chairperson of the Non-Aligned Movement.

Through his work in the Non-Aligned Movement and as a global leader, Mandela connected with people across the political spectrum. He developed a close relationship with Muammar Qaddafi, the authoritarian leader of Libya. Following the bombing of an American airplane over Lockerbie,

Scotland, in 1988 by Libyan agents, the United States wanted to try the suspects in the States, and Qaddafi's regime was under UN-imposed sanctions for his refusal to turn them over. Mandela flew to Tripoli in 1999 to personally close the deal—Qaddafi would hand over the suspects and the United Nations would drop its sanctions. Qaddafi's acceptance of the agreement was based on his personal trust in Mandela, and the incident was resolved peacefully.[59]

As his time in office went on, Mandela's propensity for a more delegative leadership style increased, especially on domestic issues. Internationally, however, he remained a flexible/pragmatic leader. On both domestic and international fronts he fought for respect of human rights. It is important not to forget that Mandela and the ANC came into power in South Africa without any experience in leading a large and complex country in a period of the relative global turmoil that followed the end of the Cold War.

Nelson Mandela is a complex and multidimensional individual whose legacy is as massive as it is contested. His open-mindedness in the face of a setting that, quite literally, defined issues in terms of black and white enabled him to find practical solutions to problems. Whether in school, in the midst of the struggle, during his long prison sentence, in negotiations with the government, or during his transformative presidency, Nelson Mandela listened to all sides of an issue before coming to a conclusion. He serves as an example to South Africa and to the world as a leader who sought office not for personal power, but in order to implement change and reform a broken and unjust system.

Mandela passed away on December 5, 2013. He was a member of the Group of Elders, a small group of older statesmen and women who support peace. The group also includes Kofi Annan, who had these words to say about Mandela after his passing:

> For me, his most important lesson was that he never sought power for the sake of power. Time and again, he invested his authority in strong, democratic institutions that would actually outlast any individual leader. Even founding the Elders was an expression of his belief in an idea that was larger than himself.[60]

NOTES

1. Robert O. Keohane, "International Institutions: Two Approaches," *International Studies Quarterly*, 32, 4 (1988): 379.

2. The Nelson Mandela Foundation, *The Life & Times of Nelson Mandela*, accessed August 20, 2013, at http://www.nelsonmandela.org/content/page/timeline.

3. Ibid.

4. Anthony Sampson, *Mandela: The Authorized Biography* (New York: Random House 1999), 67.

5. The Nelson Mandela Foundation, *The Life & Times of Nelson Mandela.*
6. Ibid.
7. Ibid.
8. Sampson, *Mandela*, 316.
9. The Nelson Mandela Foundation, *The Life and Times of Nelson Mandela.*
10. Ibid.
11. Nelson Mandela, *Long Walk to Freedom* (New York: Back Bay Books 1994), 10.
12. Sampson, *Mandela*, 10–11.
13. Mandela, *Long Walk to Freedom*, 11.
14. Nelson Mandela, quoted in Sampson, *Mandela*, 11.
15. Sampson, *Mandela*, 11–12.
16. Mandela, *Long Walk to Freedom*, 20.
17. Sampson, *Mandela*, 13.
18. Mandela, *Long Walk to Freedom*, 50.
19. Ibid.
20. Ibid., 22.
21. Ibid., 46.
22. Ibid., 42–53.
23. Ibid., 52.
24. Ibid., 50–53.
25. Gerald Shaw, "Lazar Sidelsky," *Guardian*, http://www.theguardian.com/news/2002/may/27/guardianobituaries.nelsonmandela.
26. Ibid.
27. Mandela, *Long Walk to Freedom*, 110–111.
28. Ibid., 113.
29. Ibid., 115.
30. Ibid., 117.
31. Ibid., 123.
32. Sampson, *Mandela*, 69.
33. Ibid.
34. Mandela, *Long Walk to Freedom*, 133.
35. Ibid., 355.
36. Lionel Bernstein, "Rivonia: Telling It As It Was," *African National Congress*, July 2, 1988. http://www.anc.org.za/show.php?id=3762.
37. Mandela, *Long Walk to Freedom*, 362–368.
38. Ibid., 362.
39. Ibid., 521–522.
40. Sampson, *Mandela*, 193.
41. Mandela, *Long Walk to Freedom*, 372.
42. Bernstein, "Rivonia."
43. Sampson, *Mandela*, 312.
44. Ibid., 210.
45. Ibid.
46. Ibid., 213.
47. Ibid., 214.
48. Nelson Mandela, "Address to the US Congress," *Alternatives: Global, Local, Political*, 15:4 (1990): 453–458.
49. Ibid, 457.

50. Nelson Mandela, "South Africa's Future Foreign Policy," *Foreign Affairs*, 72, 5 (1993): 86.
51. Ibid., 87.
52. Mandela, *Long Walk to Freedom*, 19.
53. Nelson Mandela, "Inaugural Address," Pretoria, South Africa (May 10, 1994).
54. Sampson, *Mandela*, 488.
55. Ibid., 528.
56. Ibid.
57. Ibid., 549.
58. Ibid.
59. Ibid., 555–556.
60. Statement by Kofi Annan in December 2013. http://theelders.org/e/Nelson-Mandela-message/.

21

Devils to Angels: Addressing the Cases along a Continuum

Jean Krasno

The leadership case studies in this volume are psychobiographies "at a distance," meaning none of the authors knew these leaders or had any direct, personal contact[1] with them or insight into their characters. All the information comes from speeches, biographies, and other documents. While this method has limitations, it allows us to gather information on a greater variety of personalities and add to the literature in the field of political psychology and the study of leadership. Our contribution here is to examine the psychological development of these leaders through available sources and apply this to an understanding of their political motives and Decision Making style. Many of our authors speak and read the language of the specific leader, allowing us to access sources that may not have been available in previous analyses. We use an examination of early childhood experiences, utilizing the approach undertaken by Alexander and Juliette George in their analysis of Woodrow Wilson where they explain Wilson's compulsive behavior through a study of his struggles with a very controlling father. However, we also rely on the work of other political psychologists who have shown the importance of experiences in adulthood that have shaped beliefs, personality, and decisions.

As stated in Chapter 1, all leaders are charismatic and enjoy the attention that comes with leadership. Yet the personalities of leaders are differentiated by specific behavioral traits that tend to cluster around a particular type. We identify four overall types: authoritarian, chaotic/impulsive, delegative, and flexible/pragmatic. We found that no leader fully embodies one type, excluding all other behavioral traits outside that type. Leaders practice a range of behaviors, depending on the times or the context of the situation at hand. Nevertheless, we found in studying the leaders for this volume that both men and women tend to fall predominantly within one type with some overlap. For example, an authoritarian leader who generally practices tight control may at times become impulsive or at other times may be forced to delegate some decisions to others. But an authoritarian leader would never go to the opposite extreme of seeking compromise or becoming conciliatory or reach out to understand an opposite viewpoint.

As you have seen in reading the previous chapters, we have arranged the book to reflect the four leadership types described in Chapter 1. Here I will not repeat all the detailed, contextual assessments of our leaders and references covered in the chapters, but will merge the individual studies to create a larger picture of our research. We discovered in examining this group of leaders that the types tended to converge into a graduated continuum rather than maintaining distinct boundaries between behavioral styles. In addition, our continuum is more of a winding path rather than a straight line. The continuum begins with those leaders who exhibit extreme, even violent, authoritarian behavior: our *Devils*. This chapter will highlight some of the characteristics that place each leader along the continuum.

The traits that characterize an authoritarian personality are the regular practice of control, requiring the agreement and obedience of both the inner and outer circles at all costs. The leader has a belief system that is dogmatic, closed-minded, and highly ideological. He or she is narcissistic, exhibits self-aggrandizement, must be the center of attention even to the point of cult of personality, can never be wrong, and is obsessive compulsive. Authoritarian leaders seek power as an end in itself, to compensate for an extreme lack of self-esteem. This archetype displays ego-defensive behavior that is aggressive, manipulative, and secretive, a tactic that is used to stifle disagreement and solidify control.

THE DEVILS: AUTHORITARIAN LEADERS IN NONDEMOCRATIC SOCIETIES

Examples of the extreme type in our sample are Muammar Gaddafi, Saddam Hussein, and Fidel Castro. Comparing their early childhoods, we see a pattern of ego-defensiveness to compensate for either parental abuse through regular beatings, abandonment—in the case of Saddam Hussein—or a sense of inadequacy brought about by constant ridicule. Power and control for these leaders became an ego-defensive means to build self-esteem. Their ability to achieve power, however, came from their intelligent, strategic-minded, and persuasive qualities. These particular leaders, who actually came to power through force, may have originally sought power to instigate change, but ultimately power became an end in itself and protecting that power gave birth to extreme violence. Cultural norms that tolerate or even embrace violence are fertile soil for extreme violent behavior. The historical, cultural environment of authoritarian control, for example, in Libya, Iraq, and Cuba, through monarchies, dictators, or colonial rulers, enabled a tolerance or acceptance of authoritarian control within these societies. The cult of personality then perpetuates the violence through fear or loyalty to the "great" leader.

Muammar Gaddafi

Muammar Gaddafi was raised in a proud nomadic tribal culture in Libya. Yet when he attended school in a town 18 miles away, he was ostracized for being poor. This created in him resentment toward his middle-class bourgeoisie classmates who had attacked his proud heritage. Muammar joined the rebels who wanted to rid Libya of the British and overthrow the complicit monarchy. As a victim, he could identify with all of Libya as a victim of colonialism. Gaddafi admired Egyptian leader Gamal Abdel Nasser, and joined the army as Nasser had done, eventually overthrowing the Libyan King Idris. His autocratic control of Libya did not allow for any opposition, and he was able to hold onto power for some 40 years. His brutality was not just exercised to defeat any opposition to his leadership but was also manifested in his sponsorship of terrorism and most particularly his support for the bombing of the civilian aircraft over Lockerbie, Scotland. Yet he could also be pragmatic and yield to compromise in order to hold onto power. He demonstrated his latent pragmatism in 2003, after the Iraq invasion earlier that year, when he finally made an agreement with the West to give up his WMD program. However, in 2011, his Bedouin tribal pride and instinct for survival ultimately was his tragic flaw. Unable to relinquish power, he refused to accept any compromise or a peaceful transition of power, but instead threatened that those who opposed him, specifically in Benghazi, would be hunted down "street by street, house by house." He had been able to compromise to hold onto power, but not to peacefully surrender power, and ultimately, he was murdered by his own people.

Saddam Hussein

Saddam Hussein's early childhood was tragic. His father died, or disappeared, before Saddam was born and his mother gave him away at birth to an uncle. After his uncle was sent to prison, Saddam was returned to his mother, and his stepfather often beat and degraded him. As a child, he was unwanted and therefore never was able to bond or create personal attachments. Saddam's ruthless behavior demonstrates this lack of empathy. Maureen Buckley and Carolyn Saarni explain that the attachment relationship of an infant with the caregiver is the primary context in which a child's emotional life develops. To survive, the infant must elicit response in the caregiver and form the notion that the world is a safe place. If this bond does not form, the infant may see the world as an unsafe environment and cannot trust others. Vigilant for signs of threat, a child, even into adulthood, may display either aggressive or submissive behavior as a means of self-protection. This can lead to becoming a bully or a victim. Buckley and Saarni also add that this sense of being a victim can be influenced by culture (the victim of colonial abuse) as well as cognitive growth.[2]

Saddam, in order to hold onto power, ordered the deaths of his political opposition and even had his two sons-in-law murdered for disloyalty. He used chemical weapons against the Kurds in northern Iraq and persecuted the Shi'a population in the south. He put in place a cult of personality, assuming the role of the messenger of God. Yet, through his tight control, he kept Iraq together as one country. In the end, however, he was found living in a hole in the ground, brought to trial, and ultimately hanged to death in a scene of violence that reflected his own brutality.

Fidel Castro

Like Gaddafi and Saddam, Fidel Castro was a talented orator, a natural leader, and a rebel. He too overthrew an entrenched and violent dictator and instituted his own Cuban version of Communism in an essentially agrarian society. While Castro grew up in a middle-class family, he witnessed poverty and injustice all around him. He resented his autocratic father, who sent him away at a very young age to get an education, where Fidel was maltreated and often had little food to eat. His sense of abandonment led him to see himself as a victim, and his personal desire for justice and dignity fed into an inner anger that later manifested itself into a drive to lead the Cuban people out of their own victimized status. Violence as a means of achieving power was a way of life in Cuban politics, and Castro's biography indicates that he was also fascinated by violence. One story that emerges from his youth states that on the way to Havana in a car with some of his friends, Castro demanded that the driver stop the car because he wanted to shoot something. Castro emerged from the car, took out a gun, and began shooting cows in a field by the road. When Castro came to power at the age of 32, he became the autocrat that he had so hated in his father and the long line of Cuba's dictators. But he believed that he knew the answers to Cuba's problems and only he could lead the country. Like other authoritarian leaders, he also believed that he could never be wrong. Castro sought power to change Cuban society and he did do that, while repressing any opposition. Though he never instituted the means for power sharing or any mechanisms for the peaceful transition of power, he did pass the leadership of the country to his brother, Raul, when his own health began to fail.

THE LESS DEVILISH: AUTHORITARIAN LEADERS WITH A NONVIOLENT STREAK

Gaddafi, Saddam, and Castro all rose to power through the military, utilizing the hierarchical structure of the institution as well as its projection of power, which suited their personalities. Milton Rokeach explained in his study of dogmatism that authoritarian personalities are often drawn to the military.[3] In addition, the traditional political culture of their countries accepted authoritarian leaders and violence as a norm. Two other authoritarian leaders also rose through the military and exhibit our list of traits under the authoritarian typology, but do not manifest the same kind of violence as our *Devils*. In these two cases, the traditional political culture included mechanisms for the people to express their views that placed a certain amount of restraint on the extent to which these leaders could use pure violence. These next two leaders along our continuum are Gamal Abdel Nasser of Egypt and Hugo Chávez of Venezuela.

Gamal Abdel Nasser

Nasser, like the previous leaders, had a turbulent childhood and was sent away at an early age to live with an uncle and go to school. The uncle was absorbed in political activities and barely cared for the child, and Nasser developed a sense of abandonment. He had been close to his mother and missed her when he was sent away. Tragically, his mother died while Nasser was away and the family kept it a secret from him for several months until he returned home for school vacation. Nasser was doubly wounded by her death and the secretive way his father handled the news. When his father remarried soon after his mother's death, Nasser never forgave him and there was no bond with the father. Nasser turned to books and discovered in them the role models that his family could not provide.

His sense of lack of control over his own life was reflected in Egypt's lack of control over its destiny through British colonialism. His mission to oust the British and their puppet King Farouk married well with restoring Egypt's self-esteem as well as his own. In contrast to our *Devils*, however, Nasser chose role models through his reading that renounced violence, and while Nasser did not shy away from eliminating his opposition, he often chose to send them into exile and put them under house arrest or in jail, rather than outright murder. He sought power but not as an end in itself, and he instituted many needed reforms. However, his mistrust of the military as a competing source of power weakened that institution to the extent that they became bogged down in a senseless war in Yemen and were desperately unprepared for the 1967 war with Israel. It was a war that Nasser himself had instigated through self-aggrandizing and bombastic language that was really intended to gain popularity within the Arab world. The Egyptian check on its leaders, while not through institutional means like free and fair elections, nevertheless can be very persuasive through massive demonstrations and people turning to the streets, as we have seen recently. Thus, when Nasser offered to resign after the 1967 humiliating defeat, the street restored him to power, and he remained in office until his death in 1970.

Hugo Chávez

Hugo Chávez also rose through the military and was attracted by its hierarchical control and discipline. Although Venezuela is considered democratic, the criteria defining democratic institutions—a free press, free and fair elections, and a participatory opposition—are weak and its history is more authoritarian than democratic. So Chávez is included in this group because of his similarity to the others discussed above. Like some of the other authoritarian leaders in our study, his parents sent him away along with an older brother, to live with an ailing grandmother. When he was finally able to go to school, the other students and the teacher ridiculed and humiliated him for his worn and disheveled clothing, which reflected his poor status and his family's poverty. Humiliated and feeling abandoned by his parents and given the responsibility beyond his young age of caring for an elderly grandmother, Chávez developed a strong need to defend his ego and restore his self-esteem. Rising to power through the military and using his persuasive oratory gift, Chávez adopted an identification with the Venezuelan hero Bolivar. He developed a strategy of deifying Bolivar and then narcissistically attaching himself to this messianic image. After attaining power, he worked tirelessly to reduce and eliminate the opposition, which he would refer to as evil. He created an in-group that he controlled and an out-group that was considered the enemy.

While operating as an authoritarian type, he could also be impulsive and called for sudden meetings that everyone would be required to attend. He professed that anyone could speak, but he would often punish those who spoke up, especially those who might criticize his actions or policies. Yet his goal was to alleviate poverty, something he had known fully as a child. He enacted policies that benefited the poor, nationalized many industries that had profited only the wealthy class, and distributed the revenues to build communities, schools, and jobs. When a showdown developed over rewriting the constitution, faced with the loss of power, he was able to make compromises on provisions within the new constitution that he had wanted adopted. Nevertheless, by vilifying the opposition, limiting a free press, and removing constructive criticism, he divided the country, pitting one side against the other, instead of governing through compromise and reconciliation. After his death and the loss of his charismatic personality, he has left behind a legacy of division in Venezuela instead of a political culture that represents all the people.

Emperor Hirohito

The Emperor Hirohito of Japan is difficult to classify into one of our types. He lived in a militaristic and authoritarian political culture and his decision making, through his upbringing and socialization, adapted to that political reality. Therefore, we have classified him here as authoritarian within an undemocratic society. Hirohito was named Emperor of Japan, following his father's death in 1926, at the age of 25 and became the highest authority in the Empire of Japan. In contrast to the previously discussed authoritarian leaders, he did not grow up in a country victimized by colonial rule; he represented a colonial power. He was raised at birth as the crown prince and was given every privilege of that position. He was taught that his family was heroic and responsible for the uniting of the empire and its creation. Through his training, he was instilled with the belief that he was the embodiment of his heroic ancestors and because of this, he could not fail. At play, he was always allowed to win. We do not see in him any sense of abuse or victimization. Yet by this very creation of an unreal, fantasy world, he was unprepared for the realities of war. In addition, the military in Japan had taken over the political system and did not allow dissent.

At the time of the decision to attack Pearl Harbor in 1941, Japan had expanded its empire to the extent that to maintain control of its territory, it needed vast amounts of energy resources. When the United States threatened to cut off its source of oil needed to operate Japan's vast military, the leadership was forced to make a decision. Rather than reaching a compromise with the United States, which would result in shrinking the empire, the military leaders devised a plan to attack the U.S. base at Pearl Harbor, which they hoped would intimidate the United States and end the oil embargo. However, since Japanese culture saw Hirohito as the highest authority, the military would need his approval to proceed. According to our research here, it appears that Hirohito was torn between approving the attack and giving his disapproval. He appeared aware of the possible consequences of drawing the United States into the war in the Pacific rather than achieving the desired outcome through intimidation, as the military tried to convince him. In discussions with some of his advisers, he expressed his doubts about the attack. However, later in his own words, Hirohito explained his ultimate decision to authorize the bombing. He appeared afraid that if he did not go along with the military's decision, they might assassinate him as they had done with others who had disagreed with their policies. His death would end the royal lineage and bring down the Imperial House of Japan. Playing a role in his decision was also his socialization in the belief that Japan, and he as the Emperor, could not fail. Therefore, his priority of preserving the Imperial House of Japan, and his own life, prevailed, with the hope, or gamble, that the military's strategy might be correct.

AUTHORITARIAN LEADERS IN DEMOCRATIC SOCIETIES

Harry S. Truman and Henry Stimson

In August 1945, on the other side of the globe in Washington, D.C., two men contemplated the ultimate retaliatory response to Hirohito's decision that had facilitated the attack on Pearl Harbor a few years earlier. Harry S. Truman and Henry Stimson sat huddled in an office laying out the decision to use the most devastating and terrifying weapon ever developed in human history, the atomic bomb. That August, the United States dropped two bombs, one on the city of Hiroshima, Japan, and shortly afterward, the second one flattened Nagasaki. Were these men evil? What would lead them to rationally make such a profoundly horrific decision? Millions had already died in the war; other cities had been flattened in Europe (Coventry in England and Dresden in Germany, for example) and the United States was already fire-bombing Tokyo. Were they desensitized to the suffering and simply saw these massive weapons as just another step-up in the violence?

We could argue that no one completely understood the aftermath of radiation sickness and contamination, so they might be forgiven on that score. Yet these two generally, highly moral men made a rational decision that they believed would quickly end the war. Were there other choices? Yes. They could have invited Japanese leaders to witness a demonstration of the bomb, like the Trinity test at Alamogordo. But there were doubts that a test would be successful and, as we know now, there were only the three bombs. The weapon that decimated Hiroshima most likely alone would have ended the war, but the two men rationally decided that without waiting, a second bomb was needed. We can surmise there were three goals: (1) to clinch the end of the war through a Japanese full surrender, not a negotiated or compromised solution; (2) to test both types of bombs: nuclear (Hiroshima) and plutonium (Nagasaki); and (3) to fully demonstrate U.S. power to the Soviets. To calculate such a decision, Truman and Stimson had to have seen the Japanese as the faceless *outgroup*, not mothers carrying babies, not nurses and doctors at the hospital caring for the sick, people eating breakfast, children going to school, a city full of people. It was war and that is how decisions were made. But would we do it again? Probably not; we haven't.

Not Just a Man's World

There were no women in our *Devils* category at the extreme end of the spectrum; however, there are a number of female leaders that fall into the authoritarian type. Margaret Thatcher and Golda Meir both demonstrate predominantly authoritarian leadership traits. Their management style is hierarchical and controlling, but they have all emerged through democratic systems that place limitations on purely autocratic behavior. They are also neither narcissistic nor create a cult of personality in the same way as the extreme authoritarian types. They do not display any propensity for violence like our *Devils*, but Thatcher and Meir did oversee periods of war.

Margaret Thatcher

Margaret Thatcher, born Margaret Hilda Roberts in October 1925, grew up in the conservative town of Grantham, Lincolnshire, in the United Kingdom. Her father, Arthur Roberts, not only supported his daughter but also promoted her ambitions to become a leader, offering her the best in private education and building in her an unyielding self-confidence and interest in politics. This is in total contrast to Saddam Hussein's childhood, where he was abandoned by his mother and berated and abused by his stepfather. It is also in contrast to the childhoods of Gaddafi, Castro, Chávez, and even Nasser, all of whom had little or no support from their parents and often faced threats to their ego.

Margaret's father also instilled in his daughter religious Methodist traditions rooted in hard work, moral certitude, and discipline. She was trained to be assertive, and did not develop the traits of ego-defense. Her personality reflected her confidence, even self-righteousness, in her view of right and wrong, a clear black-and-white belief system. As prime minister, she asserted unprecedented control, not the normal British collegial style.

She also grew up in World War II and that experience taught her to deplore appeasement. During the Falklands crisis, she built on that experience to strongly implore the House of Commons not to appease Argentine aggression on these British island territories. During the crisis, Thatcher formed a war cabinet, which she ran as a military-command post. When asked for the authority to sink the Argentine cruiser, the Belgrano, she readily gave her permission, which resulted in killing the 368 persons onboard. Thatcher was willing to use force and appeared to those around her in no mood to compromise. She was the first and, until now, the only female prime minister of the United Kingdom. She was called the *Iron Lady* for a reason: tough, authoritarian, and uncompromising.

Golda Meir

Like Margaret Thatcher, Golda Meir was the first and only female prime minister of the State of Israel. Unlike Thatcher, however, Golda did not have the support of her father, yet she was similarly controlling and outspoken. Born of a Jewish family in Kiev in 1898, then a part of the Russian Empire, as a girl she moved with her mother and sister to Milwaukee, Wisconsin, to join their father, who had gone before to find a better life. Her father wanted his two daughters to follow the traditional role for women of getting married and raising a family. When Golda wanted to finish high school and become a teacher, her father strongly disapproved. Stubborn in her ambitions, at 15 Golda ran away from home to join her older sister, Sheyna, in Denver, Colorado. As a girl still in Russia, Golda had witnessed harsh discrimination against Jews, who through pogroms had been forced to abandon their possessions and become homeless. This experience shaped Golda's mission in life, to help the Jewish people. When she did marry, she did not take her married name, Meyerson, and insisted that they move to Palestine, where she worked to raise money to fight the 1948 war that created the State of Israel.

Like Thatcher, she had a strong sense of moral certitude and believed that she knew what was best for the Jewish people—her personal moral mission. She did not seek power but stubbornly sought to enact her vision for Israel and carried out many policies that strengthened the country. She was the prime minister from 1969, shortly after the 1967 Six Day War, until 1974. As prime minister, authoritarian and controlling, she surrounded herself with an insulated group of advisers who generally agreed with her, referred to as Golda's kitchen cabinet because they often met at her home around the dining table. Faced with the issue of what to do with the Palestinian people after occupying the West Bank and Gaza, her moral certitude failed her. She vacillated on what was the right thing to do: keep the Holy Land together within the State of Israel or secure a purely Jewish state and give up the Occupied Territories. Her indecisiveness allowed unregulated settlements to spring up on the West Bank. Always seeing things in black and white, she was unable to find a compromise solution, a dilemma that plagues Israel today.

She saw Arabs as the *outgroup,* whom she stereotyped as weak and untrustworthy. She had no desire to meet and discuss a peaceful, compromise solution with Nasser or any of the other Arab leaders. Her inflated self-confidence and belief in Israel's superiority left the country vulnerable to attack in the 1973 Yom Kipper War. She resigned in 1974 and died in 1978, just at the time of the Camp David Accords, a compromise peace agreement with Egypt carried out by others.

AUTHORITARIAN MIXED TYPES

In this section, I will examine and discuss leadership personalities who are predominantly authoritarian but who also include a mixture of traits from our chaotic/impulsive and in some cases delegative type. They are narcissistic and controlling, dogmatic—seeing issues in black and white, stubborn, secretive, and generally unwilling to compromise. The chaotic/impulsive type includes traits like being unable to focus, frequently changing policy without careful thought, making sudden policy changes, and exhibiting impulsive behavior. The delegative personality type is complex and can develop due to differing motivations. At first we thought the delegative leader liked the authority and prestige of office, but absent much interest in governing would then delegate administrative work to others. But what we found was more complicated. Sometimes leaders need to delegate in order to simply spread out the work load, but others make a regular pattern of doing so because they have confidence in themselves and trust in others and their ability to do the work effectively. In that sense, these leaders do not have to be in control at all times. Our mixed types utilize a combination of approaches. However, as we discovered, authoritarian leaders may delegate from time to time, but not regularly, and they do not demonstrate an interest in compromise or seeing other points of view.

Silvio Berlusconi

Silvio Berlusconi, born outside Milan, Italy, in 1936, began his early life under fascism, not by foreign occupation but under the control of Italian dictator Benito Mussolini, who transformed Italy through legal, extra-legal, and violent means. Silvio's father was absent during much of his early years, serving in the Italian military and then escaping to Switzerland when Nazi Germany occupied Italy in 1943. As a young boy, Silvio suffered through bombing raids, going regularly to the train station, hoping to see his absent father descending from the train. To a young child, this sense of abandonment and lack of control, especially during the violence of war, can permanently affect personality and establish a strong need to be in control.[4] One day, Silvio—again waiting at the train station—saw his father emerging down the steps of the train. As he says, it was the happiest day of his life. Yet a child, not yet aware of the world, can often blame himself for his father's absence. He can permanently feel the need to earn his father's love and attention. When the war ended in 1945, Berlusconi was sent away to a strict Catholic boarding school whose rules did not permit the students to go home much during the school year, increasing Silvio's sense of separation from his parents. We saw this separation anxiety develop in Hugo Chávez, Fidel

Castro, and Gamal Abdel Nasser as well. As a youth, Silvio was often ridiculed for his short stature, and this also permanently affected his ego-defensiveness, like the way Chávez was ridiculed for his poverty, or the way Gaddafi's more bourgeois classmates made fun of his tribal, rural manner. Silvio Berlusconi's life appears to be dominated by both the need for control and the need to be the center of attention.

Berlusconi is bright, extroverted, and gregarious and has a lively and witty sense of humor, which has endeared him to his public. He became a talented entrepreneur and built that penchant for success into a political career, serving twice as prime minister, 1994–1996 and 2001–2006. An admirer of Mussolini and his authoritative hold on power, Berlusconi maintained a hierarchical and controlling management style in both his business dealings and as prime minister, manipulating laws to serve his personal interests and those of his inner circle. His narcissism led him to create a messianic myth, claiming to be the *Jesus Christ of politics* and depicting himself as *the patient victim*, the suffering martyr.[5] He considered himself above the law and became embroiled in any number of legal scandals. He could be impulsive in his need for attention and his philandering. Therefore, for our research, we have classified him as authoritarian and impulsive, but not delegative, and only compromising if it meant holding onto power, similarly to Hugo Chávez.

Eva Peron

Eva Peron, often referred to by the diminutive Evita, never held formal office but with her glamour and strong personality on the global stage as First Lady of Argentina, she became a model for future Latin American women to move into the spotlight in leadership positions. She is an example of a personality that includes traits from all our four types. Her husband and president of Argentina, Juan Peron, like Berlusconi, admired Mussolini and, while in the Argentine military, had even served with Mussolini's army in the early years of the war. Argentina had aligned itself with fascism and was ostracized following the war, something Eva tried to ameliorate in her famous trip to Europe in 1947 as described in detail in the chapter devoted to Eva in this volume. Born in 1919 in a village in rural Argentina, Eva was the illegitimate daughter of a wealthy rancher, Juan Duarte, who ultimately allowed the children of his secret second family to take his name before he died. Eva witnessed throughout her childhood the stark differences between the wealthy upper class of her father and the abject poverty and injustice endured by her mother with her five children.

Beautiful and with a talent for stage and radio, she was invited to a gala where she met Juan Peron, then secretary of labor, and they fell in love. After they were married in 1945, she campaigned with him for the presidency, which he won in 1946. Evita immediately used her position as First Lady to launch many social programs: providing housing for the poor and education for poor children and establishing well-organized and humanely administered schools for orphaned children. She carried with her the pain and suffering of her childhood, which shaped her dedication, even obsession, with helping the poor. She was adamant and controlling in her oversight of these programs, finding it difficult to delegate to others, and did so only when she was too exhausted to do it herself. She had to be pragmatic and flexible in dealing with her husband, the president, so she could continue her work.

Evita was well aware of the importance of her glamour, which she saw as giving pride and hope to the lower classes. Relentless in her work, she wore herself out, not eating well and working such long hours that she became very ill and died in 1952 at the young age of 33. Shortly before she died, she had established her own political party and was beginning to talk about running for the position of vice president.

She was narcissistic in her own way and enjoyed the power she was handed, but she strategically used it to achieve her social goals. Ironically, Juan Peron's later wife, Isabela Peron, became the first female president of Argentina and the first female president in Latin America.

FLEXIBLE AND PRAGMATIC TYPES

Angela Merkel

Moving back to the European continent, Angela Merkel, the first female chancellor of Germany, offers another example of a groundbreaking woman. Elected in 2005, she is still serving as chancellor and leader of the Christian Democratic Union at this writing. Born Angela Kasner in Hamburg, her father, a Lutheran pastor, moved the family when Angela was only six weeks old back to his hometown, then located in communist East Germany. Growing up under the Soviet-style regime, Angela witnessed the antagonism against religion by the state and repression carried out by the secret police. The contradiction of a religious upbringing in a nonreligious society foreshadows the dichotomies Merkel exhibits in her personality and leadership style. Unlike authoritarian leaders Castro, Chávez, and Berlusconi, she experienced a normal childhood and adolescence with caring parents.

But also unlike Thatcher, her father could often be critical to the point of being cold to Angela. In fact, even after her accession to the office of chancellor, the good pastor publicly rejected his daughter's politics. He expected perfection in his children while simultaneously admonishing them not to let teachers notice them for fear of reprisals against the church. Angela retains some of that secretiveness today. She became a highly intellectual young woman whose teachers found her uninspiring and lacking ambition, but whose classmates recognized her as an outgoing leader. The version of Merkel that her classmates saw clearly represented the truer picture, considering her meteoric rise from political neophyte to general-secretary of the CDU in a mere eight years. Bright and a good student, she earned a degree in physics. When Germany reunited in the 1990s, Angela was recognized as competent and hardworking, and Chancellor Helmut Kohl saw her as a strong symbolic bridge between the East and West.

As the first female chancellor of the largest economy in Europe, Merkel had to learn the nuances she faced that men did not. Her physical appearance endured incessant scrutiny whereas her male predecessors' went unnoticed. But contrary to her male colleagues, a great part of her strength as a leader rests with her ability to set her own ego aside in order to build consensus, both domestically and internationally. Her flexibility in governing and her collegial management style manifest themselves in her cabinet. In negotiating her first, very fragile governing coalition, she allowed the junior partner to hold key ministries while remaining focused on her longer-term strategic goals. She fosters genuine debate in cabinet meetings, seeks out opposing positions, and encourages ministers to take active roles in crafting policy. And she encourages them to take credit for doing so, as well. Consequently, Merkel has successfully weathered a number of crises in managing the European Union and the Euro Zone by balancing the interests of the German people and the German economy with the health of the European Union. She has also successfully maneuvered through the political agendas of other heads of state. By indulging her natural curiosity, she avoids the dogma and ideological sterility that often plagues party politics.

Benazir Bhutto

Benazir Bhutto was shot in the head and killed in 2007 by opponents during her third campaign to become prime minister of Pakistan. The details of her life are covered in the chapter dedicated to her in this book, so I will give only an overview here to demonstrate why we have placed her in the pragmatic/flexible type. When elected prime minister the first time in 1988, like the other women in our book, she had been the first female prime minister not only of her country but also within the entire Muslim world. As leader of the Pakistan People's Party (PPP), Benazir served from 1988 to 1990 and again from 1993 until she was overthrown in 1996.

Born in 1953 as the eldest of four children into a wealthy, political family in Pakistan, Benazir had the best of education. She attended Harvard for her BA, and went on to Oxford University for graduate work. Unlike other Muslim fathers, Benazir's father, Zulfikar Ali Bhutto, wanted his daughter to achieve her highest capacities and groomed her for political life.

Zulfikar, the founder of the PPP, was president of Pakistan from 1971 to 1973 and was then elected prime minister from 1973 to 1977. He often took his children along when he met with foreign diplomats and insisted that Benazir accompany him when he met with Indira Gandhi, prime minister of India at the time, to witness the negotiations for a peace agreement between the two countries that lasted for many years. Both her parents showed great confidence in her, and Benazir developed a high sense of self-esteem.

The death and martyrdom of Benazir's father lifted Benazir into the leadership of the PPP and the position of prime minister where she enacted many policies in support of women. She freed many women from prison, supported women's right to work and choose employment, worked to repeal all discriminatory laws against women, and promoted female literacy and education. In addition, some 100,000 women were trained to work in rural areas in the field of health and family planning. Her government also allowed the revival of trade unions and removed censorship of the media. During her tenure, she also prevented Shari'a law, which discriminates against women from becoming the law of the land. Her managerial style was collegial and she was both flexible and pragmatic in trying to achieve reform. Nevertheless, she appeared to be ahead of her time, as she was overthrown a second time in 1996, and much that she had accomplished was undone by her successor. Undeterred, however, she was determined to try again in 2007, but was cut short by her tragic end.

Ellen Johnson Sirleaf

Ellen Johnson Sirleaf, born in Liberia in 1938, won the presidency in 2006 as the first female president of Liberia and the first on the African continent. Liberia was emerging from a violent time and a horrific civil war. Sirleaf, like Angela Merkel, is still in office at the time of this writing. She has been both pragmatic and flexible in putting together a government that has included her opposition and even some of her previous enemies. In that way, she has demonstrated an open-minded acceptance of different points of view and a belief that it is better to bring the opposition into the government than let them fester and return the country to conflict. She is confident in her ability to communicate with all sides and finds agreeable solutions through her collegial management style. Ellen's father, a lawyer, was elected to Liberia's House of Representatives as the first indigenous member. President Tubman often appointed her father to foreign delegations, and her father frequently brought diplomats to their home, introducing Ellen to politics at an early age. She describes her father as distant, however, and her mother, a teacher, became her primary role model. Her mother was a devout Catholic and served as a traveling pastor, unusual for a woman in those days. She eventually opened her own school.

Ellen married young in 1956 in her senior year in high school to a man seven years her senior and had four children with him. The marriage turned disastrous for Ellen as he increasingly verbally and physically abused her and their union ended in divorce. Instead of allowing the trauma to demoralize her, Ellen also took these lessons to heart and became determined to support women's rights. Like Benazir Bhutto, Ellen Johnson Sirleaf attended college in the United States at the University of Colorado and later obtained a master's in public administration at Harvard's Kennedy School of Government in 1971. These were important years for her in building her sense of self-esteem.

Women had played an important role in Liberia in attempting to bring an end to the violent civil war, and their support for Ellen helped her become elected to her first term in 2006. As president, Sirleaf has included women in high positions in the government to head the ministries of commerce, justice, finance, youth and sports, gender, and development. Like her mother, she has led an effort to educate girls. Infant mortality rates have significantly declined from 152 per thousand births to 74, indicating that the health of mothers has improved dramatically. She is open to working with others across the political spectrum and has stated that she believes that governments must respond to changing times, representing her flexible attitude. Unlike our authoritarian types, she has only sought power to implement policies that protect and support women and stabilize the economy and security of Liberia, enabling her to become reelected in 2011. In recognition of her work, in 2011 she was awarded the Noble Peace Prize along with two other women for their commitment to bettering the lives of women.

William Jefferson Clinton

Bill Clinton is a clear example of flexibility and pragmatism. At times he appeared to backtrack and abandon policies he had previously supported, but overall, his approach to politics was balancing the art of the possible. Clinton served two four-year terms as president of the United States, from 1993 through 2000. He is open-minded, highly self-confident, optimistic, and competitive. He demonstrates only a moderate drive for power, and this was primarily for the purpose of achieving the goals he set out to accomplish.

He suffered a sense of abandonment at an early age; his father died before he was born and his mother left home shortly after his birth to attend school. After her return, she was often out partying and eventually married Roger Clinton, who was an abusive alcoholic. She showered Bill with affection, but placed him in a terrifying home life situation. Bill learned survival techniques by outshining everyone at school and building faith in his capacity to overcome obstacles. His use of charm and wit and his unfailing persistence enabled him to achieve both his personal and political goals.

Through his own suffering, he was able to empathize with those who were also suffering and would often express his ability to feel their pain.

As president, he wanted to move the Democratic Party to the center, which meant at times he ignored the more socialist agenda of the party loyalists. On the other hand, he preempted the Republican Party's agenda of cutting spending, achieving a balanced budget, and reforming welfare. Because the Republicans could not attack him for his more moderate policies, they went after him personally with devastating effects. Yet the economy grew and thrived under Clinton, and he is known today for leaving a strong economy as his legacy. Clinton also wanted to focus on domestic issues and stay out of foreign affairs. Unfortunately, this led to his disastrous lack of leadership on the Rwandan genocide. The horrific results of his dithering forced him to grasp a leadership role in international affairs and that proactive stance carried him through the rest of his presidency.

Achieving the presidency in 1993, shortly after the end of the Cold War, Clinton's leadership overlapped with many of the other leaders in this study. He also benefited from Gorbachev's peaceful end to the global tensions created by the East-West divide. The unification of the world economy meant that the World Trade Organization could emerge and Clinton embraced the new organization. Though a very conservative Senate held him back and most notably Jesse Helms as chairman of the Foreign Relations Committee, Clinton's progressive aspirations overlapped with those of Kofi Annan and Nelson Mandela during those years. He signed both the Statute of the International Criminal Court and the Comprehensive Test Ban Treaty. Even though these instruments have still not been ratified, he demonstrated that he understood the forward vision of the world they embody. Bill Clinton may not have finished achieving his goals. The Clinton Global Initiative is growing, and if his wife Hillary Clinton wins the presidency in 2016, he could become something we yet don't even have a name for, "First Gentleman?"

OUR ANGELS: OCCUPYING THE OTHER END OF OUR CONTINUUM AND COMBINING FLEXIBILITY WITH DELEGATION

While the reader may disagree with our classifications and may want to move our personalities around, after carefully examining our case studies, we have decided to go out on a limb and classify the remaining leaders as our *Angels.* We acknowledge that our *Devils* did some things that were at times beneficial to their countries, ousting a colonial power or modernizing the economy or social structure. In the same vein, we also acknowledge that our *Angels* can be criticized for deficiencies and flaws. But on balance, these leaders have significantly used their positions to make very positive changes.

While we found that many leaders' behavioral patterns included some delegation, we discovered that among our selected group, our delegative archetype does not constitute a dominant characteristic on its own. At first, we envisioned a leader who enjoyed the prestige of the office but was not particularly interested in governing, handing off these tasks to others. But we found that those leaders who tended to delegate did so because they trusted others and had enough confidence in themselves to choose the right people and manage them from a distance. In this section, we discuss Mikhail Gorbachev, Václav Havel, Kofi Annan, and Nelson Mandela.

Mikhail Gorbachev

Of all the leaders we discussed in our study, Mikhail Gorbachev is most likely the person whose decision making affected the entire world in the most significant manner. His decisions to open a dialogue with the West, withdraw Soviet troops from Afghanistan, and refusal to use force in the fall of 1989 to prevent East Germans from passing through the gates into West Berlin led to the fall of the Berlin Wall and brought about a peaceful end to the Cold War. Previous Soviet leaders had done just the opposite, and a closer look at Mikhail's life sheds light on his personality and belief system that shaped these major decisions.

Born in 1931 in a small farming village near Stavropol in the southwestern section of the Republic of Russia—near today's border with the state of Georgia—Mikhail grew up experiencing the hard life of poor farmers. On one side of his family were staunch communists, participating loyally with collective farming, while the other side refused to participate in the cooperatives, hiding grain from the authorities. When the Nazis arrived in his village during World War II, the entire village suffered Nazi brutality, and Mikhail's grandfather had to hide the boy in the attic. Under Stalinism, both his grandfathers became victims of communist political repression and the Soviet secret service, the KGB. One grandfather was sent to prison, barely escaping execution, and the other was exiled to Siberia. As a child, Mikhail worked alongside his father in the fields. Within his own family, he listened to the arguments on both sides of the issue of communism as it affected poor rural life.

His experience and knowledge of rural life, the increased repression and poverty imposed on village farmers by Stalinist policies, and his more worldly education at the university combined to shape his belief system and sense of ethics. He became curious and open-minded, especially toward understanding different systems and different points of view.

Upon becoming secretary general of the Communist Party and leader of the Soviet Union in 1985, he immediately began to try to reform the system through his plan *perestroika*, but found that the system was so corrupt and bankrupted—having spent huge portions of the budget on the military—that his policies were not effective and even appeared chaotic. The rationale for building such a large military was based on the notion that the West was the enemy, but as Gorbachev traveled outside the Soviet Union, he discovered that this was a myth created to cut the Soviet people off from knowing anything about the prosperity of the Western world. The Soviet system was built on intense secrecy to protect the prerogatives of the inner circle. However, this very secrecy thwarted adaptability and the kinds of innovations that were blossoming outside. When Gorbachev launched his *glasnost* policy of openness, encouraging greater dialogue and a more free press, he faced a backlash. Hence, his domestic policy, though desperately needed, was not popular.

Yet his openness was well received in the foreign policy realm. He worked in a collegial style with his advisers and delegated much of foreign policy to his trusted foreign minister, Edward Shevardnadze. He also participated directly in meetings with Margaret Thatcher of the UK and U.S. leaders, making a strong impression of himself as someone they could finally talk to in a reasonable way. His speech at the United Nations in 1985 offered for the first time the hope that an open dialogue could take place between the East and the West. In 1989, when he withdrew Soviet troops from Afghanistan, that hope grew and he was applauded in November 1989 for not sending troops to prevent the outflow of people into West Berlin. If the Soviet military had used force at that time as they had done before, there would have been a bloody confrontation. He was awarded the Nobel Peace Prize in 1990 for his decisions to unfold a peaceful solution to end the Cold War, and the world was grateful.

More than any of the other leaders in our study, Gorbachev's decision to not use force in 1989 and to end the Cold War peacefully may have had the greatest impact on world politics and the freedom for our other leaders to enter the world stage. The end to East-West tensions brought about the emergence of Lech Walesa and Václav Havel in Europe. In Africa, the elimination of the threat of communism enabled the release of Nelson Mandela from prison and through his leadership gave the world a new role model for peaceful reconciliation. Had the Cold War continued, Kofi Annan would not have been able to launch his agenda to address the advancement of human rights and the rule of law, reduce poverty through the Millennium Development Goals, and introduce the Responsibility to Protect.

Václav Havel

Václav Havel was never awarded the Nobel Peace Prize, though some believe this was a gross oversight by the committee. Born in Prague, Czechoslovakia, in 1936, Havel, like his contemporary, Mikhail Gorbachev—born five years earlier and hundreds of miles away—grew up experiencing the brutality of Nazism, the violence of World War II, and the repression of communism. Unknown to the two men, their search for knowledge and truth and their open-minded ability to understand a spectrum of viewpoints would lead them to the same goal: a more open and free society. However, Havel's search for freedom had to wait for Gorbachev's decision not to use force in 1989. Unlike Gorbachev, Havel was born into a wealthy cosmopolitan elite family of intellectuals.

Despite the previous elite status of his family, Václav formed a humble personality and stated that he longed to be accepted by others to relieve his sense of loneliness. Yet he was very comfortable with himself and spent long stretches of time thinking and forming ideas, both philosophical and political. He stated that he was often embarrassed by praise. He was very critical of the repression brought about by the communist system and found a way of expressing this resistance through the guise of literature in the form of fiction and fantasy. His first major play, *The Garden Party*, was presented as part of the Theater of the Absurd. He was a prolific writer, and his works would carry political messages hidden within the subtext of the story. However, following the crackdown connected to the 1968 Soviet invasion of Czechoslovakia, Havel's works were banned, and he spent several years in and out of prison as a dissident. Plagued by bouts of pneumonia, nevertheless, Havel used his time in prison, the longest period from 1979 to 1983, to reflect upon his own sense of ethics and opposition to the communist system. His resistance and detention resulted in Havel becoming a symbol of the struggle and social unrest. His writings became more hopeful as he sensed change was coming; little did he know that change would be the result of the decisions made by Communist Party leader Mikhail Gorbachev.

Elected president in 1990, he began to put his goals into effect, first by announcing the end of the Warsaw Pact and then by insisting on the withdrawal of Soviet troops in Czechoslovakia. Reflecting his open-minded belief system and perhaps his sympathy for fellow prisoners, he offered a broad amnesty to those imprisoned during the communist regime. Perhaps the most controversial and boldest of his decisions was regarding the split of Czechoslovakia into two separate states. Even though he personally felt the country should stay intact, he allowed the people to make that decision through a popular referendum, thus delegating this momentous determination to the people. By doing so, he facilitated a peaceful transition rather than allow festering resistance to lead to upheaval and possible conflict. He died in 2011, having been able to participate in and witness the outcome that he had so presciently hoped for and believed was coming.

Kofi Annan

While Kofi Annan never served as a head of state, his leadership as secretary-general of the United Nations (1997–2006) has had a profound effect not only on the organization but on the world as well. He saw his role as secretary-general in a unique way, to use the symbolism and visibility of the office as a bully pulpit to launch and prioritize such norms as human rights, and humanitarian intervention and to fight poverty through strategies like the Millennium Development Goals. Born in Kumasi, Ghana, in 1938, he, like Nelson Mandela, was raised in a traditional tribal system as a member of the dominant Ashanti tribal group. Even though his father was not an elected tribal chief, he often operated as such and the Ashanti king spent many evenings at the Annan household, discussing the issues of the day. Kofi spent hours observing the traditional leadership style and process of silently listening, even for hours, to all points of view. Only after everyone had spoken would the chief synthesize the differing positions and make a decision, relying on the cultural tradition of patience, negotiation, and reconciliation. Annan as secretary-general was known for his patient listening and even silence during meetings and discussion. What others might have mistakenly interpreted as disinterest was in fact his Ghanaian style of listening and absorbing. In Ghana, as in many African cultures, the sense of community and reconciling differences in order to work together take preference rather than a more Western adversarial style. We cannot say that all African leaders follow this path, but Kofi Annan embraced this style and brought it with him into his leadership and decision making behavior.

Probably the most profound adult experience for Annan that shaped his later goals and motivations was the genocide in Rwanda in 1994, something that also deeply affected President Bill Clinton. Annan was deeply hurt by the immense tragedy, and shortly after taking office in 1997, he began to examine the whole notion of humanitarian intervention and led the way to shaping the new norm we now refer to at the Responsibility to Protect.

Kofi Annan's management style is also reflected in his pragmatic and flexible leadership type. He always wanted to work as a team, telling his staff to keep in constant dialogue with everyone and set aside time to thrash out ideas. He regularly delegated leadership on various issues to others and was careful to surround himself with intelligent and independent thinkers. However, his *cabinet* meetings were not the roiling affairs that Clinton enjoyed. He was not the competitive type, but used the meetings to absorb ideas and listen.

Kofi Annan was awarded the Noble Peace Prize in 2001 along with the United Nations as a whole for their contribution to global peace. Even after leaving office, Annan has been sought out to mediate complex peaceful solutions and succeeded in finding a workable solution to the conflict in Kenya in 2008. He was again asked to be the joint envoy of the United Nations and the League of Arab States for Syria in 2011, but stepped down in August 2012 when he found that the members of the Security Council were not unified in their support.

Annan never sought power at all, let alone for its own sake. He had been a member of the staff at the United Nations when he was asked to take on the role of secretary-general. Yet he embraced the opportunity to advance humanitarian norms within the goals of the organization. He fits well into Rokeach's open-minded personality with his ability to seek differentiated information about other points of view. Based on his optimism for change, he took advantage of his position as a world leader to give a voice to the voiceless, and through his concept of the Millennium Development Goals, he offered hope to those most vulnerable. While his life experiences shaped his personality and decision making, he actively developed his inner response to these events in a manner that made him the moral leader he has become.

Nelson Mandela

Nelson Mandela led the African National Congress (ANC) in its struggle to end the discriminatory policy of apartheid in South Africa, and was awarded the Nobel Peace Prize in 1993 for his work. Like Kofi Annan, Mandela was raised in a traditional African tribal system where he, similar to Annan, was in the privileged position of observing the daily work and decision making process of the paramount chief and Regent of the Thembu people. As in Annan's Ghana, the Regent would listen silently for hours to his tribesmen. Then he would synthesize their perspectives and give a decision that would integrate all opposing views, the purpose being to keep together all the people in one inclusive community. Thus both men, Annan and Mandela, developed the skill of building consensus and listening to all sides of an issue. To strive for reconciliation was one of the primary goals of both leaders, yet doing so without sacrificing the higher values of human rights, equal treatment under the law, and democracy.

In addition to his childhood experiences, Mandela was also shaped by events later in his life. By high school, Nelson, like Kofi, led students in protests against the school's undemocratic policies. We can see from this period that Mandela was already developing a strategy for resistance. As an adult, because of his opposition to the system of apartheid, Mandela was sentenced to life in prison. However, instead of harboring anger and thoughts of revenge, Mandela utilized his 27 years in prison to contemplate and focus his beliefs. Like Václav Havel, who also spent years in jail for his political opposition, Mandela's health suffered, but he continued to lead the ANC from prison and continued to convey his hopes for change, drawing on his childhood education in reconciliation.

Like Havel, imprisonment increased his public image as a moral leader, and upon his release in 1990, he resumed his political work to end apartheid. Elected as the first black president of a newly multiracial democracy in South

Africa in 1994, Mandela immediately exercised an inclusive management style, bringing into the government representatives of the opposition and delegating work to trusted people, particularly his deputy president, Thabo Mbeki. Serving one term only, he was adamant that South Africa maintain a system of democracy and not fall into a cult of personality or exclusionary policies that had led other African countries to suffer under dictatorships and constant military coups. Nevertheless, like Havel and even Annan and others waiting in the wings, Mandela had to wait to realize his goals until Mikhail Gorbachev stepped into the Soviet leadership and brought a peaceful end to the hostilities of the Cold War that had reached into every continent.

A FEW CONCLUDING REMARKS ABOUT THE STUDY

We set out in this research to study the personalities of a set of leaders to analyze how they made decisions on critical issues and what factors came into play in shaping their behavioral traits that make up our typology. We wanted to select leaders from different continents over time and to include both men and women. In this sense, we hoped to add to the literature of research and writing in the field of political psychology. We had an idea of how these leaders would fit into our types, but in the end we learned much more than we had anticipated, particularly about the astounding commonalities in childhood and adult experiences among this group of people who never knew each other or met only in later life, once they had become leaders. We had no idea of where each personality would fit in our continuum, nor had we even envisioned a continuum initially. We started out with a general theory, but the study really evolved in a more inductive rather than deductive manner. We did not realize until we put all the chapters together that most of our *Angels* had actually been awarded the Nobel Peace Prize.

I want to be clear that the results of this qualitative study do not show that the traits in our types create leaders. On the contrary, leaders must be intelligent, highly motivated, charismatic, verbally persuasive, and energetic and must be able to connect with the times and the mood of the people. I argue that the behavior and decision making styles of those leaders are shaped by personality and personality is shaped by childhood and adult experiences. I also want to be clear that we accept that there are innate characteristics as well as learned behavior.

Psychologist Paul Bloom states that humans are emotional beings, and empathy and morality grow from that natural state. Even babies demonstrate empathy, and Bloom explains that all morality grows out of empathy.[6] In a later publication, Bloom elaborates on this theory by proposing that certain moral foundations are products of biological evolution: yes, the survival of the fittest. Being moral may have a genetic base. It may have been selected "in" because it leads to the preservation of the specie more than amoral behavior. We are social beings and need each other's assistance to survive, hence natural selection operating at the group level.[7] Empathy on a larger scale can lead to caring about people far away who may be suffering from discrimination or starvation. We see Kofi Annan working to better the lives of people in all reaches of the globe and Nelson Mandela willing to accept life in prison or even death to support the end of suffering under apartheid. But empathy and moral emotion can be either encouraged in a child, thwarted, or left to languish. A parent can say, "Don't hit Johnny. You would not like it if Johnny hit you. It hurts, and you don't want to hurt him." This is taught, but if there were no innate sense of empathy, all this teaching would not make a difference. This becomes just as important with our empathetic leaders as with our group of violent and brutal bullies. If there is no bond between the infant child and the parent, then the primary context in which a child's emotional life develops is severed. With no emotional development, there is no empathy. Paul Bloom explains that psychopaths lack moral emotion, so if they succeed in life, it is because they are good at faking it: love, loyalty, empathy, "while cold-bloodedly plotting for their own benefit."[8] Saddam Hussein could fake sorrow by crying at a meeting while the people he had condemned were removed from the room and taken to their deaths.

All of our violent authoritarian leaders suffered some kind of childhood abuse, beatings, neglect, or even abandonment. Even some of our less-violent authoritarian leaders had some experience with abandonment, leaving them with a greater need for control. Yet how do we explain those who had no trauma in childhood later becoming authoritarian leaders, however nonviolent? This will need more examination, but one thread weaves throughout these leaders, which would also find explanation in Rokeach's work on dogmatism.[9] These leaders grew up in households where strict religious beliefs and training were in terms of black and white, right or wrong. They were taught to accept their belief system as the only correct one and all others as wrong, with no attempt to understand differing points of view. Another explanation might be found in the work of Jean Piaget, *The Moral Judgment of the Child.* According to Piaget, the brain of a child develops over time where at a younger stage the child absorbs the rules but is unable to understand the larger picture of fairness or moral balance. A more substantive understanding grows as the child develops, and by the age of 10 or 12, the moral fairness of an interaction supersedes the rules.[10] Therefore, a possible explanation for our non-trauma, authoritarian group might be both the black-and-white training of a strict religious upbringing and somehow a fixation on rules without developing a greater sense of the overall moral picture. On the other hand, our pragmatic and flexible leaders had supportive parenting and, even in some cases, training in forming empathy for other points of view and in building skills in reconciliation. Kofi Annan's deep empathy with the suffering brought about by the genocide in Rwanda led eventually to the creation of the norm Responsibility to Protect.

In conclusion, we invite students and scholars to debate our findings, rearrange our types, and add to the discussion. This study is by no means exhaustive, and we hope that other researchers will want to add new personalities and expand and build on our research.

NOTES

1. One exception to this is that Jean Krasno worked with Kofi Annan in publishing his papers.
2. Maureen Buckley and Carolyn Saarni, "Skills of Emotional Competence: Developmental Implications," in *Emotional Intelligence in Everyday Life,* ed. Joseph Ciarrochi and Joseph P. Forgas (New York: Psychology Press, 2006), 56–57.
3. Milton Rokeach, *The Open and Closed Mind: Investigations into the Nature of Belief Systems and Personality Systems* (New York: Basic Books, 1960), 344.
4. Buckley and Saarni, "Emotional Competence," 56–57.
5. Oliver Burkeman, "Silvio Berlusconi Is Not Jesus Christ," *Guardian,* February 14, 2006.
6. Paul Bloom, *Descartes' Baby: How the Science of Child Development Explains What Makes Us Human* (New York: Basic Books, 2004), 111–119.
7. Paul Bloom, *Just Babies: The Origins of Good and Evil* (London: The Bodley Head, 2013), 8–18.
8. Bloom, *Descartes' Baby,* 112.
9. Rokeach, *The Open and Closed Mind,* 109–131.
10. Jean Piaget, *The Moral Judgment of the Child* (New York: The Free Press, 1965).

Selected Bibliography

Aburish, Said K. *Nasser: The Last Arab*. New York: St. Martin's Press, 2004.

Adsera, Alicia. *Fertility Changes in Latin America in the Context of Economic and Political Uncertainty*. Chicago, IL: University of Chicago Press, 2005.

Alexander, Anne. *Nasser Life and Times*. London: Haus Publishing, 2005.

Annan, Kofi with Nader Mousavizdeh. *Interventions: A Life in War and Peace*. New York: Penguin Press, 2012.

Babbitt, Eileen F. "Ethnic Conflict and the Pivotal States." In *The Pivotal States: A New Framework for US Policy in the Developing World*, edited by Robert Chase, Emily Hill, and Paul Kennedy, 338–359. New York and London: W.W. Norton and Company, 1999.

Barnes, John. *Evita, First Lady: A Biography of Eva Peron*. New York: Grove Press, 1978.

Berlusconi, Silvio. *L'italia Che Ho in Mente*. Milan Arnoldo Mondadori Editore S.p.A., 2000.

Bhutto, Benazir. *Daughter of Destiny*. New York: Harper Perennial, 2007.

Bhutto, Benazir. *Reconciliation: Islam, Democracy and the West*. New York: HarperCollins, 2008.

Bix, Herbert P. *Hirohito and the Making of Modern Japan*. New York: HarperCollins, 2000.

Bloom, Paul. *Descartes' Baby: How the Science of Child Development Explains What Makes Us Human*. New York: Basic Books, 2004.

Bloom, Paul. *Just Babies: The Origins of Good and Evil*. London: The Bodley Head, 2013.

Blundy, David, and Andrew Lycett. *Gaddafi and the Libyan Revolution*. London: Weidenfeld & Nicolson, 1987.

Bourne, Peter G. *Fidel: A Biography of Fidel Castro*. New York: Dodd, Mead, and Company, 1986.

Buckley, Maureen, and Carolyn Saarni. "Skills of Emotional Competence: Developmental Implications." In *Emotional Intelligence in Everyday Life*, edited by Joseph Ciarrochi, and Joseph P. Forgas, 51–76. New York: Psychology Press, 2006.

Byrd, Peter. *British Foreign Policy under Thatcher*. Oxford: Philip Allan, 1988.

Campbell, John. *Margaret Thatcher: The Grocer's Daughter*. London: Jonathan Cape, 2000.

Cazorla-Sanchez, Antonio. *Franco: The Biography of the Myth*. Abingdon, UK: Routledge, 2013.

Chatani, Seiichi. *Shōwa Tennō: Sokkin tachi no Senso* [The Shōwa Emperor: War from the Perspective of the Aides]. Tokyo: Kobunkan, 2010.

Chávez, Hugo, and Marta Harnecker. *Understanding the Venezuelan Revolution: Hugo Chávez Talks to Marta Harnecker.* Translated by Chesa Boudin. New York: Monthly Review Press, 2005.

Clinton, Bill. *My Life.* New York: Alfred A. Knopf, 2004.

Close, David. *Nicaragua: The Chamorro Years.* Boulder, CO: Lynne Rienner, 1999.

Cordesman, Anthony. *Weapons of Mass Destruction in the Middle East.* London: Brassey's, 1991.

Coughlin, Con. *Saddam: The Secret Life.* London: Macmillan, 2002.

Crassweller, Robert D. *Peron and the Enigmas of Argentina.* New York: W. W. Norton & Company, 1987.

Daalder, Ivo H. "Knowing When to Say No: The Development of US Policy for Peacekeeping." In *UN Peacekeeping, American Policy, and the Uncivil Wars of the 1990s,* edited by William J. Durch, 35–67. New York: St. Martin's Press, 1996.

DeLuca, Anthony R. *Gandhi, Mao, Mandela, and Gorbachev: Studies in Personality, Power, and Politics.* Westport, CT: Praeger Publishers, 2000.

Denzau, Arthur T., and Douglass C. North. "Shared Mental Models: Ideologies and Institutions." In *Elements of Reason: Cognition, Choice, and the Bounds of Rationality,* edited by Arthur Lupia, Mathew D. McCubbins, and Samuel L. Popkin. Cambridge, UK: Cambridge University Press, 2000.

Direnzo, Gordon J. *Personality and Politics.* Garden City, NY: Anchor Books, 1974.

Dower, John. *The Most Terrible Bomb in the World.* N.p.: DK Publishing Book, 2001.

Durch, William J., and James A. Schear. "Faultlines: UN Operations in the Former Yugolavia." In *UN Peacekeeping, American Policy, and the Uncivil Wars of the 1990s,* edited by William J. Durch, 193–274. New York: St. Martin's Press, 1996.

el-Khawas, Mohamed A. *Gaddafi: His Ideology in Theory and Practice.* Brattleboro, VT: Amana Books, 1986.

Elizalde, Rosa Miriam, and Luis Báez. *Chávez Nuestro.* Havana: Casa Editora Abril, 2005.

Elles, Diana. "The Foreign Policy of the Thatcher Government." In *Thatcherism: Personality and Politics,* edited by Kenneth Minogue, and Michael Biddiss, 95–104. Basingstoke: Macmillan, 1987.

Encarnación, Omar G. *Spanish Politics: Democracy after Dictatorship.* Cambridge, UK: Polity Press, 2008.

Favor, Lesli J. *Eva Perón.* Singapore: Marshall Cavendish Corporation, 2010.

Fernandes, Clinton. *The Independence of East Timor: Multilateral Perspectives.* Eastbourne, UK: Sussex Academic Press, 2011.

Ferrari, Georgio. *Il Padrone Del Diavolo: Storia Di Silvio Berlusconi.* Milan: Camunia, 1990.

Fraser, Nicholas, and Marysa Navarro. *Evita: The Real Life of Eva Peron.* New York: W. W. Norton, 1996.

Fujiwara, Akira. *Showa Tenno no Ju-go Nen Senso* [Fifteen Years of War under Emperor Showa]. Tokyo: Aoki Shoten, 1991.

Fumimaro, Konoe. *Heiwa heno Doryoku: Konoe Fumimaro Shuki* [An Attempt to Seek Peace: The Diary of Konoe Fumimaro]. Edited by Kanjiro Tanaka. Tokyo: Nihon Denpotsushinsha, 1946.

Gabriel, Jiri, Lubomir Novy, and Jaroslav Hroch, eds. *Czech Philosophy in the XXth Century: Czech Political Studies, II.* Washington, DC: Council for Research in Values and Philosophy, 1994.

Gaddis, John. *The United States and Origins of the Cold War*. New York: Columbia University Press, 2000.

Gardiner, George. *Margaret Thatcher: From Childhood to Leadership*. London: William Kimber, 1975.

Genovese, Michael. *Women as National Leaders*. Newbury Park, CA: Sage Publications, 1993.

Gentile, Benito Mussolini with Giovanni. "The Doctrine of Fascism." In *Fascism Doctrine and Institutions*, edited by Benito Mussolini. Rome: Ardita Publishers, 1935.

George, Alexander L., and Juliette L. George. *Presidential Personality and Performance*. Boulder, CO: Westview Press, 1998.

Gilmore, Robert. *Caudillism and Militarism in Venezuela, 1810–1910*. Athens: Ohio University Press, 1964.

Ginsborg, Paul. *Silvio Berlusconi: Television, Power, and Patrimony*. London: Verso Press, 2005.

Gonzalez, Victoria. "Somocista Women, Right-Wing Politics, and Feminism in Nicaragua: 1936–1979." In *Radical Women in Latin America, Left and Right*, edited by Victoria Gonzalez and Karen Kampwirth, 41–78. University Park: Pennsylvania State University Press, 2001.

Gorbachev, Mikhail. *Memoirs*. London: Bantam Books, 1996.

Gorbachev, Mikhail. *Размышления О Прошлом И Будущем* [Thinking About the Past and the Future]. Moscow: Terra, 1998.

Gordin, Michael. *Five Days in August: How World War II Became a Nuclear War*. Princeton, NJ: Princeton University Press, 2007.

Gordon, Michael R., and General Bernard E. Trainor, *Cobra II: The Inside Story of the Invasion and Occupation of Iraq*. New York: Pantheon Books, 2006.

Gorenberg, Gershom. *The Accidental Empire: Israel and the Birth of the Settlements, 1967–1977*. New York: Times Books, 2006.

Gott, Richard. *Hugo Chávez and the Bolivarian Revolution*. New York: Verso, 2005.

Grachev, Andrew. *Gorbachev*. Moscow: Vagrius, 2001.

Greenstein, Fred I. *Personality and Politics: Problems of Evidence, Inference, and Conceptualization*. New York: W. W. Norton & Company, 1975.

Guevara, Aleida. *Chávez, Venezuela, and the New Latin America: An Interview with Hugo Chavez*. New York: Ocean Press, 2005.

Harris, John F. *The Survivor: Bill Clinton in the White House*. New York: Random House, 2005.

Harris, Lillian Craig. *Libya: Qadhafi's Revolution and the Modern State*. Boulder, CO: Westview Press, 1986.

Harvey, Robert. *American Shogun: General MacArthur, Emperor Hirohito and the Drama of Modern Japan*. New York: The Overlook Press, 2006.

Hata, Ikuhiko. *Hirohito: The Shōwa Emperor in War and Peace*. Kent: Global Oriental, 2007.

Havel, Vaclav. *The Power of the Powerless*. New York: M.E. Sharpe, 1985.

Havel, Vaclav. *Disturbing the Peace: A Conversation with Karel Hvizdala*. New York: Alfred A. Knopf, 1990.

Havel, Vaclav. *Open Letters: Selected Writings 1965–1990*. New York: Alfred A. Knopf, 1991.

Havel, Vaclav. *Summer Meditations*. Translated by P. Wilson. New York: Vintage Books, 1992.

Havel, Vaclav. *To the Castle and Back.* Translated by P. Wilson. New York: Alfred A. Knopf, 2007.

Heckel, Margaret. *So Regiert Die Kanzlerin.* München: Piper, 2009.

Hellinger, Daniel. *Venezuela: Tarnished Democracy.* San Fransisco: Westview Press, 1991.

Hermann, Margaret G. "Assessing the Foreign Policy Role Orientations of Sub-Saharan African Leaders." In *Role Theory and Foreign Policy Analysis,* edited by S. G. Walker, 168–198. Durham, NC: Duke University Press, 1987.

Hermann, Margaret G. "Assessing Leadership Style: Trait Analysis." In *The Psychological Assessment of Political Leaders: With Profiles of Saddam Hussein and Bill Clinton,* edited by Jerrold M. Post, 178–212. Ann Arbor: University of Michigan Press, 2003.

Hermann, Margaret G. "William Jefferson Clinton's Leadership Style." In *The Psychological Assessment of Political Leaders: With Profiles of Saddam Hussein and Bill Clinton,* edited by Jerrold M. Post, 313–323. Ann Arbor: University of Michigan Press, 2003.

Hodgson, Godfrey. *The Colonel: The Life and Wars of Henry Stimson, 1867–1950.* Lebanon, NH: University Press of New England, 1992.

Höhler, Gertrud. *Die Patin: Wie Angela Merkel Deutschland Umbaut.* Zürich: Orell Füssli Verlag, 2012.

Hudson, Valerie. "Chapter One: Foreign Policy Decision Making." In *Foreign Policy Decision Making (Revisited),* edited by Richard Snyder, H. W. Bruck, and Burton Sapian, 1–17. New York: Palgrave/MacMillan, 2002.

Irokawa, Daikichi. *The Age of Hirohito: In Search of Modern Japan.* New York: Free Press, 1995.

Jankowski, James P. *Nasser's Egypt, Arab Nationalism, and the United Arab Republic.* Boulder, CO: Lynne Rienner Publisher, 2001.

Janis, Irving L. *Groupthink: Psychological Studies of Policy Decisions and Fiascoes.* Boston, MA: Houghton Mifflin, 1982.

Janis, Irving L. *Crucial Decisions: Leadership in Policy Making and Crisis Management.* New York: Free Press, 1989.

Joesten, Joachim. *Nasser: The Rise to Power.* London: Odhams Press, 1974.

Kampwirth, Karen. *Women and Guerilla Movements.* University Park: Pennsylvania State University Press, 2002.

Kampwirth, Karen. *Feminism and the Legacy of Revolution.* Athens: Ohio University Press, 2004.

Karsh, Efraim, and Inari Rautsi. *Saddam Hussein, A Political Biography.* New York: Free Press, 1991.

Kato, Yoichi. *Shōwa Tennō to Sensō no Seiki* [The Shōwa Emperor and the Century of War]. Tokyo: Kodansha, 2011.

Kawahara, Toshiaki. *Tennō Hirohito no Shōwashi* [The Emperor Hirohito and the History of Shōwa]. Tokyo: Bungeishunju, 1983.

Kawczynski, Daniel. *Seeking Gaddafi: Libya, The West and The Arab Spring.* London: Biteback Publishing, 2011.

Kille, Kent. *From Manager to Visionary: The Secretary-General of the United Nations.* New York: Palgrave Macmillan, 2006.

Kille, Kent, ed. *The UN Secretary-General and Moral Authority: Ethics and Religion in International Leadership.* Washington, DC: Georgetown University Press, 2007.

Kinzer, Stephen. *Overthrow! America's Century of Regime Change from Hawaii to Iraq.* New York: Times Books/ Henry Holt, 2006.

Koenigsberg, Richard. *The Psychoanalysis of Racism, Revolution, and Nationalism.* New York: Library of Social Science, 1977.

Krasno, Jean E., ed. *The Selected Papers of Kofi Annan.* 5 vols. Boulder: Lynne Rienner, 2012.

Kriseova, Eda. *Vaclav Havel: The Authorized Biography.* New York: St. Martin's Press, 1993.

Kurbjuweit, Dirk. *Angela Merkel: Die Kanzerlin Für Alle?* München: Carl Hanser Verlag, 2009.

Lacouture, Jean. *Nasser: A Biography.* London: Alfred A. Knopf, 1973.

Landman, Todd. *Issues and Methods in Comparative Politics: An Introduction.* Abingdon, UK: Routledge, 2000.

Lane, David. *Berlusconi's Shadow: Crime, Justice, and the Pursuit of Power.* London: Penguin, 2005.

Langguth, Gerd. *Angela Merkel: Aufstieg Zur Macht.* 2nd ed. München: Deutsche Taschenbuch Verlag, 2008.

Large, Stephen S. *Emperor Hirohito and Shōwa Japan: A Political Biography.* London: Routledge, 1992.

Leonard, Melinda. *The Desk Studies of Colombia, Guatemala, and Nicaragua.* New York: International Rescue Committee, 2001.

Leuchtenburg, William E. *In the Shadow of FDR: From Truman to Barack Obama.* 4th ed. Ithaca, NY: Cornell University Press, 2009.

Ludwig, Arnold M. *King of the Mountain.* Lexington: University Press of Kentucky, 2002.

Lupia, Arthur, Mathew D. McCubbins, and Samuel L. Popkin, eds. *Elements of Reason: Cognition, Choice, and the Bounds of Rationality.* Cambridge, UK: Cambridge University Press, 2000.

Malloy, Sean. *Atomic Tragedy: Henry Stimson and the Decision to Use the Bomb against Japan.* Ithaca, NY: Cornell University Press, 2008.

Mandela, Nelson. *Long Walk to Freedom.* New York: Back Bay Books, 1994.

Manning, Paul. *Hirohito: The War Years.* New York: Dodd, Mead & Company, 1986.

Maraniss, David. *First in His Class: A Biography of Bill Clinton.* New York: Simon and Schuster, 1995.

Martinez, Luis. *The Libyan Paradox.* London: Hurst, 2007.

McCoy, Jennifer L., and David J. Myers. "Introduction." In *The Unraveling of Representative Democracy in Venezuela,* edited by Jennifer L. McCoy, and David J. Myers, 1–8. Baltimore, MD: Johns Hopkins University Press, 2004.

Meir, Golda. *My Life.* New York: Putnam, 1975.

Meisler, Stanley. *Kofi Annan: A Man of Peace in a World of War.* New York: John Wiley and Sons, 2007.

Merkel, Angela. *Mein Weg.* Hamburg: Hoffmann und Campe Verlag, 2004.

Metoyer, Cynthia Chavez. *Women and the State in Post-Sandinista Nicaragua.* Boulder, CO: Lynne Rienner, 2000.

Mishra, Robin, ed. *Angela Merkel: Macht Worte.* Freiburg im Briesgau: Herder, 2010.

Miyamoto, Seitaro. *Tennokikansetsu to Sono Shuhen: Mittsu no Tennokikansetsu to Showashi no Shogen.* [Emperor Organ Theory and Related Theories: Three Types of Emperor Organ Theory and the History of the Showa Period]. Tokyo: Yuhikaku, 1980.

Monti-Belkaoui, Janice, and Ahmed Riahi-Belkaoui. *Gaddafi: The Man and His Policies.* Aldershot, UK: Ashgate Publishing, 1996.

Morison, Elting. *Turmoiland Tradition: A Study of the Life and Times of Henry L. Stimson.* New York: Atheneum, 1963.

Newton, Michael. *The Path to Tyranny: A History of Free Society's Decent into Tyranny.* Phoenix: Eleftheria Publishing, 2010.

Niblock, Tim. "The Foreign Policy of Libya." In *The Foreign Policies of Middle East States,* edited by Raymond A. Hinnebusch, and Anoushiravan Ehteshami. Boulder, CO: Lynne Rienner Publishers, 2002.

Oakley, M. L. *On the Make: The Rise of Bill Clinton.* Washington, DC: Regnery, 1994.

Oquist, Paul. *The Sociopolitical Dynamics of the 1990 Nicaraguan Elections.* Lanham, MD: Rowman & Littlefield, 1992.

Pargeter, Alison. *Libya: The Rise and Fall of Gaddafi.* London: Yale University Press, 2012.

Payne, Stanley G. *The Franco Regime, 1939–1975.* Madison: University of Wisconsin Press, 1995.

Payne, Stanley G. *A History of Fascism, 1914–1945.* Madison: University of Wisconsin Press, 1995.

Perón, Eva, and Juan Domingo Perón. *La Razón De Mi Vida.* Buenos Aires: Peuser, 1951.

Piaget, Jean. *The Moral Judgment of the Child.* New York: Free Press, 1965.

Ponniah, Thomas, and Jonathan Eastwood, eds. *The Revolution in Venezuela: Social and Political Change under Chávez.* Cambridge, MA: Harvard University Press, 2011.

Post, Jerrold M. "Assessing Leaders at a Distance: The Political Personality Profile." In *The Psychological Assessment of Political Leaders: With Profiles of Saddam Hussein and Bill Clinton,* edited by Jerrold M. Post, 69–104. Ann Arbor: University of Michigan Press, 2003.

Post, Jerrold M. "Leader Personality Assessments in Support of Government Policy." In *The Psychological Assessment of Political Leaders: With Profiles of Saddam Hussein and Bill Clinton,* edited by Jerrold M. Post, 39–61. Ann Arbor: University of Michigan Press, 2003.

Post, Jerrold M., Stephen G. Walker, and David G. Winter. "Profiling Political Leaders: An Introduction." In *The Psychological Assessment of Political Leaders: With Profiles of Saddam Hussein and Bill Clinton,* edited by Jerrold M. Post, 1–7. Ann Arbor: University of Michigan Press, 2003.

Pym, Francis. *The Politics of Consent.* London: Hamish Hamilton, 1984.

Quarterman, Mark. "UN Leverage in East Timor." In *Leveraging for Success in United Nations Peace Operations,* edited by Jean Krasno, Bradd C. Hayes, and Donald C. F. Daniel, 141–168. Westport, CT: Praeger, 2003.

Ramonet, Ignacio, and Fidel Castro. *Fidel Castro, My Life: A Spoken Autobiography.* Translated by Andrew Hurley. New York: Scribner, 2006.

Rattray, Captain R. S. *Ashanti Law and Constitution.* Oxford: Clarendon Press, 1929.

Reduzzi, Giglio. *Berlusconi: The Truth About Italy's Much Maligned Premier.* Dallas, TX: St. Paul Press, 2010.

Renshon, Stanley, ed. *The Political Psychology of the Gulf War: Leaders, Publics, and the Process of Conflict.* Pittsburgh, PA: University of Pittsburgh Press, 1993.

Renshon, Stanley. *High Hopes: The Clinton Presidency and the Politics of Ambition.* New York and London: Routledge, 1998.

Renshon, Stanley. "Psychoanalytic Assessments of Character and Performance in Presidents and Candidates: Some Observations on Theory and Method." In *The Psychological Assessment of Political Leaders: With Profiles of Saddam Hussein and Bill Clinton*, edited by Jerrold M. Post, 105–133. Ann Arbor: University of Michigan Press, 2003.

Renshon, Stanley. "William Jefferson Clinton's Psychology." In *The Psychological Assessment of Political Leaders: With Profiles of Saddam Hussein and Bill Clinton*, edited by Jerrold M. Post, 277–302. Ann Arbor: University of Michigan Press, 2003.

Rhodes, Rod. "From Prime Ministerial Power to Core Executive." In *Prime Minister, Cabinet and Core Executive*, edited by Rod Rhodes, and Patrick Dunleavy, 11–37. London: Macmillan, 1995.

Rogan, Eugene. *The Arabs: A History*. New York: Basic Books, 2011.

Rokeach, Milton. *The Open and Closed Mind: Investigations into the Nature of Belief Systems and Personality Systems*. New York: Basic Books, 1960.

Ronen, Yelmdit. *Gaddafi's Libya in World Politics*. Boulder, CO: Lynne Rienner Publishers, 2008.

Ruoff, Kenneth J. *The People's Emperor: Democracy and the Japanese Monarchy, 1945–1995*. Cambridge, MA: Harvard University Press, 2001.

Sadat, Anwar. *Revolt on the Nile*. New York: The John Day Company, 1957.

Salas, Miguel Tinker. *The Enduring Legacy: Oil, Culture, and Society in Venezuela*. Durham, NC: Duke University Press, 2009.

Sampson, Anthony. *Mandela: The Authorized Biography*. New York: Random House, 1999.

Sherwin, Martin. *A World Destroyed*. New York: Vintage Books, 1987.

Sirleaf, Ellen Johnson. *This Child Will Be Great*. New York: HarperCollins, 2009.

Simons, Geoff. *Libya: The Struggle for Survival*. London: MacMillan, 1993.

Simonton, Dean Keith. *Why Presidents Succeed: A Political Psychology of Leadership*. New Haven, CT: Yale University Press, 1987.

Skowronek, Stephen. *The Politics Presidents Make: Leadership from John Adams to Bill Clinton*. Cambridge, MA: Harvard University Press, 1997.

Slater, Robert. *Golda, the Uncrowned Queen of Israel: A Pictorial Biography*. Middle Village, NY: J. David, 1981.

Smith, William C. *Authoritariansim and Crisis of the Argentine Political Economy*. Stanford, CA: Stanford University Press, 1989.

Snow, Edgar. *Red Star over China*. 1938. Reprint, New York: Random House, 1961.

Staten, Clifford. *The History of Nicaragua*. Westport, CT: Greenwood Publishers, 2010.

Steinberg, Blema S. *Women in Power: The Personalities and Leadership Styles of Indira Gandhi, Golda Meir, and Margaret Thatcher*. Montreal, QC: McGill-Queen's University Press, 2008.

Stephens, Robert. *Nasser: A Political Biography*. New York: Simon and Schuster, 1971.

Stille, Alexander. *The Sack of Rome: How a Beautiful European Country with a Fabled History and a Storied Culture was Taken over by a Man Named Silvio Berlusconi*. New York: Penguin Press, 2006.

Stone, William F., and Paul E. Schaffner. *The Psychology of Politics*. New York: Springer-Verlag, 1988.

Suedfeld, Peter, Karen Guttieri, and Philip Tetlock. "Assessing Integrative Complexity at a Distance: Archival Analyses of Thinking and Decision Making." In *The Psychological Assessment of Political Leaders: With Profiles of Saddam Hussein and Bill Clinton*, edited by Jerrold M. Post, 246–270. Ann Arbor: University of Michigan Press, 2003.

Taylor, Julie. *Eva Perón: The Myths of a Woman*. Chicago, IL: University of Chicago Press, 1979.

Terasaki, Hidenari. *Shōwa Tennō Dokuhakuroku: Terasaki Hidenari Goyogakari Nikki* [Records of the Self-Remarks by the Emperor Shōwa: Diary of Terasaki Hidenari]. Tokyo: Bungeishunju, 1991.

Thatcher, Margaret. *The Downing Street Years*. London: Harper Collins, 1993.

Thatcher, Margaret. *The Path to Power*. London: HarperCollins, 1995.

Timmerman, Kenneth. *Weapons of Mass Destruction: The Cases of Iran, Syria, and Libya*. Los Angeles: Simon Wiesenthal Center, 1992.

Titus, David A. *Palace and Politics in Prewar Japan*. New York: Columbia University Press, 1974.

Traub, James. *The Best Intentions: Kofi Annan and the UN in an Era of American World Power*. New York: Farrar Straus, and Giroux, 2006.

Vaccaro, J. Matthew. "The Politics of Genocide: Peacekeeping and Disaster Relief in Rwanda." In *UN Peacekeeping, American Policy, and the Uncivil Wars of the 1990s*, edited by William J. Durch, 367–407. New York: St. Martin's Press, 1996.

Vandewalle, Dirk. *A Modern History of Libya*. New York: Cambridge University Press, 2006.

Urban, George. *Diplomacy and Disillusion at the Court of Margaret Thatcher*. London: I. B. Taurus, 1996.

Wainstock, Dennis. *The Decision to Drop the Atomic Bomb*. Westport, CT: Greenwood Publishing Group, 1996.

Wetzler, Peter. *Hirohito and War*. Honolulu: University of Hawai'i Press, 1998.

Wilson, Dick. *The Long March: The Epic of Chinese Communist Survival*. New York: Viking Press, 1971.

Winter, David G. "Assessing Leaders' Personalities: A Historical Survey of Academic Research Studies." In *The Psychological Assessment of Political Leaders: With Profiles of Saddam Hussein and Bill Clinton*, edited by Jerrold M. Post, 11–38. Ann Arbor: University of Michigan Press, 2003.

Winter, David G. "Motivations and Mediation of Self-Other Relationships." In *The Psychological Assessment of Political Leaders: With Profiles of Saddam Hussein and Bill Clinton*, edited by Jerrold M. Post, 306–312. Ann Arbor: University of Michigan Press, 2003.

Wohlstetter, Roberta. *Pearl Harbor: Warning and Decision*. Stanford, CA: Stanford University Press, 1962.

Woods, Kevin M. *The Saddam Tapes: The Inner Workings of a Tyrant's Regime, 1978–2001*. Cambridge, UK: Cambridge University Press, 2011.

Woodward, Bob. *Veil: The Secret Wars of the CIA 1981–1987*. New York: Simon & Schuster, 1987.

Yamada, Akira. *Showa Tenno no Senso Shido* [The Leadership of Emperor Showa in Wartime]. Tokyo: Showa Shuppan, 1990.

Yamada, Akira. *Ososugita Seidan* [The Decision Made Too Late]. Tokyo: Showa Shuppan, 1991.

Yamamoto, Shichihei. *Showa Tenno no Kenkyu: Sono Jitsuzo wo Saguru* [The Study of Emperor Showa: His Real Image]. Tokyo: Shodensha, 1989.

Young, Hugo. *One of Us*. London: Macmillan, 1989.

Zanatta, Loris. *Eva Peron: Una Biografia Política*. Buenos Aires: Sudamericana, 2009.

Zonis, Marvin. "Leaders and Publics in the Middle East: Shattering the Organizing Myths of Arab Society." In *The Political Psychology of the Gulf War: Leaders, Publics and the Process of Conflict*, edited by Stanley A. Renshon, 269–292. Pittsburgh, PA: University of Pittsburgh Press, 1993.

About the Contributors

Monika Adamczyk is a graduate of Yale University, where she earned a BA in Political Science and Environmental Engineering. She has worked for various nonprofits conducting foreign policy and security research. She is also a contributor to two short books on the social and labor history of Oak Ridge, TN, and Hanford, WA, during the Manhattan Project, which were published by the Atomic Heritage Foundation.

Emad Abdel Karim Baniyounes was born in November 1960 in Dair Abu Said, Jordon, and earned his Bachelor of Science degree from Umm Al-Qura University, Mecca, Saudi Arabia, in Islamic Mass Communications. He came to the United States in 1988 and became the owner and president of E & E export and import company and of Wala General Contracting, responsible for major building renovations in New York City and the surrounding metropolitan area. In 2010, he was elected to Jordan's 16th Parliament, and was also elected member of the Finance Economic Committee and the Energy Committee. Emad has been Jordan's delegate to the Mediterranean/European Parliament and its Environment Committee and has organized various charitable organizations to support women's and children's rights in Jordan. In 2014, he returned to New York and has completed an MA degree at the City College of New York in International Relations.

Helen Baxendale holds a Bachelor of Philosophy with majors in History and Political Science from the Australian National University. She graduated with First Class Honours and the University Medal for Political Science in 2011. Her Honours thesis on the political rhetoric of Barack Obama was awarded the L. F. Crisp Prize. Helen's research interests include comparative government and politics, political leadership, and political rhetoric. In addition to her research interests, Helen has observed political decision making at close quarters, having worked as a researcher and adviser to a senior member of the Australian Parliament. Her chapter in this volume was the product of a short course of study under Professor Jean Krasno at Yale

University in July 2009, made possible by the International Alliance of Research Universities.

Salem B. S. Dandan is a PhD fellow at the Department of Political Science, University of Copenhagen, Denmark. In addition, he is part of the Copenhagen Middle East Research Project (COMER), which is a cooperation between the University of Copenhagen and the Royal Danish Defense College. He is also a guest-researcher at Kings College, London. His PhD thesis investigates how states utilize armed nonstate groups as proxies in the greater Middle East, with special focus on Iran. Particular emphasis is on the use of Hezbollah and Hamas, and the motivations, strategies, and cost that influence the patron-proxy relationship. He has published a wide variety of articles on civil-military relations in the greater Middle East and on armed-non-state groups.

Nicole DiMarco received her BFA in Theater with a minor in English Literature from Pace University and MA in International Relations from the City College of New York. She worked under the advisement of Dr. Jean Krasno to complete the thesis that has been excerpted for this book. Nicole has long been concerned with the issue of women's rights and has volunteered her time to many women's organizations, including Women for Afghan Women in Queens. She teaches English and Drama at Xavier High School in New York City.

Christopher Hammond began studying Nelson Mandela with Mac Maharaj, former Minister of Transportation in the Mandela administration, during his undergraduate education at Bennington College. Hammond recently completed his MA degree in International Relations at the City College of New York (CCNY), writing his thesis on the role of international cooperation in addressing transnational threats. He is currently completing an internship in U.S. State Department. Prior to this, he interned at the United Nations in the Department of Peacekeeping Operations, where he worked with Professor Jean Krasno and a research team from the City College of New York (CCNY) to complete a survey of data collection methods used in post-conflict societies.

Jean Krasno is a tenured member of the faculty as a Lecturer in the Department of Political Science at CCNY, where she held the position of Director of the MA Program in International Relations from 2011 to 2014. She is also a Lecturer and Associate Research Scientist at Yale University, where she has taught courses on the United Nations, UN peacekeeping, and International Organization since 1995. She was Executive Director of the Academic Council on the United Nations System from 1998 to 2003 when the organization was housed at Yale. Dr. Krasno received her PhD from the City University of New York Graduate Center in 1994. Some of her publications include *The United Nations and Iraq: Defanging the Viper,* co-authored with James Sutterlin (2003), Greenwood/Praeger Publishers, and *The United Nations: Confronting the Challenges of a Global Society,* editor (2004), Lynne Rienner Publisher. In 2005, Dr. Krasno was authorized by former UN Secretary-General Kofi Annan to organize his papers for publication, a project housed within the Colin Powell Center at CCNY. *The Annan Papers,* a five volume set, were published by Lynne Rienner Publishers in March 2012.

Peter Marcus Kristensen is a PhD fellow at the Department of Political Science, University of Copenhagen, Denmark. His research focuses on the sociology of the international relations discipline, specifically how rising non-Western powers cope with Western intellectual hegemony. His doctoral research project "Other Worlds Restored: Rising Powers and the Problem of Peaceful Change" studies non-Western perspectives on International Relations in the case of China, India, and Brazil. His articles have recently appeared in peer-reviewed journals like *International Political Sociology, International Studies Review, International Studies Perspectives, Journal of European Public Policy,* and *Pacific Review.* The chapter on Gadaffi is an updated version of a paper he wrote for Professor Jean Krasno's class on decision making and political psychology at Yale University in 2009.

Sean LaPides is a researcher and writer with the Research Foundation-City University of New York. He holds an MA in International Relations from City College of the City University of New York. He worked with Jean Krasno at the Colin Powell Center as Senior Research Associate on *The Annan Papers.* Formerly an international marketing director in London, his interest in world affairs stems from his experiences in Asia and Europe, with a particular specialization in Germany. His research interests include political psychology, collective memory, international law, and global governance. He currently resides in the San Francisco Bay area.

Robert Lattin is a Policy Analyst and the Deputy Communication Director for the Democratic Foreign Affairs Committee in the U.S. House of Representatives. He has an MA degree in International Relations from the City College of New York and a Bachelor of Science degree in Near Eastern Studies from the University of Arizona.

Natasha Zemtsova Miller was born in the City of Novocherkassk, Rostov-on-Don region, south Russia. She earned her bachelor's degree in

Psychology at the Don State Technical University, Rostov-on-Don, Russia. After completing her studies in Russia, she moved to New York City to continue her education. Natasha earned her MA degree in International Affairs at the City College of New York. Political psychology and role of personality in politics have been in the scope of Natasha's professional interest since 2008. Since 2013, Natasha has worked for the United Nations, Department of Peacekeeping Operations, Office of Operations, as a Team Assistant.

Evette Rivera's professional history has been in the fields of communications, education, and humanitarian affairs. As a journalist, she published various articles concerning politics and education. She graduated from the City College of New York in June 2011 with an MA in International Relations and wrote her thesis on child marriage. Soon after, she worked as a consultant for the UN Department of Public Information in New York and later researched for the UN Population Fund in Bangkok on the issue of child marriage in South Asia. Evette currently lives in Thailand, working on projects that service urban refugees.

Shun Sakugawa is a recent graduate of the MA program in International Relations at the Jackson Institute of Global Affairs, Yale University. His focus of study at Yale was U.S. foreign policies and its decision making process in the context of East Asian Politics. He holds a BA in International Relations from the University of Tokyo.

Charlotte Scaddan is Information Officer at the United Nations, where she promotes UN priority issues through social and digital media. She is a member of the small team—named Best Social Media Team 2013 by the Digital Diplomacy Review—managing the UN presence on a range of social media platforms, with millions of followers. Charlotte has a degree in History from University College London and an MA degree in International Relations from the City College of New York, where she was awarded the prize for Best Graduate Student in International Relations.

James Suggett is a student in the Master's Program in International Relations at the Colin Powell School for Civic and Global Leadership at the City College of New York (CUNY). He received a graduate research fellowship in 2013–2014, which he used to study Portuguese in Brazil and carry out comparative research on modern Brazilian political institutions. James currently works as a writing tutor at CCNY's Writing Center and as a part-time program assistant in the Skadden, Arps Honors Program in Legal Studies. Before coming to CCNY, James lived in Venezuela, where he worked as a staff writer and editor for Venezuela Analysis, organized study abroad delegations, and was a volunteer teacher at La Escuelita del Barrio Pueblo Nuevo y Simon Bolivar.

He also previously worked as a student activist coordinator and a research assistant in Washington, D.C. He holds a master's degree in Public Administration from CCNY and a bachelor's degree in History with a focus on the Global South from UC San Diego.

Marcin Szudek, a native Polish speaker, was born in Gdansk, Poland, the heart of the Solidarity Movement, where Lech Walesa worked in the shipyards. Marcin immigrated to the United States in 1998 and received his bachelor's degree from Hunter College in Political Science and Economics. He is now completing his MA degree in International Relations at the City College of New York. He currently works at a Manhattan-based nonprofit organization assisting veterans transitioning into the civilian workforce.

John Tumminia lives in Greenwich Village in New York City and has an MA in International Relations from the City College, City University of New York. A dual citizen of the United States and Italy, he has traveled to over 100 countries reporting for his blog, www.flyingnorth.net.

Jakub Robert Walko is currently a member of BlackRock's Corporate Governance and Responsible Investment team, where he works to facilitate improvements in the structure and transparency of public companies. He joined the team from Glass, Lewis & Co., where he helped private and government institutions fulfill mandates of Socially Responsible Investing. Previously, he was involved in the areas of disarmament and humanitarian aid at the United Nations. Jake holds a BA in Economics and Political Science as well as an MA in International Relations with a focus on international law. His research interests include political psychology, behavioral finance, and systems of governance and compliance. Jake divided his early years between Central Europe and the United States and currently lives in New York City.

Index